Praise for Heather Cox Richardson's

TO MAKE MEN FREE

"A readable and provocative account of the many paths that Republicans have taken to their current state of confusion."
—*New York Times Book Review*

"The book offers a lively survey of Republican politics in all its diversity, from the 'transformational presidency' of Abraham Lincoln (to borrow a 21st-century term) to the conservative ascendancy of Ronald Reagan." —*Washington Post*

"The most comprehensive account of the GOP and its competing impulses...an important contribution to understanding where we are today." —*Los Angeles Times*

"At its Lincolnian best, the G.O.P. has been not just grand but good. In *To Make Men Free*, the eminent political historian Heather Cox Richardson superbly brings the Republican Party's history to life, while offering sharp and often surprising interpretations of its rises and declines, when it heeded Lincoln's legacy and when it did not."

—Sean Wilentz, author of *The Rise of American Democracy: Jefferson to Lincoln*

"Heather Cox Richardson tells a great story, full of fascinating figures, of how the Republican Party has enjoyed extraordinary political success in a country full of poor people, while doing much to serve the rich. It's a vital chapter in the history of American conservatism."

—Eric Rauchway, professor of history,
University of California, Davis

"In *To Make Men Free*, one of our most admired historians takes on one of the most important topics of our past and present: the 160-year story of the Republican Party. From Abraham Lincoln to George W. Bush, from Radical Republicans to Movement Conservatives, Heather Cox Richardson recounts the GOP's dramatic history with unimpeachable insights and crisp, vivid writing. How did the antislavery party become the party of the Solid South? How did the antitrust party of Theodore Roosevelt become the party of Wall Street and the Club for Growth? In this brisk account, Richardson make sense of a twisting tale that shapes our lives every day."

—T. J. Stiles, Pulitzer Prize–winning author of *The First Tycoon: The Epic Life of Cornelius Vanderbilt*

"Heather Cox Richardson has written a much-needed book: a comprehensive and balanced history of the Republican Party. The prose is engaging, the research is deep, the argument is persuasive; *To Make Men Free* is the work of a major talent at the top of her craft."

—Ari Kelman, Bancroft Prize–winning author of *A Misplaced Massacre: Struggling Over the Memory of Sand Creek*

"[An] opinionated history.... Richardson aptly ends by wondering if the modern Republican Party 'will find a way to stay committed to the ideals of its founders.'"

—*Publishers Weekly*

"Heather Cox Richardson's concise history of the Republican Party shows how a party that once saw government as the guarantor of equal opportunity for all morphed into today's intransigently antigovernment, antitax, antiregulation GOP. Richardson convincingly demonstrates that the Republican Party has oscillated throughout its history between equal opportunity and protection of property rights as its lodestar. Those seeking clues to how the GOP might evolve in the future will want to read this important book."

—Ruy Teixeira, coauthor of
The Emerging Democratic Majority

"A rich portrait of the thinking and times of Abraham Lincoln and those closest to him in the founding of the Republican Party... perceptive and persuasive.... Readers of Richardson's history of the GOP will come away with a good sense of the complex path that led the party to the abnegation of the Lincoln legacy." —*Washington Spectator*

"Sharp and readable." —*Open Letters Monthly*

"Richardson makes a bold, pertinent argument.... A hard-hitting study that will surely resonate with ongoing attempts to regenerate the GOP."

—*Kirkus*

"This is a highly intelligent, absorbing book that offers a window into the history of the Republican Party from its hopeful inception under Lincoln through its deserved failure under George W. Bush. Heather Cox Richardson defines three cycles of Republican principles as the party toggled between the meaning of the Declaration of Independence, which promised equality, and the Constitution, which protected private property. Touting the Constitution, Republicans tied themselves to business and rejected social welfare as socialism. These two principles were entwined in the recent Conservative movement, bringing economic disaster and a chaotic and warlike foreign policy. Breaks under Theodore Roosevelt and Dwight Eisenhower, following Lincoln's path, were fruitful but doomed respites. This book raises the question of whether Republicans deserve to survive as now constituted. It is essential reading in this election season and beyond."

—Aida D. Donald, author of *Lion in the White House: A Life of Theodore Roosevelt* and *Citizen Soldier: A Life of Harry S. Truman*

TO MAKE
MEN FREE

TO MAKE MEN FREE

A HISTORY OF THE
REPUBLICAN PARTY

HEATHER COX RICHARDSON

BASIC BOOKS
New York

Basic Books
Hachette Book Group
1290 Avenue of the Americas, New York, NY 10104
www.basicbooks.com

Printed in the United States of America

First Trade Paperback Edition: November 2021

Published by Basic Books, an imprint of Perseus Books, LLC, a subsidiary of Hachette Book Group, Inc. The Basic Books name and logo is a trademark of the Hachette Book Group.

The Hachette Speakers Bureau provides a wide range of authors for speaking events. To find out more, go to www.hachettespeakersbureau.com or call (866) 376-6591.

The publisher is not responsible for websites (or their content) that are not owned by the publisher.

Library of Congress Cataloging-in-Publication Data
Richardson, Heather Cox.
To make men free: a history of the Republican Party / Heather Cox Richardson.
pages cm
Includes bibliographical references and index.
ISBN 978-0-465-02431-5 (hardcover)—ISBN 978-0-465-08066-3 (e-book)
1. Republican Party (U.S.: 1854-)—History. 2. United States—Politics and
    government. I. Title.
JK2356.R44 2014
324.273409—dc23
2014026434

ISBNs: 978-0-465-02431-5 (hardcover), 978-1-5416-0062-1 (paperback),
978-0-465-08066-3 (ebook)

LSC-C

Printing 1, 2021

For Nancy Evans

CONTENTS

Introduction

In 1862, in the midst of the Civil War, Republican Justin Smith Morrill stood up in Congress to defend his party's novel invention: an income tax. The government had the right to demand 99 percent of a man's property, Morrill thundered. If the nation needed it, "the property of the people...belongs to the government." The Republican Congress passed the income tax—as well as a spate of other taxes—and went on to create a strong national government. By the time the war ended three years later, the Republicans had fielded an army and navy of more than 2.5 million men; had invented national banking, currency, and taxation; had provided schools and homes for poor Americans; and had freed the country's four million slaves.

A half century later, when corporations dominated the economy and their millionaire owners threw their weight into political contests, Republican Theodore Roosevelt fulminated against that "small class of enormously wealthy and economically powerful men, whose chief object is to hold and increase their power." Insisting that America must break up this class in order to return to "an economic system under which each man shall be guaranteed the opportunity to show the best that there is in him," Roosevelt called for government to regulate business, prohibit corporate funding of political campaigns, and impose income and inheritance taxes. He demanded a "square deal" for the American people.[1]

In the mid-twentieth century, Republican president Dwight Eisenhower reiterated the earlier Republican calls for economic opportunity and applied them on an international scale. Believing that economic inequality bred war and that in the nuclear age war threatened humanity itself, Eisenhower sought to prevent international conflict by raising standards of living everywhere. He recoiled from using American resources to build weapons alone, warning, "Every gun that is made, every warship launched, every rocket fired signifies, in the final sense, a theft from those who hunger and are not fed, those who are cold and are not clothed." He called for government funding for schools, power plants, roads, and hospitals.[2]

At these crucial junctures in American history, Republicans have taken the stand that economic opportunity is central to the American ideal and that it is government's responsibility to make it possible for everyone to rise. At other times, the Republicans have thrown their support behind America's wealthiest men: Congress has passed laws that benefit businessmen—has even permitted businessmen to write legislation—and has blamed those who fell behind for their own poverty. While claiming to be championing "laissez-faire" government, Republicans and the policies they pursue have been anything but evenhanded; they have protected an increasingly small wealthy population at the expense of America's majority.

Over the one hundred and sixty years of their history, Republicans have swung from one pole to another: sometimes they have been leftists, sometimes reactionaries. Today, once again, the Republican Party has positioned itself on the far right. How did the Republican Party—the party of Abraham Lincoln, Theodore Roosevelt, and Dwight D. Eisenhower—become the party of today?

The journey has not been straightforward.

Since its formation in the 1850s, the party has, in three different eras, swung from one end of the political spectrum to the other. In each of these cycles, Republicans have replayed the same pattern. In their progressive periods they have expanded the vote, regulated business, and raised taxes. As a result, wealth became widely distributed and the economy strong.

Yet each time the party has sponsored progressive legislation, it has sparked a backlash from within its own ranks. After Lincoln, and after Roosevelt and Eisenhower as well, Republican leaders gradually turned against their own reforms in favor of protecting the interests of the rich. Their argument was always that taxes redistribute wealth, interfering with the fundamental right to property. Adamant that hardworking white men not see their fortunes transferred to lazy African Americans and immigrants, they cut funding for education and social welfare programs. As Republican policy shifted, and the machinery of government was enlisted to promote big business, wealth moved upward. And each time—in 1893, in 1929, and most recently in 2008—these periods of reaction were followed by a devastating economic crash.

There is nothing at all random about the Republicans' ideological shifts. They reflect the GOP's ongoing renegotiation of the party's—and the nation's—central unresolved problem: the profound tension between America's two fundamental beliefs, equality of opportunity and protection of property.

This tension has driven American political life since the nation's earliest days. The Declaration of Independence promised citizens equal access to economic opportunity. This was the powerful principle for which poor men were willing to fight the American Revolution, but it was only a principle; it was never actually codified in law. When the Founding Fathers wrote the Constitution, the supreme law that established the American nation, they assumed that the country's vast resources would ensure equality of opportunity. Worried instead about social stability, they enshrined in the Constitution another principle: that property rights must be protected.

In the economic, social, and political chaos of the Revolution and its aftermath, political leaders were much more concerned with putting out fires and hammering out plausible solutions to governing a raw country than they were with foreseeing problems that might arise in lands that were still unsettled. But western settlement became central to American life soon after the Constitution was ratified. As it did, Americans discovered that the principles of equality of opportunity and protection of property contradicted each other, and that that contradiction threatened American democracy itself.

During the American Revolution, Daniel Boone crossed the Appalachian Mountains to explore the land to the west of Virginia and returned with stories of "Kentucke," a land abundant in natural resources. As soon as the war ended, Americans rushed to lay claim to the region's riches. Once there, they quickly discovered that equality was not the inevitable result of economic freedom. Some men settled on better land than others; some had family money; some were just lucky, and quickly, those men accumulated more than others.

This rapid stratification of wealth revealed that the disparity between the Declaration of Independence and the Constitution made America's new democracy inherently unstable. Along with their wealth, Kentucky's landowners gained political power, which they used to secure legislation that promoted their interests at the expense of poorer settlers. They justified their actions with the Constitution's mandate that property must be protected. Wealthy men came to control government by working with lawmakers who shared their values and influencing voters by buying the channels through which they got information. Gradually, the laws they put in place circumscribed other men's ability to rise, and wealth moved upward. Equality of opportunity faltered.

As soon as national legislators saw what was happening in Kentucky, they tried to address the disparity between the Declaration of Independence and the Constitution. In 1787, when the Articles of Confederation were still in force, the congress assembled under that document passed the Northwest Ordinance, which was designed to prevent wealthy men from dominating the new western lands. The measure outlawed both primogeniture and slavery, systems that the men who wrote the Northwest Ordinance—including Thomas Jefferson, author of the Declaration of Independence—believed were instrumental in concentrating wealth. Over the next fifty years, as a handful of wealthy slave owners tightened a stranglehold on the South, it remained possible for poor men to rise in the northern lands protected by the Northwest Ordinance. By the 1850s, as the grandsons of America's Founding Fathers came of age, the contrast between protection of property in the South and opportunity in the North was stark.

America's 1848 acquisition of vast western lands from Mexico brought the two systems into conflict. Southern leaders insisted that the Constitution's protection of property— including their property in slaves—was the nation's fundamental principle, and they demanded the right to spread slavery to the new lands. But the struggles of Kentucky's poor settlers had shown northerners that slavery was incompatible with economic opportunity, and they opposed its western spread. By 1854, when southern slaveholders, who made up about 1 percent of the population, came to control the White House, the Senate, and the Supreme Court, they pushed to establish their program as the law of the land. It began to seem as if America would abandon the promise of equality in favor of the protection of property.

Certainly slave owners expected this outcome. They explained that their leadership was God's will; he had proved he favored them by making them richer than other Americans. According to these increasingly powerful men, society functioned best when workers with little intelligence and no aspirations simply did as they were told, producing food, clothing, housing, and all the other basic requirements of human society. Thanks to this hardworking majority, southern leaders, men at the forefront of civilization and refinement, could direct their attention to advancing human progress. The labor of those below freed them from the need to get their hands dirty. They proclaimed loudly that this system was the pinnacle of human achievement.

Their vehement defense of their way of life revealed slave owners' uneasy awareness of just how unstable their system was. It depended on keeping those at the bottom of society from political power. If they were allowed to vote, slaveholders explained, they would demand a larger share of the wealth they were producing and would launch a revolution by "the quiet process of the ballot-box," as one southern leader warned. Eventually, angry voters would turn to leaders who promised to promote equality and pledged to level the economic playing field.[3]

It was this very scenario that inspired the creation of the Republican Party. Northern men who aspired to better themselves rejected the idea that they were part of a permanent underclass meant to serve the rich; they reiterated the promise of the Declaration of Independence that every man was created equal. They argued that national prosperity could grow only from a strong and broad base, not from the top down, and they insisted that the government must guarantee all men equal access to economic opportunity. Aware that these northern men threatened their political dominance, slave owners vilified them and tried to manipulate the political system, insisting that the nation teetered on the edge of revolution.

But northerners went on to organize the Republican Party to push back against the control of government by the wealthy slaveholders. We "are for both the *man* and the *dollar*; but in cases of conflict, the man *before* the dollar," Abraham Lincoln explained. The Republicans, inspired by the need to guarantee that rich men would not dominate the government and take away economic opportunity for all, came together to take back the country.[4]

In 1860, the Republicans put Lincoln into the White House, and southerners promptly left the Union. Their absence opened the way for members of the new party to reshape the national government according to their principles. As they pivoted from one crisis to another to fund and fight the Civil War, they fundamentally changed the government, turning it from protecting the wealth of propertied men to promoting economic opportunity for everyone. In the 1860s, prodded by the needs of the Union cause, the Republican Party created a new, strong national government that worked to develop the economy from the bottom, educating young men and giving them land to farm. Finally, when the circumstances of the war permitted it, they tried to make America into a land where every man, regardless of race or background, could rise through hard work. They abolished slavery, then gave freedmen the vote to enable them to protect their own economic interests.

Civil War Republicans explicitly rejected the idea that they were enacting welfare legislation. Rather, they argued, it was a legitimate use of the government to expand economic growth that benefited everyone. Their arguments were popular, and their legislation won bipartisan support. The Founding Fathers had neglected to guard against the wealthy dominating government and subverting it to their own ends, but Lincoln's Republican Party had addressed that omission by protecting the economic independence its members believed lay at the heart of American liberty. It seemed the nation had, at last, found a political system that would fulfill its original promise to promote widespread prosperity.

Almost as soon as the Civil War ended, the Republicans' egalitarian vision came under attack. The war had required Americans to pay national taxes for the first time in history, and when government-funded programs helped ex-slaves and immigrant workers, opponents saw the very redistribution of wealth southern leaders had predicted. Eastern Republicans, whose industries flourished under the party's economic policies, began to focus on protecting their interests rather than promoting opportunity. Within just a few years, they drove the party to embrace the ideas it had just fought a war to expunge. By the 1870s, more than thirty years before Russia's Bolshevik Revolution, powerful Republicans were railing against the "socialism" and "communism" that might lead government to redistribute wealth to African Americans and immigrant workers through public works projects and social welfare legislation paid for with tax dollars. The party began to focus on defending the interests of big business, and money and power concentrated at the top of society. In the 1880s, voters turned to the Democrats, and the Republican Party took steps to restrict voting and jiggered the electoral system to stay in power. When their efforts failed and voters returned a Democratic government to power in 1892, Republican leaders predicted economic disaster, encouraged investors to shun the stock market, prompted a run on Treasury gold, and precipitated a national economic crash.

Within the span of about fifty years, the Republican Party had taken the nation to opposite extremes. In the 1860s, party leaders had launched an innovative drive to expand opportunity, but within a generation, the Republican effort to enable working men to rise had turned to the defense of property. Property was the heart of individualism, Republicans argued, and any effort to regulate business or to levy taxes was a direct attack on the American system. Unregulated capitalism meant that wealth concentrated at the very top of the economic ladder, consumption faltered, and an inevitable depression crashed down. Once the driving agents of economic security, Republicans had become engineers of economic disaster.

The tension between the commitment to equal opportunity and the quest to protect property created a vicious cycle. The country was in thrall to a pattern that would recur each time the party rededicated itself to its founding principles. It would become the central story of the Republican Party.

Just as Lincoln adapted the American vision of freedom to the challenges of westward expansion, Theodore Roosevelt and Dwight D. Eisenhower adapted it to the crises of their own eras: industrialization and international conflict. Lincoln, Roosevelt, and Eisenhower each believed that government must not privilege any specific economic interest, neither stacking the deck for the rich nor redistributing wealth to the poor. It should work to promote the interests of all hardworking Americans, the group that by the 1870s had come to be called the middle class. The vision of these three presidents, at critical moments, revived what was best about the Republican Party.

As Lincoln had done before him, Roosevelt recognized the danger of a system that forced increasing numbers of workers into poverty and concentrated wealth and power in the hands of a few. He came of age during the 1880s, the height of early American industrialization, when wealth was gathered in the hands of business owners, who built empires that rested on the labor of millions of unskilled urban workers. Opposing the industrialists' iron control over government, Roosevelt turned back to the original Republican vision, adapting it to the particular moment in which he governed. He called for government regulation of business and promotion of education to guarantee a level playing field for all Americans. His actions forced national leaders again to take measures to protect economic freedom.

The backlash against this second expansion of the middle class was quick and dramatic, especially after the labor and racial unrest following World War I. Republicans accused workers and African Americans of plotting to bring the Bolshevik Revolution to America and demanded full-throated support for capitalism from all Americans. When the party resumed control of the government in the 1920s, its leaders slashed taxes and business regulation, insisting that a strong business sector would create wealth that would make everyone prosper. "The chief business of the American people," said Republican president Calvin Coolidge, "is business."[5]

As had been true thirty years before, wealth concentrated at the top of the economic scale and declining purchasing power among the majority of Americans destabilized the economy. When the 1929 crash wiped out disposable income, there were not enough consumers to fuel a recovery.

Americans clamored for government aid, but President Herbert Hoover echoed the big business Republicans of the 1890s. He and members of his administration blamed greedy and lazy American workers for the crash and insisted that the government must not intervene in the economy: the only things that would spark a recovery were lower taxes and pay cuts for public employees. The Great Depression settled over the country.

The language and the pattern were familiar. They had been honed in the aftermath of the Civil War and provided a potent blueprint for the next decades of Republican leadership, although they had more to do with the habits of the Republican Party than they did with the reality of modern life.

At the end of World War II, the cycle began again. Dwight Eisenhower renewed the Republican effort to expand the middle class and adapted that effort to the modern era. Facing the challenge of leading a superpower in a bitterly divided nuclear world, Eisenhower fervently believed that America must promote widespread economic prosperity across the globe to prevent the political extremism that sparked wars.

Like Lincoln and Roosevelt before him, Eisenhower revived the classic Republican view of government and set out to use it to guarantee American freedom in the postwar world. Under his direction, the middle class expanded, and the country thrived. But once again, a racist and anti-immigrant backlash in the 1960s and 1970s tied the party firmly to big business in the next decade. In an uncanny echo of the ideas of the 1890s and the 1920s, Republican economists embraced the old idea that deregulation and unfettered capitalism would create wealth that would trickle down to everyone in society. It took until the new millennium, but once again the government's aggressive promotion of big business led to wealth stratification and, inevitably, in October 2008, economic collapse.

Three great presidents, Abraham Lincoln, Theodore Roosevelt, and Dwight D. Eisenhower, advanced a new, progressive vision of America, only to have their vision come under attack from forces within their own party. In each era, opponents of government activism used racism, xenophobia, and antitax rhetoric to destroy Republican programs designed to advance economic opportunity. Party leaders then tied the party to big business, abandoning entrepreneurs and small businessmen as well as rising workers. Wealth moved to the top echelons of society, until, in each era, a crash destroyed the economy.

The Republican Party repeatedly has swung from being the party of the middle class to the party of the rich, following pathways laid down during the peculiar years of the Civil War and its aftermath. It is impossible to understand the crossroads at which the Republicans stand today without understanding how this pattern, established in the late nineteenth century, would go on to repeat itself, first during the era of Theodore Roosevelt, then during the era of Dwight Eisenhower.

But the history of the Republican Party does more than simply show the trajectory of a political party. It explains why, since the Civil War, the nation has swung between progressivism and reaction, and why government efforts to level the economic playing field between individuals and corporations have been first embraced and then later attacked as "communism." These swings expose the tensions inherent in America's peculiar brand of government: how can a democracy promote individual economic opportunity at the same time it protects property?

1

The West as a Land of Promise

The story of the Republican Party starts in the late eighteenth century, in what was then the American West. Immediately after the Revolutionary War, Americans in Kentucky saw firsthand that the Constitution had a flaw that undercut the equality promised in the Declaration of Independence. The nation's fundamental law had not provided any way to prevent the wealthy from taking over the government and using it for their own benefit. One of the families that suffered profoundly from this omission was that of the man who would come to define the Republican Party: Abraham Lincoln.

In 1831, when he was twenty-two, Abraham Lincoln packed his few belongings and left his father's home. He set out on his own, traveling west to the wild Sangamo Country in the southwest part of the Illinois frontier, where settlers were slicing furrows through the purple and white and golden wild-flowers that bent in the endless winds, carving out rough farms from the deep grass prairies. In Sangamo Country, families

15

lived in rough cabins made of chinked logs, cooked corn and small game over open fires, and made do with whatever furniture they could knock together. They built small towns with gristmills, dry goods stores, and whiskey sellers, working their way up to economic security in a raw land.[1]

Lincoln's 1831 journey was part of America's dramatic nineteenth-century westward expansion. Decades earlier, as ragged soldiers were fighting the American Revolution, Daniel Boone had crossed the Appalachian Mountains to explore the land on the other side. The story of his travels appeared in 1784, a year after the Revolution ended, and it established for Americans what the West would mean for the new nation. Boone's West was a paradise. The soil was rich for farming, sparkling rivers could power mills, and there were prime animals fattened for hunters. It was a place where even an impoverished wanderer like Boone could prosper "in peace and safety, enjoying the sweets of liberty, and the bounties of Providence." Boone described the people who trekked across the mountains after him as ideal Americans, polite and hospitable, and so eager for education that they immediately set up schools. Boone's West was the heart of America, where every man could rise and build a thriving, educated community.[2]

Boone's distant relative Abraham Lincoln, grandfather of the future president, heard Boone's stories about the West. Lincoln sold a large parcel of land in his home state of Virginia and bought at least sixteen hundred acres in Kentucky. Then he joined the migrants leaving the settled states, bringing his wife and five children across the mountains to the new land. With the help of his three sons—Mordecai, Josiah, and Thomas—he cleared trees and brush to plant fields. Quickly, he accumulated property: by 1785, he owned more than five thousand acres.[3]

But this rich land was not unoccupied, and its inhabitants did not want new neighbors. In 1786, while the Lincoln men were working in one of their clearings, Indians attacked. They killed Abraham as Mordecai ran for a gun and Josiah ran for help. Eight-year-old Thomas stayed with his father. He was still beside his father's body when Mordecai, hastening back, shot an Indian coming toward the boy, a story that would grow over the years until it was one of the few things Thomas would pass on to his own son.[4]

His boys' lives after Lincoln's death revealed a political flaw in the idea that the West was a land of opportunity for everyone. The elder Lincoln had done well in Kentucky, but his sons would not share his fortune. Kentucky lands were still part of Virginia, and Virginia's primogeniture laws were in force there. Thus Abraham's eldest son, Mordecai, inherited all of his father's property. Mordecai became a wealthy Kentucky planter who bred racehorses, but his younger brothers, Josiah and Thomas, fell into poverty. Forced to work as a day laborer, Thomas, and presumably Josiah, never learned to read.[5]

Thomas worked hard as a farmer and occasionally as a carpenter to make up some of the ground the primogeniture laws had taken from him. Eventually, he bought his own farm. In 1806, he married Nancy Hanks, a young woman from a similarly rising family, and the two began to put down roots. They lived in a log cabin with a dirt floor and a single window, but they had a feather bed with a woven coverlet, a loom, and a spinning wheel, and Thomas was elected to minor positions in the community. In 1807, a daughter, Sarah, joined their household. Thomas Lincoln moved his wife and daughter to a new farm in Hardin County, Kentucky, in 1809. On February 12 of that year, Nancy and Thomas Lincoln welcomed their first son, naming him Abraham, after Thomas's dead father. It seemed to the Lincolns and their neighbors, who shared corn shuckings and barn raisings, that their hard work might be able to turn the West into the world of prosperity that Boone had promised.[6]

But by the time young Abraham was six, it was becoming clear to Thomas that his work had been in vain. Kentucky permitted slavery, and planters began to buy up great swaths of its rich land, on which they worked their gangs of slaves. The price of land rose, putting pressure on small farmers like Lincoln, who could afford only poorer and poorer fields. Worse still, the land in what was by now the new state of Kentucky had not been carefully surveyed. It seemed that no one, including Thomas Lincoln, had a clear deed to his property. Fights over land ownership flooded the courts, but only wealthy planters had enough money to hire lawyers to establish their deeds. Finally, unable to defend the title to his property, Thomas Lincoln had to leave Kentucky.[7]

The Declaration of Independence had stated that all men were created equal, and the American Revolution had promised to make men independent, but the Founding Fathers had not guarded against the power of wealthy men to control the machinery of government for their own benefit. This omission haunted men like Thomas Lincoln.

In 1816, Lincoln took his family across the Ohio River to what would become the free state of Indiana. This Territory had been organized under the Northwest Ordinance, a law passed by Congress in 1787 under the Articles of Confederation shortly after Kentucky's political problems became obvious. The Northwest Ordinance was based on an earlier measure drafted by Thomas Jefferson, the primary author of the Declaration of Independence, and was designed to prevent the control of the West by an economic elite. It prohibited both primogeniture and slavery in the new western lands north of the Ohio River. Congress expected these prohibitions to prevent the development of a class of wealthy men who could monopolize resources and take over the government. Thus the measure would, in theory, preserve American independence and upward mobility for all.

Thomas Lincoln certainly hoped so. He moved his family to a free state not because he hated slavery on moral grounds— although he did—but because slavery fed an oligarchy that was the antithesis of American independence. Only in a free state would he be free from slave owners, who seemed able to manipulate the machinery of government so that it worked only for them. In Indiana, where the government did not favor a very wealthy class, he could hope to rise to prosperity.

But Thomas Lincoln never managed to get his feet under him after moving to Indiana. Just as he and nine-year-old Abraham began the back-breaking work of clearing the unbroken forest for planting, Nancy Hanks Lincoln died, leaving eleven-year-old Sarah to keep house for her father, her brother, and her teenaged cousin Dennis Hanks. Thomas remarried quickly, bringing Sarah Bush Johnston and her three children from Kentucky to Indiana, but he was too old and broken to rebuild. In 1830, he gave up on Indiana and moved to Illinois to start again.[8]

Young Abraham found the work of hacking a farm out of wilderness dull and exhausting. The young man wanted to think, to read and write, but his aging father needed his muscle, and Abraham sowed seed, hoed fields, grubbed roots, cut trees, made fences, and harvested crops both at home and for farmers to whom his father hired him out for wages that legally belonged to Thomas. The young Lincoln disdained his father's apparent disregard for learning and lack of ambition. He had every intention of making the dream of western prosperity mean more for him than chopping weeds in the hot sun.[9]

In 1831, finally an adult, Abraham Lincoln set out to make his mark in the world, as did thousands of other young men in this dynamic era. But making it on his own wasn't much easier for the young Lincoln than it had been for his father. He settled in the town of New Salem, a village of about a hundred people on a bluff above the Sangamon River, where he failed as a storekeeper, then cobbled together various jobs, eking out a living splitting rails and making deliveries. Government appointments—as a postmaster and surveyor—kept him afloat and made him well known. In 1834, voters elected him to the state legislature.[10]

Elected office gave Lincoln the time and confidence to start studying law. When his term in the legislature was up, he moved to Springfield, the new state capital, where he formed a law partnership first with a prominent lawyer, John T. Stuart, and then, when Stuart went to Congress, with politician and circuit court judge Stephen T. Logan. By 1844, Lincoln's practice was lucrative enough to enable him to start his own firm. Two years later, after he had made his name riding the circuit around the state to try cases in local courthouses, he was elected to the US House of Representatives.[11]

Lincoln had risen to become a man of substance. After much hemming and hawing, in 1842 he had married Mary Todd, a well-connected and politically astute woman who also hailed from Kentucky, and they started a family that eventually included four sons. By 1844, the Lincolns lived in their own small but substantial home, valued at twelve hundred dollars.[12]

As a boy grubbing roots in Indiana, Lincoln had dreamed of a comfortable future that included having enough to eat, a home, and work that employed his considerable brain rather than just his considerable brawn. That dream, it seemed, had finally come true. Lincoln, like young men around him who had hoisted themselves from work shirts and log cabins into frock coats and frame houses, believed America was a land where a fellow could become anything he wanted, if only he worked hard enough.

Then, in 1854, that freedom to rise came under sudden and dramatic attack. After passage of the Missouri Compromise in 1820, slavery had been prohibited in the fertile western plains above the southern border of Missouri, the lands that would eventually become the states of Kansas, Colorado, Nebraska, Wyoming, Montana, South Dakota, and North Dakota. In 1854, a Democratic senator from Illinois, Stephen A. Douglas, proposed the Kansas-Nebraska Act, a measure that threatened to overturn the Missouri Compromise and open these millions of rich acres to slavery.

Men across the North recoiled from this attempt to inject slavery into land that had been free for more than thirty years. The first to take a stand against it were abolitionists, who opposed slavery everywhere, but although vocal, they were always a minority of the northern population. Many dismissed them as crackpots, and many more found their leaders insufferably self-righteous radicals, even if their hearts seemed to be in the right place.[13]

Then Horace Greeley, the abolitionist editor of the terrifically influential *New York Tribune*, expanded the struggle against the proposed Kansas-Nebraska measure beyond abolitionist circles by using an abolitionist concept to reframe the bill as an economic and political threat to white men. By the 1850s, the South was America's richest region by far, and its society was dominated by about 1 percent of its population. A very few large planters, who controlled more than 90 percent of the South's wealth and owned more than half its slaves, swayed southern politics. Abolitionists had developed the idea that this "Slave Power" was determined to dominate America by taking over the government; Greeley insisted that the Kansas-Nebraska proposal proved that the Slave Power had succeeded. The problem with the measure, he explained, was not that it would hurt slaves (although obviously it would). The problem was that it would close off the West for free white workers, who could never compete with rich slave owners. What southerners wanted, he wrote, was to control the government in order to push their economic system over the entire continent. According to Greeley, a Slave Power threatened to subvert American equality.[14]

Greeley's argument signaled that the issue of slavery would eventually sever the nation's major parties along regional lines. Greeley adhered to the Whig Party, whose members tended to be entrepreneurs and professionals who wanted the government to develop the economy by dredging rivers and clearing harbors, building a road across the new states of the Northwest, and raising tariffs to protect domestic industries. Douglas's Democratic Party, in contrast, served the wealthy southerners who demanded that the government stay small so that it could never meddle in their affairs. The two parties could stitch their northern and southern constituencies together only so long as their policies were nationally oriented and slavery remained a local institution that did not impinge on the lives of northerners.

But the Kansas-Nebraska Act convinced northerners that slavery directly threatened their society. Greeley's argument made good sense to men like Lincoln. Why wouldn't rich southerners try to take over the whole country, just as they had taken over Kentucky? Once established in the West, wealthy slave owners would monopolize the region's resources at the expense of small farmers and influence state governments to pass laws that enabled them to stay in control. America would become an oligarchy.

With northerners convinced that they were under attack by a southern Slave Power, passage of the Kansas-Nebraska bill fueled one of the nation's most important political realignments: the formation of the Republican Party. After Douglas introduced the Kansas-Nebraska bill in Congress, angry northerners had begun threatening to toss out the old, corrupt parties that seemed increasingly subservient to the Slave Power and talked of creating a new political party dedicated to preserving economic opportunity. When Congress passed the measure on May 8, 1854, it seemed they had little choice. The Kansas-Nebraska Act "took us by surprise—astounded us," Lincoln later recalled. "We were thunderstruck and stunned; and we reeled and fell in utter confusion." Northerners had lived their adult lives confident that the West would remain open for people like them—poor but hardworking, ambitious young men—to rise. Suddenly that promise was broken.[15]

On May 9, the morning after Congress had passed the Kansas-Nebraska Act, Maine congressman Israel Washburn invited about thirty antislavery representatives to meet at the rooms of his friends, Massachusetts representatives Thomas D. Eliot and Edward Dickinson (whose talented daughter Emily was already writing poetry), in Mrs. Crutchett's select board-inghouse at the northwest corner of Sixth and D Streets in Washington. The men who called the meeting were northern Whigs, and the men who came to it entered the elegant room as members of a variety of political parties, but they all left committed to a new northern organization that would stand against the spread of slavery into the West. They called them-selves "Republicans," hoping to invoke Thomas Jefferson—who had called his own political party Republican—and recall the principles of the Declaration of Independence.[16]

With the defection of so many prominent men from their old party affiliations to a new organization, Horace Greeley decided to cast his lot with the Republicans. In an editorial in his *New York Tribune*, he called for an end to "party names and party shackles" and urged northerners to come together to resist the extension of slavery and to stand firm against rich slave owners. With the conversion of Greeley, the Republicans won a powerful new voice. They had also begun the process of enlisting influential newspaper editors and rhetoricians in their behalf, a tactic that would help to make the Republican Party the key player in American politics for the next century and beyond.[17]

Momentum built for northerners to join the new political movement dedicated to opposing the spread of slavery into the West. Men came together in anti-Nebraska meetings and paraded through towns to protest the bill; women made anti-Nebraska flags. Conventions across the North called upon all free men to fight together "for the first principles of Republican Government and against the schemes of aristocracy, the most revolting and oppressive with which the earth was ever cursed or man debased." Stephen Douglas joked that he was so unpopular he could have traveled from Boston to Chicago by the light of his own burning effigies.[18]

That summer, Abraham Lincoln was arguing the biggest case of his legal career and remained aloof from Republicans, although he shared their anti-Nebraska sentiments. But in the fall, he began to articulate a new political ideology that aligned with the new party. In October, before an audience in Springfield, Illinois, Lincoln asserted that the Declaration of Independence rather than the Constitution embodied America's fundamental principle: equality. He explained that the Founding Fathers had prohibited slavery in the West with the Northwest Ordinance, and he reminded listeners that Thomas Jefferson himself had sponsored that law. Opposition to the extension of slavery was thus a bedrock American principle, even if the Constitution's protection of property bolstered the institution where it already existed. Those trying to confine slavery to the South, Lincoln maintained, were on the side of America's political angels.[19]

In the midterm election of 1854, northerners decimated the ranks of congressmen who had voted for the Kansas-Nebraska Act. There were 142 northern seats in the House of Representatives; voters put "anti-Nebraska" congressmen in 120 of them. Anti-Nebraska coalitions elected 11 senators and swept Democrats out of state legislatures across the North. Almost immediately, anti-Nebraska forces in Illinois began plotting to get the new Illinois legislature to elect Lincoln to the US Senate (for in the nineteenth century, state legislatures still chose the state's senators). They failed—barely—to pull the different factions together behind Lincoln, but it was clear that he would be a major force in Illinois politics in the future.[20]

Lincoln retreated back to his law practice, but like everyone else in the North, he could not ignore the dramatic events of 1854. It seemed that a Slave Power was bent on taking over the nation and only a new political organization could stop it.[21]

The events of the next few years would convince northerners that their fears about the Slave Power were prescient. Between 1855 and 1858, proslavery men tried to subvert democracy in Kansas, beat a senator almost to death on the floor of Congress, and took away Congress's power to legislate over slavery in the West. Each of these events had a different catalyst, but Republicans saw them as proof that a cabal was taking control of the nation. In 1858 Lincoln would tie them together in his famous House Divided speech, clearly defining the Republican fear that America was under deliberate siege.

The first scene of the drama was set in the new Kansas Territory, which had been carved out of the West by the Kansas-Nebraska Act. That law established that voters were to decide the status of slavery in Kansas Territory, but Congress had not spelled out how or when that would happen. The disastrous result of that omission was that proslavery and antislavery factions essentially went to war. Over the course of summer 1856, guerrilla warfare in Kansas caused about two hundred deaths and destroyed around two million dollars in property.[22]

Republicans interpreted the bloody events in the new Territory as part of a larger attempt to pervert democracy. Who would determine the future of Kansas: the antislavery settlers, who made up the majority, or a proslavery faction that had grabbed power through violence and fraud and set up a draconian proslavery government? It seemed the latter. Republican newspapers, led by the *New York Tribune* and the *Chicago Tribune*, published stories of an antislavery minister tarred and feathered and sent down a river on a raft, arbitrary arrests of free-state men, election fraud, and finally rumors that the government was planning to try all free-state men for treason in front of proslavery judges and juries. But the Democratic president, Franklin Pierce, sided with the proslavery faction and declared that antislavery men were outlaws.[23]

The conflagration burned back to the East, where the fight over Kansas engulfed Congress. In mid-May, proslavery Democrats denounced the free-state men as rebels, and free-state men demanded an investigation into Kansas election fraud and violence. In the midst of the furor, abolitionist senator

Charles Sumner of Massachusetts delivered a speech that, far from settling the problem, triggered an attack that added fuel to the fire.

Sumner's speeches were widely read, widely reprinted, and widely influential. They were larded with foreign-language quotations and erudite references, but they were also incendiary and full of extreme accusations and language that was barely on the right side of respectability. His 1856 speech "The Crime Against Kansas" compared the political struggle in Kansas to the rape of a virgin slave girl by her master. If that wasn't edgy enough for the Senate floor, Sumner lingered over a long, lurid description of elderly South Carolina senator Andrew Pickens Butler dallying with his "mistress," the "harlot" slavery, and threatening to take his state out of the Union if everyone did not share his infatuation with her. To serve their "madness for Slavery," Sumner claimed, men like Butler had bought up the press, lawyers, judges, and even the president, all of whom did their bidding. The Slave Power was trying to force slavery on the unwilling settlers of Kansas; an oligarchy was trying to deprive American citizens of their rights.[24]

Sumner's speech was so shocking that even committed Republicans distanced themselves from it, and from him. Then, suddenly and dramatically, a southerner seemed to demonstrate that the senator from Massachusetts was terribly right.[25]

On May 22, two days after Sumner finished speaking, a representative from South Carolina came up behind him as he sat writing at his desk during a recess and beat him unconscious with a heavy walking stick. The attacker, Preston Brooks, was Senator Butler's cousin, and he was infuriated by Sumner's verbal assault on the elderly man and his characterization of the South. As southern senators looked on, Brooks rained blows on Sumner until his weapon broke. The senator was left sprawled on the floor, badly bruised and soaked in blood from two bone-deep slashes on his head.[26]

Sumner might be annoying, and he might espouse the abolitionist cause many found distasteful, but he was an elected senator speaking for his constituents on the floor of the Senate. That he should be beaten almost to death for his words while southern senators stood by and watched seemed to demonstrate the truth of his position. The Slave Power threatened the right of white northerners to be represented in their government. Its adherents were willing to go to any extreme— even kill an elected senator—in order to push their agenda. Across the North, mass meetings condemned the attack "not only as a cowardly assault upon a defenceless man," as one supporter wrote to Sumner, "but as a crime against the right of free speech and the dignity of a free state."[27]

Increasingly, men turned toward the new political party that promised to stand up to the Slave Power. Abraham Lincoln was one of them. Although he had continued to speak against the spread of slavery after the passage of the Kansas-Nebraska Act, Lincoln had been unwilling to abandon the established Whig Party for the new coalition. Finally, in late May 1856, he left the Whigs and cast his lot with the Illinois Republicans. In recognition of his growing influence, they asked him to give the final speech of their convention. Embracing the theme of the hour, he called for everyone to stand against the influence of the Slave Power.[28]

Opposition to the Slave Power was the dominant theme of the 1856 presidential election. Republicans nominated a prominent western adventurer, John C. Frémont, on a platform that opposed the extension of slavery into the West. Another new party, the Know-Nothings, whose signature issue was opposition to foreigners and Catholics, nominated Millard Fillmore, the last Whig president, on a platform that opposed both slavery and immigration. Even the Democrats nodded to popular fear of a Slave Power conspiracy by nominating for president the bland Pennsylvania Democrat James Buchanan; he had been out of the country for several years as minister to Britain, giving him apparent distance from any southern cabal.

Although politicians of all parties were talking about the Slave Power, the election revealed that the country had not yet fully realigned over the slavery question. The Democrats had enough national support to put Buchanan into the White House, and the Whigs could bring southern votes to Fillmore, but Republicans ran strong for a brand-new party. Their candidate won only about a half a million fewer votes than Buchanan, out of a total of about four million votes cast. Ominously for Democrats, Frémont and Fillmore together polled four hundred thousand more votes than Buchanan.[29]

People had voted for Buchanan in the hope that he would calm the sectional tension, but instead he fed the growing crisis by giving Republicans more proof that the Slave Power was taking over the government. In his inaugural address, Buchanan noted that the Supreme Court would soon calm the situation in Kansas by deciding a case that had sat before it for a year, a case that would establish when a Territory could decide the slavery question. "To their decision, in common with all good citizens, I shall cheerfully submit, whatever this may be," Buchanan announced.[30]

Only days later, the Supreme Court handed down the *Dred Scott* decision. Among other things, this decision established that Congress had no power to stop slavery from spreading into any western Territory. To outraged northerners, it looked like a setup. Democrats with deep southern ties dominated the Court, and they had delayed the decision until after the presidential election to keep from alarming northern voters.

For the decision certainly alarmed them. The Court had declared the Missouri Compromise, a law northerners held sacrosanct, unconstitutional. And, perhaps most galling, the decision appeared to prove that Buchanan already knew of its outcome when he spoke so approvingly of it at his inauguration. Northerners howled. Newspaper editors poured vitriol on the decision. The acerbic Horace Greeley put it best when, the day after the decision came down, he announced that it was "entitled to just so much moral weight as would be the judgment of a majority of those congregated in any Washington bar-room."[31]

In June, the Illinois Republican Party nominated Lincoln to run for Douglas's Senate seat in the 1858 election. Lincoln accepted in a speech history knows as the House Divided speech, which painted in everyday images the conspiracy to turn the nation over to slave owners. In Lincoln's formulation, Stephen, Franklin, Roger, and James—Stephen Douglas, who had written the Kansas-Nebraska Act; former president Franklin Pierce, who had presided over its passage; Chief Justice Roger Taney, who had recently declared that Congress had no authority to prohibit slavery in the West; and President James Buchanan, who threw his weight behind the Taney court— were all building a house that Lincoln used to symbolize the nation. When they were through, Lincoln warned, Americans would find that the carpenters had fitted slavery into every beam and nail in the framing. Slavery would be integral to every part of the nation: the South, the West, and, eventually, the North.[32]

In July, a concerned Douglas returned to Illinois to rebut Lincoln, and for the next three months the two men battled over the extension of slavery. Douglas insisted that self-determination was the true genius of American democracy and that the question of slavery must fall to western settlers themselves. African Americans had no inherent rights, according to Douglas: "This government of ours...was made by the white man, for the benefit of the white man, to be administered by white men." Lincoln stood firm on the Declaration of Independence. He warned that if Americans started to make exceptions to the principle of equality, there was no obvious place to stop: "If one man says it does not mean a negro, why not another say it does not mean some other man?" As the two men debated their positions across Illinois, Lincoln suggested that Douglas and the Democrats were bankrolled by rich slave owners working to destroy America. Poor Republicans, though, had "to fight this battle upon principle, and upon principle alone." Although Lincoln lost to Douglas in 1858, his principles continued to gain momentum.[33]

But what were those principles? Republicans had made it clear exactly what they stood against, but they had not yet explained what they stood for. Finally, in 1859, responding to a speech South Carolina Democrat James Henry Hammond had delivered in the Senate, Lincoln articulated a Republican vision for

America. In their speeches, these men laid out two dramatically different visions of America, visions that had contended since the nation's earliest days and whose defenders would continue to struggle for supremacy for the rest of the nineteenth century and the twentieth—and into the twenty-first.

In March 1858, on the floor of the Senate, James Henry Hammond gave a speech that laid out the worldview of southern slave owners. Hammond was a perfect foil for Republicans. He was a wealthy and well-connected slave owner with predatory sexual appetites, which ruined the lives of his white nieces as well as those of his slaves. His sense of mastery was unparalleled.[34]

Hammond described an America that sounded a lot like an oligarchy. When things were ordered correctly, he explained, the bottom of society was made up of drudges: stupid, unskilled workers who were strong, docile, and loyal to their betters. He called these workers "mudsills," a reference to the timbers of a building that were driven into the ground to support the loftier structure above. Members of this mudsill class would never rise. They were too stupid, for one thing, and they were happy where they were. On this mudsill, according to Hammond, rested higher civilization—those gentlemen who led "progress, civilization, and refinement," men like him. It was right for southern slave owners to control the country, he said, because they were the wealthiest men in the nation, proving that they alone had figured out a true system of political economy.

The southern system was the only safe one, Hammond explained. Members of the mudsill must have no say in government, for if they did, they would demand a redistribution of wealth. So long as they had no political power, their stupidity—and cupidity—could never challenge the system that Hammond insisted worked so well. The North, he warned, used white men as its mudsill and thus courted disaster. Northern workers had a terrible potential to destroy society because, unlike Black slaves, they could vote. Indeed, they made up the majority. If they worked together, "Where would you be?" he asked. The government would be overthrown and property redistributed.

Hammond didn't worry about the apparent discrepancy between the concept of American democracy and his insistence that the upper class should rule. He believed that the idea of self-government was never intended to be more than a general principle. Regular people should not be "annoyed with the cares of Government." Their role was only to elect one or another set of leaders, and these leaders would make all the decisions. Even then, he believed, Congress could actually do very little. No matter what a majority of the people might want—or how big that majority was—Congress could not do anything unless it was explicitly enumerated in the Constitution. According to Hammond, the nation was frozen into a state that favored a wealthy elite.[35]

Men like Hammond—slave owners with more than fifty slaves who made up the planter class—spoke authoritatively for the South. But most southern whites were much poorer than those at the top of society. They tended their own farms with the help of their wives and children and, if they were lucky, a slave or two. And yet, a complicated mix of racial and class ideas made white southerners buy in to Hammond's vision. So long as they thought they could rise in America, and so long as slavery maintained a clear line between themselves and the African Americans alongside whom they lived and worked, southern whites shared an interest in maintaining the institution. In the antebellum years, southern thinkers had bolstered this racial line with religious and cultural arguments that bound white southerners more and more tightly to the slave system. Ministers defended the religious purity of slavery to their congregations; in turn, southern whites had come to believe that the culture slavery supported was the only true American way. By the time Hammond spoke in 1858, most white southerners believed profoundly in the sanctity of a slave system that served only the very top 1 percent of families in the American South.[36]

But northerners like Abraham Lincoln disagreed. Hammond's vision of an American society divided between the dim drudges and the rich and powerful was not only deeply troubling to them; it was also profoundly insulting. Lincoln had grown up in uneducated poverty and had, himself, sweated in the dirt and heat of the fields. He had, though, set out as a young man, moving to the river bluffs of the Illinois frontier to better himself. He had worked hard as a hired hand and as a clerk and had studied passionately to make up for his lack of opportunity. Was it really true, as Hammond suggested, that he was stupid and content to serve others for a pittance his whole life? Was it true that he was dull timber on which his betters should rest?

The idea was ludicrous.

In September 1859, Lincoln spoke at the Wisconsin Agricultural Fair, held at Milwaukee's fairgrounds, and used the opportunity to reply to Hammond's argument by articulating a new theory of political economy. With successful farmers at the fair prodding their prize cattle around dusty animal rings and exhibiting the vegetables they had coaxed out of the earth, Lincoln denied that men were bound forever to the station in which they were born. Instead, he outlined a worldview that would stand against that of Hammond's to become the heart of the fledgling Republican Party.[37]

Lincoln ridiculed the idea that the wealthy should control society. That canard had the equation backward, he explained. Laborers, not rich men, created wealth. In the nineteenth century most Americans worked directly on the land or water. Men like Lincoln saw farmers wrestling wheat and potatoes out of the ground with harrows and hoes; fishermen fighting the seas to reach rich shoals and fill their holds with cod; miners swinging picks to uncover gold; lumberjacks ripping saws through forests to make lumber. They saw the individual worker as the fundamental element in a healthy economy. Labor, they believed, created value by turning natural resources—earth, fish, gold, trees—into something a worker could sell.

From the idea that labor created value came a number of other principles. First of all, Republicans believed that anyone willing to work could rise to economic prosperity. A man's ability to work was his money in the bank, in effect, and there was no excuse for an able-bodied man or his family to live in poverty. A good God would not have created a world in which man's inevitable fate was to suffer from want. Instead, the Almighty had created a world in which there were plenty of resources for everyone. So long as men were willing to work, the world had unlimited plenty.

Everyone in this sort of economy shared the same interests. The way a healthy American society operated, Lincoln told the Milwaukee farmers, was that "the prudent, penniless beginner in the world, labors for wages awhile, saves a surplus with which to buy tools or land, for himself; then labors on his own account another while, and at length hires another new beginner to help him." What was good for the individual worker was, ultimately, good for everyone. There was no conflict between labor and capital; capital was simply "pre-exerted labor." Except for a few unproductive financiers and those who wasted their wealth on luxuries, everyone was part of the same harmonious economic system.

This harmony depended on the protection of property and the right of every man to accumulate as much as he could. The chance to become wealthy would motivate a man to work hard, but fear that government policies might endanger his hard-earned wealth would dim his enthusiasm for labor. Then, too, if property were not safe, those who had already accumulated capital would send it overseas, depriving other men of the chance to rise. The nation, and the men in it, would stop getting richer.

For all their defense of private property, though, men like Lincoln adamantly opposed great accumulations of wealth. Rich men who sought to monopolize land, money, or the means of production were undermining the natural harmony of economic interests and endangering the entire country. If a few people came to dominate money or resources, rising laborers would be forced to work for them forever or, at best, would have to pay exorbitant prices for the land they needed to become independent. That was what had happened in Kentucky, and what men like Lincoln worried would happen across the nation if the Slave Power had its way.

A key way to guarantee economic independence, Lincoln told the Milwaukee audience, was to promote education. A man's brain guided, directed, and protected his labor, so every mind must be cultivated and improved to help men rise. Those who believed workers were the mudsill of society wanted their workers to have strong backs and weak minds. To this, Lincoln responded, "Free Labor says 'no!'" Only universal education could prevent oppression of hardworking men, he said, whether from "crowned-kings, money-kings, [or] land-kings."

Hammond and men like him rested their politics on the Constitution's protection of property and their worldview on the idea that workers and employers constantly competed for primacy. But Lincoln looked back to the ideas of equality outlined in the Declaration of Independence to envision a new and prosperous future. All men were included in the Declaration of Independence, he insisted, and what was good for individuals was good for society. Now that Americans had the good fortune to be able to create new communities in the West, it was imperative that they honor the principle of equality of opportunity for every man. Only the exclusion of slavery from the new western lands would enable every man—white as well as Black—to rise.[38]

Although he did not talk about it in Milwaukee, Lincoln had also given significant thought to Hammond's argument that Congress was so bound by constitutional limits that it could not respond to the popular will for new initiatives. To Lincoln, this simply made no sense. He had watched

New Salem die because the settlers there—willing workers, eager to bring prosperity to their region—did not have the resources to dredge the Sangamon River to increase their river trade. To say that the government could not engage in the sort of economic development that would have saved New Salem would leave much of the nation mired in poverty, all for lack of a small investment that could clear the way for enterprising young men to get to work. Lincoln believed that the government must respond to popular desire for it to do work that was too big for individuals.[39]

This conviction meant that Lincoln's approach to governing was profoundly different from that of antebellum Democrats. He believed that government should be "nonpartisan," acting in the interests of all citizens, rather than catering to the voters of whichever party was in power. Political contests enabled different interests to hash out policies acceptable to the majority of voters. In contrast, Democrats saw politics not as a forum for developing policy but as the battleground for parties. By the 1850s, they held onto national power not through policy so much as through attacks on their opponents and through the "spoils system"—for to the victor go the spoils—in which the party that won an election used the government to advance its own interests. Party leaders distributed government jobs to supporters in a system known as patronage. Although this seemed like a crass system of payoffs to its opponents, Democrats argued that the only way a nation could command the allegiance of its citizens was to tie them to the government through the machinery of politics. Lincoln's emphasis on nonpartisanship meant that the Republicans would have a vision of the interests of the nation as a whole and a language to promote that vision, which Democrats, with their focus on opposition and inactivity, did not.[40]

By 1859, Lincoln had brought together these two important concepts in a worldview that would soon become that of the Republican Party. His concern about the growing power of slave owners in the 1850s had convinced him that, rather than privileging an economic elite, the government must leave the economic playing field free for hardworking individuals to rise. By 1859, the idea of a level playing field had combined with his conception of nonpartisan politics to suggest that "equality" might mean something more active than simply staying out of the way of the man on the make. Republicans like Lincoln were ready to adopt the idea that the government should actively promote individual economic advancement.

In spring 1860, when Republicans in the House of Representatives offered their first major piece of legislation, they gave voters a concrete example of what Republican economic activism would mean. A recession during the Buchanan administration had tanked government revenues and thrown men out of work, especially in northern cities. To fill the empty Treasury and create jobs, Republicans called for sweeping new tariffs, which were essentially taxes on manufactured goods arriving from Europe.

The government had traditionally raised money with tariffs, but whereas past tariffs had protected only manufacturing businesses, in spring 1860 Representative Justin Smith Morrill of Vermont introduced a tariff that also protected agricultural, mining, and fishing products. Sugar, wool, flaxseed, hides, beef, pork, corn, grain, minerals, dried and salted fish, and so on would all be protected.

Morrill explained that the proposed bill rested on Republicans' belief that everyone shared a harmony of interests. What helped one group would inevitably help another. The most important part of the economy was the most fundamental one: the conversion of raw materials into consumable products. The Morrill Tariff would support those working in primary industries, and Morrill explained that a strong foundation of upwardly mobile farmers and workers would make America an economic powerhouse. The bill's supporters were clear about what they were doing: they declared it the province of government to advance policies that promoted "the prosperity and happiness of the whole people." With a jab at the mudsill theory, Morrill noted that the government should treat all Americans "as members of one family, all entitled to equal favor, and no one to be made the beast of burden to carry the packs of others."[41]

Republicans got the Morrill Tariff through the House in May 1860. Southerners stopped it in the Senate, enabling Republicans to highlight the difference between their governing plans and those of the Democrats.

In the run-up to the election of 1860, no one was more eager to delineate those differences than Abraham Lincoln. Hindsight makes the emergence of the Republican Party look preordained, but in fact 1860 was a critical year for its definition and ultimate success. And no one did more to define the Republican Party in 1860 than the lanky westerner with a sense of humor.

Republican leaders were divided between radicals, who wanted sweeping national action against slavery everywhere, and conservatives, who simply wanted to return to the time before the Kansas-Nebraska Act turned everything upside down. That split threatened disaster for the party. If party leaders nominated a radical for president, more conservative western Republicans would shift away from the new party and line up to support the presidential candidacy of northern Democrat Stephen Douglas. To combat this backlash toward conservatism, Lincoln urged more radical party leaders to moderate their public stands. He spoke often and wrote widely, emphasizing that the principles he had laid out in his debates with Douglas should not be compromised.

Although Lincoln was an increasingly important national figure, it was not a given that he would be the new party's standard-bearer in the 1860 election. Many men vied for the presidential nomination, and a gambler in 1859 would have put his money on radical New York senator William Henry Seward, who had the nation's chief political backroom dealer, Thurlow Weed, behind him. The humorless abolitionist Salmon Portland Chase from Ohio also had followers. On the other side of the party, so too did conservative Edward Bates from the border state of Missouri, who had never actually joined the Republican Party but had won antislavery credentials by emancipating his own slaves.[42]

In February 1860, New York City Republicans eager to undercut Seward invited Lincoln to come east to give a speech. Lincoln understood that this invitation would give him the opportunity to reach a new audience. Going all out to make a positive impression, he picked a complicated topic that would highlight his intelligence and logic, and he bought a new suit. Then he made the three-day train trip from Springfield, Illinois, to New York City and took rooms at the luxurious Astor House. Only hours before his speech, he had his picture taken by fashionable photographer Matthew Brady. A true artist, Brady quickly realized he should celebrate rather than try to conceal Lincoln's great height. He photographed the six-foot-four-inch frontiersman standing, rather than sitting, and placed him in front of a classical pillar beside a pile of books, his angular cheekbones and dark eyes gazing pensively at the camera, the westerner come east.

Shortly after eight on the evening of February 27, Lincoln rose nervously to address the capacity crowd at New York's Cooper Union. Fifteen hundred men had crowded into the hall. They were shocked by the speaker's rough, awkward looks. Then he began a dry recitation of his argument in a high-pitched voice with a backwoods accent, and their worst fears were realized: they had been bamboozled into listening to a backcountry hick.

As he spoke, though, Lincoln warmed to his topic, and by the time he got to the end of his ninety-minute speech, listeners were on their feet cheering. Lincoln undercut Senator Douglas's accusation that Republicans were radicals, establishing through careful logic that it was rather Democrats trying to spread slavery who were radicals, Democrats who were dangerously sectional. Republicans were the ones whose philosophy echoed the national vision of the Founding Fathers. The next day New York newspapers reprinted the speech and hailed the event, putting 170,000 copies of the address into the hands of readers. Lincoln's Cooper Union speech had made him a household name and pulled the Republicans firmly away from radicalism.[43]

Lincoln's supporters then pulled off a dramatic coup: they arranged for the May 1860 Republican convention to be held in Chicago, giving their candidate a home-field advantage. When the convention met, Lincoln had the support of the Illinois delegates, of course, and outside his home state he was "the second choice of everybody," one supporter noted. On the third ballot the momentum swung his way. Chase and Seward had lost. While a number of men wept with joy at Lincoln's nomination, kingmaker Weed wept with disappointment.[44]

The party's platform reiterated that Republicans defended the principles of the Declaration of Independence, going so far as to quote the document's famous assertion "that all men are created equal; that they are endowed by their Creator with certain unalienable rights; that among these are life, liberty, and the pursuit of happiness; that to secure these rights, governments are instituted among men, deriving their just powers from the consent of the governed." It insisted that the normal condition of Americans was freedom, and charged that Democrats were attacking that principle because they were subservient to slave owners. While states must be able to determine the status of slavery within their own borders, the "new dogma" that slavery must spread everywhere in the West was dangerous and revolutionary political heresy.

The platform went on to call for policies to advance national development. Republicans endorsed tariffs to protect every branch of the economy; the distribution of land to promote farming; legislation to protect the equal rights of immigrants; the clearing of rivers and harbors for maritime trade; and the construction of a transcontinental railroad. Republicans invited all citizens—"however differing on other questions"—to support their ticket.[45]

The Republicans were finally united, but the Democratic Party split in two, into a moderate northern wing that nominated Stephen Douglas and a fervent proslavery southern wing that nominated John C. Breckinridge. Based in the middle of the country, primarily in Virginia, Kentucky, and Tennessee, a new Constitutional Union Party, whose adherents basically wanted the slavery question to go away, nominated its own candidate and called vaguely for Americans to honor the Constitution and enforce the laws. With four candidates in the race and Democrats slashing at each other more than at Lincoln, the Republicans finished first in November. They won majorities in both houses of Congress and elected their presidential candidate with slightly less than 40 percent of the vote, a winning plurality.

Less than a hundred years after Daniel Boone blazed a trail to Kentucky in search of economic opportunity, and with the experience of men like Thomas Lincoln still fresh in their memory, Republicans had fashioned themselves as the defenders of American liberty, the guarantors of economic fairness and equality. In 1860, only six years after they had organized, they put Abraham Lincoln into the White House.

2

Government of the People, by the People, for the People

As soon as it became clear that Lincoln had been elected, southern congressmen began to resign. By picking up and going home, these Democrats handed control of the government to the fledgling Republican Party. Within months the nation would be embroiled in a cataclysmic civil war. As they fought the war and paid for it, Republicans would reconceive the nation according to their principles. Pushed and pulled by the exigencies of the battlefields but always guided by their worldview, Republicans over the next four years hammered out a new, active role for government that would make it easier for hardworking men to rise. In the process, they both constructed a new concept of American freedom and branded as disloyal the Democrats who opposed them. But no matter how fervently Republicans talked about equality, as early as 1864 it was apparent that their economic policies were creating a class of extremely wealthy men, a discrepancy between ideology and reality that would not bode well for the future.

The Republicans' expansion of government's role in the economy grew first from desperation. When Lincoln took office, the nation was in dire financial straits. Not only had South Carolina, Mississippi, Florida, Alabama, Georgia, Louisiana, and Texas already left the Union—and it would obviously take money to fund the effort to get them back—but the new president inherited from the previous administration a sixty-five-million-dollar deficit, along with outstanding short-term Treasury notes soon coming due. There was nothing in the Treasury to pay these notes. The government needed money fast. Republicans began constructing policy largely by the seat of their pants, but the result was a new financial and revenue system that tied every American firmly to the national government.[1]

Lincoln's secretary of the Treasury, Salmon P. Chase, knew little about finance; Lincoln had given him the post to keep the Ohio man's insatiable ambition from making trouble for the new administration. In his first effort to raise money, Chase simply followed precedent: he turned to private bankers for funds. He offered three million dollars in bonds to New York financiers. But when bankers refused to pay anything near par for the bonds, the game changed. Chase netted some badly needed cash, but northerners began to snarl that financiers were disloyal.[2]

Popular anger at bankers made Republicans begin to codify their rather vague principle that America's people were the foundation of its wealth. While Chase continued to worry that he needed the support of the nation's financiers, Congress began to shift financial measures away from bankers and toward the American people. This was practical, but it also nicely reinforced the Republican conviction that average citizens, rather than the wealthy few, were the heart of the nation. Quickly, necessity became deliberate policy. Over the next two years, Congress would create a new financial system that rested on the widespread participation of regular people across the country rather than on large loans from eastern bankers.

The process of rebuilding the nation's financial system began as soon as Confederates fired on Fort Sumter in Charleston Harbor. Lincoln called for seventy-five thousand volunteers to suppress the rebellion, then called Congress into emergency session in July 1861 to find the money to put them in the field. Republicans understood that taxes were imperative, but they had little sense of how to levy them. Everyone threw something into the pot. The first revenue measure was a cobbled-together mess of different tariffs and taxes: a higher tariff on sugar, tea, coffee, and liquor; a twenty-million-dollar direct tax on the states, letting states figure out how to raise the money; and a novel income tax of 3 percent on annual incomes over eight hundred dollars.

The measure was intellectually incoherent, drawing from different precedents and different theories, but it did reflect Republican ideas in one important way: it distributed the financial burdens of the war evenly among rich and poor, East and West, businessmen and farmers. The tariff duties on necessities would fall disproportionately on the poor. The direct tax, which almost all states funded through a land tax, would hurt poor western farmers but barely touch wealthy eastern businessmen. To address these inequities, Senator James F. Simmons, a very wealthy—and somewhat shady—cotton trader from Rhode Island had proposed the income tax. The chairman of the Senate Finance Committee, the irascible but staunchly principled William Pitt Fessenden of Maine, enthusiastically seconded the idea, despite the fact that such a tax would fall disproportionately on the eastern states. An income tax would mean that "the burdens will be more equalized on all classes of the community, more especially on those who are able to bear them."[3]

There was very little discussion of this revenue measure since it came up as the first battle of Bull Run revealed just how unprepared for war the government really was. Instead of the decisive victory that northerners had expected from their troops, the battle turned into a rout, with panicked Union soldiers sprinting from the front, throwing aside guns and rucksacks as they ran. Rumors that Confederate cavalry would sweep into Washington on the heels of the fleeing soldiers convinced Congress that it must protect the capital immediately. It authorized an army of five hundred thousand men and quickly passed the undigested tax bill. Lincoln signed the measure into law on August 5, 1861.

The Union limped through the rest of the summer, but the collapse of the nation's banking system in the fall prodded congressmen to make their first major effort to move financial policy toward popular funding. Since the 1830s state banks, chartered by state governments, had managed America's banking, circulating their own currency backed—or not—by securities. Before the Civil War, northwestern banks had supported their currency with southern bonds. When secession made those bonds worthless, northwestern currency collapsed. Without money, trade stopped and business stagnated. By fall 1861 an economic crisis loomed as the region's farmers faced marketing the year's crops without a circulating medium.

Chase suggested solving the problem by replacing state bank notes with new national bank notes and leaving the rest of the banking system unchanged, but eastern financiers recoiled at even this mild adjustment. Opposed to any plan that might hamper the circulation of their profitable currency, they tried to demonstrate just how important the banking industry was to the country. In late December 1861, as Congress worked to create the new national bank notes Chase wanted, New York bankers stopped redeeming their notes in gold. Specie payment was a standard option rarely exercised by customers, but it reassured people that bank notes represented real value. A refusal to redeem notes in gold created panic as bank paper essentially became worthless, making people who held the notes of the suspending bank or who had deposits in it worry—with great justice—that their wealth had just evaporated.

Suspension sparked a domino effect as suspension by one bank made depositors of other banks rush to take their money out in gold before it, too, disappeared. Since banks kept only a fraction of their capital in gold on hand, the rush meant the next tier of banks had to suspend, and so on. When the New York banks stopped redeeming in specie, a run on the Treasury meant the national government had to suspend, too. The New York banks had precipitated the Union's economic collapse. Left unchecked, the banking crisis would take down the war effort.[4]

Their early purchase of government bonds had stretched New York banks' reserves, and bankers were undoubtedly under pressure, but administration men and Republicans in general were convinced that eastern bankers were deliberately trying to force the government to cater to them. Major banks in Ohio and Indiana did not suspend specie payments until the New York banks' suspension caused a run on their gold, adding further evidence to the argument that suspension was a political, rather than a financial, decision. Newspapers across the country condemned the "presumptuous and insolent banks" and suggested that if bankers were going to prevent Congress from fixing the country's financial crisis, then it was high time "the people" reined in their power.[5]

Rather than bowing to Wall Street's pressure, Congress abruptly cut bankers out of financial decision making and rested government finances on the strength of the American people in general to fund government obligations. It created paper money backed not by private capital, as notes traditionally were, but by government credit, which would enter circulation when Secretary Chase used it to pay the government's bills. The Legal Tender Act provided for the issue of $150 million of notes for use as legal tender in payment of all debts, public and private. This measure would keep the government from going "into Wall Street, State street, Chestnut street"— the centers of American financial power—"or any other street begging for money," said its congressional sponsor. It would "assert the power and dignity of the Government." "We are all in favor of the citizens of the Republic becoming its *creditors*, rather than the *debtors* of the bankers and capitalists," one Ohio man wrote to his congressman. Newspapers claimed that the cry in the streets was "Down with the banks, and give us a national currency."[6]

The measure passed, although Republicans from New York, New Jersey, and New England—all areas with strong banking interests—either voted no or showed a remarkable lack of enthusiasm for it. Lincoln signed the Legal Tender Act on February 25, 1862. America had a new, national currency that rested not on private capital controlled by state banks but on the stability of the national government, supported by regular Americans.[7]

The notes, printed with green ink on the back, were wildly popular and spread across the country quickly. With their history of unstable state banks, westerners, especially, liked the national money and grabbed at it "like a duck at a worm," one congressman noted. Only four months later, Congress authorized the issue of another $150 million worth of greenbacks. Government money seemed the path to the future.[8]

The new money could be used immediately, but it would start depreciating just as quickly if the government didn't have funds to back it. The war was costing the Treasury two million dollars a day, and the government was borrowing for regular expenses. If credit failed, so would the war, and everyone knew it. When Chase failed to get bankers to buy more bonds without a large discount, congressmen knew they needed to develop a major new revenue measure. Even conservative Republican newspapers declared, "There is not the slightest objection raised in any loyal quarter to as much taxation as may be necessary."[9]

In March 1862, Congress began debating a sweeping tax bill that would change American revenue policies forever. This measure, H.R. 312, became the foundation for Republicans' wartime taxation. It was designed to distribute the burden of taxation evenly and to work in tandem with new Republican tariffs to promote national economic growth.[10]

The new tax bill reflected Republicans' commitment to economic fairness as well as their increasing interest in consolidating power in the national government. It distributed taxes to consumers indirectly through 3 percent taxes on manufactured goods. Since this tax was regressive and could not be levied at a high enough rate to raise the necessary money without unduly burdening the poor, Republicans expanded the income tax they had invented the previous year. The new version had two tiers: a tax of 3 percent for incomes over six hundred dollars—a good living in 1862—and a tax of 5 percent for incomes over ten thousand dollars. "The weight [of taxation] must be distributed equally," explained Justin Smith Morrill, "not upon each man an equal amount, but a tax proportionate to his ability to pay."[11]

Republican congressmen shifted revenue collection from states to the national government. The new bill created an Internal Revenue Bureau in the Treasury Department, the foundation of what would become the Internal Revenue Service. Congressmen did not endorse this idea enthusiastically. Democrats abhorred the idea of a stronger federal government, and even Republicans worried that the new bureau would create an army of officials to harass people and suggested that it would be very popular to leave federal tax collection to states. Morrill was adamant, though, that the federal government should have the power to raise money itself. It had a right to "demand" 99 percent of a man's property for an urgent necessity, he declared. When the nation required it, "the property of the people . . . belongs to the Government."[12]

Republicans fell in line behind Morrill. They pointed out that it would be more expensive for each state to revamp its current system to collect the new taxes than to create a new federal system. Additionally, they noted that national taxes had an economic and psychological value. If people were personally invested in the government, they would have a personal sense of responsibility for its survival and stability. Unanimously, Republicans rejected an amendment that would give the states control of collecting the new taxes.

The new bill also nurtured industry. Democrats and western farmers favored taxes on raw materials, believing that such taxes would fall primarily on eastern manufacturers. This would hobble industry, but the new taxes, which fell across the economy generally, would not. Even more significant, congressmen knew quite well that if American manufacturing were to bear the proposed 3 percent tax on manufactures, it would have to be protected by higher tariff walls, to which Congress was turning its attention. And tariffs, after all, were Morrill's spur for economic growth.

Congress passed H.R. 312 in late June, as Union soldiers retreated down the Virginia peninsula before the Army of Northern Virginia and its new commander, General Robert E. Lee. The bad news from the battlefields made it all too apparent how imperatively the government needed money.

Lincoln signed the measure on July 1, but even before the tax bill was adopted, Congress had begun to debate a new tariff bill. Based on the Morrill Tariff, the new measure set the average rate on imports at about 37 percent, and cut the free list in half. "If we bleed manufacturers we must see to it that the proper tonic is administered at the same time," said Morrill, "or we shall have destroyed the goose that lays the golden eggs." Congress passed the tariff bill with little debate, and Lincoln signed it into law on July 14.[13]

The editor of *Harper's Weekly* summed up the Republicans' new revenue system. "Congress has passed a tax law, and a tariff," he wrote. "The two are co-ordinate parts of one integral system."[14]

The new tax and tariff laws were comprehensive, but they wouldn't start producing significant revenue for months. To pump money into the Treasury right away, Chase had to sell more bonds, but this turned out to be problematic. The new taxes and a good harvest made most Americans increasingly optimistic about the nation's financial situation, but bankers continued to insist on sweet discounts on bond sales. The public and Congress were so infuriated by the bankers' demands that Chase had little choice but to try something new: to turn away from the bankers and toward the man—and woman—on the street. The government would stop focusing on the sale of large blocks of bonds to bankers and would instead mass market them, one at a time, to individuals.[15]

Because the government did not have the marketing network it needed to sell bonds directly to the public, Chase turned to a Philadelphia banker who had cooperated with the Treasury in the past and who was hungry for more business. This financier, Jay Cooke, stood in dramatic contrast to the uncooperative New York bankers. Whereas New Yorkers had resolutely shut Chase out of their circle, Cooke had peppered Chase with letters, flattered him, invested money for him, and entertained his fashionable daughter. Cooke even picked up the expenses Kate Chase charged when she redecorated her father's stately Washington home. Cooke was politically savvy, but he was also honest and hardworking and firmly devoted to the Union cause.

In October 1862, Chase appointed Cooke the general subscription agent for the country, offering him a sales commission from which he was to hire agents and buy advertising. Cooke fully grasped that his appointment represented a momentous change for government finances, making the public, rather than bankers, the mainstay of the Treasury. He threw himself into his job, assuring Chase that he would not only sell bonds but also "enlighten the whole community fully and constantly on the subject of the nation's resources and finances." He did so aggressively. Cooke advertised widely and reported each day's sales in the press. He set up rivalries between cities, encouraging residents to buy more than their neighbors. He wrote editorials hawking the bonds and badgered newspaper editors to do the same. And he hired agents, lots of them, who spread out through the mining towns of the West, the conquered towns of the South, and throughout the North, urging women as well as men to buy government bonds. Soon Cooke was reporting sales of more than one hundred thousand dollars a day.[16]

By fall 1862, to fund a war of unprecedented scope, the Republicans had changed the country's entire system of finance and revenue. They had divorced the Treasury from eastern bankers, resting it instead on the farmers, miners, fishermen, and small business people they believed were the backbone of the American economy. For the first time, ownership of the American government was widespread. Every American conducted his or her business in national currency. Every American who bought anything paid national taxes. Every American with money to spare owned a bond, a piece of the government. Every American had an interest in making sure the Union survived and prospered.

The demands of the war would also bring to life Lincoln's vision of an activist government that nurtured the economy. Before the Civil War, the government had done very little: it conducted foreign affairs, collected customs duties, delivered the mail, and maintained a small army in the West. Democrats had repeatedly shot down economic initiatives out of fear that if the government started intervening in the economy, it would only be a question of time until it interfered with slavery. But with Democrats now in a minority, Republicans quickly began to experiment with government activism.

Their first step, the 1862 Homestead Act, embodied the heart of Republican beliefs. The law granted citizens—or immigrants who announced their intention of becoming citizens—one hundred sixty acres of western land once they had lived on it for five years. This law put the power of the government behind the Republicans' vision of America. In the past, the Treasury had raised money by selling off western land to speculators. Now, though, rich men would be cut out, and poor farmers would win title to land through their own hard work. Republicans insisted this policy would be far more valuable to the nation than short-term cash from land sales because it would provide individuals with the means to rise. If men had land on which to grow crops, they would produce agricultural surpluses, which they could sell for cash. In turn, they would use that cash to buy manufactured products. This would stimulate the entire economy, enabling free men to "contribute to the greatness and glory of the Republic" as they "develop[ed] the elements of a higher and better civilization," said the bill's sponsor, House Speaker Galusha Grow of Pennsylvania.[17]

This long-term vision had a short-term benefit. Republicans pointed out that successful farmers buying manufactured goods would, of course, be paying the new taxes Congress was in the process of levying. "Every smoke rising from a new opening in the wilderness marks the foundation of a new feeder to Commerce and the Revenue," wrote Horace Greeley. The great West would "pour the wealth of empires at our feet," claimed Representative William Windom of Minnesota, if only Congress would make it possible for the labor of willing men to rouse the "giant energy of productiveness" asleep there.[18]

President Lincoln signed the bill on May 20, 1862. "We have now abandoned the public lands as capital," mused Morrill, "with the design of deriving a larger revenue from those who may settle upon them and make them fruitful."[19]

Republicans did not expect that impoverished young men could carve productive farms out of the wilderness without any guidance. Taking a leaf from Lincoln's speech at the Milwaukee Agricultural Fair, they also put the muscle of the national government behind education. Information was key to increasing production, they maintained, and thus imperative for the nation.

Republicans started by creating a Department of Agriculture to spread knowledge about modern farming practices. Lincoln rarely prodded Congress on domestic legislation, but in late 1861 he reminded Congress that agriculture, which all agreed was the nation's most important industry, the foundation of all others, had no bureau or department of government devoted to it. Distributing information about regional crop conditions and new methods of farming would enable farmers to work more efficiently, benefiting both farmers and the nation. Republicans jumped on Lincoln's suggestion, especially since larger crops would enable northern farmers to export food to drought-stricken Europe and bring desperately needed gold into the country. Even the chairman of the Senate Finance Committee, William Pitt Fessenden, who hated the idea of appropriating money for anything other than war funding, noted that in exchange for "seed money," the country would be "richly paid over and over again in absolute increase of wealth. There is no doubt of that." In a bipartisan vote, Congress passed a bill creating a Department of Agriculture, and Lincoln signed it within days of signing the Homestead Act.[20]

Only weeks later, Republicans tackled one of the most important educational measures the country has ever seen: the creation of public universities. Before the Civil War, only youngsters from wealthy families could afford the cost of higher education. Republicans worried that a lack of schooling would keep talented young men of modest means from successfully navigating the increasingly complex economy of the modern world.

Antebellum attempts to fund public colleges had foundered on the intransigence of southerners, who adhered like limpets to the idea that Congress could do nothing that was not expressly enumerated in the Constitution. With southern

Democrats now out of the government, Representative Morrill introduced a bill that would give each state thirty thousand acres of western land for each of its senators and representatives. The states would sell those lands and invest the proceeds in a fund to support agricultural colleges.

Many Republicans who favored the land-grant college plan opposed taking time and money from the war effort while Lee was harrying Major General George B. McClellan and his army across the Virginia peninsula. Morrill disagreed. Far from being inappropriate when the nation was desperate for money, he insisted, the bill was imperative. Knowledge would enable farmers to produce bigger crops and more efficiently. The bill was "demanded by the wisest economy." Just as Republican theorists argued, Morrill explained that farmers would produce surpluses, which they would sell, accumulating capital with which they would buy more manufactured goods. The entire economy would boom. Not incidentally, the government would raise more in taxes.

A majority of Republicans agreed, and the bill passed. Lincoln signed the Land-Grant College Act into law on July 1, 1862. The Republicans had laid the groundwork for America's system of public state universities.[21]

Thus far, Congress had taken new steps to promote economic development, but it had not claimed dramatic new powers for the government. That changed on the day Lincoln signed the bill creating the land-grant colleges, when he also signed a bill creating a transcontinental railroad corporation. The Union Pacific Railroad Act was another far-reaching piece of legislation designed to develop the country. It was different than other Republican laws, though; with it, Republicans embraced a new, expansive vision of the government's relationship to the economy.

From the 1830s, when waves of easterners first began the long trek to the Pacific Coast, to the 1860s, the overland trip from the settled states to the West Coast was daunting. Emigrants usually made the arduous journey by wagon, negotiating dry plains and raging rivers, drought and quicksand, two mountain ranges, tornados, rain, hail, snow, and various Indian tribes eager to protect their land before, at long last, the travelers reached their destinations. The trail was lined with bones of animals for which the trip had been too taxing and with graves of migrants who had fallen to cholera, or to snakebite, or childbirth, or any of the other deadly dangers waiting along the way. Easterners wanted an easier way to go west.

Republicans put a call for a transcontinental railroad in their platforms in 1856 and 1860 on the grounds that one was "imperatively demanded by the interests of the whole country," but any such plan ran up against Democratic insistence that economic development was beyond the scope of the federal government. The Civil War abruptly changed the debate. Southern Democrats were gone, and the government needed gold from western mines. Moreover, building the railroad would spread the northern system of free labor westward, weakening the chance that slavery could spread there. "We were slandering our constituents when we said that we were paralyzed or restricted by their will from adopting the great and beneficent measures for improving the physical and moral condition of our country," said an Indiana representative. If the government would spur development, one railroad supporter thundered, America would become "the greatest nation of the earth."[22]

Republicans had to solve two problems to construct a railroad, one legal and one practical. The legal problem was that only states or organized Territories could charter a corporation, and a transcontinental railroad would have to run through unorganized land. The practical problem was that no businessmen wanted to fund a risky and expensive project when there were plenty of safe, profitable wartime industries in which to invest. Railroads had always followed development, not preceded it, but the transcontinental was to be built before a region had settlers or trade to use it.

To get the railroad under way, Congress boldly expanded the role of the national government in the economy by declaring its power to charter a corporation. The Union Pacific Railroad Company was much like a state corporation—it was established to provide a public service—but at the national level. Congress gave to the UP a four-hundred-foot right-of-way across the country, offered the company ten sections of land per mile, and permitted it to sell US bonds to fund construction (although it required the company to repay the bonds and their interest).

With this act, Congress assumed the role of developing the economy at a national level as state legislatures had done locally. Although congressmen stopped short of giving the new corporation permission to operate within states, they did expand federal involvement there, too. The new measure provided land grants and bond issues to railroad companies within Kansas and California to build branches of the new railroad that ran through those states. Finally, it provided government oversight of the project. If the companies failed to complete their task, the government would assume control of the railroad.

The bill passed by a bipartisan vote and became law on July 1, 1862. The editor of the *American Railroad Journal* identified the passage of the bill as the beginning of "a new era in the history of our public works." Never so restrained, at the *New York Tribune* Horace Greeley trumpeted that "the clouds that have long darkened our National prospects are breaking way, and the sunshine of Peace, Prosperity, and Progress will ere long irradiate the land."[23]

By mid-1862, Republicans had reconceived the national government to reflect their ideology, turning away from the wealthy and tying the government tightly to poorer men and women—the mudsills—working their way up to economic prosperity. Democrats opposed much of what Republicans were trying to do, but for the most part they muted their opposition because Republican policies were so popular. That all changed in fall 1862, when Lincoln tried to weaken the Confederacy by warning that he would free slaves within Union lines the following year if Confederates did not lay down their arms. Democrats so hated the idea of free African Americans that they launched an all-out attack on Lincoln and Republicans. But they didn't stop there. They began to attack the war itself, preferring to let the South go than to free "the niggers." This strategy initially produced some electoral wins, but when the war began to go well for the Union, it hobbled Democrats with a reputation for treason that would stick to them for generations.

Democrats fired their first salvo against Black freedom when Lincoln decided in summer 1862 to undermine the South by freeing the slaves of rebels who didn't lay down their weapons. Doing this would take away the slaves the southern army was using to dig entrenchments, bury the dead, cook, tend the wounded, and so on, forcing officers to take white soldiers from the battlefields to do those jobs. It would also guarantee, once and for all, that antislavery England would not recognize the Confederate government. In September, after the Battle of Antietam provided enough of a victory that emancipation wouldn't look like desperation, Lincoln released the Preliminary Emancipation Proclamation, announcing that the slaves in any region still under Confederate control on January 1, 1863, would be forever free.

Democrats exploded. Republicans had misled them into a war for emancipation by playing on their loyalty to the Union, they told voters before the midterm elections. Soldiers were putting their very lives on the line for Black people. Abolitionists, not southerners, were the nation's real enemy.

Their attack worked. Republicans got shellacked in the 1862 elections. They lost twenty-two seats in the House while the Democrats picked up twenty-eight. Illinois and Indiana went Democratic. Worse, so did New York, Pennsylvania, and Ohio, a bad sign for 1864 as these three states commanded the largest numbers of electoral votes in the North. New York elected a Democratic governor. Especially in the Midwest, voters had indicated that they could no longer give their loyalty to the Republicans. Democrats didn't want "no damned black Republicans" around. In Lincoln's Illinois district a Democrat replaced a Republican.[24]

But Lincoln played his defeat at the polls in such a way that it redounded to Republicans' benefit. Rather than forcing emancipation down Americans' throats, Lincoln offered to give way entirely. He suggested three new constitutional amendments to safeguard slavery for the rest of the nineteenth century, provide compensation for the slaves of any loyal slave owner, and pay African Americans to move to the West or to another country. Lincoln thus gave notice to northern voters that they would get what they asked for, so they had better be careful to choose wisely.[25]

Northerners who still hated the Slave Power were horrified by the suggestions that slavery could continue for almost forty more years and that they might have to pay slave owners to end it. Rather than greeting Lincoln's conservative initiative with relief, they pushed back. Republican leaders and major newspapers demanded that Lincoln take a stronger, not a weaker, line against slavery. Now complaining not that the administration was too radical, but that it was too conservative, they called for immediate emancipation.

With momentum behind emancipation, Lincoln attended the traditional New Year's Day reception at the White House on January 1, 1863, shaking hands with well-wishers. In the evening, he retired to his office with a small group of witnesses and signed the Emancipation Proclamation. "If my name ever goes into history, it will be for this act," he told the men around him, "and my whole heart is in it." To quiet Democratic cries that free Black men would murder their former owners,

Lincoln enjoined African Americans not to resort to violence, except in self-defense. To address Democratic charges that free Black men were lazy and would need public assistance, the president urged them to work faithfully for wages. He also welcomed Black men into the army to fight for their country.[26]

The editor of the *New York Times* rejoiced that the power of slavery in America had been forever broken. The proclamation "marks an era in the history, not only of this war, but of this country and the world," he wrote.[27]

But the struggle was hardly over. Democrats continued to carp that Republicans were using the power of the government to help African Americans at the expense of white men. Constantly, they highlighted the devastating news from the battlefields, where men were dying in horrific firefights or expiring from disease, and argued that the government was destroying white men to elevate Black people. Democrats' insistence that the government was hurting white people to favor African Americans would echo into the future.

At the same time, Democrats' virulent opposition to Lincoln and emancipation meant that in 1863 they unwittingly wove treason into the very fabric of their party's popular identity. After the Union armies stumbled through the first two years of the war and Democrats' success in the 1862 midterms suggested that the conflict might well end in an armistice, confident Democrats were blindsided in summer 1863 when the military tide abruptly turned. At Gettysburg, Pennsylvania, on the first three days of July, Union soldiers wiped out a third of Lee's fighting force and broke the military might of the Confederacy. No sooner had northerners begun to celebrate when the telegraph wires hummed with news of the surrender of

Vicksburg, Mississippi, on July 4, which gave the Union control of the Mississippi River, bisecting the Confederacy and dramatically curtailing its ability to move food, goods, and troops.

Just as the Union was cheering major military victories, Democrats in New York City rioted against the administration. The timing could not have been worse for their cause. Rather than seeming like people with legitimate complaints about a government that appeared to be murdering its soldiers for no good reason, the protesters appeared to be attacking the government just as it started to be successful. They came across as anti-success as much as antiwar.

The riots were sparked by a new federal draft, which took enrollment of soldiers away from the states and gave it to the national government. Democratic newspapers screamed that the Republican government was conscripting poor white men into its mismanaged war to die to "free the nigger." In mid-July, the *New York Times* called the draft a "national blessing" that would settle, once and for all, whether or not the government was strong enough to compel men to fight for it. Democrats were calling for resistance to the draft, but for his part, the editor of the *New York Times* was willing to bargain that the majority of Americans loved their country. The editor scorned the Democrats who threatened to take matters into their own hands to stop the government's enrollment of soldiers. "Let them do their worst," he sneered.[28]

They did. On July 13, Democrats attacked draft officers with rocks and clubs. Rioters spread through the city, burning the homes and businesses of New Yorkers prominent in the Republican Party. As the muggy afternoon wore on, black storm clouds rolled into the sky, mingling with the smoke from the fires. Late in the day, the mobs turned their wrath onto the city's African American residents. They torched the Orphan Asylum for Colored Children, leaving hundreds of orphans homeless. Then they beat twelve Black men to death. One cart driver, leaving a stable at about eight o'clock after putting up his horses, strayed into their path. Several hundred men and boys beat him to death, then hanged him, then set fire to his body. When the rioting ended four days later, about 120 people were dead.[29]

The draft riots made the Democrats look anti-American. Their image fell still further when news reached northerners of the Battle of Fort Wagner, fought just two days after the riots ended. On July 18, two Union brigades took heavy losses as they attacked the fort at the mouth of Charleston Harbor. What made this attack so important, then and to history, was that it was fought by the first Black regiment: the Fifty-Fourth Massachusetts. The contrast between Black soldiers dying for the Union and white mobs railing against the government was stark. No fair-minded American could miss it.[30]

Voters turned against the Democrats. In elections held in the fall, Republicans made up much of the ground they had lost the previous year. In the crucial state of Ohio, which had slid far toward southern sympathy, the Democratic gubernatorial candidate lost by more than one hundred thousand votes, and the Republicans picked up three-quarters of the seats in the next legislature. In New York, too, Republicans won handily, taking nearly two-thirds of the legislature.[31]

With Democrats losing ground, Republicans identified their own party with a new, progressive nation that turned for its founding principle to the equal right of every man to rise through his own labor, the very principle Abraham Lincoln had articulated in 1859 to refute James Henry Hammond's elitism. In mid-November 1863, at the dedication of a national cemetery at Gettysburg, President Lincoln transformed Republican principles into poetry. What Americans were fighting for, he reminded them, was equality before the law and government freed from the control of an oligarchy.

With the Gettysburg Address, Lincoln redefined the nation. Firmly planting the roots of America in the Declaration of Independence rather than the Constitution, he reminded listeners of the political equation that had given birth to the Republican Party. The genius of America, he insisted, was the equality that the Founding Fathers had not managed to enshrine in the nation's laws. The trials of the Union were the trials of human self-government. Was it possible for men to create a civil society governed by laws that treated everyone equally? Or would such a society always devolve into an oligarchy? Would free men fight to preserve their right to self-government? Or would the armies of an elite inevitably outlast those of a people's government? The fate of the Union would answer those questions once and for all, and President Lincoln well knew the whole world awaited the answer. He called for Americans to resolve that "government of the people, by the people, for the people, shall not perish from the earth."

Lincoln made this principle the centerpiece of his 1864 reelection campaign. He ran that year not as a Republican but as a member of the National Union Party, a new organization designed to gather all Americans behind a government that stood for every man's equal right to rise. The symbol of that principle was an amendment to the Constitution—the thirteenth—which prohibited slavery except as punishment for crime. The Senate had developed and passed the amendment in spring 1864, using in it the language of the Northwest Ordinance, the law passed after legislators had seen wealthy men take over Kentucky. While the first twelve amendments to the Constitution had limited the power of the national government, the thirteenth increased it, putting Congress in charge of guaranteeing freedom.

Here, in forty-three words, was the principle that had forced Lincoln into politics. The Thirteenth Amendment marked the end of an economic system that had enabled a few rich men to control the nation. It codified the idea that Congress should respond to the will of the people, not bow to the demand of men like James Henry Hammond that it be hamstrung by the limits of the original Constitution. It declared all men free.

During the congressional debate on the new amendment, Republicans reiterated again and again that America's economic future depended on the end of slavery. The slave system represented monopoly and oligarchy, and it must die. Once free labor spread through the entire nation, America would bloom. Black men would work hard and flourish, but so would white men, currently kept down by a system that privileged the wealthy. With the death of slavery, Massachusetts senator Henry Wilson thundered, "The wronged victim of the slave system, the poor white men...impoverished, debased, dishonored by the system that makes toil a badge of disgrace...will... begin to run the race of improvement, progress, and elevation."[32]

In four short years Republicans had changed the entire premise of the relationship between the national government and its citizens. They had worked to build economic prosperity from the bottom of society rather than from the top, in an ever-expanding harmonious system. But by 1864 there was a troubling disparity between Republican ideology and reality. Party members spoke of defending the common man, but the truth was that the wartime economy had created great fortunes. And the Lincoln administration could not survive without the support of the men who controlled those fortunes. Republicans generally managed well the balancing act between their support for workers and their need to work with moneyed men, but as the war dragged on tensions between rich and poor, East and West, were putting terrific strain on the country. To keep the Union together behind the war effort, Republicans had to soothe disaffected voters at both ends of the economic spectrum, while emphasizing that theirs was the only party that was truly American.

With their wartime legislation, Republicans had focused on making opportunities available and guaranteeing that individuals could keep what they earned, believing that one man's success would create the capital to enable others to rise. This made a great deal of sense in the preindustrial world from which men like Lincoln came, where business was done on a human scale and enterprises usually hired only a few individuals who knew their employer personally and worked with him closely.

But the war years had opened a chasm between manufacturers and workers, and Republican ideology offered no obvious remedy to close it. The imperatives of the war, along with the Republicans' legislation, had nurtured a booming manufacturing sector with huge factories worked by hundreds of employees who never saw, let alone worked with, their employer. Owners made sums of money unimaginable before the war, usually from government contracts funded by taxpayers, while wartime inflation consumed workers' wages. As the economic gap between owners and employees widened, workers became isolated from their employers; there were no longer shared community activities or informal interactions where workers could voice their concerns about workplace safety or ask for higher wages.

A new class of financiers, too, had emerged. Like the large manufacturers, they seemed divorced from hardworking Americans. They were rich and made their money by riding the swells and troughs of the financial markets as war news made investors either jubilant or skittish. Men gambling in money, influenced by the fortunes of the Union armies, seemed to be making a killing off the deaths of soldiers.

Before the war, there was nothing in Republican economic theory to address the problem of great wealth accumulated by means other than slavery. When, by 1864, it was becoming clear that the postwar economy would not be the rural world Republicans had envisioned, many people started to grumble about the fortunes being made under Republican policies. Poorer men started to drift toward the Democrats, who accused Republicans of becoming the very elitists they had organized to destroy. "New England manufacturers are getting richer every day," one Democrat exploded, "richer and richer and richer.... They are ... becoming the owners of this country.... They are getting all the protection of the Government."[33]

To reassure hardworking Americans that the administration had their interests at heart despite its recent courting of moneyed men, Republicans gave more aid to the farming West. Investment in the transcontinental railroad had been slow, so in spring 1864 Congress doubled the land grant offered to the Union Pacific and increased the amount of money it could raise. Investors snapped to attention, and workers began to hammer rails across the plains.

Republicans also worked to import workers to the western fields. The nation had been gripped by nativism in the 1850s, with Democrats, especially, complaining that immigrants competed with native-born men for scarce American jobs. Many men who later joined the Republican Party had participated in the immigrant bashing, but when the Republican Party formed, its economic theory challenged the idea that laborers competed against each other. If labor created value, as they argued, there was no need for workers to fight over a limited number of jobs. The more laborers a country could attract, the more wealth they would create, and the better for everyone.[34]

The circumstances of the war years reinforced this Republican theory. The drain of men to the battlefields meant there was a shortage of men in northern fields, and by harvest time of 1862, western newspapers claimed that the West could use one hundred thousand additional laborers. Republicans gradually came to like the idea that new immigrants would spread the northern system of free labor across the West, increasing production as they kept slavery from getting a foothold.

Republicans had organized western Territories as quickly as possible during the war—Colorado, Nevada, and Dakota Territory in 1861; Idaho and Arizona Territory in 1863; and Montana Territory in 1864 (along with Nevada as a state)—configuring the West almost as it looks today. But there was no point in organizing those lands if there was no one to live in them. Immigration was the solution. As one poorly educated man wrote to his senator, "Protect Emegration and that will protect the Territories to Freedom."[35]

By 1864, Republicans were strongly in favor of immigration. That year, as farmers faced another season with too few hands, Congress passed "an Act to encourage Immigration": a law permitting businessmen to import workers, appropriating money to provide for impoverished immigrants upon their arrival, and guaranteeing that no immigrant could be drafted until he announced his intention of becoming a citizen.[36]

Republicans could not afford to lose the common people, but they desperately needed the support of eastern businessmen and the Wall Street community, too, for if wealthy men slid away to the Democrats, Republicans would lose control of government, and the best the Union could hope for was a negotiated peace with the South. First Lincoln himself worked to appease businessmen by pushing back against Congress when it moved to issue more of the popular greenbacks. He urged congressmen to create instead national banks backed by national bonds whose rock solid value would keep bank notes at par, a plan that promised to stop the inflation that businessmen loathed. Congress obliged—grudgingly—and in 1863 and 1864 America got a national banking system to replace state banks.

Then, in an 1864 revision of the tax and tariff laws, Congress increased the manufacturing tax to 5 percent and raised the income tax brackets to 5 percent for incomes from six hundred to five thousand dollars, to 7.5 percent for incomes from five to ten thousand dollars, and to 10 percent for incomes over ten thousand dollars. But it refused to put higher taxes on a tiny upper bracket, arguing that such a tax would target a few very rich men unfairly. Wealthy men unhappy with the new taxes could take comfort from new tariff rates: they went up to around 47 percent to "shelter and nurse" domestic industry.[37]

The most important way in which the Lincoln administration tried to cater to businessmen, though, was with the 1864 vice presidential nomination. In a convoluted intrigue, congressional radicals at the party's convention tried to force Secretary of State Seward, whom they perceived as too conservative, out of the cabinet. To do this, they pushed Daniel S. Dickinson, a pro-Union Democrat from New York, for the vice presidential slot. They wanted Dickinson not because they liked his politics, but because if he became vice president, Seward would have to resign since it would be impolitic for New York to have both the vice presidency and the secretary of state post. Stuck in the vice presidency, the Democrat could do no real damage, and the radicals would have undercut conservatives in the cabinet.

But Lincoln could not afford to lose Seward. The president valued his secretary of state for his own merits, but more important, Seward was the protégé of the most important backroom dealer in the country, New York's Thurlow Weed. Weed was an older man—born in 1797—and his sympathies were with New York's businessmen. He had always believed that the wealthy and well-connected should control the nation's politics and business; he just hadn't wanted northern leaders to be shut out by those from the South. His inclinations meant that as the Republicans moved toward average Americans, he threatened to move away from the Republicans. If Weed turned to the Democrats, he would take Wall Street men with him, and the Republicans would lose the election.[38]

When radicals tried to push the secretary of state out of the cabinet, Lincoln could appease Weed by defending Seward. To cover their tracks, radicals clumsily claimed that the only goal of their machinations was to bring Union Democrats into the Republican fold. Lincoln took them at their word and quietly threw his weight behind another pro-Union Democrat, Andrew Johnson, whom Lincoln had appointed the military governor of Tennessee after the state had been retaken from the Confederates. With the support of New York's delegates, Johnson won the vice presidential slot. Seward's position was safe, Weed was happy, and New York's business community stayed behind Lincoln. But the stage was set for a national tragedy.[39]

Delegates to the 1864 Republican convention in early June emphasized that theirs was the party of all good Americans. Technically, it was not even a Republican convention, for organizers had changed the party's name to the National Union Party to make it easier for Democrats to vote Republican in this election without supporting the party they believed was made up of "nigger worshippers." They deliberately chose a southern city for the meeting and made the convention's temporary chairman Robert Breckinridge, the slave-owning uncle of John Breckinridge, who had run for president in 1860 as the Deep South's staunchly proslavery candidate. Delegates to the convention met in Baltimore on June 7 and got down to business.[40]

In their deliberations, delegates made it clear that, so far as they were concerned, the Republican Party was the only legitimate political organization in the nation. Every American citizen had a duty to maintain the integrity of the Union, Republicans said, and to destroy, once and for all, the Slave Power. At the same time, they endorsed the expansion of government to defend individual opportunity and economic growth. By 1864, Republicans stood against aristocracy and for the equal opportunity of anyone willing to work hard. They stood for a government that promoted economic growth, and they welcomed to the nation anyone, of any color, who was willing to contribute to that growth. Democrats opposed all of this, including, after 1863, the defense of a Union they believed catered to Black people. In effect then, in the minds of Republican officials, the Republican Party had become indistinguishable from the nation. In 1864, anyone who believed in America and in the sacrifices of the men who had died for the country must vote Republican.[41]

Nonetheless, in summer 1864, it seemed the Republicans' delicate balancing act had been for naught. Democrats had nominated for president the popular Union general George B. McClellan on a platform that called for an immediate armistice to stop the carnage. The idea of an end to the slaughter gained ground as General Ulysses S. Grant, who had taken command of the Union armies in March 1864, launched a war of attrition to destroy the Confederacy. In May and June, more than 17,500 Union soldiers were killed or wounded at the Battle of the Wilderness, 18,000 at Spotsylvania, and another

12,500 at Cold Harbor. The mounting casualties made Lincoln despair of reelection. Even Horace Greeley had abandoned the war effort and begged the president to negotiate with southern leaders in order to save the "bleeding, bankrupt, almost dying country."[42]

Then the prospects changed. In late August, Rear Admiral David Farragut took control of Mobile Bay, the last port the Confederates held in the Gulf of Mexico east of the Mississippi River; it was a prize that had eluded the Union for more than two years. On September 2, General William Tecumseh Sherman captured Atlanta, a city of symbolic as well as real value to the Confederacy, and set off from there to smash his way to the Georgia coast. Three weeks later, when Confederate soldiers under General Jubal Early threatened Washington, Major General Philip Sheridan and his men chased them eighty miles down the Shenandoah Valley. Jubilant Republicans asked the Democrats whether they still believed the Union's cause was a failure.

Voters answered that question emphatically. Reelecting Lincoln meant committing to fight on until victory, and re-elect him they did. Resoundingly. Voters gave the president a majority of 212 to 21 in the Electoral College and a popular majority of 55 percent of their votes. Among soldiers, Lincoln won 78 percent of the vote. Republicans fared well down the entire ticket. They took all but 40 of the 185 seats in the House of Representatives, and all but 11 of the 54 seats in the Senate. Republicans also took every state house except that of New Jersey.[43]

As if to reward Americans' faith, the Union's military triumphs continued. Each win seemed to set the stage for a new nation to be constructed as soon as the Confederacy disbanded. The question was no longer whether the country would survive, but rather what sort of nation would emerge from the conflagration. To that, President Lincoln had given much thought. His recent landslide showed that Americans backed the vision he had shaped in 1859, and he pushed hard for its completion. He asked Congress to pass the proposed Thirteenth Amendment to the Constitution and send it off to the states for ratification.[44]

When Congress took up the measure, Democrats continued to argue that African Americans were inferior to whites and that Republicans were trying to create a despotism that served "the negro." It was Republicans who brought a new tone to the debate. No longer on the defensive, they aggressively championed their creation of a new, strong national government that advanced the interests of all hardworking men. They rejected Democratic defense of states' rights, pointing out that states' rights was the dogma of the past and had done America no favors. The new principle of the country was that the national government was paramount. Congressman Thomas Jenckes of Rhode Island put the new American nationalism clearly when he demanded, "If we are not a nation, what are we?"[45]

Republicans insisted that with freedom the law of the land, America would prosper. Freedom would remove artificial supports for slave owners and artificial obstacles in the way of African Americans. Both would now run the race of life with the equal protection of the law, free to rise—or sink— according to their own merits. With freedom, production would quadruple, Ohio congressman James Ashley insisted:

once capital was secure and laborers inspired to work for their own betterment, he rhapsodized, the country "would blossom like the rose." Free labor would, he said, make America "the most powerful and populous, the most enterprising and wealthy nation in the world."[46]

After significant wheeling and dealing, the measure passed with just over a two-thirds majority. When the final aye vote put the measure over the top and the Speaker of the House announced the tally, the galleries and the floor broke out into wild cheers. Men hugged each other and cried. Antislavery congressman George Julian recalled that he felt he "had been born into a new life, and that the world was overflowing with beauty and joy." He considered it an extraordinary privilege to be able to record his name on "so glorious a page of the nation's history."[47]

Lincoln signed the measure on February 1, 1865, and sent the Thirteenth Amendment off to the states for ratification. Finally, it seemed, the promise of the Declaration of Independence would be codified in the US Constitution.

The Thirteenth Amendment embodied the theory for which Republicans had organized, but congressmen knew they must take steps to sustain southerners until newly free workers could reshape the South's economy. The spring months, before greens and livestock are big enough to eat, are always a lean time in agricultural areas. But in the South in 1865, things weren't just hard; they were desperate. Invading Union armies had destroyed homes, farmland was gone to weeds, draft animals had been killed, heirloom seeds had been lost. Hungry refugees, former slave owners and former slaves both, tramped the roads in despair. They were in very real danger of starving to death.

Congress recognized their plight and shortly after passing the Thirteenth Amendment voted to provide relief for both white refugees and freedmen who had been displaced by the war. It created a new bureau within the War Department to provide food, medical care, and resettlement on abandoned lands to loyal southerners. Signaling that this was solely in response to the disruption of the war and that, under normal circumstances, men should be able to provide for themselves, Congress limited the operation of the new Bureau of Refugees, Freedmen, and Abandoned Lands to the duration of the war plus one year. Lincoln signed the measure on March 3, 1865. Ironically, this measure, passed in charity, would be the opening wedge against Republican policies almost as soon as the artillery fell silent.[48]

After addressing southern destitution, congressmen beavered away to finish their work before Lincoln's second inauguration; they had to work all night from Friday, March 3, to midday Saturday, catnapping at their desks to finish up before the ceremony. They adjourned the congressional session ten minutes before noon. Since the new Congress was not slated to convene until early December, they would be able to scatter to their distant homes before the summer heat made the capital unbearable.[49]

On Saturday, March 4, 1865, Lincoln took the oath of office for the second time. For days Washington had been socked in with rain, and the morning did not look auspicious. Men stood ankle deep in the muddy streets along the route of the inaugural procession. Still, bands played as troops of African American and white soldiers escorted the president to the Capitol. As Lincoln prepared to take the oath, the weather broke. By noon, the time Lincoln was sworn in, the skies had cleared and the sun shone down.[50]

The physical contrast between this man and the one who had placed his hand on the Bible exactly four years before was shocking. Lincoln was bent, bone-weary, his faced deeply lined. In place of his anxiety and anticipation at the time of his first inaugural were maturity and the certainty of a job well done.

The nation had changed as dramatically as the president in the past four years. In March 1861, a weak government faced a rebellion with a tiny army and an empty treasury. By 1865, the Republicans had created a government that had commanded more than 2.5 million soldiers and sailors, distributed western land, created national money, invented national taxation, chartered a national corporation, and had assumed a 2.5-billion-dollar debt. By 1865, a newly strong American government commanded the support of its citizens.

And they were happy to give it their loyalty. That government not only had prosecuted a victorious war—for it was clear to everyone that the Confederacy's end was near—but also had spurred a flourishing economy. Northerners had lost loved ones and poured money into the cause, but they had emerged from four years of turmoil in far better shape than they had foreseen in 1861. Before the war, the North had struggled with an economic recession; by 1865, it was prosperous. Ships bustled in harbors from Portland and Philadelphia to Detroit and Milwaukee, and in London and Shanghai, moving goods that newly flush northerners brought into their increasingly comfortable homes. The Republicans' active government had created a strong and growing middle class, whose members had fought to defend the government during the war and now used government money and owned government bonds, paid government taxes and attended government-funded colleges, and gave their wholehearted allegiance to the nation. The government had organized the West on the principles of free labor—the object for which northerners had gone to war in the first place—and there was every expectation that those same principles would spread to the Pacific and, perhaps, beyond. The war had been traumatic, but the sacrifice had paid off.

The whole world seemed to be beginning anew. Poet Walt Whitman thought the very heavens reflected the fortunes of war. After months of fog and clouds, the weather had cleared. "The western star, Venus, in the earlier hours of evening, has never been so large, so clear," Whitman wrote. "It seems as if it told something as if it held rapport indulgent with humanity, with us Americans."[51]

News from the front continued to favor the Union. Grant's men ground their way toward Richmond, and Confederate armies crumbled as starvation and despair stalked the South. Finally, on April 9, Grant received a message from Lee requesting a meeting to discuss terms of surrender. Grant met the southern general in the tiny Virginia town of Appomattox Court House, where Lee surrendered the Confederacy's main army. Grant sent the soldiers home to plant their spring crops. The war was not over—there were still three southern armies in the field—but it was clear to everyone that the Confederacy's death was simply a matter of time. This realization incensed the mentally unstable actor John Wilkes Booth, who clung to the ideals of the Old South. On the morning of April 14, he scribbled in his diary: "Our cause being almost lost, something *decisive* and great must be done."[52]

Lincoln, too, could finally see the end of the war. On the same day that Booth mused on the need for a southern hero, one of Lincoln's longtime associates remarked that he had never before seen the president looking so cheerful. The weary strain of the war years had begun to ease. Lincoln was relaxed and jovial that evening as he and his wife set off to Ford's Theater to watch actress Laura Keene in *Our American Cousin*. The president was enjoying the play in his theater box, laughing at the farce under way on the stage below him, when Booth stepped up behind him and pulled a trigger.[53]

President Lincoln died at 7:22 the following morning.

3

Republicans or Radicals?

Lincoln could not have imagined that the pro-Union Democrat he wanted as his running mate in 1864 to calm Wall Street would become the sole leader of the nation for seven of its most crucial months. But so it happened. On April 15, less than three hours after Lincoln had breathed his last, Andrew Johnson took the presidential oath of office in his rooms at Kirkwood House on Pennsylvania Avenue. With Congress out of session, Johnson was now in charge of what he called the "restoration" of the Union. In the seven months before Congress reconvened in December, Johnson would undermine Lincoln's vision of the nation and in the process warp American politics for generations to come.[1]

Even as they mourned the loss of the president, Republicans rejoiced that the war was over. The contest between a slave economy and free labor had been decided on battlefields at the cost of billions of dollars and more than six hundred thousand American lives—but the North had won. At long last the Slave Power had been defeated. Poor men and rich men would run the race of life on equal terms.

Republicans expected to rebuild the southern economy on the basis of free labor. They believed that the monopolization of southern lands by rich planters had retarded the region's growth, forcing poor whites, as well as Black slaves, into ignorance and poverty. They wanted to bring schools to the former Confederacy and put families on their own farms, rebuilding the South into a model economy of educated, upwardly mobile workers.

Although he had been elected on their ticket, Johnson did not share Republicans' vision. Secession had divided him from his southern Democratic colleagues but not from his Democratic political principles. With Congress in recess, he worked as fast as he could to restore the Union along the lines northern Democrats wanted before Republican congressmen came back to Washington and started meddling. His actions ignited a pitched battle between himself and Congress, a battle that would cripple the spread of a free labor economy to the South and produce rhetoric to undercut government activism until the present. Thanks to Booth's bullet, Lincoln's 1864 nod to Andrew Johnson in order to appease New York businessmen opened the door to the destruction of the Republican Party's original principles.

Johnson set out to wrench the Republicans' new activist government back to what it had been in the days before 1860. Stuck in the mind-set of an antebellum Democratic politician, he believed in the old-fashioned rule of party and saw politics as war. The object of winning an election was not to advance policies—since government shouldn't do much of anything—but to put party leaders into office. Johnson recognized that Republicans' use of the government to advance individual prosperity was enormously popular—and that it threatened to consign Democrats to oblivion. Johnson also knew that only the peculiarity of the 1864 election had made him welcome, briefly, on the Republican (or National Union) ticket. With the war won and Lincoln gone, few party members would support Johnson.

As president, Johnson set out to resuscitate the antebellum political system dominated by the Democratic Party, with himself at its head. Over the course of the summer he pardoned all but about fifteen hundred former Confederates, either by proclamation or presidential pardon, returning them to positions of authority in southern society. He required only that southern states ratify the Thirteenth Amendment abolishing slavery, declare secession illegal, and default on Confederate debts before they could be readmitted to the Union. Since he pardoned ex-Confederates and refused to endorse Black voting, Johnson guaranteed that the same men who had taken the South out of the Union would be responsible for bringing it back in.[2]

Southern leaders half-heartedly met the president's demands, then joined him in trying to re-create the antebellum world. Within each state, through a series of laws together dubbed "Black Codes," they bound former slaves to white employers and guaranteed the dominance of white people in the South. In Mississippi, courts could "apprentice" Black children to masters and mistresses; Black men could be arrested and fined if they did not sign year-long contracts, then "hired out" to anyone who paid their fines—a system that essentially threatened uncooperative African Americans with new language for the old system of being sold into slavery. In Alabama, Black men couldn't own guns, and chain gangs legally replaced whipping and branding as punishment for crime. In South Carolina, African Americans could not sell corn, rice, peas, bacon, chickens, or any farm products without written permission from their employer. Florida joined most other southern states in punishing "vagrancy" with forced labor. Nowhere could a Black person testify against a white person in court, and the punishment for breaking a law was whipping or sale into slavery.[3]

When officials from the Bureau of Refugees, Freedmen, and Abandoned Lands set up federal courts to protect Black southerners, ex-Confederates cried foul at what they saw as government intrusion into relations with people they still thought of as theirs. Although a third of the 150,000 rations the bureau provided in summer 1865 went to white people and cases were decided in favor of employers 32 percent of the time, disaffected southern whites dubbed it the "Freedmen's Bureau" and insisted that it promoted the interests of African Americans over whites. They began to redefine the Civil War as a struggle over states' rights rather than slavery. They had foreseen this stranglehold of federal officials, they claimed, and had taken up arms in anticipation of it. They, not the Yankees, had been the true defenders of American principles.[4]

Republicans looked on, aghast, as Johnson and white southerners took only months to erase the hard-earned fruits of victory. Adding insult to injury, the 1870 census would count African Americans as whole persons rather than three-fifths of a person, as they had been counted as slaves, and the South's representation in the House of Representatives would increase. If Johnson's plan were permitted to go forward un-challenged, wealthy southern whites would be more powerful after the Civil War than they had been before it.

In November 1865, a writer for the *New York Times* noted that white southerners misunderstood what it meant to return to the Union. They expected to come back to a nation that looked as it did in 1861. Southerners did not see that north-erners' attitudes about government had evolved during the war and that their attitudes must also change. Southerners clung to outmoded states' rights ideas because they had not learned a better system, whereas northerners had learned to give up states' rights for the common good. Southerners' loyalty to states' rights was a fallacy that must be "educated out of them," according to this writer. Until it was, white southerners might be willing to submit to the federal government, but they would always make objections "in which the 'honor' of their States will figure largely."[5]

Johnson's actions put Republicans in a difficult spot. They were horrified at his restoration of authority to antebellum southern leaders, but they were also unwilling to push too hard against a president who had, after all, been elected on their own ticket. Once Congress was back in session, they hoped to be able to work with him to rebuild the South in a way that did not look quite so much like the antebellum slave system. But when Congress reconvened in early December, the president refused to compromise with Republicans even when they tried to protect the very basic tenets of free labor in the South. Instead, he fought them tooth and nail. In the short term, Johnson's intemperate attacks hobbled the establishment of free labor in the South. But they also had far-reaching consequences: Johnson linked government activism and benefits for Black people in a negative equation that would echo into the future.

Johnson greeted Congress on December 4, 1865, with the happy news that the country had been reconstructed. He had moved the process along as quickly as possible, he explained, because a continued military presence in the South would have cost tax money, created a large patronage system, and "envenomed hatred" among white southern Democrats. All that remained to do, he announced, was for Congress to admit newly elected southern representatives to their seats. They were already in Washington, marveling at the changes the war years had wrought on what only four years before had been a sleepy southern town.[6]

Republicans scorned Johnson's cheery message. Southerners had indeed elected representatives to Congress— including many of the same men who had taken the South out of the Union. Georgia was a bit behind the other states in its choice of senators, but it would soon elect Alexander Stephens, the vice president of the Confederacy, to Washington. With Johnson backing the southern state governments that were squeezing Black southerners into quasi-slavery, it seemed to Republicans that the system they had worked so hard to destroy had sprung back, phoenix-like. The South might have lost the war, but it appeared to have won the peace.

Congressional Republicans wanted no part of Johnson's "restoration." They refused to seat the South's representatives and appointed a committee of fifteen congressmen to come up with a new plan to reintegrate the South into the Union. The committee began to hear the testimony of ex-slaves, southern whites, and army officers about conditions in the South. Meanwhile, Congress tried to jumpstart free labor in the region. It passed a bill to expand the duties of the Freedmen's Bureau, enabling it both to put impoverished southerners—white as well as Black—onto homesteads and to establish schools. The expanded Freedmen's Bureau bill also provided for federal courts throughout the South wherever Black Americans could not participate in the local court system. The bill did not limit these operations to the former Confederate states; it covered the Black and poor white populations in the border states as well.[7]

In addition, Congress passed a bill giving Black southerners all the civic rights southern states denied them. It declared that everyone born in America (except certain American Indians) was a citizen, entitled to all the rights of citizenship, including the right to make contracts, sue, testify in court, own property, and share the same legal penalties, no matter what local laws or customs established.[8]

Republicans considered these bills relatively uncontroversial, designed primarily to formalize the work the Freedmen's Bureau was already doing. The measures advanced Lincoln's belief in education and opportunity for all and would provide the legal basis for repairing the damage inflicted on the South by the slave owners who had monopolized its resources. The new bills would establish homesteads worked by educated Americans across the South and enable every man to defend the value of his labor and property in court. They would sow the seeds of a thriving society of free workers, and would integrate the South into the free labor economy that appeared to be so successful in the North and West. Both bills passed with overwhelming majorities.[9]

To Johnson, though, these measures were anathema. He recognized that the Republican use of the government to promote individual economic success was enormously popular in the North. He had every reason to expect that extending that program into the border and southern states would be equally popular among the poor farmers, white and Black, who made up the majority of the South's population. These people clamored for schools and homes, and it was reasonable to assume that any political party providing those things would be popular. If Republicans continued their efforts to develop a strong middle class, Democrats were finished.

So Johnson took a stand against what he saw as a dangerously strong Republican Party. In February 1866, he vetoed the Republicans' two new bills and delivered veto messages that laid out a formula for opposition to government activism that has endured until the present. Johnson combined southern fears of a roiling underclass, traditional racism, hatred of taxation, and states' rights into an attack on Republican efforts to bring a free labor economy to the South. He smeared the Freedmen's Bureau as evidence of the terrible perversion of the government: Republicans had turned the limited government mandated by the Constitution into a grasping behemoth that worked not for all but rather for the service of a "special interest." That favored group was made up of lazy ex-slaves who wanted a redistribution of wealth.[10]

Johnson's opposition to the new measures did not rest on racism alone, although that was at the heart of it. The sticking power of his argument came from his linkage of racism to the dangers of an active government, a connection that resonated with northern Democrats still convinced that Lincoln had sent white men to the slaughter for the benefit of African Americans. Johnson warned that the new plan would put agents in every county and parish in the South, creating "immense patronage" that would grow continually. The party in power could count on the votes of those employees. It could also count on the support of the entire Black community, support that did not mean, in these days before Black suffrage, votes. Johnson's listeners, raised on stories of a dangerous Black underclass that wanted a redistribution of wealth, would have understood his concern about Black political involvement as a threat that Republicans would use Black men as a revolutionary army.

Johnson estimated the cost of the new system at more than twenty-three million dollars a year for the agents alone—more than the entire federal budget in any year of John Quincy Adams's administration, he pointed out—plus more for the soldiers who would have to defend them. Who would pay this exorbitant sum? Taxpayers. Johnson singled out the white southerners who were taxed even though their representatives had not yet been readmitted to Congress, but the larger formula was clear. According to him, Republicans were planning to get taxpayers across the country to pay for a growing bureaucracy that catered to lazy African Americans. Johnson insisted that Republicans were engaging in reverse racism, singling out freedmen for protections that the law had never given specifically to white men.[11]

Johnson's portrait of the bills was fiction, based partly on his delusion of what Black life was like in the South—only twelve days before, he had informed an astonished delegation of former slaves that they did not really understand the South or slavery—and partly on his calculation of what would work to build his own political support. The equation he developed in these crucial vetoes—that government activism equaled special help for minorities paid for by hardworking taxpayers—grew out of the peculiar circumstances of the postwar years, but it became the equation that opponents of government activism have used ever since. Johnson's attack on the new Republican approach to government established a connection between racism and government activism that would resonate far into the future.[12]

Johnson's obstructionism pushed Republicans toward stronger and stronger measures as they tried to build a free labor economy in the South. First they overrode Johnson's vetoes of the Civil Rights and Freedmen's Bureau bills (although they had to jettison the homestead and education provisions of the latter). Then they turned to producing their own master plan for constructing a free labor nation.

A horrific riot in Memphis, Tennessee, in April 1866, made the need for government action clear. Sparked when white police officers attacked the Black federal soldiers they saw as a threat to white supremacy, the riot highlighted just how vital it was to find a way for ex-slaves to participate safely in southern society. In the struggle, white mobs killed thirty

African Americans, wounded fifty more, and destroyed property valued at one hundred thousand dollars. The mayor did nothing to stop the riots; his supporters weakly suggested his negligence was because he had been too drunk to function.[13]

The Memphis riot added urgency to the Republicans' plan for reconstruction. By April, the Committee of Fifteen had heard months of testimony from southerners, white and Black, about the conditions in the war-torn region, and congressmen's northern constituents, appalled at what the committee uncovered, urged Congress to declare its own program for the South. Finally, on the last day of April 1866, members of the committee introduced into Congress the joint resolution that would become the Fourteenth Amendment to the Constitution.[14]

The amendment was a moderate and inexpensive way to move the nation forward. Avoiding Johnson's complaints, it called for neither redistribution of wealth nor special legal status for African Americans. Instead, it made every man equal before the law. It overturned the *Dred Scott* decision and established that any person born or naturalized in America (except the same Indians who had been excluded in the Civil Rights Bill) was an American citizen. To address the problem that would result from the upcoming 1870 census, in which Black people would be counted as one whole rather than as three-fifths of a person, the committee proposed that congressional representation for the southern states be based on population, as with all states, but that southern representation be reduced in proportion to the number of men a state refused to allow to vote. The committee prohibited from holding elected office anyone who had sworn to support the Union and then broken that oath in order to join the Confederacy (this provision swept in the military and political officers who had switched allegiances in 1861 and meant that many officials in Johnson's new governments were ineligible for their posts). The amendment also closed loopholes that southern states had found to protect their war debt. Finally, like the amendment that preceded it, the Fourteenth Amendment increased the strength of the federal government by giving Congress the power to enforce its provisions. Both houses of Congress agreed to the amendment on June 18, 1866, and sent it off to the states for ratification.

Congress required southern states to ratify the amendment before being readmitted to the Union. Republicans hoped that the amendment would protect Black rights, adjust representation according to suffrage, nip future secessionists' ambitions in the bud by invalidating the Confederate debt, and keep the South from falling into obviously disloyal hands. And if things didn't go as hoped, the amendment gave the national government the power to step in to set things right.

Johnson hated the proposed Fourteenth Amendment. He hated its broad definition of citizenship; he hated its assertion of national power; he hated its disfranchisement of the southern leaders he backed. Most of all, though, he hated that it offered a moderate route to reunification that could be supported by most Americans. If it were ratified by the states, it would destroy his chances of rebuilding a dominant national Democratic Party.[15]

Johnson fought back. He told southern politicians to ignore Congress's order to ratify the Fourteenth Amendment.

He assured them that Democrats would win the 1866 midterm congressional elections, and once back in power, Democrats could repudiate Republican "radicalism" and allow Johnson's plan for reconstruction of the Union to proceed. Energized ex-Confederates made the summer of 1866 a bloody one. In July, when a Unionist convention in New Orleans called for taking the vote away from ex-Confederates and giving it to loyal African Americans, white mobs attacked the building where the convention was in session. The ensuing riots killed thirty-seven Black people and three white delegates to the convention.[16]

Rather than condemning the violence in the South, Johnson egged it on. He insisted that his policies were the only constitutional means of restoring the Union, denounced Congress as an illegal body (because it had not seated southern representatives), called certain Republican congressmen traitors who should be hanged, and, shockingly, compared himself to Jesus Christ, saying he was willing to be a martyr to the cause of small government.[17]

Johnson's extremism and his supporters' violence created a backlash. Northerners were not willing to hand the country back to the Democrats who were rioting in the South and to a president who compared himself to Jesus. Rather than rebuking the Republicans, voters repudiated Johnson. Republicans won a two-thirds majority of Congress in the 1866 elections, enabling them to override any veto Johnson chose to throw down.

Now firmly in control of rebuilding the South, the Republicans tried to enforce the policies they had established with the Fourteenth Amendment. But in every southern state other than Tennessee (where locals so hated their native son Johnson that they ratified the Fourteenth Amendment just to spite him), whites had ignored Congress's reconstruction plan. To begin to move their program forward, Congress passed the Military Reconstruction Act on March 2, 1867. This act divided the ten unreconstructed southern states into five military districts and, as Johnson's plan had done, required new constitutional conventions to rewrite the state constitutions. Unlike his plan, though, the new law permitted Black men to vote for delegates to the conventions. It also required the new state constitutions to guarantee Black suffrage and to ratify the Fourteenth Amendment.

The Military Reconstruction Act created a new relationship between individuals and the government that reflected Republican principles. It dramatically expanded the suffrage to give every adult male a voice in the making of laws and policies, and the new voters were not the sorts of men who had traditionally been seen as good candidates to influence politics. In the past, theoretically at least, voters were men who owned property and thus had a stake in the community and stability. Theoretically, they had enough education to understand issues and to vote for men who would protect their interests.

Ex-slaves turned that formula on its head. Very few owned property, and fewer still were educated (since it had been a crime in the antebellum South to teach a slave to read). What freedmen did have, that most southern whites did not, was a fervent loyalty to both the government and free labor. Republicans gambled that when it came to voting for policies that they believed would promote the good of the nation, these loyalties would outweigh the disadvantages of poverty and ignorance. "What is wanted in the mass who vote is the desire for right result, freedom from selfish motive and willingness to trust in wise guidance," as one Republican put it.[18]

The Military Reconstruction Act reflected Republican confidence in free labor. In the short term, party members were willing to depend on the goodwill and good sense of poor Black voters. But in the long term, the new system would succeed only if voters quickly gained property and knowledge. The act was the capstone of the Republican program for the country. It put the health of the nation into the hands of the people at large, in the confidence that they would work hard, get an education, and push the government to do what was best for everyone.

It is hard to overestimate the significance of the Military Reconstruction Act. With it, Republicans asserted that all men, poor and underprivileged as well as rich and educated, should have a say in American government. They also committed the nation to a system of government that backed individual economic prosperity and promoted education. Both elements—prosperity and education—were required, and if either fell through, voters would be swayed by economic dependence or by demagogues, and the republic would fall. Leading Republican politician James G. Blaine later reflected that the Military Reconstruction Act was of "transcendent importance and . . . unprecedented character. It was the most vigorous and determined action ever taken by Congress in time of peace. The effect produced by the measure was far-reaching and radical. It changed the political history of the United States. But it is well to remember that it could never have been accomplished except for the conduct of the Southern leaders."[19]

The Military Reconstruction Act was the last gasp of Lincoln's Republican Party. Over the next five years, party members would abandon their commitment to equality and tie the party to big business. Events in the South set the stage for this transformation: southern whites portrayed the enforcement of the Military Reconstruction Act as James Henry Hammond's nightmare vision come to life. Tied as it was to a defense of slavery, Hammond's warning about a grasping underclass had gotten little traction in the North before the war. Indeed, instead of swaying northerners to his way of thinking, Hammond's argument had done the opposite, pushing Republicans to defend workers. But after the war, as urban workers began to organize politically, many northerners began to worry that Hammond had been on to something.

The unraveling of the Republican vision began almost as soon as the Military Reconstruction Act passed in March 1867, when the idea behind it—that every man should have a say in the government—came under powerful attack. These attacks started in the South, where many whites were willing to work with the government to create a healthy free labor economy, but many more were not. White southern Democrats carried into the postwar years not only scars but also a growing realization that the modern world had shoved their antebellum society so far into the past that it almost seemed the stuff of legend. Once quaint southern cities and elegant plantation homes were now charred ruins; once productive fields were now weed-choked meadows; once healthy young men were now corpses or scarred veterans; once happy wives and children were now ragged refugees. And there was no way for the South to rebuild along traditional lines, for during the war, international cotton markets had reoriented themselves toward Egypt and India rather than the American South. Cotton had been the region's main export and chief generator of the income that had made white southerners the nation's wealthiest Americans before the war, but now cotton prices were unstable and dropping.

Still, most white southerners clung to the past. The Republicans' new system would bring economic and political leveling to a hierarchical society firmly divided by race. It would include former slaves in the economy and government and give poor white men a say equal to that of elites. For the first time in southern history, all men—Black as well as white, poor as well as rich—would have the same political voice. The Republicans' experiment took the government out of the hands of a wealthy elite and gave it to all men, and most white southerners wanted no part of this new way of doing business. Fully aware that the Republican plan would destroy the traditional South, southern state leaders refused to participate in it. They came up with a simple way to stymie Congress: they refused to enroll voters. State officials declared that they preferred to remain under military rule than to permit African Americans to vote.

Republicans in Congress had to pass three more enabling acts to put the Military Reconstruction Act into motion. Eventually, they put the army in charge of registering voters. This seemed to be the only way to get southern whites to engage in the process of rebuilding their governments without slavery, but it presented the enormous problem of putting the military in charge of voting. The mix of soldiers and elections is never comfortable, and though in this case it seemed imperative, Democrats instantly accused the Republicans of setting up a military dictatorship. With that dictatorship, they charged, Republicans would advance the very scenario James Henry Hammond had predicted: the radical redistribution of wealth.

Republican attempts to spread free labor across the South fueled Democratic fears. To lead political organizations—called Union Leagues—in the Black community, Republican leaders recruited upwardly mobile Black southerners who embraced the principles of the free labor system and who called for self-help, education, and thrift. But the vast majority of the former slaves enrolling to vote in the South were far more radical than Union League leaders. They were uneducated, semi-skilled, and impoverished, and their first experience of free labor had been devastating as former masters had cheated them of wages and had tried to impose on them a system as close to slavery as possible. From their perspective, the employer-employee relationship had been superimposed directly over the master-slave relationship. They had little confidence that they could rise to economic prosperity through hard work. Instead, they believed they must organize to demand fair wages and fair treatment from their former masters. They advocated land confiscation, went on strike against employers, and called for social welfare programs that would have to be funded with taxes.[20]

This more radical version of Republicanism also attracted poorer white farmers who had always resented rich plantation owners. By late 1866, small farmers were facing ruin after repeated crop failures. They were broke and hungry. They were also furious that Johnson had returned to power the very men they blamed for dragging the prosperous South into the war, a war that had destroyed their homes, their livelihoods, and their kin.[21]

These angry and poor southerners, Black and white both, were the very men Republicans were welcoming into southern politics at the point of a bayonet. The Republicans "are the champions of the poor man as against the rich," the *Montgomery Advertiser* warned. Rumors circulated that ex-slaves were organizing as a military force. For ex-slaves and their families, threatened by white vigilantes, arming themselves was an obvious thing to do, but hostile white observers saw their worst fears coming to life. They had always said that the end of slavery, letting the mudsills have a say in society, would launch a revolution. It was only a question of time, it seemed, before armed Black men would demand a redistribution of wealth.[22]

In the North, the Republican sweep of the 1866 elections had removed moderate Democrats from office, leaving only die-hard extremists in solidly Democratic districts. This meant that there were no powerful northern Democrats willing to check the revival of Hammond's worldview. Democratic extremists gleefully echoed their southern colleagues. Republicans were trying to "'organize a hell' in the South" and put "the Caucasian race" under "their own negroes."[23]

To that bald racism they tied the growing Republican government, which by 1865 had about fifty-three thousand workers who drew about thirty million dollars in salary. According to Democrats, Republicans were trying to take over the government permanently. They argued that Republicans had fomented a war in order to have an excuse to impose high taxes. With that money, they paid the salaries of party members they put into government jobs. Now Republicans were using trumped-up stories of violence against ex-slaves to inflate the government even further with the Freedmen's Bureau and the Military Reconstruction Act. Since the Republican government employed them, members of this army of officials would, of course, continue to support Republican candidates. It was only a question of time until the entire country was in thrall to this single-party behemoth.[24]

Racism reinforced the horror of this specter. Tax dollars would employ not just white men, Democrats insisted, but also Black men too lazy to work in the fields for a living. Because Republicans would be dependent on Black votes to stay in control, soon African Americans would hold all government offices in the South. The nation's leading Democratic newspaper, the *New York World*, claimed there would soon be "negro governors, negro mayors of cities, and negro occupants of every grade of office State and municipal."[25]

Even aside from the issue of office holding, Black men would allegedly corrupt American society. According to Democrats, Black voting would lead to a redistribution of wealth, just as antebellum southern planters had warned. Legislators with Black constituencies would create programs that catered to Black voters, and the only way to pay for those programs would be to levy money from hardworking white men. And since impoverished African Americans would not have to pay taxes, they would see no need to use tax money wisely, making government programs "among the most wasteful and corrupt that ever existed." They would "perpetuate robbery," making "extravagant expenditures" for roads, schools, hospitals, asylums, and other public institutions. According to Democrats, government programs for African Americans meant that white men would be ground into poverty.

It was not just the South that was at risk, but the entire nation, Democrats claimed. To get Black votes, politicians would have to promise African Americans "special legislation," enabling the Black minority to dictate national policy. The *New York World* warned that African American voters would swing the election of the next president, who would have to do their bidding.[26]

At best, this formulation was a willful misreading of the southern situation. At worst, it was a downright lie, aided and abetted by the newspaper stories written by southern reporters for the newly organized Associated Press, who were overwhelmingly ex-Confederates. Either way, it established the argument that the Republicans' use of the federal government was not designed, as Lincoln had advocated, to create an economy of upwardly mobile individuals. Rather, it was designed to do what James Henry Hammond had charged: redistribute wealth.[27]

The idea that every man should be able to rise and have a say in government seemed like a lovely idea when antebellum Republicans were talking about hardworking slaves in the distant South. But conditions had changed in the North during the war, and suddenly a number of Republicans were beginning to cool on the idea of universal suffrage at home. What was unsettling them was the rise of labor unions. America had never had a well-organized labor movement. Some urban workers had formed craft unions before the Civil War, but the war had wiped out even that level of organization. The drain of men to the battlefields and to the western mines kept unemployment low and wages steady, and few workers tried to organize. Those who did failed spectacularly when their employers convinced the government that their labor force was deliberately weakening the Union war effort. Government leaders sent soldiers to break the unions and defend war production.[28]

As soon as the war ended, though, workers began to organize. During the fighting, real wages had not kept up with inflation, and deteriorating working conditions in the growing factories had gone unaddressed in the all-out hustle to provide for the troops. Urban laborers worried that the war, waged to guarantee the ability of all workers to rise, had actually caused them to be left behind. Soon after the shooting stopped, they struck for better conditions and an eight-hour workday.

In August 1866, the country's first general labor union organized. This first meeting of the National Labor Union was no minor affair: it drew sixty thousand people. Most workers calling for organization simply wanted a chance to rise to comfort, but the resolutions developed by the group's leaders after the convention declared that workers must join unions to reform the abuses of the industrial system. These ideas were not especially popular in America, but neither were they unique: Karl Marx supported the National Labor Union's effort to organize workers. He saw its work as similar to his own efforts in Geneva with the International Workingmen's Association.[29]

The rise of organized workers took Republicans by surprise. Their definition of "workers" had been shaped in their antebellum rural towns. When they had constructed their ideas about political economy, they had envisioned individuals working for small proprietors or local farmers, slowly accumulating bank deposits, starting families, and gradually becoming proprietors themselves. Suddenly—to their minds—they were confronted with individuals who seemed to want to accumulate wealth by manipulating the laws rather than by working.

How would the Republican Party adjust to the rise of labor unions? Would it support workers' organizations or not? Some party members greeted unions as the logical outcome of a war against oligarchy. After all, the Republican Party had come together to protect workers in the first place, they reasoned. That the economic elite had gone from owning slaves to owning factories made little difference. These Republicans took their cue from the Republican Party's roots in the West and reasoned that the party's mission was to prevent the rich from controlling society.

But others recoiled from labor organization, and they were the ones who would hold sway. The war years had shifted the Republicans' center of gravity. Once northern Democrats regrouped after secession, Republicans could no longer rely on westerners as their electoral base. It was impossible to retain control of the national government without controlling New York, and as Lincoln had recognized by 1864, it was impossible to hold New York without having the support of Wall Street. A stand against wealthy employers that might have succeeded before the war would go nowhere after it. Eastern businessmen saw nothing good in labor organization.

In 1867, a dramatic public debate ignited by Senator Benjamin Wade of Ohio forced the party to step back from workers. Wade, who had been a cattle drover and worked on the Erie

Canal before studying law and entering politics, led those who saw class activism as the next step in the party's commitment to free labor. His fiery oratory lifted him to prominence, and in March 1867 the Senate had chosen him its president pro tem, in effect making him the nation's acting vice president. Opponents worried that he would run for president in 1868.[30]

In summer 1867, Wade joined a number of senators as they traveled to the West to see the land they had protected from slavery. In mid-June, their train stopped in Lawrence, Kansas, where Wade gave a rousing set of remarks. It's not entirely clear what he actually said, as he spoke without notes and later contested the account given by the only reporter present. The reporter trumpeted that Wade had declared war on property; he had celebrated the destruction of slavery and predicted that the next fight in America would be the struggle between labor and capital. "Property is not equally divided," the reporter claimed Wade said, "and a more equal distribution of capital must be worked out." Congress, which he now led, had done much for ex-slaves and must now address "the terrible distinction between the man that labors and him that does not."[31]

The speech became headline news because the reporter wrote for the *New York Times*, which by 1865 staunchly advocated the interests of New York City businessmen. The editor of the paper refused to let the issue die even when Wade and the other senators present insisted that Wade had been misquoted. The *New York Times* claimed that Wade was a demagogue painting a false picture of the American economy. Every hard worker could succeed in America, it maintained: "Laborers here can make themselves sharers in the property of the country,—can become capitalists themselves,—just as nine in ten of all the capitalists in the country have done so before them,—by industry, frugality, and intelligent enterprise." Trying to get rich by force of law would undermine society. Wade and other radicals were simply trying to redistribute wealth. If they succeeded, they would destroy America.[32]

The *New York Times*'s coverage of the speech unsettled many Republicans. Their leaders had always argued that the potential for national economic growth was unlimited, that increasing production would lift everyone to prosperity. Yet Wade seemed to be saying that labor and capital were locked into a struggle over limited wealth, just as Democrats claimed. Wade's actual remarks were probably intended to draw attention to the ugly reality that Republican wartime legislation had benefited industrialists more than their workers and that this inequality must be addressed. Republicans had widely discussed this issue during the war and acknowledged it explicitly in debates over graduating the income tax. But the *Times* reported that Wade had described the American economy as a war between labor and capital. This sounded perilously like the horrific world described by James Henry Hammond.[33]

The tension between Republicans who supported the right of every man to have a say in his government and those who worried about radicalism created an interparty rift that would, within a decade, make Republicans the party of big business. The problem started with a struggle over tactics. With white southerners howling about Black rights and the tide running against Wade and his comments on labor, it seemed to most Republicans imperative to reassure voters that they were not radicals and to take a moderate stand before the 1867 fall elections. But Benjamin Wade and Charles Sumner, two of the most powerful Republicans in the Senate, tacked in the opposite direction. They thought the Republicans needed to be more aggressive in the fight for equal rights, not less. They demanded far stronger reconstruction measures in the South, including a requirement that plantation owners give land to their former slaves before they could be pardoned, and also the establishment of Black suffrage in the North as well as the South. Fully aware that such radical proposals would lose voters in the upcoming elections, potentially giving Democrats control of Congress and likely killing what Republicans had achieved for equality, congressional Republicans bottled up these proposals in committee.[34]

Outraged, Sumner gave an interview to a reporter in which he blamed members of his own party for the failures of Reconstruction. Worse, he named names. He castigated elderly statesman William Pitt Fessenden for acting in ways "akin to insanity" and dismissed him as a backwoods hick. While Sumner was rude about his equals, he was downright insulting about the younger men in Congress, who, he implied, simply didn't understand their business. Sumner's older colleagues were furious, but more damaging was the enmity of one of the younger men, New York's Roscoe Conkling. Conkling was a touchy egotist who never forgot a slight. The feud between the two would break the party in half, and the ensuing destruction would doom the Republican commitment to equality.[35]

Everyone followed the upcoming elections nervously. Had Americans taken their government out of the hands of an outmoded economic oligarchy only to hand it to radical workers? In the end: no. The elections were "a crusher for the wild men," one Republican sighed with relief. In the South, voters elected moderate delegates to constitutional conventions. Opponents shrieked that the delegates were Black radicals, but in fact only about 30 percent were Black and almost all were from the 10 percent of the Black community that embraced moderate Republicanism. Most of the rest were native white men; about 25 percent were white men who had moved south after the war. In the North, voters also opted for moderation. They turned a number of Republicans out of office—including Ben Wade. New York's Roscoe Conkling moved up to the Senate, the start of his meteoric rise to prominence at the expense of older Republican radicals like Wade and Sumner.[36]

In February 1868, radicals in the lame duck Congress made a last stand with an effort to remove Johnson from office. The House voted 126 to 47 to impeach the president. The articles of impeachment listed Johnson's disregard for specific laws but more generally they indicted his "attempt to bring into disgrace, ridicule, hatred, contempt and reproach, the Congress of the United States." To great effect, they used quotations from his speech comparing himself to Jesus.[37]

But senators were not as eager as members of the House to get rid of the president. Moderate Republicans bore no love for Johnson, but they were troubled by the idea that a president could be discarded simply because he disagreed with Congress. They also recoiled from the idea of putting Benjamin Wade—who was still president pro tem—in the White House. The Senate vote was 35 to 19 for conviction, one vote short of the necessary two-thirds. Seven Republicans—including Sumner's nemesis William Pitt Fessenden—joined with twelve Democrats to keep Johnson in the White House. Republicans had begun to step away from the likes of Sumner and Wade.

With Republicans divided between those who wanted to stand behind Black rights and organized workers, and others who worried that labor activism would lead to a redistribution of wealth, party managers took a diversionary tack that would become a standard weapon in party leaders' rhetorical arsenal. They worked to attract voters by promoting the idea that only Republicans loved the country. Shortly before the 1868 Republican National Convention, General John A. Logan presided over a meeting to organize Civil War soldiers and sailors into a political body. Although it was not yet named, this would be the precursor to the Grand Army of the Republic, an organization quickly dubbed the GAR. The meeting declared that the troops earnestly and actively supported the Republican Party as the only political organization true to the principles of loyalty and equality before the law.[38]

With soldiers' and sailors' support, General Logan nominated U. S. Grant for president on a platform that harked back to Lincoln and classic Republican free labor theory. In their platform, Republicans condemned Democrats, blamed the problems of the last few years on Johnson—who was never really a Republican, they insisted—and promised that their program would carry the nation forward to the prosperity free labor promised. Grant got every single vote in the convention. The real question was who would become the vice presidential nominee. This would tell whether radicals or moderates would control the party.[39]

The contest was between Ben Wade, who was, after all, then next in line for the presidency, and Reuben Fenton, governor of New York and a consummate wire-puller. Wade appeared to have it sewn up, but Fenton threw his votes to the moderate Speaker of the House, Schuyler Colfax of Indiana, making Colfax the vice presidential nominee. New Yorkers had silenced the radicals.[40]

Grant's letter of acceptance was one of calm deliberation. He pledged that if elected he would administer the laws in good faith, economically, and "with the view of giving peace, quiet, and protection everywhere." Peace and the universal prosperity it would bring would reduce taxes and retire the national debt. His letter was brief but showed the talent for powerful language that later made his memoirs such a tour de force. Grant ended his letter with the famous words "Let us have peace."[41]

The Republicans won in November. Voters rejected the economic radicalism that pitted workers against the wealthy, utterly rejected Johnson's southern policy, and stood firm on a free labor system in the South. Mostly, though, voters endorsed the idea of peace. Grant promised a calm, fair way to get beyond the hatreds of the war, and after four years of a shooting war and three more of animosities that often boiled over into violence, Americans were ready for a rest.

They also hoped for the prosperity they had been expecting ever since Lincoln and his colleagues started talking about the backwardness of the Slave Power. Republicans confidently predicted that, now that sullen southern whites had been resoundingly defeated, southerners would pull together with the rest of the nation to build a free labor economy. When that happened, the entire nation would prosper. The South's fields would flourish, commerce would revive, entrepreneurs would develop new resources, immigrants would pour into the country, and the economy would boom. Then, the Philadelphia *Daily Evening Bulletin* reported, "The great Republican party will have the proud satisfaction of knowing, by positive proof, that it has been right all through this contest, and that the principles and policy advocated and sternly adhered to, have at last secured permanent peace to the country."[42]

4

Abandoning Equality

Washington was wrapped in cold mist on March 4, 1869, but neither the puddles on the muddy streets nor the threat of a downpour from the dark clouds overhead dampened the spirits of the thousands who lined the streets to see the man who had won the Civil War sworn in as president. As the carriage carrying the president-elect approached the Capitol, cheers erupted from the crowd and a half dozen brass bands struck up clashing tunes. Spectators surged forward. Silence fell as Salmon P. Chase, now chief justice, administered the oath of office. After Grant kissed the Bible, a twenty-one-gun salute and cheers from the crowd greeted the new president. According to an enthusiastic newspaper reporter, the noise thundered out to the American people "that the Administration of Andrew Johnson has passed away, and that the reign of Grant and loyalty, and truth and patriotism, has begun."[1]

In his inaugural address, Grant spoke as if the Johnson administration had never happened, but the new president could not erase the four years that had passed since he had accepted General Lee's surrender. To many Americans, Grant represented the best impulses of the war years: a principled dedication to equality and individual opportunity and a willingness to defend them to the death. But the political struggles since 1865 had disabused northerners of the idea that the new nation was going to move forward with its people reunited and in accord. In politics, Johnson had hardened the arguments of the Democrats and given power back to their white southern adherents, allowing them to continue to hammer on racism and class fears in a national context. The mutterings of a nascent labor movement and the shift of the Republican Party's center of power from the West to the East had helped to spread those fears to moderate Republicans.[2]

Grant was also in the singularly unenviable position of having to adjust the Republican Party's message so it would appeal to voters in the South as well as the North. Before the 1868 election, Republicans had realized that if they were going to campaign on the argument that their program for reconstructing the southern states had been a great success, they couldn't very well continue to keep those states out of the Union. Doing so would seem to prove the Democrats' charge that Republicans had no intention of ever permitting them to gain enough power to control the government again. So in June, Congress had readmitted the seven states that had met its requirements for readmission: Alabama, Arkansas, Florida, Georgia, Louisiana, North Carolina, and South Carolina. With these states rejoining the Union, Grant would have to make the Republican message appealing to southern as well as northern voters.

But members of his own party quickly undercut Grant's effort to get the entire nation to embrace the North's free labor economy. In 1869, as Grant took office, Americans grappled with the question of the proper role of government in the postwar nation. Was government activism the way to promote equal opportunity for every man, as Republicans insisted? Or did it threaten to destroy the nation's principles—and thereby the nation itself—by sucking taxpayers dry to cater to the lazy masses who kept corrupt politicians in power?

A peculiar and intensely personal struggle for control of the party during Grant's first term meant that Republicans would come to favor the latter interpretation. Older Republican statesmen, led by Charles Sumner, refused to accept the upstart general as the head of the party, and in their determination to wrest power from him, they attacked the party's reconstruction policy. In its place, they adopted a disdain for workers, white and Black, akin to that expressed by James Henry Hammond and instead championed the western cowboy, who they insisted was the antithesis of lazy ex-slaves and urban workers, as the true American individual. In 1872, they split the party and attacked administration men for maintaining an active government that they insisted was redistributing wealth. They lost the election but convinced most party members that Lincoln's active government, designed to promote equality of opportunity, was socialism. By 1872, Republicans had turned against the very government activism that had defined the party at its birth.

The struggle for control of the Republican Party began as soon as Grant took office. Like Lincoln before him, President Grant was a poor westerner; though educated at West Point, he was never a cultured man. He was a brilliant general and, it later turned out, a brilliant writer, whose *Memoirs* helped to spark the realist movement in American literature, but he was never welcome in Washington's established political circles.

Grant's biggest detractor within the party was Senator Sumner, whose pomposity had gotten worse in the years since he had become the symbol of northern victimization by southern tyrants. Sumner believed himself to be a grand statesman and the true leader of the Republican Party, delivering from on high the only acceptable policies on reconstruction and foreign policy. Sumner had scorned Grant during the 1868 campaign, declaring him completely unqualified for the presidency. In a sense, Sumner was right; Grant's training had given him different skills than those of a canny politician.[3]

The general's expertise was in military management, where leaders led and success depended on letting ability trump politics. Grant started his presidency expecting that, as in military leadership, politics would take a back seat to the needs of the country. With that in mind, he considered it a matter of pride to ignore the advice of Republican congressmen when he made appointments, thereby trying to rid himself of the ties of influence. Quickly, though, slighted Republicans began to accuse him of "cronyism" for his attempts to avoid the usual political channels, and Grant felt he had to appoint at least some of their candidates to office.[4]

His efforts did not smooth the growing tension among party leaders, and when Sumner and his friends made little effort to hide their contempt for the rough westerner who had become president, Grant began to move toward those who did not act as if his ascension to the White House was the best joke of the season. One of the congressmen eager to work with Grant was the man Sumner had alienated the previous summer: New York senator Roscoe Conkling. Conkling was a brilliant man and an extraordinary speaker, but he was also vain and proud, carried a grudge to extraordinary lengths, and hated to be touched by any but his most intimate friends, an odd foible for a nineteenth-century politician who had to glad-hand his way through rough-and-tumble crowds. Conkling's talents could have led him to the top of national politics, but he preferred to replace Thurlow Weed and rule the state of New York.[5]

Grant needed New York's support. It was the wealthiest state, with the largest congressional delegation—thirty-two members—and the most electoral votes: it would have thirty-five in 1872, six more than Pennsylvania's twenty-nine; thirteen more than Ohio's twenty-two; fourteen more than Illinois's twenty-one. No other state had more than fifteen, and most of the rest didn't break ten. With that sort of weight, New York usually decided the presidency. Grant had barely lost the state in 1868 and had squeaked out his victory thanks to southern Black voters; switching New York's thirty-five electoral votes to his column in 1872 would almost certainly secure his reelection. Grant could do the math as well as anyone. He was eager to work closely with New York Republicans.

Cordiality between Conkling and Grant grew into an alliance when Grant's first major policy initiative threw him into a fight with Sumner for control of the Republican Party. Like Lincoln, Grant's primary political focus was on economic growth. The president badly wanted America to annex the island of San Domingo (now the Dominican Republic) to establish markets for American goods in the Caribbean. Grant neglected official diplomatic channels and assigned to his own private secretary, Orville Babcock, the task of traveling to San Domingo to negotiate a treaty for annexation. Grant did not confer with the powerful leader of the Senate Foreign Relations Committee—Charles Sumner—until Babcock and the signed treaty were already back in Washington.[6]

By then, Grant had learned that he had to play politics, but it was too late to appease Sumner. On a Sunday night in early January 1870, the senator was having dinner with two reporters when his servant interrupted to say the president was at the door. Walking over from the White House to give Sumner the deference the senator believed was his due, Grant had come to tell Sumner he was about to submit the San Domingo treaty to the Senate for its approval.[7]

What happened next would cause such a breach between the two men that it would tear the Republican Party apart. Grant apparently assumed that Sumner would follow the president's lead and support the treaty. Before the president left, one of the newspapermen asked Sumner whether he approved. Although the newspaperman believed the senator gave Grant his cheerful assurance that he would support the measure, Sumner later insisted that he had only promised to give the matter his careful consideration. In fact, Sumner worked with Senate Democrats to defeat the president's pet project. Grant believed Sumner deliberately killed a treaty that offered a brilliant naval base and the key to American control of the Caribbean after having explicitly promised to support it. Sumner's condescending dismissal of the measure made the president abandon any hope of working with Sumner and his friends.[8]

For political support, Grant turned away from the older, first generation of Republican politicians like Sumner, who were so powerful in their own right they could thwart the president. In their place, he turned to younger men whose power bases were still small and who were eager for presidential favor. Chief among these men was Conkling, who had shared Grant's enmity for Sumner since the older senator's impolitic words of the previous year. When Conkling took over leadership of the Republican Party in New York, his position at Grant's right hand was secure.

The breach between Grant and Sumner began to divide the party leadership into two camps. Grant removed from government positions the men he had appointed at Sumner's request. In retaliation and, as usual, unable to believe that anyone's opinion was more important than his own, Sumner launched repeated broadsides at the president in summer 1870, condemning him as the ignorant puppet of designing men. His friends cheered him on, but other Republicans, horrified at the idea of yet another split between Congress and a president, began to slide away from Sumner and his self-righteous declarations.[9]

With control of the Republican Party seeming to hang in the balance in summer 1870, unexpected political events in the far-off state of Missouri took on extraordinary significance. Missouri suddenly seemed to be a microcosm of the nation itself, the experiment that would answer the question of whether the Republicans' expanded government would promote equality or foster despotism. It had been the only slave state north of the Missouri Compromise line, and the divided loyalties of its people made the Civil War there especially brutal. During the war, Missouri's secessionists and Unionists had clawed at each other. Among the secessionists were Quantrill's Raiders—the guerrilla gang in which Jesse and Frank James cut their teeth—who would ride into a Union town on horseback, guns blazing in both hands, and mow down civilians before disappearing as quickly as they had come.

The random violence of these guerrillas radicalized Missouri Republicans. When a convention met in St. Louis in the last months of the Civil War to revise the state constitution, Unionist delegates tried to undercut the guerrillas by guaranteeing that no one but staunch Republicans could vote or hold political office in the state. They took the suffrage away from anyone who had ever, in any way, helped the Confederates, even by something as minor as delivering a letter or offering a meal to someone who supported the South. Although this radical measure made sense in an area torn apart by guerrilla warfare, it also meant that all but the most devout Republicans were prohibited from voting. Since jurors were chosen from the poll lists, it meant that no one but Republicans could sit on juries. Unionists also required that preachers, lawyers, and teachers take a sweeping loyalty oath. As a result, Republicans would not only control polls and juries in the state but also monopolize all religions, classrooms, and legal proceedings.[10]

The constitution became known as the Drake Constitution, after the leader of the Missouri Republican Party, Charles Drake; Republicans' angry opponents called it the "Drakonian

Code." Voters ratified it in June 1865 by a vote of 43,670 to 41,808, an astonishingly close result considering that only Republicans were welcome at the polls. The new constitution immediately faced popular outrage, for the official establishment of a single political party worried even people who were not ex-Confederates. The constitution faced even more criticism after Congress readmitted southern states to the Union in summer 1868, for readmission meant that Democrats in former Confederate states had political rights now denied to Democrats in the Union state of Missouri. But Drake and his men were unwilling to cede any power. Their iron grip on the state looked quite unlike American republicanism not only to Democrats, but also to many moderate Republicans, who joined with Democrats to fight the Drake machine.[11]

An odd coincidence made events in Missouri crucial to the outcome of the struggle between Grant and Sumner. The key player in Missouri's challenge to Drake and his men was Carl Schurz, a close friend of Charles Sumner. Schurz was an important Republican leader who had fought in the German revolution of 1848, fled to America when it failed, and arrived in the New World carrying a torch for republican government. Schurz had been a staunch Republican since the party's early days, turning the oratorical skills he had honed rallying German students to what he saw as the same revolutionary impulse in America. He had brought the vital German American population into the Republican fold, helping to swing the critical election of 1860, served as ambassador to Spain, and fought on the battlefields of the Civil War's eastern theater.[12]

After the war, Schurz had toured the South at President Johnson's request and wrote a devastating report on conditions there that played into the hands of radical Republicans. But Schurz was always wary of political extremes. His own flirtation with radicalism had stopped dead in 1848 when he met Karl Marx and found him arrogant and obnoxious. Marx's condescension had repelled many who might well have become followers, Schurz later recalled, including, it seems, himself.[13]

Schurz worried that Republicans were moving toward despotism. In 1868, he spoke widely across Missouri in favor of Grant and the Republican ticket, but in the same election cycle he took on Charles Drake, who had been elected to the US Senate in 1866 and ran the state as if it were his fiefdom. Missouri's other Senate seat was opening, and Drake expected the state legislature, which he pretty much ran, to put one of his cronies in the spot. Schurz badly wanted the seat for himself, and he undertook to wrench it from Drake's machine.[14]

Schurz and his friends insisted that Drake's inexorable control of the state was incompatible with the republican government they had repeatedly risked their lives to defend. When Schurz's men began to court legislators, Drake played into their hands with his arrogant contempt for the well-respected German American leader. Worse, he insulted the immigrants on whose votes many legislators depended. The Republican caucus in the state legislature gave the Senate seat to Schurz. He went to Washington for the congressional session starting in March 1869, insisting that he stood for purifying the Republican Party of dictators like Drake not only in Missouri but throughout the entire administration.[15]

The history of the West was different from that of the rest of the country, and Schurz's stand against machine politicians reverberated across the nation because it caught the mood not just of Missourians, but of settlers in the western plains generally. The government had had little to do with eastern settlement, but Washington politicians had been uniquely responsible for American migration to the plains. They had enticed farmers west with the Homestead Act, transported emigrants with subsidized railroads, determined boundaries with government surveys, and used US troops to protect settlers from Indians. And yet, the timing of that migration, which took place primarily during the politically charged years after the Civil War when Democrats insisted that Republicans were creating a government that discriminated against hardworking white men, meant that the inhabitants of the region developed a hearty dislike of the very government that had made their settlements possible. Their hatred developed alongside the cattle industry, which boomed as Texans moved the huge herds of cattle that had multiplied during the war to eastern markets, army posts, and Indian agencies, where the government kept herds to supply the bimonthly rations called for by treaties with tribes.

The cattle industry's rise right after the Civil War meant that it would play a peculiar and important role in American politics. Most cattlemen and the white cowboys they hired were ex-Confederates who had fought in the war, a war that left them with nothing but the clothes on their backs and the ability to handle a horse and a gun. They had little love for the US government, and their attitude did not improve as they did business. They resented federal laws that prohibited the killing of Indians, and insisted that US army officers, who still hated their former enemies, cheated them when buying cattle and favored Union cattlemen. Seeing the Unionists they despised get preferential treatment from the government confirmed the opinion of ex-Confederate cattlemen that federal officials were corrupt.[16]

The timing of the cattle industry's growth meant that cowboy imagery grew to have extraordinary power. Entangled in the vicious politics of the postwar years, Democrats, especially those in the old Confederacy, imagined the West as a land untouched by the Republican politicians they hated. They developed an image of cowboys as men who worked hard, played hard, lived by a code of honor, protected themselves, and asked nothing of the government. In the hands of Democratic newspaper editors, the realities of cowboy life—the poverty, the danger, the debilitating hours—became romantic. Cowboys embodied virtues Democrats believed Republicans were destroying by creating a behemoth government catering to lazy ex-slaves. By the late 1860s, cattle drives were a feature of the plains landscape, and Democrats had made cowboys a symbol of rugged individual independence, something they insisted Republicans were destroying.[17]

A Democratic newspaper editor in Missouri brought together the western dislike of the government with Democratic opposition to the Drake machine in Missouri. Former Confederate John Newman Edwards argued that the newly strong Republican government in the state was actively persecuting hardworking Americans. His newspaper, the *Kansas City Times*, attacked the Drake machine as a prime example of dangerous government overreach, and in his hands, Jesse James, who had graduated from being a Quantrill Raider to robbery and murder, became a hero. When the Republican governor offered a reward for James's capture, Edwards began to print letters from the outlaw that portrayed him as the innocent victim of a political witch hunt. James insisted he had not committed the crimes charged to his account (although he certainly had), but he could not turn himself in because he was an ex-Confederate Democrat. With the state's lawyers, judges, and jurors all staunch Republicans, he couldn't get a fair trial. In Edwards's columns, and soon in the hearts of Democrats across the country, Jesse James became the symbol of a good, hardworking man persecuted by a corrupt government.[18]

The image of the western individualist standing against a corrupt eastern government became a key part of America's political mythology when Carl Schurz used it to bolster Sumner's attack on President Grant. Schurz had gotten himself elected to the Senate by tapping into western resentment with his attacks on the dictatorial Drake machine. Then, in summer 1870, when control of the national party seemed to hang in the balance, Schurz enlisted the same western rhetoric to indict the entire Grant administration.[19]

Everyone knew Schurz's assault was coming when Missouri Republicans met to choose a gubernatorial candidate, and everyone understood that his attack would signal a fight over the direction of the Republican Party. So when party members met in Jefferson City, national politicians and reporters crowded into the convention to watch what would happen. Those hungry for drama were not disappointed. Drake refused to cede control, and Schurz and his supporters walked out of the convention and to the other end of the Capitol building to organize their own political campaign. They called themselves "Liberal Republicans," in a reference to the classic liberal idea that individuals must be protected from the overreach of the state. They nominated for the governorship B. Gratz Brown, a former senator with preternaturally huge ears who joined them despite strong ties to Drake, and they promised to let ex-Confederates participate in Missouri public life again. Grant's political bosses worked hard to squelch the Liberal Republicans, but Schurz and his people won the election, putting Brown into the governor's chair by joining with Missourians fed up with the Drake machine.[20]

Fresh from the victory in Missouri, Schurz took the fight for western-style individualism to the president and the national Republican Party. In a powerful speech on the floor of the Senate in December 1870, he insisted that the Republicans had lost their principles and were now working solely to consolidate their power. The president, Schurz charged, had thrown in his lot with machine politicians. Grant had tried to defeat the Liberal Republicans, purging all but staunch Drake men from state offices and levying a fee on officeholders to fund the campaign against Schurz and Brown. Grant's only excuse, Schurz said, was that he was a political novice misled by calculating advisers who were not his true friends and who had "prostituted" his administration.[21]

Schurz's attack on Grant encouraged Sumner to take an even stronger stand against the president. The senator from Massachusetts had convinced himself that the party was replaying the crisis of the 1850s, when Republicans had attacked a powerful minority—the Slave Power—that was trying to take over the government. The San Domingo treaty was like the Kansas-Nebraska Act, he insisted: it was an attempt by a corrupt president to force slavery on an unwilling territory. In his speeches on what he saw as a replay of the 1850s, Sumner was at his intemperate best. Democrats repeated his broadsides on the president with such glee that Conkling charged Sumner with aiding the wrong party.[22]

But Sumner had badly miscalculated his own strength in a Congress that now included southerners and westerners. Wounded when his friend of twenty years, Grant's secretary of state Hamilton Fish, sided with the president, Sumner refused to speak to Fish. By early 1871, Conkling noted with relish, Sumner's attitude had made it impossible for the White House to work with the Senate Foreign Affairs Committee. Clearly Sumner would have to be removed from the chairmanship of this important committee, or the country could not engage in diplomacy.[23]

When the Forty-Second Congress convened in March 1871, the Republican caucus removed Sumner from his coveted chairmanship. Schurz and others tried to defend their friend and longtime Republican leader, but they were outvoted by new Republicans and Democrats. Back at the White House, Grant was unusually cheerful and remarked that he had had to make an example of Sumner "to teach these men they cannot assail an administration with impunity."[24]

Grant had won the battle, but the war was not over. The party had split, and Republicans like Sumner and Schurz insisted that they alone honored the party's true principles. While Grant's men focused on patronage and policies that would enhance their own local power, these "liberal" Republicans talked of national policy and principle. They believed that Grant and his small-minded cronies were out to line their own pockets. In contrast, they offered the image of an individual, hardworking man—symbolized by the western cowboy—who could rise and thrive if only the government would stay out of his life.

The seemingly petty personal struggle within the Republican Party had huge repercussions for both the party and the nation. Ironically, for Sumner had begun his political career as a principled abolitionist and styled himself the nation's chief defender of African American rights, his crusade against Grant would destroy Republicans' efforts to establish a fair system of free labor in the South. It would also end Republicans' dedication to equality of opportunity, their party's fundamental principle.

The fight between Sumner and Grant began to turn important Republican newspapers against the administration after Grant's men pushed the senator out of the chairmanship of the Foreign Affairs Committee. Sumner was an insufferable egotist, but he was also an elder statesman of the Republican Party. His principled stand against slavery had been a driving force behind opposition to the Kansas-Nebraska Act back in 1854, and no one had forgotten—or *could* ever forget—that he had been beaten almost to death on the floor of the Senate as he stood up for Republican principles.

Horace Greeley's *New York Tribune* was the first newspaper to back Sumner against the administration, and its defection started a cascade. Greeley had been an early leader of both abolition and the Republican Party, and he had trained a number of the nation's leading journalists, who revered him. His backing of Sumner swung other editors into the Sumner camp. Sumner might have been imprudent, and even bitter and unjust in his words about the treaty to annex San Domingo, Greeley's protégé at the *New York Tribune* Whitelaw Reid mused, but his opponents were power-hungry thugs. Repeatedly, Greeley begged Republicans to abandon Grant before the 1872 presidential campaign.[25]

Greeley's attacks on the president began to shift Republican principles away from the defense of equality. The former abolitionist abruptly abandoned the idea of a free labor system in the South, vilifying the administration's defense of ex-slaves in order to turn voters against the president. In 1870, Grant was facing what amounted to an armed rebellion in South Carolina, where members of the Ku Klux Klan terrorized Republican voters and any African American they suspected of Republican sympathies (which meant virtually all of them). Klan mobs whipped their victims, cut off their ears, hanged them, burned them, or if the victims were unusually lucky, simply warned them to abandon everything they owned and flee to save their lives. South Carolina's governor told the president he could no longer maintain order in the state, and Grant asked Congress for power to send in troops to destroy the Klan. He must have assumed he would have the support of Republicans, especially the former abolitionists in their ranks, like Greeley, for such a mission.[26]

But the mercurial editor was willing to abandon Black Americans if it meant he could score points against Grant. Beginning in 1871, the *New York Tribune* adopted Democratic rhetoric to assail the administration's "meddling" in the South, which was unnecessary, Greeley alleged, and was actually causing the South's problems. When a Senate committee began to investigate the Klan, the *Tribune* dripped with contempt. Southern Unionists were repeating the "same old, old story of murder, intimidation, and proscriptive oppression" to keep themselves in power, it declared. The *Tribune* echoed Schurz's position that the only way to calm the South was to treat ex-Confederates with kindness and charity. It cheered on those challenging Grant.[27]

Greeley's sudden support for Democratic ideas opened up a new front in the southern war against Black rights. It suggested to southern whites a different approach to oppose Black voting. The old abolitionist had no patience for southerners' racism, but by 1871 it was clear he had a weak spot for James Henry Hammond's argument that those at the bottom of society should not participate in politics. During the unusually harsh winter in 1871, when New York City workers had asked the Democratic city government for jobs to get them through an economic slowdown, Greeley had exploded. The problem was not a lack of work, he scoffed; the problem was the workers. Poverty came not from unemployment, he insisted, but from profligate spending, intemperance, and laziness.[28]

Playing to Greeley's biases, Democrats in South Carolina, who had been backing the Ku Klux Klan, resurrected the economic part of Hammond's argument and began to complain about their Black neighbors in terms of labor rather than race. To show that it was dangerous to give mudsills the vote, they insisted that the first South Carolina legislature elected after Black suffrage had immediately set out to redistribute wealth. The legislature, which had a Black majority (eighty-eight Black Americans and sixty-seven white), levied taxes on large landowners to raise funds to rebuild the shattered state. The same legislature had also approved the use of state money to provide land to settlers—usually freedmen—at low prices.[29]

The conjunction of these two measures infuriated South Carolina Democrats, who railed in racist agony against the "crow-congress," the "monkey-show" that they insisted was deliberately expanding the government and prostituting it to the interests of ex-slaves. African American voters were plundering white property owners. One observer commented that, with prominent white South Carolinians disfranchised and African American men voting, "a proletariat Parliament has been constituted, the like of which could not be produced under the widest suffrage in any part of the world save in some of these Southern States." Disgruntled Democrats organized a "Tax-Payers' Convention" to protest what they insisted was a law designed by workers to redistribute wealth.[30]

This formulation played far better in the North than a purely racist formulation would have, especially because northerners had a ready-made illustration at hand of what a worker's government would mean. In spring 1871, in the wake of the Franco-Prussian War, workers took over the city of Paris and established the Paris Commune. American newspapers plastered details of the Commune on their front pages, describing it as a propertied American's worst nightmare. They highlighted the murder of priests, the burning of the Tuileries Palace, and the bombing of buildings by crazed women who lobbed burning bottles of newfangled petroleum through cellar windows. The Communards were a "wild, reckless, irresponsible, murderous mobocracy" who brought to life the chaotic world James Henry Hammond had foreseen in 1858.

Newspapers reported that workers in Paris had taken over the government with a plan to confiscate all property and transfer all money, factories, and land to associations of workmen.[31]

Thanks to Greeley, Republicans had been sliding away from the idea of free labor in the South; the troubles in Paris made them slide away from the idea of free labor in the North as well. Republican newspapers across the country warned readers that what was happening in Paris might easily happen in America. They pointed out that Karl Marx's International Workingmen's Association for the emancipation of the working classes had established headquarters in New York City in 1867, and although members of the First International believed they were defending workers against combinations of capital the same way Lincoln's Republicans had, many Americans feared the men they called "Internationals" or "Communists," a term that in this early incarnation reflected only the idea that workers wanted wealth redistribution rather than that they advocated any organized political philosophy. Organized laborers "are agrarians, levelers, revolutionists, inciters of anarchy, and, in fact, promoters of indiscriminate pillage and murder," the *Boston Evening Transcript* charged. The *Philadelphia Inquirer* insisted that the Internationals were at war against capital and property and would force anyone who owned anything—even a small plot of land—to divide it with those who had nothing. This philosophy, it said, appealed to poor, lazy, vicious men who would rather steal from the nation's small farmers and mechanics than work themselves. *Scribner's Monthly* warned: *"the interference of ignorant labor with politics is dangerous to society."*[32]

Greeley brought growing concerns about workers in politics full circle by telling readers that the problems in South Carolina were precisely the same as those in Paris: workers were taking over the government. On May 1, 1871, a landmark article on the front page of the *New York Tribune* claimed that African Americans in South Carolina were socialists, and, as voters, they held the balance in elections. The state was split along racial lines, but the problem was not racial, the *New York Tribune* explained—it was what Hammond had predicted: African Americans were radical levelers. Ex-slaves were "ignorant, superstitious, semi-barbarians" who were "extremely indolent, and will make no exertion beyond what is necessary to obtain food enough to satisfy their hunger."[33]

To these lazy louts, Republicans had given the vote, which gave them "absolute political supremacy." They elected to office demagogues who talked of class warfare and promised to take wealth away from hardworking white South Carolinians and give it to idle African Americans. This was what the new taxes were for, the *New York Tribune* said. Ignoring the very real needs of a state rebuilding from a war that had destroyed its cities, its fields, and its people, the correspondent reported that property owners were being robbed to support the "Nigger Government." Workers were plundering the state's treasury and confiscating wealth through taxation. "The most intelligent, the influential, the educated, the really useful men of the South, deprived of all political power, ... [are] taxed and swindled by a horde of rascally foreign adventurers, and by the ignorant class, which only yesterday hoed the fields and served in the kitchen."[34]

Greeley endorsed the sentiments of Georgia Democrat Robert Toombs, a staunch secessionist and the first Confederate secretary of state, who explicitly compared ex-slaves to the Paris Communards. Republicans argued that Black voters would quickly gain the education they needed to be good citizens, Toombs said, but what had happened in Paris proved that education did not necessarily mean a man was fit to vote. The mob in Paris had been intelligent, but "they were the most dangerous class in the world to be trusted with any of the powers of government." The only way to create a stable society was to have a property requirement for voting. Without such a requirement, "the lower classes…the dangerous, irresponsible element" would control government and "attack the interests of the landed proprietors." According to Toombs, "Only those who owned the country should govern it, and men who had no property had no right to make laws for property-holders." Only ten years after Republicans had gone to war to stop the slave owners' view of the world from becoming the law of the land, the New York Tribune, the first Republican newspaper, was endorsing the slave owners' vision.[35]

In the end, the Tax-Payers' Convention called only for economy in the South Carolina government, hardly a grand conclusion to a meeting that promised to save the country. But in its wake, the peculiarities of electoral politics in New York meant that Republican newspapers across the country followed Greeley's lead. Anxious to pull New York City away from Democrats, and thus keep control of New York's thirty-five crucial electoral votes, editors turned Hammond's language against working-class Democrats in the North and suggested that what was going on in South Carolina was also happening in New York. Both were being ruled by "irresponsible non-property-holders."[36]

To illustrate their point, Republicans went after the powerful Tweed Ring, which controlled New York City and stayed in power with the votes of Irish immigrants. William Marcy Tweed bought voters' loyalty with jobs on public works projects, paid for, of course, with taxes. In July 1871, the *New York Times* launched an exposé of the Tweed Ring. Cartoonist Thomas Nast made the attack more powerful when he began to draw pictures of Tweed as a swollen vulture fattening on the public treasury. In Nast's hands, Tweed symbolized the corruption of government by uneducated poor voters who wanted easy government jobs.[37]

By the fall, Republicans were taking a stand against laborers in politics. At the *Nation*, E. L. Godkin worried about the corruption of the government by urban factory workers. When they tried to push a labor candidate for Massachusetts governor, they revealed, he wrote, "the organization, prematurely and under false colors, but still the organization of such a commune as America would now supply." Looking at the rising numbers of industrial workers and the conditions of city life, famous reformer Charles Loring Brace warned Americans, "In the judgment of one who has been familiar with our 'dangerous classes' for twenty years, there are just the same explosive social elements beneath the surface of New York as of Paris."[38]

Greeley's stance against African Americans and workers swung support away from the government activism associated with the Grant administration. Now with a national platform, Schurz and his fellow reformers hoped to defeat Grant in 1872 and return the Republican Party to the individualism that they argued was its original principle. They planned to pull "the best elements" of both parties into the Liberal Republican movement and destroy the political power of African Americans and organized workers, who, they thought, elected politicians to pass laws that would redistribute wealth.[39]

Schurz and his fellow reformers believed they could beat the Republican administration, despite its extensive patronage network, because of the support they commanded from important newspaper editors. No one knew better than Republicans that political contests were won in the media. Some editors had come onboard because of Grant's attack on Sumner, some opposed Black voting, some opposed workers' organization; whatever the reason, Murat Halstead of the *Cincinnati Commercial*, Horace White of the *Chicago Tribune*, William Cullen Bryant of the *New York Evening Post*, Charles A. Dana of the *New York Sun*, Colonel William Grosvenor of the St. Louis *Missouri Democrat*, and E. L. Godkin of the *Nation* all crafted their editorials to boost the Liberal Republicans. Most important, the movement had the support of Horace Greeley, who had been instrumental in constructing the early Republican Party.[40]

Elder Republican leaders who found themselves pushed out of Grant's inner circle by his new, younger supporters fed anti-Grant stories to their old friends in the media. The different newspapers picked up each other's tales of Grant's alleged corruption, nepotism, and perfidy. Perhaps most powerfully, Greeley continued to attack the southern Republican governments, blaming Grant for their failure and charging that they were confiscating the wealth of white property holders through "oppressive taxation" to redistribute it to lazy African Americans.[41]

Liberal Republican newspapers took a stand against labor organization, too. The *Chicago Tribune* announced in January 1872 that "those who style themselves 'the working classes'" needed to be taught "a few sound truths of political economy." As they became increasingly visible in politics, said the Chicago paper, their ignorance was painfully evident. The *New York Tribune* warned that a worker at a labor reform convention in Connecticut had hinted that if workers didn't get a better shake, he would "resort to the revolutionary violence of the Paris Commune." Shortly thereafter, the *Chicago Tribune* turned back to the situation in South Carolina. Claiming that the state had been run deeply into debt by improvident men, it called for wealthy South Carolinians to control the state again, for they were the ones who knew how to manage property.[42]

Delegates to the Liberal Republican Convention, meeting in Cincinnati on May 1, had great hope that they could purify American politics. Their movement had grown and was attracting "New Departure" Democrats, who were willing to forget the issues of the war and move forward to develop the southern economy. These Democrats held themselves apart from "Bourbon Democrats," who styled themselves after the French Bourbon kings and professed loyalty to the old southern aristocracy, which had been, they said, swept under by a rabble. New Departure Democrats were ready to support the Republican free labor vision, which Liberal Republicans promised to revive even as they rejected the original Republican idea that government should level the economic playing field between rich men and poor men.[43]

Since journalists controlled the convention, it was no surprise that the Liberal Republican platform was a concise version of their newspaper themes of the past six months. It called for equality of all men before the law; the preservation of the Thirteenth, Fourteenth, and Fifteenth Amendments; universal amnesty for ex-Confederates; and the removal of federal troops from the South. It castigated the spoils system for making government an instrument of "partisan tyranny," "personal ambition," and "selfish greed." It sought to break the power of patronage by calling for an impartial civil service to run government. It also demanded that no president serve for more than one term. After hearing the platform, delegates cheered for "the Second Declaration of Independence."[44]

Then disaster hit. For their presidential candidate, Schurz and the senior politicians at the convention hoped to draft Charles Francis Adams of Boston, Lincoln's ambassador to England, the son of President John Quincy Adams, and the father of Henry Adams, who taught at Harvard and edited the influential *North American Review*. But Whitelaw Reid and other New York operators had arranged to throw the nomination to Horace Greeley. As Schurz stood aghast, Reid lined up the votes to make Greeley the Liberal Republican nominee for president.[45]

Greeley, the erratic editor who had championed Lincoln but then turned against him; who had called for peace, then war, then negotiations; who had demanded harsh reconstruction measures, then called those measures unconstitutional, was now the party's candidate to move the country toward unity and a prosperous future. Greeley, who had excoriated the South and southerners as evil incarnate, was now to court their votes. Greeley, who had put in writing that he hated Democrats, was now asking for their support.

As a sop to Schurz, the convention nominated Missouri governor B. Gratz Brown for vice president, but the damage was irreparable. Henry Adams, a member of the very demographic the Liberal Republicans needed, dismissed the nomination and backed Grant. He reflected that any Liberal Republican president must be exceptionally discreet, strong, and stable to hold back reactionary southerners who would expect dividends for their votes against Grant. This was precisely what Greeley was not. He was, Adams said, "putty." With brutal accuracy, the *New York Times* noted that the bottom had fallen out of the Liberal Republican movement.[46]

The Liberal Republicans forced into play one more faction that would cement the Republicans' shift away from their original principles. New York bankers and businessmen threw their weight into the 1872 contest. Before the war, the New York business community had generally backed the Democrats, who defended the cotton production that supported the entire American economy. During the war, businessmen were willing to flirt with Republican policies, but in the early postwar years, their concerns about what they saw as Republican radicalism made them lukewarm supporters of the party. The rise of the Liberal Republicans lit a fire under them. They worried profoundly about the alliance between Liberal Republicans and Democrats, for if the new party won, it would return a number of former Democrats to office. Affluent men might be nervous about Republican radicalism, but they knew their businesses had boomed under the economic policies of Republican administrations, and Democrats had made no secret of their determination to dismantle those policies. Bankers and businessmen were just as determined to make sure they couldn't. The opposition of the business community to the Democrats pulled the Republican Party into its orbit, and Republican ideology continued to drift away from its original focus on equality.

After the war, Democrats had viciously attacked Republican economic policies. They backed the repayment of government bonds in depreciated currency, a plan that would have decimated the value of bankers' holdings. They had taken a stand against the Republican tariff system that put walls around American industries and promised a return to the prewar system of tariffs for revenue only. Dropping tariff rates would leave fledgling industries unprotected from European competition. There was no way that bankers or businessmen were going to stand by and let Democratic policy replace the Republican emphasis on economic development.

New York bankers took the lead against Liberal Republicans for two simple reasons. First, they controlled the bulk of the nation's capital. Second, New York was by far the most important state in the country in an election, but the state was always balanced on a knife's edge: generally the Democrats controlled New York City and the Republicans the rest of the state. So it was in New York that Republicans put their primary efforts (although they fought hard for Pennsylvania and Ohio, too).

In 1872, prominent New York banker Henry Clews worried that the Liberal Republicans' control of so many important Republican newspapers would doom any Republican candidate but Grant, who was a popular war hero and a devil people knew. But the Liberal Republicans had stirred up so much ill feeling toward the president, it was not clear that he could win renomination. Believing that if the party chose another candidate, it could well lose, Clews threw himself behind Grant. He did so, he said, because "I believed the sacredness of contracts, the stability of wealth, the success of business enterprise, and the prosperity of the whole country" depended on Grant's reelection. "Of course," he continued, "I knew that Wall Street business would boom in the wake of this general prosperity," adding, "of course, I expected to share in Wall Street's consequent prosperity."[47]

Clews organized the business community to support Grant. He got leading businessmen from both parties to call a mass meeting at Cooper Union to back the president's reelection. Addressing the packed hall, and the crowds outside, Republican leaders complimented Grant and tore apart former colleagues who had joined the Liberal Republicans. The ideas, principles, and policies of the Republican Party were greater than any man, Clews and his people said; they were stronger than the party itself. The Liberal Republicans could not come up with any policy quibbles with the Republican Party; their objections were solely personal, driven by petty ambitions.[48]

Republican leaders warned that if the Democrats regained power through the Liberal Republicans, the country would move backward. Democrats would tear apart the new nationalism the North had fought to maintain and would return the nation to a worship of states' rights. They would destroy the new national currency and the national banking system that had brought prosperity. And they would insist that the government pay them for the loss of their slaves. The Democrats, and their Liberal Republican enablers, were "poison."[49]

With its long-standing friendliness toward the business community, the *New York Times* began to swing to Grant's support. It cheered on the president and celebrated the Cooper Union meeting, declaring that the meeting represented all right-thinking Americans. Not only "the mercantile class" attended but also "representatives of the mechanics and laboring men," who understood that putting Democrats into power was madness.[50]

Administration Republicans gathered in Philadelphia in June to renominate Grant and reiterate Republican principles. Insisting that Republican policies benefited everyone, they pointed out that Republicans had freed the slaves, created equal citizenship, and established universal male suffrage. They had given land to settlers and passed a protective tariff to promote the development of the entire country. They defended both white and Black workers, and in their platform they even nodded to the idea of women's suffrage, although they were circumspect about it: "The Republican party is mindful of its obligations to the loyal women of America for their noble devotion to the cause of freedom. Their admission to wider fields of usefulness is viewed with satisfaction, and the honest demand of any class of citizens for additional rights should be treated with respectful consideration."[51]

When the Democrats held their noses and endorsed Greeley and Brown at their July convention, it seemed that Grant could overcome the Liberal Republican newspaper crusade against him. No matter how badly they hated Grant, many Democrats would simply not be able to stomach Greeley.[52]

Clews and his gang in New York still had a card to play. Clews was quite aware that the only newspaper in New York City that had not yet swung to the Liberal Republicans was the *New York Times*. So when New York Republicans set out to nominate a gubernatorial candidate at their state convention in August, Clews torpedoed the expected nomination of someone the editors of the *Times* didn't like. Instead, he forced through the elderly Democrat John A. Dix as the Republican nominee for governor. Dix was not in on this scheme, and he actually declined the nomination before Grant twisted his arm to accept it. The plan worked. The *New York Times* declared that "General Dix was the very best man that could have been chosen." It enlisted on the side of Grant in the upcoming contest, giving the Grant men the most powerful mouthpiece in the country to make their case for the president's reelection.[53]

Desperate to stop Grant, the Liberal Republican press did all it could to undermine the president. Along with the Democrats, the Liberal Republicans poked at scandal after scandal, but none stuck. By the fall it was clear that their only shot at taking the administration down was to link the Grant administration directly to something big. The obvious place to look for a scandal was in the close relationship between government and business, which was becoming increasingly unpopular with the public. Since the war, Democrats had harped on the idea that the Republicans were using the votes of duped African Americans to stay in power in order to help the very wealthy. They based this argument on their long-standing opposition to tariff and, later, tax legislation, arguing—inaccurately—that from the very beginning of the Civil War those measures had been designed to funnel wealth upward.

Wartime Republicans were not deliberately enriching the wealthy at the expense of the working man, but their actions in the postwar years gave even supportive voters reason to pause. The Republican conviction that everyone shared an interest in increasing production meant that party officials eagerly sought the help of businessmen in devising policies to promote growth. Often the relationship between public officials and businessmen got too close, as when Jay Cooke picked up the shopping bills of Treasury Secretary Chase's extravagant daughter. After the war, leaders from both parties worked more and more closely with businessmen as everyone tried to push a chaotic postwar nation toward economic growth.

The sordid underside of this cozy relationship was exposed to public view on January 6, 1872, when Edward D. Stokes shot railroad baron James Fisk Jr. on the stairs of New York's Grand Central Hotel, inflicting a wound that would kill Fisk the next day. "Diamond Jim" Fisk was a barrel-chested former peddler with an elaborately waxed moustache who had risen to become a swash-buckling financier. He was well known for his lavish displays of wealth, his cut-throat greed, his generosity, and his voluptuous show-girl mistress, who took the place of his long-suffering wife on Fisk's arm at shows and fancy dinners. Fisk and Stokes had been business partners until Stokes walked off with Fisk's mistress. Then the two men publicly accused each other of financial improprieties in their business dealings. Their animosity was widely known; the shooting shocked people but did not surprise them. Word of Stokes's attempt on Fisk's life raced through the city. Crowds gathered outside the hotel for the latest news, and the story became a national sensation.[54]

The shooting tore open growing public nervousness over the relationship between government and business. Both Fisk and Stokes had been deeply involved in the Erie Railroad, which had bought the goodwill of the New York legislature by working with William Marcy Tweed's Tammany Hall. The railroad and political rings made a financial and political union that controlled the state, opponents charged. That Tweed himself came to Fisk's deathbed to pay his respects gave teeth to such accusations. Republican newspapers made hay of the Erie Ring and its connection to Tammany Hall, flaying Democrats for their willingness to let businessmen dictate government policy.[55]

But the same argument could be turned just as easily against the Republicans. In June 1872, Congress declined to extend the income tax and chose instead to fund the government through increased tariffs. Republicans had always seen the income tax as an extraordinary war measure and had provided for it to expire in 1870 before extending it to 1872. There was little agitation to extend the tax then since the Treasury was running a surplus; nonetheless, workers noted that Congress chose to end a tax on wealthier members of society while maintaining tariffs that hit workers every way they turned.[56]

Voters were already worried that an active government was ripe for corruption by special interests at the bottom of society, but increasingly in 1872 they worried that men at the top of society were just as dangerous. Liberal Republicans, who promised a return to even-handed government unswayed by any special interest, could turn this fear to their advantage if they could just find a way to tie the administration directly to an Erie-like scandal. If they could prove that Grant Republicans were corrupting the government to line their own pockets, they might overcome Greeley's weaknesses among voters. Schurz tried to implicate Grant in some War Department scandals, but doing so only hurt his own credibility. Then, in September 1872, Charles Dana at the *New York Sun* broke the story the Liberal Republicans needed: the Credit Mobilier scandal.

Like the Erie scandal, the Credit Mobilier scandal involved a railroad: this time the Union Pacific. Dana claimed to have evidence that a principal in the Union Pacific Railroad, Republican congressman Oakes Ames from Massachusetts, had bribed a number of key Republican lawmakers to pass legislation benefiting the railroad. "The Vice-President of the United States, the Speaker of the House of Representatives, the chosen candidate of a great party for the second highest office in the gift of the people, the chairman of almost every important committee in the House of Representatives—all of them are proven, by irrefutable evidence, to have been bribed," Dana wrote.[57]

In fact, Dana's evidence was deeply problematic. He had a list of names with dollar amounts next to them on the back of a letter Ames had written. But the list was not in Ames's handwriting, and the man who produced the list had admitted in court that he had written it himself, claiming that it reflected his memory of a conversation he had overheard. But

Dana buried that significant information deep in his paper. On his front page, he insisted that there was no doubt the Republican politicians were guilty. They had devised policies for their newly active government that would not advance economic opportunity generally but rather line their own pockets at the expense of American citizens. No one with any respect for America would vote to keep the Republicans in power now, he announced. The *New York Tribune* picked up the story and ran with it. So did the rest of the Liberal Republican press. And so, for that matter, did gleeful Democrats.[58]

For their part, administration Republicans were outraged. "Bribing me to support Pacific Railroad interests is just as incredible as that I should need to be bribed to vote the Republican ticket," sputtered the vice president. Republicans seemed honestly surprised that their willingness to invest in the country financially as well as politically should be seen as somehow inappropriate. The whole point of the Republican worldview, after all, was that all Americans shared a harmony of interest. If a project was good for economic development, it was good for everyone. The government should support it; the wealthy should invest in it; the workers should build it. Republican officials had operated this way during the Civil War; capitalists had operated this way ever since. The accusation that congressmen investing in a great national project had been bribed to do so struck administration Republicans as a pathetic effort to boost the Liberal Republicans. They charged Dana, Greeley, and the other Liberal Republican editors of "prevarication," "slanders," and "utter falsity."[59]

This last-ditch effort of the Liberal Republicans to spike the Grant campaign failed. Most Republicans were convinced that only a straight Republican ticket could protect the results of the Civil War. Capitulating to Liberal Republicans, along with what seemed to be their unholy alliance with Democrats, threatened to throw African Americans back under the control of their former masters. It would give southern Democrats a larger say than ever in national affairs (since African Americans would be counted as whole people, rather than three-fifths of a person, after the 1870 census). For their part, African Americans stuck to Grant even when Sumner half-heartedly encouraged them to vote for the Liberal Republican ticket. As Frederick Douglass famously put it, "The Republican party is the ship and all else is the sea."[60]

Democrats could have helped the Liberal Republicans, but they refused to do so. Voting for Greeley was simply too much for them. Most stayed home or, in places like New York, swung to the Republicans. Grant was reelected in a landslide with more than 55 percent of the popular vote. He took every state except Georgia, Kentucky, Maryland, Missouri, Tennessee, and Texas, whose electoral votes totaled only 63 to Grant's 286.

Although Grant was reelected, the struggle for control of the Republican Party marked a sea change in both the party and the nation. By declaring war on the administration, Sumner and Schurz and the Liberal Republicans had split the party and bled older, principled Republicans out of power. Men like Roscoe Conkling and other machine politicians took their place.

Ironically, in their quest to preserve the principles of Lincoln's Republican Party, the Liberal Republicans doomed those very principles. In order to take down President Grant, Liberal Republicans had adopted the language of Democrats who opposed Republican ideals in general. Drawing from Hammond's old argument that poor men would always vote to give themselves government benefits, Liberal Republicans had tarred administration Republicans as corrupt demagogues who promised wealth distribution to lazy African Americans in order to keep themselves in power. Once there, Liberal Republicans charged, they not only catered to Black voters but also did the bidding of the very wealthy. Their policies redistributed wealth from hardworking Americans to the undeserving at the bottom of society and at the top. This, of course, was what the Democrats had been saying since the Civil War, but their rhetoric had not gained traction in the North until the Liberal Republicans legitimized it.

The confluence of events of 1871 turned northerners against ex-slaves, and they also determined that the maturing Republican Party would not champion organized workers. When Liberal Republicans went after ex-slaves as lazy schemers, they opened the door to attacks on New York City immigrants and eventually to a blanket condemnation of workers as a separate interest attacking the harmonious system that guaranteed American prosperity. And thanks to the popular image of the western cowboy, they had a ready-made foil for the socialistic eastern worker. The rush of financiers and businessmen to support the Republican Party in 1872 grafted that condemnation of workingmen onto the maturing party. After 1872, regardless of the economic realities of industrialization and modernization, Republicans would cling to their prewar definition of good American workers as hardworking men who believed they could rise on their own merits. Republicans would dismiss labor organization as being an un-American plot to redistribute wealth.

Beginning with the election of 1872, administration Republicans could also count on hefty war chests funded by businessmen. By refusing to adapt their ideas to the realities of postwar industry, Democrats pushed businessmen firmly into the Republican Party. Most industrialists and financiers were determined to prevent the return to power of Democrats, whose postwar economic policies they abhorred. By the time of Grant's second term, business interests were beginning to take over the Republican Party.

The Liberal Republicans delegitimized the argument of the Civil War Republicans that a strong national government should promote general prosperity by creating economic opportunities for men on the make. After 1872, Republicans argued just the opposite. They tended to deride any effort to use tax money for programs that helped society in general as "communism" or "socialism," regardless of what the actual goals of the legislation were or of who was proposing it. Increasingly, they echoed the prewar Democratic argument that wealthy men should dominate society.

Lincoln's policy of helping every man work his way up had been jettisoned by his own party after only twelve years.

5

Republicans and Big Business

Whereas the peculiarities of the 1872 election prompted Liberal Republicans to divide the world into hard workers and lazy louts who wanted a handout, the politics of the next few years cemented that division into the regular party. Over the next two decades, a new generation of Republican leaders solidified the party's swing toward big business. They abandoned the idea that the economy grew from the bottom up and began to argue that it grew from the top down. Refining the belief of Republican founders that everyone shared a harmony of economic interests, they insisted that legislation protecting business benefited all hardworking Americans: strong businesses would create jobs, more people would find work, and the country would grow. Republican officials insisted on a high tariff to protect industry. They cut taxes and attacked any sort of regulation. Then, ignoring the fact that the industrial system they promoted was driving growing economic inequality, Republicans argued that workers trying to survive on pennies a day or farmers operating at a loss had only themselves to blame: they were lazy. Instead of buckling down to work, these people expected a handout from government, paid for by tax dollars collected from men who *were* hard workers.

After the election, former Greeley supporters continued to carp that African Americans and organizing workers wanted a redistribution of wealth. South Carolina had fallen into socialism, they warned, where "they who lay the taxes do not pay them, and...they who are to pay them have no voice in the laying of them." Anti-Grant Republicans made similar complaints, saying that workers employed on government contracts building roads and courthouses, dredging harbors, and so on seemed dangerously similar to South Carolina's ex-slaves. One editor worried that "much of the manual labor required by cities, States, and the General Government" was procured on "thoroughly communistic principles." He claimed—incorrectly—that mechanics who supposedly did as little as possible to collect a paycheck made more money than their betters, men of education who had positions of responsibility.[1]

Increasingly, Republicans echoed these charges, even though the idea that the nation was sinking under wealth-redistributing taxation was ridiculous. In the fiscal year that ran from June 1871 to June 1872, the Treasury spent $270 million, much of it on funding the interest on national bonds. Less than 36 percent of the total expenditures—about $130 million—came from taxes; most of the rest came from tariffs. Indeed, tariffs brought in so much money that the Treasury ran a surplus of $94 million. In today's money, that would mean that the Treasury made expenditures of $4 billion, collected a little less than $2 billion in taxes, and ran a surplus of $1.4 billion. This was hardly the picture of a nation sinking under a program of wealth redistribution. But the reality stood very little chance against the power of Republican rhetoric, pushed, as it was, in the nation's most powerful newspapers.[2]

In this atmosphere of growing dislike for politically active workers, Republicans expanded their definition of wealth distribution to include anything that impinged on the freedom of businessmen to do whatever they wished. No longer did Republicans focus solely on the idea that tax-funded contracts would redistribute wealth to lazy voters. In the mid-1870s they began to insist that government regulation of business in any way was, itself, a redistribution of wealth.

That change developed after midwesterners joined together to challenge pro-business government policies. These "Grangers," as they were called, urged farmers to elect to office men who would stand against railroads and "middlemen"— the grain buyers and elevator operators who set the prices farmers would get for their crops. Grangers insisted that in America officeholders should work for the people, not, as one said, for monopolies and "men whose pockets are well filled with money, who want special legislation to replenish their own coffers." In the 1870s, Grangers elected a number of senators, representatives, and governors. Granger-led legislatures in the Midwest promptly passed laws regulating railroad rates and the fees that elevator operators could charge farmers. The Granger Laws, as they were known, established the principle that government should oversee business practices.[3]

Businessmen recoiled at the Granger Laws. They roared that government regulation of business limited a man's ability to accumulate all he could and thus was a redistribution of wealth. With their abhorrence of "communism," Republicans echoed the businessmen's opposition to any government regulation. The staunchly Republican *Chicago Tribune* bemoaned that communism was creeping into the country: "The spirit of Grangerism, Workingmanism, Communism, Grievanceism, or by whatever name the present fever among those who assume to themselves the title of 'the industrial and producing classes' may be termed, appears to be growing apace throughout the United States." It warned that the International was making America "the battle-ground in the war that Communism is waging upon society" and urged Americans to keep their eyes open to the dangers it threatened.[4]

After the nation slid into a severe recession in 1873, Republicans and workers fought bitterly and openly for control of economic policy. The failure of Jay Cooke's bank on September 18 precipitated the Panic of 1873, and the interconnection of finance capitalists, especially in railroad securities, meant that after Cooke's house went under, banks and brokers tumbled like dominos. Henry Clews's bank failed. Stocks plummeted. The New York Stock Exchange shut down for ten days. Production slowed. Factories closed. Wholesale prices collapsed. And unemployment soared.[5]

The economy had been softening for months before the crash, but Americans were shocked when it hit, and they scrambled for some way to explain the sudden collapse. Businessmen and workers had very different explanations for the crisis, both centered in recent financial policy. From the 1790s until 1873, American law had allowed currency to rest on either gold or silver, but silver was so expensive it was rarely coined. By the 1870s, newly discovered western mines promised to drop the price of silver, and as the economy had weakened, farmers and entrepreneurs rejoiced that silver currency would increase the money supply and make it easier to borrow. Established businessmen and bankers, though, insisted that the threat of inflation caused by the prospect of an increased money supply made capitalists afraid their money would be wiped out if they invested in new businesses. This insecurity, they said, was the cause of the economic downturn.

The Republican Congress sided with moneyed men. It demonetized silver in February 1873 during a routine reworking of the nation's currency laws, a move that dramatically reduced the money supply just when it needed expanding to stimulate the sluggish economy. Interest rates had gone up, and western farmers found themselves unable to do business without currency or credit. (Ironically, tight money also worried investors, who shied away from new projects, including the Northern Pacific Railway, whose bonds Jay Cooke had counted on selling to stay solvent.)

After the crash, workers blamed the change in the currency laws—which they dubbed the "Crime of '73"—for their troubles and demanded that the government stop privileging wealthy eastern businessmen and start protecting workers. But Republicans dismissed their clamors. Protecting businessmen so they felt comfortable investing in new projects *was* protecting workers, they said, since businessmen created jobs when they invested their money. Anyone arguing that the government must help out workers and farmers was attacking the very system that made America great.

Voters disagreed. Fed up with the Republicans' pro-business legislation, they threw seventy-seven Republican representatives out of office in 1874. The next year, for the first time since the Civil War, Democrats, with their conviction that the government must level the playing field between workers and business, controlled the House of Representatives.

With Democrats again viable, the 1876 election of a successor to President Grant turned on the question of what, exactly, Republicans stood for. They claimed to be the party of the common man, using an active government to expand the economy so everyone could rise. They told voters they stood against "utterly incompetent" traitors who had tried to destroy the country first on the battlefield and then by attacking Republicans' successful economic policies. Republicans warned voters against trusting unworthy, cowardly, and incapable Democrats. But Democrats charged that Republicans had become the party of the rich, winning elections by attracting Black voters with promises of handouts and then moving money upward to the nation's wealthy elite.[6]

The two presidential candidates reflected their party's position. Republicans had to placate former Liberal Republican reformers as well as Grant men, so they turned away from frontrunner Senator James G. Blaine, who had been tainted by accusations that he had taken railroad bribes. Instead, delegates nominated a dark horse, Ohio governor Rutherford B. Hayes, who was known neither as a reformer nor as corrupt.

For their part, Democrats promised vaguely to bring back economic prosperity by "reforming" government, getting rid of the waste and bureaucracy that sucked up tax dollars, and cutting government's ties to business. For president, they nominated New York governor Samuel J. Tilden, well known and well loved by reformers for his long fight against the corruption of Tammany Hall.[7]

On election night, grave robbers tried to steal Abraham Lincoln's body, setting a fitting tone for what would turn out to be a frightful election. Thanks in part to Republican reformers unhappy with Hayes and still determined to bring down the Grant men, Tilden won 51 percent of the popular vote to Hayes's 48 percent, a difference of about a quarter of a million votes. But Tilden was 1 vote short of the 185 Electoral College votes he needed. Each side promptly accused the other of fraud.[8]

Victory depended on returns from Oregon and from the southern states that still had Republican governments: South Carolina, Florida, and Louisiana. The returns of each state were disputed, and Congress appointed a fifteen-member commission to figure out which ones to accept. Four months after voters had cast their ballots, and by a straight party vote of eight to seven, the Republican majority of the committee decided that Hayes had won all four of these states and thus the presidency.[9]

The Republicans kept the White House, but their victory seemed to prove that they and their wealthy supporters were determined to control the government regardless of the will of the people. During the four-month fight, railroad barons promised southern businessmen that they would use their influence to see that government funding went to the southern transcontinental railroad the businessmen desperately wanted if their states' electoral commissions would ignore the Tilden majorities and throw their electoral votes to Hayes. When states did, indeed, support Hayes, Tilden men concluded that big business was determined to continue feeding at the public trough regardless of what that did to the fundamental principles of American government.[10]

That conviction grew stronger when it seemed that Grant would back the choice of wealthy businessmen with bullets. Furious when Congress handed the election to Hayes, northern Democrats insisted that they would inaugurate Tilden by force if they had to. Secret military clubs formed throughout the Midwest to support Tilden, and the Democratic governor of Indiana was reported to be organizing the state militia for war. Grant responded by warning that he would deal with violence by declaring martial law. Tilden supporters believed they were seeing the destruction of the American republic at the hands of an economic oligarchy backed by the military power of the state.[11]

Once inaugurated, President Hayes did his best to defuse that fear. Immediately, he appointed a Democrat as postmaster general—a plum position for distributing patronage as every hamlet had its own postmaster—to indicate that he would not use federal patronage to shore up southern Republicans. Hayes also refused to use the military to defend Republican state governments in the South. In South Carolina, Wade Hampton, the "reformer" candidate for governor, had won the popular vote, but his supporters had run a violent campaign that undoubtedly kept Republicans from the polls. The Republican incumbent holed up in the state house surrounded by soldiers, insisting that because the election had been so corrupt he should remain in office. Hayes warned that he would not continue to use federal troops to protect Republican state governments, and in April 1877, he removed the troops from around the South Carolina State House (although not from the South in general), permitting Hampton to take over as governor.[12]

But Democrats held on to the idea that the Republicans had perpetrated the "Great Fraud of 1876" to perpetuate their political empire. As soon as Hayes took the oath of office, they began to assail him as "His Accidency." Beginning to electioneer for the midterm elections even before the 1876 election was settled, Democrats insisted that Republicans had stolen the presidency and were determined never to give up power.[13]

If accusations that Republicans were determined to run the country for the benefit of their rich constituents seemed quite believable when Hayes took office in March 1877, by the end of July they seemed incontrovertible. That month the country's first national strike erupted. Beginning in West Virginia when the Baltimore and Ohio Railroad cut wages 20 percent, the strike spread along the rail lines to Maryland, Pennsylvania, Illinois, and Missouri, shutting down the nation's railway system. Mobs destroyed ten million dollars in property; clashes between workers, police, and company men left one hundred people dead.[14]

Organized workers hoped that the Great Railroad Strike was the opening salvo in a war against the oligarchy that appeared to be running the country, but Republicans as well as many Democrats saw instead a scene that looked much like the Paris Commune. Allan Pinkerton, the founder of the strike-breaking Pinkerton Detective Agency, claimed the strike offered proof that "we have among us a pernicious communistic spirit" that must be crushed out completely before it led to even worse disasters. Railroad director and Republican leader Thomas A. Scott dismissed laborers' complaints in disgust. Far from complaining about their pay cut, he wrote, they should consider themselves lucky as railroad men were keeping on extra hands in the recession out of the goodness of their hearts.[15]

Hayes put the muscle of the American military behind the railroad owners. He sent soldiers to the cities immobilized by the strikes, and the workers backed down. But the use of the military to back up the railroad barons only months after Grant had threatened to use it in defense of Hayes's inauguration reinforced the belief of many Americans that Republicans had gone much too far. It did not help that Thomas Scott was one of the key railroad lobbyists who had urged southerners to make Hayes president in exchange for a southern transcontinental railroad. To hostile observers, it looked like the railroad men had subverted the election and now had the army at their beck and call.

Hayes's use of the army during the railroad strike prompted Democrats to insist that the president stop using the army as a police force. In 1878, Democrats proposed the Posse Comitatus Act, which prevented the president from using the army within the US borders unless he had the permission of Congress. Republicans greeted this measure with incredulity. Senator Blaine pressed a colleague from Pennsylvania: what if a mob were destroying Scranton, where voters had just elected the leader of a labor union as mayor? Wouldn't he want the soldiers to interfere in the face of a communist mob? Apparently not: the measure passed. The *Chicago Tribune* was horrified: passage of the measure meant that no troops "shall be used to protect colored voters of the South...or to crush out Communist riots at the North."[16]

The tide was beginning to shift away from the Republicans. In the lead-up to the 1878 midterm elections, Democrats quite openly kept Black voters in the South from the polls. That, together with the continuing recession, cost Republicans the Senate. Beginning in 1879, the Democrats would control both houses of Congress for the first time since the Civil War.

Clearly, Republicans had to regain voters. But how? Should party leaders ignore complaints that they were turning the government into the tool of big business and stand firm on the idea that their legislation protected economic equality? Or should they bow to their critics and embrace reform? Republicans first attempted to garner votes from both sides, an effort that failed spectacularly, splitting the party so badly it prompted an internecine war that led to the nation's second presidential assassination. The ensuing backlash enabled Democrats to gain enough political ground to carve away at key Republican legislation.

When Hayes declined to seek renomination, Grant Republicans, led by Roscoe Conkling, insisted that the only way to retain control of the White House was to mobilize the party's pro-business machine and renominate Grant. Other party members, eager to seize power from the Conkling crowd, backed powerful Maine senator James G. Blaine. At the Republican Convention in June 1880, these factions, nicknamed, respectively, Stalwarts and Half-Breeds, lost out to a third faction, which swung the nomination to a dark-horse candidate on the thirty-sixth ballot: Ohio congressman and House minority leader James A. Garfield. Garfield was a Republican in Lincoln's mold, an unobjectionable war general and advocate for Black rights. For the second spot on the ticket, the convention tried to smooth the ruffled feathers of Conkling and his followers by choosing a Stalwart who was deeply involved in party machinations although he had never held elective office, New York's handsome man-about-town Chester A. Arthur.[17]

For their part, Democrats nominated the popular Union general Winfield Scott Hancock on a platform that excoriated Republicans for "the great fraud" of 1876, demanded a permanent end to federal protection of Black voting, insisted on overturning Republican tariff and financial policies, and called for the government to serve only the hardworking taxpayer. In a colorful attack on Republicans, whom they accused of wanting to use the government to distribute money both upward and downward, the Democrats pledged to protect the working man "against the cormorant and the commune."[18]

Republicans won the 1880 election across the board, taking both the White House and Congress. But Garfield and Arthur won by only about eight thousand votes out of almost nine million cast. This translated to a safe victory in the Electoral College, but it made clear that Republicans no longer enjoyed any kind of monopoly on the nation's political system. More worrying still was that the South went solidly

Democratic. The Republicans held all the states north of a line that ran across the middle of the country, but in the future if they lost New York—always a swing state—they would lose the presidency. Clearly the party could not expect to keep winning if it continued to try to please all factions.

A crisis after the election heightened the need for the party to consolidate around a central message. Still determined to take control of the party, and thus the nation, Conkling picked a fight with the new president over patronage in New York City. To demonstrate his power, Conkling resigned his position in the Senate, confident that the New York legislature would immediately reelect him, thus demonstrating that Conkling, rather than Garfield, was the true leader of the Republican Party in New York and thus the linchpin of the national party. (New York's other senator, Thomas Platt, joined him in resigning, earning his place in history as "Me Too" Platt.) But Conkling was wrong. New Yorkers had had enough of his petulance. After a long battle, the New York legislature sent two new senators to Washington.[19]

The terrible end of this intraparty struggle came in July 1881, when a deranged office seeker from the Conkling wing of the party shot and mortally wounded President Garfield at the Washington train station. "I am a Stalwart, and now Arthur is president!" he allegedly shouted. While Garfield lingered, in great pain, for the next two months, Americans had plenty of time to reflect on the meaning of the assassination attempt. The big business wing of the Republican Party, to which the assassin belonged, had so corrupted the meaning of government that he had felt justified in killing the president to get a job. Surely, voters thought, this was not the Republican government for which soldiers like Garfield had died only twenty years before. Just as surely, they thought, the Republican Party, controlled as it now was by the big business wing, must no longer govern the country. When he took office upon Garfield's death in September, even Arthur recognized the damage. He kept a low profile, turned away office seekers, and would make no attempt to win renomination.[20]

Voters rejected big business Republicans and put Democrats back in control of the House in the midterm elections of 1882. Once there, they promptly began dismantling policies that were based on the fundamental Republican theory that because labor created value everyone shared a harmony of interest. Democrats dismissed the idea that the nation needed as many workers as it could get, and in 1882 Congress passed the Chinese Restriction Act, prohibiting the immigration of Chinese workers but not of professionals or scholars. Old-line Republicans fought bitterly against this law, but the Democrats' argument that competition hurt laborers and helped the wealthy won out. The Chinese Restriction Act rejected the Republican theory of economic harmony and enshrined the idea of class competition in American law.[21]

Another Republican principle to go down to defeat was the idea that protective tariffs helped everyone. In every year from 1875 to 1893, tariffs brought in more revenue than the government spent; in 1881, the government ran an annual surplus of $145 million. Surpluses convinced Democrats that industry did not actually need high tariffs, but businessmen clung to them because keeping out foreign competition enabled them to monopolize industries and set artificially high prices. This sucked money from consumers and put it in the pockets of wealthy manufacturers. Insisting that the tariff must be used only for revenue, Democrats in 1883 lowered tariff rates. The reduction was small, but it forced Republicans to defend their protectionist stance as a party measure, rather than as a policy that helped the whole country.[22]

Finally, Democrats tried to prevent Republicans from controlling the country through patronage. In 1883, they passed the Pendleton Act, which established a nonpartisan system for filling civil service jobs, in an attempt to stop the politicization of government service and the consequent risk of creating a one-party political system.

Republicans, for their part, saw the Democratic resurgence as a threat to the nation's very existence. As Democrats replaced Republican economic measures with ones that protected workers, Republicans jettisoned the idea of reform and solidified around the idea that protecting big business was crucial to defending America. Anyone arguing otherwise, they suggested, was preaching un-American socialism. Republicans had finally coalesced around a clear message, but their consolidation around a pro-business worldview further alienated voters, who increasingly supported Democrats.

Republicans turned to popular media to combat the idea that government should help workers. In 1883, John Hay, who had been Lincoln's private secretary, released a potboiler titled *The Bread-Winners*. This "thoroughly American book," as *Harper's Weekly* called it, attacked labor organizers and the politicians who did their bidding. In the same year, another author took that argument further. Yale sociologist William Graham Sumner wrote a manifesto defending "The Forgotten Man." As Sumner defined him in *What Social Classes Owe to Each Other*, this person was "worthy, industrious, independent, and self-supporting." It was utterly unfair that people like him should be taxed to support the lazy. Worse, such a redistribution of wealth would destroy America by destroying individual enterprise. Sumner called for a "laissez-faire" world in which those who failed should be permitted to sink into poverty, and even to die, to keep America from becoming a land where lazy folks waited for a handout. Such people should be weeded out of society for the good of the nation. Republicans echoed Sumner's *What Social Classes Owe to Each Other*, concluding, as he did, that the answer was: nothing. Even though "his views are singularly hard and uncompromising," wrote the *New York Times*, "it is difficult to quarrel with their deductions, however one may feel one's finer instincts hurt by their apparent cruelty."[23]

In the mid-1880s, Republicans enshrined their argument against government action on behalf of workers in the nation's fundamental law. After Roscoe Conkling threw his tantrum and destroyed his political career, he turned to litigating for big business. In the 1882 case *San Mateo County v. Southern Pacific Railroad*, he insisted, based on his role as a congressman who had helped frame the Fourteenth Amendment, that Congress had intended the due process clause of that amendment to protect corporations as well as individuals. The Supreme Court did not explicitly comment on Conkling's outrageous claim in 1882, but four years later it announced that his doctrine was definitive. The principle that corporations were protected by the Fourteenth Amendment dramatically limited potential government regulation of business.[24]

Republican embrace of big business was not just philosophical; it was also practical. After 1880, with the South solidly Democratic, Republicans had to hold the northern states, especially New York, which now had thirty-six electoral votes. They could not keep New York without the support of New York's business community, including the pro-business *New York Times*. They needed businessmen's votes as well as their money for campaign literature, newspapers, speakers, and rallies—and to pay for the sorts of activity that coaxed reluctant voters into casting a Republican ballot: whiskey and small bills were sometimes more effective than arguments.

When the 1884 Republican National Convention met in June, delegates tried to acknowledge popular anger at the Grant-Conkling Stalwarts while also staying pro-business. They nominated James G. Blaine, who four years before had been the choice of the anti-Grant men. This choice infuriated the Stalwarts without going far enough for reformers. The nomination of "Blaine, Blaine, James G. Blaine; the continental liar from the State of Maine" was too much for Republicans who wanted the party to reclaim its original principles. Led by Carl Schurz, they bolted the party and pledged to vote for the Democratic nominee, Grover Cleveland, the reform-minded governor of New York. "We are Republicans but we are not slaves," the chairman of a Republican meeting declared. The party must dedicate itself to "retrenchment, purity, and reform."[25]

These independent Republicans, indignantly dubbed "Mugwumps" by party regulars, indicated the direction of the tide. Even the *Chicago Tribune* complained about the links between business and government: "Behind every one of half of the portly and well-dressed members of the Senate can be seen the outlines of some corporation interested in getting or preventing legislation." The Senate, *Harper's Weekly* noted, was "a club of rich men." This was not an exaggeration. James G. "Slippery Jim" Fair, seated in 1881, was worth a cool thirty million dollars, equivalent to more than one billion dollars in the early twenty-first century. Fair had struck it rich through his part ownership of Nevada's fabulous Comstock Lode, then plowed his money into real estate and railroads. Other senators commanded fewer millions, but their loyalty to the corporations that had made them rich was as staunch as Fair's.[26]

In 1884, popular outrage at the influence of money in politics helped put Grover Cleveland into the White House. For the first time since the Civil War, voters had rejected Republican government and elected a Democratic president. It seemed as though, just as in the 1850s, the nation was not willing to see an economic elite take over the government. But in 1884, the parties had switched sides.

Only a generation after the Republican Party had formed to make sure that all hardworking Americans could rise, its members had replaced that principle with a defense of big business that looked perilously close to antebellum slave owners' defense of their society. And, as in the 1850s, most Americans in 1884 thought their nation should stand for the opportunity of every man to rise as long as he worked hard. Republicans who backed big business—the Old Guard, as they came to be known—would try to restore Republican supremacy by stifling dissent and manipulating the political system, and although their desperate measures produced short-term victories, they were a sign of the party's fading strength. It would take a new generation of Republicans, who saw the 1884 election as a wake-up call, to reclaim Lincoln's principles and restore the party's popularity.

At the moment, Republicans recoiled from Cleveland's election. They believed that the fate of the world hung on their control of the government. Trusting the Republican Senate to stop the Democrats from accomplishing anything, Republican operatives set out to resurrect the party and protect the economic system it had created. They blanketed the country with pro-Republican pamphlets and with editorials and news stories defending the protective tariff. Their propaganda war was only the beginning, for they recognized they must rejigger the electoral system if they were to win elections. That they set out to do, first with new campaign financing and then with the addition of six new states.[27]

After the debacle of 1884, party regulars threw themselves behind the business wing of the party. For president in 1888, they bypassed party leader Senator John Sherman, who had recently wavered on the sanctity of the tariff, and turned instead to Benjamin Harrison, a Civil War veteran, former senator from Indiana, and the grandson of a former president, who would do what he was told. At the nominating convention, a New York railroad man urged the New York delegation to swing from Sherman to Harrison, thus putting the party firmly in the hands of the businessmen.[28]

Republicans believed the fate of humanity hung on the 1888 election, and their desperation made them fight dirty.

They accused Democrats of disloyalty and fraud, but more to the point, they amassed an enormous war chest. To raise money for the fight, Republican leaders drafted John Wanamaker, the Philadelphia entrepreneur who had pioneered the department store. Wanamaker created a network of committees that reached out to businessmen all over the country, touting Harrison as the businessman's candidate and warning that a Democratic victory would destroy the tariffs on which the economy depended. Money poured into the well-oiled Republican machine.[29]

A rising kingmaker named Mark Hanna organized Republican operatives to give the House back to the Republicans and elect Harrison. In the 1888 election, Republicans took the House and Senate. Although the Harrison ticket didn't run well, it did manage—one way or another—to take New York's crucial electoral votes, which put Harrison in the White House, despite losing the popular vote by about one hundred thousand votes. Harrison was a pious man, and after the election he commented to Hanna, "Providence has given us this victory." Hanna later grumbled: "Providence hadn't a damn thing to do with it. [A] number of men were compelled to approach the penitentiary to make him President."[30]

Cleveland, who had won the popular vote but lost the election thanks to Hanna's machinations, decried the takeover of government by the wealthy. But Harrison's jubilant supporters brushed off Cleveland's warning as sour grapes. They were thrilled to have secured the nation's future and interpreted Harrison's victory as a mandate for the protectionism they insisted was the key to the nation's security. This was a willful misreading of the election results as Republicans not only had lost the popular vote but also had reassured wavering voters that they would "reform" the tariff if they regained control of the government.[31]

Still, Harrison's men believed the election was an endorsement of their economic vision. In June 1889, just three months after Harrison had been sworn into office, steel magnate Andrew Carnegie published an article titled, simply, "Wealth," in the popular Republican magazine *North American Review*. Carnegie's view of a good economy sounded much like James Henry Hammond's. Great disparities of wealth benefited everyone, he wrote, for they enabled some men to cultivate the highest and best in literature and arts and "all the refinements of civilization." If such wealth were scattered to the masses in higher wages, it would undoubtedly be squandered on food and small luxuries. Carnegie parted from Hammond by defining society's elite class not by race but rather by its members' ability to work hard. This is what the Republican vision of every man being able to work his way up to comfort had become: all men had a chance to work. The talented ones would make a fortune; the rest would be society's mudsills.[32]

Once safely in office, Harrison's men turned to making sure the Democrats could never again undermine Republican policies. To do that, they reconfigured the American political system, launched a propaganda campaign, and put more emphasis on the importance of the tariff, raising rates to new highs. Their machinations gave the nation six new western states and a new fear of voter fraud but not, in the end, a Republican majority.

With the popular vote shifting away from them, Republican leaders decided that their best bet to preserve a majority was to add more states to the Union. Since the 1870s, various western Territories had petitioned to become states, but congressmen squabbled over their admission, unwilling to create states whose voters supported the opposite party. The Republican sweep in 1888 sent Democrats scrambling, well aware that once Republicans controlled Congress, they would admit only the states that favored them. Less than two weeks before he left office, Cleveland signed off on the best deal the Democrats could get. It provided for the organization of Montana and Washington as states in nine months and cut the large Dakota Territory in half, creating North Dakota and South Dakota, both of which would be admitted as states at the same time as the other two. This deal would give Republicans the three new states of North Dakota, South Dakota, and Washington, while everyone expected Montana to go Democratic.[33]

The following year Republicans brought two more western states—Idaho and Wyoming—into the Union, creating an unprecedented six new states in a single calendar year. (They were in such a hurry to admit Idaho that they bypassed normal procedures and called for volunteers to write a state constitution, which voters approved only months after it was written.)[34]

The new states would each bring in a representative to the House of Representatives, but more important to Republicans, they would each bring in two senators. Three new Republican states—and optimistic Republicans promised they could take Montana, too, which would give them four—would entrench the party in the Senate for the foreseeable future. The new senators and representatives would alter the balance of the Electoral College as each state's electoral votes equal its total number of representatives and senators. Republicans believed that by adding western states, they could block tariff revisions by holding the Senate and guarantee the election of Republican presidents by stacking the Electoral College. No longer would New York be able to swing a presidential election toward a Democrat. It was a simple and a seemingly foolproof plan.[35]

Harrison's men also worked aggressively to fill patronage posts with staunch Republicans. Cleveland had honored the spirit as well as the letter of the 1883 civil service law, but Harrison's men had no such scruples. They handed out all positions at their disposal to supporters and all the contracts they controlled to friendly industrialists. Within a week of Harrison's inaugural, horrified observers estimated there were at least seven thousand job seekers in Washington.[36]

Harrison's operatives tried unsuccessfully to pass a bill to permit federal officers to oversee congressional elections in any place where one hundred voters requested them. This would enable Black Republicans in the South to vote for members of Congress—local and state elections were explicitly excluded from the bill—and allow federal officers to keep Democratic immigrants from voting in New York City. Harrison's men insisted, in increasingly incendiary language, that the Federal Elections Bill, as they called it—opponents dubbed it the Force Bill—was designed simply to prevent voter fraud. At the same time, though, they openly boasted that the plan would dramatically increase the number of Republicans in the House of Representatives and claimed that the bill would keep the Democrats from "stealing" the next election.[37]

Finally, recognizing that they had lost all but the most extreme pro-Republican newspapers, Harrison's people bought the popular *Frank Leslie's Illustrated Newspaper* and made Harrison's ne'er-do-well son Russell its coeditor. The first issues under his direction dismissed the idea that the president was supposed to represent the whole country. Rather, Harrison was supposed to represent Republicans. That was the whole point of an election, the paper explained. "When the people elect a President and Congress, they presume that they also elect policies and men of their political faith to carry them out. They expect that all the subordinates of the Federal service will be put in full accord with the new Administration."[38]

Frank Leslie's explained exactly what that meant: "This is to be a business-man's Administration," and "business men will be thoroughly well content with it."[39]

But the war over whether business interests or the people should control the government was not over. The flexing of Harrison administration muscles in the service of business created a backlash. Within months of Harrison taking office, even moderate Republican papers complained that "the greed displayed by the office-seekers has never been surpassed in our political history." Worse was the admission of the six new states. *Harper's Weekly* pointed out that the one hundred thousand people estimated to live in Wyoming and Idaho in 1890 would have four senators and two representatives, whereas the two hundred thousand people in New York's First Congressional District had only one representative. To stay in power, Harrison's men had deliberately undercut the political power of people in populous regions, a maneuver that seemed an assault on the principle of equal representation that Republicans were supposed to hold dear. Then came the Federal Elections Bill, and moderate Republicans finally cried foul. It was not worth losing the principles of republican government just to keep Harrison in the White House. Even the *New York Times* turned against the bill, sneering that Harrison's men were desperate.[40]

The *Times* was right. The Republican administration was desperate to shore up its power because its opponents were successfully riding a rising tide of anger at the party's pro-business policies. In the 1870s, businessmen had formed pools to carve up market shares; in the 1880s, pools gave way to trusts, whose managers controlled entire industries. By 1890, trusts needed outside capital, and financiers who provided it demanded a voice in industry to guarantee their investments were as profitable as possible. A few key players dominated the boardrooms and backrooms of industry: J. D. Rockefeller, J. P. Morgan, Andrew Carnegie, and Jay Gould, men later dubbed "robber barons." Working together, they amassed fortunes. Republican tariffs protected their economic empire because they guaranteed that American business could not be undercut by foreign competition.

In contrast to those at the top of the economic ladder, workers' incomes and standards of living were collapsing. From 1877 to 1890, more than 6.3 million immigrants arrived to crowd into the teeming cities with native-born Americans who had abandoned the family farm. Flooded urban labor markets enabled industrialists to pay lower and lower wages. When workers tried to organize so they could bargain more effectively, Republicans howled about communism and wrote laws to undercut labor unions. During the 1880s, wages continued to drop and laborers' bargaining power to weaken. Workers struck for conditions that would enable them to rise if they worked hard. Mayors tended to call out the police to keep peace, but still, strikes mounted. In 1886 alone, more than 600,000 workers were on strike or locked out of jobs, and between 1880 and 1900, more than 6.5 million workers engaged in more than 23,000 strikes. Between 1865 and 1890, strikes destroyed millions of dollars' worth of property and left dozens of Americans dead.[41]

As the crisis of urban life got more and more acute, many Republicans insisted that enterprising poor men could succeed by moving west. It was wishful thinking—social mobility was much the same in western communities as in the East—but it was a powerful antidote to the idea that America's mighty industrial economy privileged the wealthy. It blamed the workers themselves for being stuck in low-wage jobs. Any young man could make it on a farm: after all, adherents said, Lincoln had.[42]

Although many people were fed up with the Harrison administration, it would be farmers misled by the idea of the West as a solution to economic troubles who would bring it down. Farmers flooded the plains after the Civil War, enticed by railroad literature that described thriving western communities. Their dreams faded when they found themselves at the mercy of the railroad men to get their crops to markets. Men who had brought their families west on the promise of success began to organize to call for more control over railroads. They developed organizations called Alliances that would buy, sell, mill, and store their products cooperatively, thus increasing their bargaining power with railroads and elevator operators. By the time of Harrison's inauguration, members of the farmers' Alliances had announced they agreed with laborers: they called for "the reform of unjust systems and the repeal of laws that bear unequally on the people."[43]

Rather than address the criticism that their legislation privileged business, Republicans fell back on the idea that farmers were either lazy or improvident. They were in debt because of their "extravagant notions," insisting on expensive machinery and eating beef and chicken instead of cheaper pork and potatoes. In the end, it appeared, they were lazy and wanted the government to take care of them. The farmers' Alliances wanted "a sort of paternal Government," Republicans charged, just as workers did.[44]

Republicans' unwillingness to address the economic inequities of their policies strengthened the growing farmers' Alliances. The summer of 1890 became known as the Alliance Summer as speakers, including the famous farmers' orator Mary Elizabeth Lease, crisscrossed the plains. Lease thundered that "Wall Street owns the country.... It is no longer a government of the people, by the people, and for the people, but a government of Wall Street, by Wall Street, and for Wall Street." She told farmers to "raise less corn and more hell."[45]

They did as she suggested. So many farmers joined Alliances that in some western states Republicans did not bother to run political tickets for the midterm elections. By summer 1890, party leaders realized they must do something to undercut the idea that they were working solely for big business or they were in serious danger of losing control of the government. In July of that year, Congress passed two laws designed to show it was on the side of the workingman. The Sherman Antitrust Act was a toothless measure that made it illegal for businesses to combine to restrict trade, but it left undefined what, exactly, restricting trade meant, leaving the way free for courts to give great leeway to business combinations. The Silver Purchase Act was also designed primarily to undercut agitators. When a bloc of westerners backed the free coinage of silver, horrified eastern Republicans countered with a plan for the Treasury to buy up the silver flooding the market and to issue more paper currency backed by gold. This would take the wind out of the sails of the silver money men while keeping currency at par and preventing inflation.[46]

Although they were willing to nod to opponents on minor issues, Republicans stood firm on the tariff. First, they spent down the budget surplus the tariff had produced as quickly as possible to prove that the government really did need the money the tariff raised. When generous pensions for Civil War veterans did not clean out the Treasury, Congress passed appropriations for millions of dollars' worth of public buildings and statues to Civil War heroes. Then, with the Treasury running dry, they insisted that what the country really needed to usher everyone to prosperity was an even higher tariff. A House subcommittee chaired by Ohio's William McKinley—who was also the chairman of the powerful Committee on Ways and Means—produced a tariff that lowered rates on a few items but raised them on everyday items, sometimes dramatically. The rate on horseshoe nails, for example, leaped from 47 to 76 percent. Democrats were furious, and even moderate Republicans were shocked. In drafting the measure,

"MCKINLEY'S PICKPOCKETS [were] PAYING A PARTY DEBT" to big businessmen, the *New York Times* charged in a bold headline.[47]

In May 1890, in a chaotic congressional session, with members shouting amendments, yelling objections, and talking over each other, Republicans passed the McKinley Tariff without any Democratic votes. They cheered and clapped at their victory. "You may rejoice now," a Democrat yelled across the aisle, "but next November you'll mourn." Democrats were right. In the November 1890 midterm elections, angry voters repudiated the Republican Party. They gave the Democrats a two-to-one majority in the House. Republicans managed to keep the Senate by four seats, but three of those seats were held by senators who had voted against the McKinley Tariff. McKinley himself lost his House seat. The government was slipping from Republican control.[48]

Defections continued. Republicans had given the upper hand to their opponents on the tariff issue, convincing a majority of Americans that the party was only interested in making the rich richer. Alliance men grabbed wavering Republicans on the left end of the spectrum by organizing into a new party, the Populist Party, that promised to take government out of the hands of "capitalists" and give it to "plain people," but moderate Republicans were also leaving the party. By November 1892, even the Republican wheelhorse *New York Times* had taken a firm stand against Harrison's men. It ran the names of prominent Republicans who were defecting to the Democrats because, it said, they believed the Republicans' tariff policy was "wrong in theory, injurious in effect, and absolutely immoral." Wayne McVeagh, who had been attorney general under Garfield, publicly reflected that the original Republican Party had ceased to exist. In its place, he sighed, "was an organization of political corruption, fostered by bounties acquired under the system of so-called protective tariff." For him, the Harrison administration was the last straw. He, too, left the party.[49]

In 1892, Grover Cleveland won the popular vote again, beating Harrison's bid for reelection by close to half a million votes. He also handily won the Electoral College. The Democrats lost twenty seats in the House, but they still retained a strong majority. Capping the Republicans' loss, the Senate flipped comfortably to the Democrats. It was a landslide, pure and simple. Instead of keeping the country Republican, Harrison's "businessman's administration" had created a backlash that turned the entire government over to the Democrats for the first time since the Civil War.[50]

Republicans were "astounded and dazed" at the Democratic landslide, as one wrote, but concluded that, rather than compromising, they must fight harder than ever for their vision of America. "Up and at 'Em," the staunchly Republican *Chicago Tribune* cried. The only good thing about the election, according to one Republican senator, was that it would finally "put an end to William McKinley, Jr.," who was a talentless favorite of the defeated Harrison. Good riddance to bad rubbish. In fact, though, Republicans did not suffer from their loss; they managed to turn the debacle to their own advantage.[51]

Republicans had insisted that the economy would collapse if voters elected Democrats, and as soon as it was clear they had done just that, Republicans turned their dire warnings into dire reality. Harrison's administration had been "beyond question the best business administration the country has ever seen," one businessmen's club declared, and losing that administration would be a calamity, especially since, according to Republicans, Democrats were really socialists and anarchists who wanted to destroy America. The *Chicago Tribune* told readers that the lower tariff and easier money Democrats promised would destroy industries and throw people out of work. But that was fine: "The working classes of the country need such a lesson.... It remains for the wise man to endeavor so to arrange his personal affairs that he will suffer least from the threatened affliction." "The Republicans will be passive spectators.... It will not be their funeral," the *Tribune* snarled.[52]

Spurred by Republican newspapers reporting an impending collapse, fearful investors pulled out of the market. The crisis was shocking, all the more so because there was no economic reason for it. Historians have pointed to overinvestment in railroads and to declining wages that hurt purchasing power to explain the crash, and although both of those things were true, they were no more true after the election than before it. In fact, economic indicators were better in late 1892 than they had been for years. Exports of agricultural products had increased dramatically in the fall after a bumper wheat crop, reducing the unfavorable balance of trade that had plagued the nation in the late nineteenth century and boosting prosperity.[53]

Nonetheless, as soon as Cleveland was elected, the nation seemed to be in terrible trouble. Gold began to flow out of the country to Europe. It did so for a number of reasons— customs receipts had dropped, and the Republicans' pension bill had drained the Treasury—but the primary problem was that Europeans stopped investing in America. Republicans had made it crystal clear that a Democratic administration would debase the currency and create rampant inflation. It made no sense to invest under such a threat, and European investors brought their money home.[54]

As conditions worsened, the outgoing Harrison administration stubbornly refused to reassure investors. By February 1893, the stock market was paralyzed. Eastern bankers begged for an issue of bonds to replenish the Treasury, but the administration announced there was no financial problem. In mid-February, financier J. P. Morgan rushed to Washington to urge Harrison to do something, but the calm of the administration men remained undisturbed. Secretary of the Treasury Charles Foster commented publicly that the Republicans were responsible for the economy only until March 4, the day Cleveland would take office. His job was to "avert a catastrophe up to that date."[55]

He didn't quite manage it. On Friday, February 17, in Wilkes-Barre, Pennsylvania, as a paymaster of the Reading Railroad Company began to hand out monthly wages, the telegraph agent at the station handed him a telegram. He read it, closed his pay window, and started his train car for Philadelphia. Fear that Reading was going under sparked a panic among the employees. Their instincts were right: the paymaster's telegram had warned him that Wall Street was boiling. Reading was slaughtered like a lamb, one reporter wrote. Sugar and lead stocks also got hammered. After Reading started to fall, "the bottom seemed to be falling out of everything."[56]

Stocks continued to plummet the next day, with Reading over the cliff first. In the first ten minutes of trading, more than one hundred thousand Reading shares changed hands. By the end of the day, more than half a million had. The market was closed on Sunday, but on Monday, the crash continued. Observers estimated that twenty million dollars evaporated on February 20. On February 23, the slaughter became universal. The Sugar Trust collapsed, and the Northern Pacific Railroad went down. Behind them tumbled the rest of the market.[57]

Panicked observers begged Harrison to relieve the crisis, but with only eight days left in his term, Harrison's men maintained that nothing important was happening. The secretary of the Treasury spent his last few days in office sitting for his portrait. Wall Street men watched the outgoing administration in disgust. "If the National Treasury Department had been retained especially to manufacture apprehension and create disturbance it could not have done more effective work," the *New York Times* grumbled. But Secretary Foster had one more parting shot. When he handed the Treasury Department over to his successor, he told the newspapers that "the Treasury was down to bedrock."[58]

Cleveland took office on March 4, 1893, with a financial panic in full swing. His attempts to appease Wall Street by adopting Republican financial measures did little to calm the crisis and destroyed his own coalition by appearing to betray the workers and farmers who elected him. Now rudderless, the economy continued to tumble while Republicans nodded sagely and urged voters to return to their standard.[59]

By 1894, desperate workers were rising against the government to demand relief, adding fuel to Republicans' charges that the laboring classes were dangerous. First, "armies" of western workers led by "General" Jacob Coxey and "General" Charles Kelly set out from fourteen states and two Territories to march on Washington, where their leaders were arrested. Then, workers at George Pullman's Palace Car Company outside of Chicago struck after Pullman cut wages five times without reducing rents in company housing or reducing officers' salaries and then fired members of an arbitration committee. By the end of June, 150,000 members of the American Railway Union had joined in, and the nation's transportation system ground to a halt. Cleveland's attorney general, a former railroad attorney, attached US mail cars to the Pullman cars, making strikers responsible for obstructing the US mail, which gave the federal government jurisdiction over the crisis. Cleveland sent troops to Chicago and to all the states on national rail lines: North Dakota, Montana, Idaho, Washington, Wyoming, California, Utah Territory, and New Mexico Territory. The ensuing clashes destroyed $250,000 in property—not as serious as those of 1877, when $5 million in property was destroyed and more than sixty lives lost—but bad enough.[60]

The events of 1894 swung popular opinion back behind Republicans. Republican papers insisted that the "tramps" marching on Washington were looters and plunderers, lazy men eager to take the property of hardworking Americans rather than working for it. Democrats stood with the mob, Republicans insisted; they wanted to use the government for their own special interests. "Men must take sides either for anarchy, secret conclaves, unwritten law, mob violence, and universal chaos under the red or white flag of socialism on the one hand," wrote the Republican general in charge of the troops ranged against the strikers in 1894, "or on the side of established government, the supremacy of law, the maintenance of good order, universal peace, absolute security of life and property, the rights of personal liberty, all under the shadow and folds of 'Old Glory,' on the other."[61]

During the desperate summer, Democrats further infuriated Republicans by appearing to tailor government policy to poor men. Democrats tried to revise the tariff, as they had promised, but the depression had changed the debate. The Treasury was no longer struggling to spend a surplus; now it badly needed money. Worse, no congressman was willing to expose industries in his district to foreign competition in the midst of a wave of plant closings and layoffs. In the end, a vicious fight yielded a bill that lowered tariffs only slightly—thus infuriating both those who wanted wholesale revision and those who wanted no revision at all. The new tariff measure instantly raised Republican cries of socialism because it made up for lost revenue by placing a tax on incomes over four thousand dollars. "The income tax is the tax that patriotic citizens vote to tax some other fellow," snarled the *Brooklyn Union*. "The man who has saved his money and put it where it works for him is not an income taxer."[62]

In preparation for the 1894 midterm elections, Republicans blamed Cleveland and Democratic policies for falling wages, unemployment, business failures, strikes, and desperation.

Businessmen poured money into Republican coffers. A Republican victory in November would dramatically improve the economy, they claimed, because turning the House over to them would mean no more changes or uncertainty.[63]

Voters agreed. The 1894 midterms reversed the 1892 landslide. Men cheered in the streets as they read the bulletins in front of newspaper offices announcing the stunning election results. Republicans gained 130 seats in the House, giving them a two-thirds majority, and regained a slight majority in the Senate, making 1894 the largest midterm turnover in the nation's history. Republicans had successfully associated their opponents with economic disaster and anarchy.[64]

The economy had begun a cautious uptick before the Republicans regained power, and that uptick continued. With Republicans in office, businessmen believed their investments were sound. "American manufacturers and merchants and business-men generally will draw a long breath of relief," the *Chicago Tribune* commented in November, just days after the Republican victory. There would be no more "molestation" of business, no more strikes, no more "industrial discontent." The Democrats had plunged the country into a panic, it wrote (completely disregarding the actual timing of the crash), and could never again hope to rule.[65]

But just in case, Republicans set out to curb the government power they had worked for thirty years to build. An active government seemed beneficial when wielded by Republicans, but if it fell into the hands of workers and farmers who were demanding the economic changes Republicans abhorred, it could rework the American economy. They were determined to reduce the amount of damage workers could do.

As soon as Congress had passed the income tax in early 1894, Republicans began to insist that the measure was unconstitutional because it gave too much power to the federal government. The great power of taxation must be left to the states, they argued; the Constitution allowed the federal government only "direct taxation." Civil War Republicans had dismissed this old understanding, under which Congress apportioned taxation by states, which in turn almost always assessed taxes on land, in 1862, when they noted that such direct taxes unfairly burdened poor farmers while leaving rich urban dwellers largely untouched. In 1894, though, Republicans had switched their stand. Federal taxation of income from rent, stocks, bonds, and so on, they said, was an unconstitutional assumption of power. The income tax was sectional and discriminatory because it would force New York and other wealthy states to bear far heavier taxes than poorer, agricultural states. "The income tax was born of a mixture of sectionalism, communism, and demagogy," wrote the *Pittsburgh Gazette*, "and whether it shall stand or fail under the constitutional test, it will hang as a millstone around the neck of the Democracy."[66]

Almost immediately, a man who owned more than five thousand dollars of stock in New York's Farmers' Loan & Trust Company challenged the constitutionality of the income tax. One of the nation's leading Wall Street lawyers argued the case before the Supreme Court, and in a five-to-four decision in 1895 the court justices fell back on an original reading of the Constitution's provision for a "direct tax" to declare the income tax unconstitutional. Any other form of taxation was an unconstitutional expansion of federal power and must not be allowed.[67]

Furious, four of the justices pointed out that the majority's decision overturned a hundred years of precedent written by the nation's ablest jurists, as well as the Republicans' own Civil War legislation. But the majority claimed that the new measure was discriminatory: it discriminated against the wealthy. By the last decade of the nineteenth century, it seemed that Republicans had come to embrace the very ideas their fathers had organized the party to oppose.[68]

In 1896, a handsome young Nebraska Democrat speaking at his party's national convention cut to the heart of the philosophies of both parties. "There are two ideas of government," William Jennings Bryan said in a Democratic echo of Abraham Lincoln. "There are those who believe that if you just legislate to make the well-to-do prosperous, that their prosperity will leak through on those below. The Democratic idea has been that if you legislate to make the masses prosperous their prosperity will find its way up and through every class that rests upon it." Democrats electrified by Bryan's speech nominated him for the presidency, and he spent the campaign courting the people. He picked up the endorsement of the Populist Party and then toured relentlessly, speaking as often as twenty or more times a day to demand that "wealth bear its due proportion of the expense of the Government."[69]

For their part, Republicans went into the 1896 presidential election bemoaning Democrats' "record of unparalleled incapacity, dishonor, and disaster" and trumpeting that they themselves stood, foursquare and solid, for hardworking, middle-class Americans. Aware that they needed new votes to combat the Democrats' growing support, they extended a tentative hand toward a new constituency, welcoming women's "co-operation in rescuing the country from Democratic and Populist mismanagement and misrule." They nominated for president William McKinley, author of the Republicans' 1890 tariff, and on the advice of his political manager, Mark Hanna, McKinley stayed home and kept his mouth shut.[70]

In place of a popular candidate, Hanna flooded the country with surrogate speakers and newspaper editorials, paid for with the corporate money that flowed into Republican coffers. Republicans charged Bryan with "class warfare" and reiterated the idea that all classes in America worked together. Anyone trying to stir up class conflict, wrote the *New York Tribune*, was an "enemy of humanity." In Utica, New York, young Republican Theodore Roosevelt told a rally that Bryan was a "demagogue" who was trying to establish "a government of the mob." He hoped to create "a red welter of lawlessness as fantastic and as vicious as the dream of a European communist." Bryan was planning to change a government of the people, for the people, and by the people into "a government of a mob, by the demagogue, for the shiftless and the disorderly and the criminal and the semi-criminal," Roosevelt stormed. When Bryan complained about the incendiary language Republicans were using to attack him and his principles, one correspondent retorted: "This is a fight for the country and the flag."[71]

With the election framed as a choice between America and anarchy, voters resoundingly supported America. McKinley won more than 51 percent of the popular vote, although Bryan carried all the southern states and every plains state except North Dakota. No longer Lincoln's party of western men-on-the-make, the Republican Party was now entirely the party of coastal businessmen. The businessman's candidate, who had been dismissed by a colleague as a has-been only four years before, was now president.

Back in office, the Republicans immediately hiked tariff rates higher than they had been before Democrats reduced them. They were spared a backlash because the discovery of gold on Bonanza Creek near the Klondike River in the Yukon Territory of Canada brought enough of the precious metal into the US economy to ease the money supply, letting up the pressure on farmers and workers. This quirk of timing gave both Democrats and Republicans what they wanted: a gold standard and an expanded currency. After a bitter twenty-five-year fight for control of the American psyche, it seemed that big business Republicans had won.

6

Republicans Become Liberals

Republicans had won the 1896 election by framing it as a choice between America and the apocalypse, but many younger Republicans who had seen the party's losses in 1884 as a wake-up call were disillusioned by the party's ties to big business. These men were Republicans through and through; they believed that Democrats were disloyal. But they hated their party's corruption and had stuck with it only because they had learned in 1884 that bolting the ticket was suicide. At the turn of the century, young Republicans led by Theodore Roosevelt, Henry Cabot Lodge, Albert Beveridge, and Robert M. La Follette would join together to bring Republicans back to an ideology that echoed Abraham Lincoln.

Lincoln's generation had reformed the government to address the crisis of westward expansion, but for this generation the crisis was that of industrialization. These younger men looked at the increasing gulf between "tramps and millionaires," as the Populists had put it, and understood that poor men could not rise to economic security in a world where the laws were all slanted in favor of their employers. Originally, protecting individual opportunity had meant a weak government that could not hamstring initiative. But Roosevelt and his contemporaries came to understand that individual success in the industrial world depended on an active, rather than a passive, government. Only an active government could corral the overreach of business and guarantee the healthy food, living conditions, education, and access to resources that would enable individuals to succeed.[1]

Curiously, though, the insistence of these men on a domestically active government sprang from their conviction that America should intervene in international affairs, where foreign powers seemed to be imposing corrupt governments that crushed the people they colonized. Older Republicans opposed foreign intervention, but younger men took their cue from the post–Civil War images of the American cowboy that had entertained their childhoods and demanded that hardworking individuals reclaim the country from wealthy eastern businessmen and spread American values to the rest of the world. And if Americans were advancing individualism and prosperity internationally, surely they must make certain they were promoting it at home. Progressive Republicans insisted that government clean up the cities, protect worker safety, inspect food, and support education. They made little headway against the Old Guard Republicans who controlled Congress, but so dramatically did they change the national conversation that they set the stage for a raft of progressive reforms under Democratic president Woodrow Wilson.

The party's shift back to its original principles started in 1884, when the Republican crisis of that year launched a new generation and a new philosophy in the Republican Party. Younger Republicans recognized that the party must acknowledge the groundswell of anger coming from those hurt by ties between Old Guard Republicans and business. They wanted the same sorts of reforms men like Schurz had demanded since the 1870s. Unlike him, though, their formative years were those of the Civil War, and they hated the Democrats, whom they blamed for trying to destroy the nation, for murdering Lincoln, and for refusing to accept their defeat. These younger Republicans wanted to operate within the party, not outside it. They began a quiet revolution in both the East and the West.[2]

The eastern ringleader was Boston's Henry Cabot Lodge, a slight man with a trim beard, who tended to tilt his head back so he led with his jaw. Lodge was a creature of privilege with an immaculate Boston pedigree, Harvard education, and friendships with men of culture. He had met Schurz in 1874 at a dinner his mother held to honor the Missouri senator after the loving eulogy he delivered at Charles Sumner's funeral. The dinner guests included Henry Wadsworth Longfellow, Ralph Waldo Emerson, and Oliver Wendell Holmes. Lodge became a reformer like these older Boston men, who had become increasingly disgusted by the crass turn of the Republican Party in the 1870s and 1880s. But, unlike Schurz and his generation of reformers, Lodge chose to reform the Republican Party from within.[3]

Lodge's developing friendship with another young Republican hardened his resolve. He had met Theodore Roosevelt at Boston's St. Botolph Club, and the two men had renewed their acquaintance before the 1884 convention. Like Lodge, Roosevelt was the son of a prominent father. He hailed from an old New York family descended from seventeenth-century Dutch colonists. The Roosevelts had spent the two hundred years from the colonial era to the late nineteenth century getting rich. Young Theodore was privileged, was well educated, and had an abiding love for America. In his lifetime, though, he had seen an idyllic world of hardworking individuals replaced by rich men who oversaw teeming cities of immigrants slaving in factories. The new industrial cities were full of foul refuse, and the germs creeping out of tenements hit Roosevelt directly. On a devastating Valentine's Day in 1884, he held first his mother and then his young wife as they died of disease within hours of each other. Like Lodge, Roosevelt worshipped Lincoln and could not bear to see the destruction of the equality for which he had died.[4]

Together, Roosevelt and Lodge plotted to put a reformer on the 1884 ticket. But these cultured youngsters, who amused reporters at the convention by applauding "with the tips of their fingers, held immediately in front of their noses," were no match for the Blaine machine. When Blaine took the nomination, though, Lodge and Roosevelt did not bolt the party as did their fellow reformers. Instead, they soldiered their way through the Blaine campaign.[5]

Older reformers berated the younger men for backing Blaine—"the continental liar"—but managed only to drive them into a fast friendship. As vituperation from Republicans who had switched sides to support Cleveland mounted, the two men came to address each other as "Cabot" and "Theodore," a rare intimacy. "Theodore is one of the most lovable as well as one of the cleverest and most daring men I have ever known," Lodge wrote the following year. "The more I see him…the more & more I love him." Hated by independent reformers, the two men turned to practical politicians in the party and happily worked with anyone who agreed with them about general principles, whatever their particular opinions.[6]

After the death of his wife, Roosevelt temporarily washed his hands of eastern politics and moved to his ranch in Dakota Territory, so Lodge's political career took off before Roosevelt's, making him the senior partner in their professional relationship. Reformers killed Lodge's 1884 candidacy for the House of Representatives by throwing their votes to his opponent, but in 1886, he was elected to Congress. When Harrison won the White House in 1888, Lodge got Roosevelt appointed to the US Civil Service Commission. In the House, Lodge was a key figure in the effort to shore up the Republican Party nationally, working to push the Federal Elections Bill. When Democrats swept the 1892 elections, Lodge figured out a way to get the Massachusetts legislature to select him as a senator despite the national trend away from his party. In 1893, Lodge went to the Capitol's upper chamber to become the statesman he had always envisioned.[7]

Together, Lodge and Roosevelt would bring reform to the Republican Party and to America. First, though, they turned to reforming the world.

A mutual interest in maritime affairs opened the way for Lodge and Roosevelt to make their mark. Both men had a soft spot for the navy. Roosevelt had been reared on his southern mother's spellbinding tales of the Confederate navy and believed that naval power was central to a nation's success; Lodge came from a family of shipping barons and had married the daughter of an admiral. In the House, he sat on the Naval Affairs Committee, where he protected the Charlestown Navy Yard just outside Boston.[8]

Congress had slashed naval funding after the Civil War to save money, and Roosevelt and Lodge thought this neglect of the navy was scandalous. A stronger maritime presence would promote American trade in the Pacific, where Germany, England, and Russia jockeyed for supremacy under the protection of their own navies. In 1890, when Roosevelt and Lodge's friend Alfred T. Mahan of the new Naval War College published *The Influence of Sea Power upon History*, arguing that successful nations must expand overseas, Lodge pushed through Congress a measure to rebuild the American navy. Then, to reward him for his help in the 1896 election, McKinley appointed Roosevelt assistant secretary of the navy, a good job but one that should have kept him out of the limelight. Rather than keeping him quiet, though, it put him in a crucial place to change the course of American history.[9]

The drive to build America's power at sea focused younger Republicans' frustration over the direction of their party. Roosevelt stewed as Americans ignored increasing Japanese interest in the Hawaiian Islands, which decades of whaling and sugar growing had made Americans think of as theirs. In early 1893, American sugar interests had overthrown the Hawaiian queen and asked for American annexation after the McKinley Tariff raised tariff rates on foreign sugar. Harrison had backed annexation, but Cleveland listened to the outraged Hawaiians and insisted on an investigation into the entire affair. By the time McKinley was in the White House, popular sentiment was heavily opposed to annexation, and the issue languished in the Senate while the fate of Hawaii remained unresolved.

Then, in 1898, a long-brewing war in Cuba exploded. Cubans had been struggling against the Spanish colonial government for decades, but a full-fledged guerrilla campaign that began in 1895 brought a new level of horror to the conflict. To put down the guerrillas, the Spanish military began a "reconcentration" policy that forced Cubans into fortified towns surrounded by barbed wire. The towns were death camps, but anyone caught outside them was hanged as a rebel.[10]

Roosevelt and his friends believed that America could not stay aloof from these volatile situations; the nation simply must take control of Hawaii, and Cuba, and also the coaling station on the Pacific island of Samoa. But few people wanted Hawaii, and establishment Republicans, worried about hurting valuable sugar interests in Cuba, resisted intervention there. Many older men remembered war and would not court it. McKinley himself was a Civil War veteran—the last of them in the White House—and was in no hurry to send Americans into battle. "I have been through one war," he remarked. "I have seen the dead piled up, and I do not want to see another." To younger Republicans, opposition to what they saw as an obvious need to assert American power seemed to prove that businessmen had emasculated American society. "The spirit of the banker, the broker, the mere manufacturer, and the mere merchant, is unpleasantly prominent," Roosevelt complained. "In political matters we are often very dull mentally, and especially morally."[11]

Young Republicans were angry over Hawaii, but they broke with their elders over Cuba. They demanded that Americans help their neighbors. Intervention would be a moral crusade to protect the innocent, spread American values, and strengthen the country. If the Republican Party truly stood against oppression, economic backwardness, and immorality, as it had claimed in the 1896 election, it must defend those values in nearby lands. A war with Spain, Roosevelt insisted, "would be as righteous as it would be advantageous to the honor and the interests of the nation." When the USS *Maine* exploded in Havana Harbor on February 15, 1898, Roosevelt shook his fist at Republican operator Mark Hanna at a public dinner and warned: "We will have this war for the freedom of Cuba . . . in spite of the timidity of the commercial interests!"[12]

Ten days after the destruction of the *Maine*, Roosevelt ordered Admiral George Dewey, who commanded the US naval squadron in Hong Kong, to rout the Spanish from their stronghold in the Philippines if the United States declared war on Spain. On April 25, 1896, it did, and the Pacific fleet steamed to Manila, where Dewey attacked the Spanish squadron with the famous line "You may fire when ready, Gridley." Six hours later, the entire Spanish fleet was flotsam. Twelve thousand Filipino and eleven thousand American soldiers had driven the Spanish forces out of Manila by mid-August. As soon as Congress declared war, more than two hundred thousand men volunteered to fight what they saw as a crusade to spread American morality overseas—and also at home, where it seemed that timid businessmen cared more for their pocketbooks than for vigor and independence.[13]

Illustrating that the roots of the war were in the idea of American individualism untrammeled by eastern politics and business, Roosevelt and other war hawks emphasized the idea of the American West as their inspiration. Buffalo Bill boasted he could "drive Spaniards from Cuba with Thirty Thousand Indian Braves," and Jesse James's brother Frank offered to lead a cowboy regiment into the war. As it turned out, Congress gave Roosevelt, not Frank James, permission to raise a cowboy cavalry regiment. According to a reporter for the *New York Times*, Roosevelt wanted "sturdy frontier heroes" who would need no training to fight. They would have their own horses and guns, and "what is more, know how to take care of themselves, live under any circumstances, and fight all the time. They need no drilling or inuring to hardship, but can give lessons in endurance and soldierly qualities to the veterans of the regular army." Roosevelt emphasized that he took his men from every part of the country and from every walk of life: Harvard men and Indians, northerners, southerners, white, Black, rich, and poor. Any man who was hardworking and independent, who "demanded only to...be judged on [his] merits," could represent America as one of Roosevelt's cowboys. The press dubbed his regiment the "Rough Riders," after the cowboys and gunfighters in Buffalo Bill's Wild West Show.[14]

For his part, Roosevelt used his position as second-in-command of the regiment to illustrate what good government looked like. He took reporters to Cuba with him, where they cultivated his image as an outsider standing up to corrupt and inefficient eastern politicians. Roosevelt complained of officials wasting time that could have been spent winning the war, and he cut through red tape to get his men supplied with rifles, tents, clothing, and transportation before other regiments. When he disagreed with military policy, he stormed to reporters that officials had no idea of conditions in the field. Within days, government leaders bowed to Roosevelt's wishes.[15]

In Cuba, those western-style American individuals smashed through the troops of an old-fashioned European empire. On June 30, 1898, 17,000 US soldiers landed in Santiago; the next day 7,000 of them charged up San Juan Hill and Kettle Hill to take the heights surrounding the city. Roosevelt's Rough Riders were part of the attack (although they charged on foot because their horses, weakened by their voyage to Cuba, had drowned when they were pushed overboard to swim to shore). When the Spanish fleet tried to escape from Santiago Harbor through the American blockade, naval ships sank all seven of them, killing 474 Spanish sailors and cutting off communication between Cuba and Spain. On July 17, the Spanish garrison in Santiago surrendered. Ten days later, Republican John Hay—who had been Lincoln's secretary as a young man, had written the 1883 novel *The Bread-Winners*, and would become McKinley's secretary of state the following month—wrote to Roosevelt that it had been "a splendid little war; begun with the highest motives, carried on with magnificent intelligence and spirit, favored by that fortune which loves the brave."[16]

As soon as Roosevelt was back in the United States, he began to campaign for governor of New York, promising he would bring into eastern government the western individualism he had championed since his time in Dakota Territory. His campaign attracted national attention. According to the *Indianapolis Sentinel* he had thrown away his political career to fight for American principles and would be as fearless and aggressive against spoilsmen as he had been against the

Spaniards when he charged up a hill under fire, yelling like an Indian. Supporters latched on to Roosevelt as the embodiment of a new America. One crowed in the *New York Times* that his career should show young men that "there is a higher and nobler ideal than the acquisition of fortune, and that service to one's country is the first duty of patriotic citizenship." His determination to push American power overseas showed "a virility and strength of character that stamp him as a true American." Unlike the old men who cowered from foreign foes, Roosevelt would maintain "the country's honor against the mewling advocates of surrender, National effacement, and 'peace at any price.'"[17]

Roosevelt's insistence that all Americans, regardless of race or class, could successfully work their way up was wishful. In fact, by the late 1890s, hard work wouldn't do much to help many urban workers, farmers, or people of color to succeed. The rise of big business had steadily eroded the ability of industrial wage laborers to earn the money that would enable them to move up. Farmers were squeezed between falling agricultural prices and rising costs. As for African Americans, their position was worse than it had been at any time since the immediate postwar years. Jim Crow laws enforced racial segregation in the South. Lynching against Blacks had jumped in 1889, during the fight over the Federal Elections Bill, and by 1898 many Americans considered it a patriotic duty to purge communities of those who would "corrupt" the vote. Ministers preached the virtues of lynching, and people sent friends photos of themselves posed with lynching victims.[18]

Still, Roosevelt had reclaimed Lincoln's ideological language, if not his inclusive vision. The government should stand behind any man who worked hard. No longer would it be held in thrall to corrupt old ways of doing business.

But should Americans spread that vision across the world? Congressmen had agreed that the United States would not take Cuba, but what about the Philippines, which were a perfect coaling station for ships plying the Pacific trade and which other nations were eager to snatch if the Americans didn't? Should America become an imperial power, like European countries? Should a country that supported political independence impose its rule on another country?

Republicans split generationally over this question. Older Republicans like Andrew Carnegie utterly opposed a colonial experiment. In articles in the popular *North American Review*, he ticked off the reasons. America didn't need new markets; it was already exporting more than any other country on earth. It was a mistake to expand into lands full of "alien races" whose people could never be American. It would be grievously expensive to administer a colonial government, as well as to maintain the army and navy necessary to defend it. Outlying possessions were vulnerable to attack, and military protection would correspondingly have to be far stronger than the United States otherwise needed. The money wasted in a colonial experiment would be far better used at home, widening waterways, digging a canal across Nicaragua, or dredging the lower Mississippi River. Finally, taking an unwilling colony would turn democracy into despotism. "With what face shall we hang in the schoolhouses of the Philippines the Declaration of our own Independence, and yet deny independence to them?" Carnegie demanded.[19]

Young Republicans like Roosevelt and Lodge thoroughly disagreed with the older anti-imperialists. And yet, it was not they, with their eastern elite upbringing, but a newcomer from the West who provided the rhetoric for Republican imperialism. Like Roosevelt and Lodge, Indiana's Albert J. Beveridge had come of age in 1884, was a staunch party man, and wanted to remake the party into a modern, progressive force. Beveridge thundered that the war with Spain was divine intervention meant to erase domestic political and economic conflicts under all-consuming patriotic expansion.[20]

On September 16, 1898, Beveridge delivered to a state Republican meeting a landmark speech titled "The March of the Flag." It tied the triumphal narrative of the older Republicans to America's expansion overseas. The Civil War proved that God had put his stamp of approval on Americans and their free labor economy, he said, and thus had given them a mission. Tracing the progress of the flag from the Revolution to the end of the nineteenth century, Beveridge explained how Americans had wrested a glorious country out of the bountiful wilderness and peopled a continent. Should they not now spread their wildly successful form of society to the rest of the world? Objections from colonized people unwilling to accept American domination only strengthened his argument, for it proved they were unable to make good decisions for themselves. The question in 1898 was not partisan, Beveridge insisted; it was American: "Shall the American people continue their march toward the commercial supremacy of the world? Shall free institutions broaden their blessed reign as the children of liberty wax in strength, until the empire of our principles is established over the hearts of all mankind?"[21]

Older Republicans recoiled from Beveridge's aggressive imperialism, but his message resonated with younger men who wanted to reclaim the nation from what they saw as the emasculation and corruption of the eastern establishment. Republicans in the middle of the country reprinted "The March of the Flag" as a campaign document. When Spain and America hammered out a peace treaty in December 1898, Filipinos were not included in the negotiations, and the Spanish surrendered control of Cuba and ceded the Philippines, Puerto Rico, and Guam to the United States for twenty million dollars. In the Senate, eastern Republicans, Democrats, and Populists did not have the votes to block the treaty. Joining the belief in American greatness with the idea of economic expansion, young Republicans had launched the country on a career of imperialism.

The nation's new overseas adventure had important domestic repercussions. If Americans were going to spread their worldview to the rest of the globe, they must produce good citizens at home as examples for others to emulate. Men like Roosevelt looked at the conditions in industrial America—the sweatshops, exhausted mothers, working children, tenements, ignorance, and grinding poverty—and worried that children reared in such conditions would never be "fitted for the exacting duties of American citizenship." The need to build a strong citizenry went hand in hand with young Republicans' imperialistic adventure, convincing rising Republican leaders like Roosevelt, Lodge, and Beveridge that something must be done to address the problems of industrial society.[22]

To cure America's industrial ills, younger Republicans resurrected Lincoln's philosophy of government. Like him, they worried that the concentration of wealth was keeping individuals from rising. Like him, they believed that it was the duty of government to prevent the very rich from taking control of the country. Like him, they wanted a strong government to promote the ability of young men to rise to economic prosperity. And, also like him, they called for an activist government to support the middle class.

Roosevelt articulated the views of the new generation: he advocated a government that would serve the needs of a powerful young nation. Explicitly taking his political principles from Lincoln's 1859 Milwaukee speech, which refuted the idea that workers were the permanent mudsill of society, Roosevelt insisted that Lincoln held the rights of property sacred, but less important than the rights of men. He was "for both the man and the dollar, but in case of conflict, the man before the dollar," Roosevelt recalled. In Lincoln's day, that principle applied to slavery; in the early twentieth century, it applied both to wealthy corporations that abused their workers and to powerful labor unions that attempted to impose their will on reluctant individuals. Like Lincoln, Roosevelt believed that the health of the nation depended on hardworking, educated individuals creating value from their labor, accumulating property, and employing others. In a world of great capitalists and masses of wage workers, the government must stand against socialism, as Republicans had argued since the 1870s. But it must also regulate big business.[23]

Repackaging Lincoln's ideas to address the crises of the industrial era, young Republicans redefined the concept of American liberalism. The "liberal" principles that Thomas Jefferson had embodied in the Declaration of Independence harked back to the ideas of English philosopher John Locke, who called for defending individuals against a big government that might hamper a man's ability to make his own way in the world. Younger Republicans believed fervently in individualism, but they also believed that protecting the liberal worldview required strong federal government regulation of business and social welfare, rather than the "laissez-faire" government celebrated by late nineteenth-century Republicans. As Beveridge declared in a speech made the night he met Roosevelt, the rabble were destroying society, but so were the very rich. Their meddling with the natural laws of trade required "rebuke, regulation, and restraint." Individuals could not make it on their own without government intervention. After Progressive Republicans came to power, the word "liberal" would still refer to the inherent worth of individuals, but now those embracing liberalism believed enabling individuals to succeed required a strong, not a weak, government.[24]

The man most closely associated with this changed concept of liberalism was Roosevelt himself. Although an easterner, he took his political inspiration from the West, where during his sojourn after his wife's death he had ridden horses, rounded up cattle, and submerged himself in what he saw as essential America: the great West, where men were independent and justice was impartial. Although Roosevelt hired both of his ranch bosses from Maine, he maintained that it was westerners who represented the ideal American. They were hardworking, loyal, helpful, and independent. Although in reality social lines in the West mirrored those of the East, Roosevelt insisted that all westerners met on terms of perfect equality.[25]

Back from Cuba in 1898, Roosevelt decisively won the New York governorship on the promise that he would bring honest western-type government back to a state that symbolized corruption. He told rallies that he would cut through red tape, cater to no special interests, and defend every hardworking man of every race and creed. Even a Democratic paper in far-off South Carolina conceded that he would "make an able Governor and would give the rascals such a shaking up as they have never had."[26]

Once in the governor's chair, Roosevelt began to divorce the government from the businesses that had come to control it. He strengthened civil service laws and cracked down on cramped and filthy sweatshops, where immigrants both lived and worked, spending their waking hours turning out piecework, falling into bed, and getting up to go right back to work. Worse in the minds of established machine Republicans, he forced corporations that operated in a public capacity—streetcar businesses, for example—to pay taxes. Businessmen fought him, but he was determined, as he said, to establish the principle that corporations "shall pay their just share of the public burden."[27]

New York's Republican establishment finally decided to bury the troublemaking Governor Roosevelt in the obscurity of the vice presidency. Roosevelt initially objected but ultimately decided that his fame would enable him to make his new version of American government national. In 1900, once again opposing William Jennings Bryan, Republicans claimed that Democrats would destroy the country while they, in contrast, had constructed the world's most successful economy, which they were unselfishly spreading across the world, along with the liberty and civil rights for which America stood. In 1900, McKinley and Roosevelt won with a comfortable six-point lead in the popular vote.[28]

Roosevelt was wrong to think he could change the course of the nation from the vice presidency. Once in office, he discovered that he could not accomplish much of anything. His only official duty was to preside over the Senate, which would not convene until December. He was so bored he asked the chief justice of the Supreme Court if it would be unseemly for him to enroll in law school to finish his degree. (Horrified, the justice offered to supervise Roosevelt's studies himself.)[29]

Roosevelt fumed, but businessmen made it clear they were not afraid of the new blood in the executive branch. On February 25, 1901, J. P. Morgan combined companies producing two-thirds of the nation's steel into the US Steel Corporation, capitalized at $1.4 billion—almost three times more than the federal government's annual budget. Then, on November 13, Morgan's Northern Securities Company joined the nation's warring main railroad interests into a new conglomerate designed to circumvent antitrust legislation: a holding company. Even the staunchly Republican *Chicago Tribune* was taken aback: "Never have interests so enormous been brought under one management." When midwestern governors suggested that their legislatures would find some way to prohibit such a powerful combination, Northern Securities officials threw gas on the fire by announcing that they would keep all business transactions and operations secret.[30]

But while industrialists had gone about business as usual, in September 1901 an anarchist with the impossible name of Czolgosz (pronounced Cho-goss) assassinated President

McKinley, and all bets were off. "It is a dreadful thing to come into the Presidency in this way," Roosevelt wrote to Lodge, "but it would be a far worse thing to be morbid about it." Mark Hanna and the Republican Old Guard were less sanguine. "I told McKinley it was a mistake to nominate that wild man at Philadelphia," Hanna moaned. "I told him what would happen if he should die. Now look. That damned cowboy is president of the United States."[31]

Roosevelt promptly demonstrated his belief that, like Lincoln, he was the president of every single hardworking American citizen. In October, he welcomed famous Black educator Booker T. Washington to the White House, just as Lincoln had welcomed famous Black abolitionist Frederick Douglass in 1863. Washington was a commanding figure with searing gray eyes, a well-known leader in both the African American community and Republican circles. Seven months before, he had published his autobiography, *Up from Slavery*, which illustrated how the Republican idea of rising through education and hard work had turned a poor slave child into an important reformer. Southern whites stormed that Roosevelt had insulted the South by dining with Washington. The president retorted: "The only wise and honorable and Christian thing to do is to treat each black man and each white man strictly on his merits as a man." Gone were the days of sectional strife: with a southern mother, a northern father, and a western ranch, Roosevelt envisioned himself as the leader of the whole nation.[32]

Roosevelt's first message to Congress, delivered less than three months after McKinley's death, honored the idea of individualism and the belief that property must be protected, but it also insisted that the government must clean up industrial

America. The government should, first of all, keep out of the country immigrants who were not going to be good American citizens, the new president explained. By this he meant anarchists, like the one who had killed McKinley, and also anyone who did not have "a strong body, a stout heart, a good head, and a resolute purpose to do his duty well in every way and to bring up his children as law-abiding and God-fearing members of the community." The government should start cleaning up factories and limiting the working hours of women and children, and it should husband natural resources for everyone rather than allowing them to be exploited by greedy businessmen. And of course, Roosevelt added, America should build a strong army and navy in order to spread these principles around the globe.[33]

For all its radical vision of government activism, Roosevelt's message relieved the party's Old Guard. Although the new president embraced reform, he opposed sweeping political and economic changes. He supported Republican policies that had shaped the post–Civil War economy; he hoped only to ameliorate the abuses the system had spawned. If reform were going to happen—and by 1901 it appeared imperative—Old Guard Republicans could take comfort that it came at the hands of a Republican rather than an economically heretical Democrat. Older men breathed a sigh of relief that Roosevelt's message was inherently conservative.[34]

Despite western outrage at the organization of the Northern Securities Company, Roosevelt did not oppose huge combinations. He did not want to destroy big business; he simply wanted the government to supervise and control corporate combinations, preventing criminality in the business world as it did in the streets. He hoped to establish rectitude through transparency. Once people actually knew what businesses were up to, the government could consider regulation or taxation to protect the public interest.[35]

Senators and businessmen who had worried that the cowboy president would slash at the trusts breathed a hearty sigh of relief that all he wanted was "transparency." That was easy enough to ignore. The *Chicago Tribune* rejoiced that Roosevelt supported business and had suggested only cautious measures to determine whether or not trusts actually were a problem. In other words, Roosevelt was simply mouthing platitudes. According to the *Tribune*, the "grave and reverend and somewhat plutocratic Senators immediately admitted in the most delighted fashion that the young and supposedly impetuous President had discussed the trust question with rare discrimination." For all his reputation as a wild radical, it seemed as if Roosevelt did not intend to reduce the power of big business at all.[36]

The *Chicago Tribune* and the business-minded senators were mistaken. Roosevelt expected Congress to clean up the system that had permitted the corruption of government by big business and the consequent dramatic migration of wealth upward. At the very least, surely it would look into the machinations that had birthed the railroad behemoth Northern Securities holding company. But senators had no intention of humoring the young president, and months passed without any legislation that took on the trusts. When northwesterners, who had a long history of contending against the railroads, began to grumble about the government's inaction, Roosevelt stole a march on Congress.[37]

In early January 1902, Minnesota sued to stop the Northern Securities Company from organizing on the grounds that such a combination violated Minnesota law. While the Supreme Court dithered over whether or not it could rule on the case, the Roosevelt administration threw a bombshell. In February, Roosevelt's attorney general told newspapers that the administration believed the formation of the Northern Securities Company violated the Sherman Antitrust Act and that he would shortly be filing a suit to keep it from organizing.[38]

Businessmen were aghast, not only because Roosevelt was going after a business combination but also because he had acted without consulting Wall Street. When J. P. Morgan complained that he had not been informed, Roosevelt coolly told him that that was the whole point. "If we have done anything wrong," said the astonished Morgan, "send your man [the attorney general] to my man [one of his lawyers] and they can fix it up." The president declined. "We don't want to fix it up," explained the attorney general. "We want to stop it."[39]

It was clear that Roosevelt intended to end the cozy relationship of business and government. "Criticism of President Roosevelt's action was heard on every side," reported the *Boston Globe*. "Some of the principal financiers said he had dealt a serious blow to the financial securities of the country." For his part, Roosevelt was unconcerned by the fulminations of the businessmen. "If the law has not been violated," he announced, "no harm can come from the proposed legal action." In late February, the Supreme Court decided it could not hear the Minnesota case; on March 10, the United States sued to stop the organization of the Northern Securities Company.[40]

In August 1902, President Roosevelt embarked on a tour of New England and the Midwest to rally support for his attack on Northern Securities. He told audiences that he was not trying to destroy corporations but rather to make them act in the public interest, just as he had done when he was governor of New York. He demanded a "square deal" for everyone. As the *Boston Globe* put it, "'Justice for all alike—a square deal for every man, great or small, rich or poor,' is the Roosevelt ideal to be attained by the framing and the administration of the law. And he would tell you that that means Mr Morgan and Mr Rockefeller as well as the poor fellow who cannot pay his rent."[41]

It was no accident that Roosevelt took his message to the Midwest. Since the early days of the Granger movement, the region had been the center of resistance to the growing power of businessmen over the government. In the Roosevelt era, Robert M. La Follette, another young Progressive Republican, led that reform. La Follette would provide a blueprint for Roosevelt to rebuild the American government along the lines Lincoln had laid out two generations before.

Like Roosevelt and Lodge, La Follette had been a child during the Civil War. He had grown up on a farm near Madison, Wisconsin, the son of a Kentucky-born father who had made the same journey to Indiana that Lincoln's father had before settling in Wisconsin. His youth in Wisconsin meant that La Follette had seen firsthand the Granger agitation of the 1870s, when northwestern farmers protested the control of government by railroad men. He rallied to those who feared the rich were taking over the country, piling up wealth to the detriment of the rest of the people. "Money is taking the field as an organized power," one of La Follette's mentors warned. "Which shall rule—wealth or man; which shall lead—money or intellect; who shall fill public stations—educated and patriotic free men, or the feudal serfs of corporate capital?"[42]

La Follette was a Republican for many of the same reasons Roosevelt and Lodge were: young men who had cheered the Union soldiers off to war could conceive of no political home outside the party of Lincoln, Grant, and Sherman. But like Lodge and Roosevelt, La Follette believed the drive for power had tied the party too closely to big business, and he worried that the Republican machine strove to perpetuate Republican rule rather than to govern the country fairly. Opposed by the local Republican machine when he ran for Dade County district attorney, La Follette became a crusader for good government, beholden to the people rather than to money interests. When he ran for Congress in 1884, he did so as a Republican, but he won as an outsider.[43]

Twenty-nine when he was elected, La Follette became the youngest member of Congress. He was a fleshy man with piercing eyes: humorless, arrogant, and utterly convinced that only his political ideas were correct. But he was also principled and in tune with the nation's growing opposition to the corruption of government by big business. He served in Congress until 1891, when a public break with Wisconsin party bosses meant he lost their political support entirely. He turned to the people, demanding that voters take back their state from the Republican machine. In 1900, they did. They elected La Follette governor, a position he held until he went to the Senate in 1906.

From the governor's chair, La Follette advanced what became known as the "Wisconsin Idea." As Roosevelt explained in his introduction to the book explaining the system, Wisconsin was "literally a laboratory for wise experimental legislation aiming to secure the social and political betterment of the people as a whole." Rather than simply talking about the need for reform, La Follette figured out how to make it happen. He called on University of Wisconsin professors, legislators, and state officials to provide technical expertise to solve social problems. Together, they crafted measures to address the state's needs. They attacked boss rule, regulated railroads, promoted graduated taxation, and backed the direct election of US senators. "All through the Union we need to learn the Wisconsin lesson," Roosevelt announced.[44]

A new magazine helped to make the midwestern project national. The popular press had widely taken up the call for reform, but its leading voice was *McClure's Magazine*. As a coffee-pot peddler in the Midwest, S. S. McClure had come to know the people in small towns and on farms, and he understood that they were interested in the same questions that absorbed reformers in Boston and New York. He built a new monthly with long in-depth articles, wooing readers in the mid-1890s with a series of articles about Lincoln by rising writer Ida Tarbell. Early biographers had portrayed Lincoln's western childhood as a life of dirt and squalor to be overcome, but in Tarbell's hands, the West became the central influence on the president's intelligence, honesty, and morals. Tarbell's Lincoln series gave *McClure's* more than 250,000 subscribers.[45]

In its January 1903 issue, *McClure's* launched a new form of journalism. That issue contained Tarbell's exposé of the

Standard Oil Company, Lincoln Steffens's exposé of the corruption of the Minneapolis municipal government, and Ray Stannard Baker's exposé of workers' violence during a coal strike. Although general denunciations of trusts, corruption, and violence were commonplace, McClure's journalists focused on the intricate workings of single entities. Their carefully detailed studies of the machinations of a single trust, a single city, and a single union electrified readers and galvanized a movement to reform the government that had bred such abuses.

Roosevelt grumbled at what he called "muckrakers," after those sorry characters in John Bunyan's seventeenth-century Christian allegory *Pilgrim's Progress* who were so busy raking up filth that they ignored Heaven. But muckraking journalists like Ida Tarbell were on Roosevelt's side, giving powerful voice to the president's progressive impulses. As McClure himself editorialized in the January 1903 issue, all three articles might have been titled "The American Contempt of Law." It was the public that paid for such lawlessness, and it was high time the public demanded that justice be enforced.[46]

Industrialists' overreach confirmed the sense that people must push back against them. In fall 1902, while the Northern Securities question still hung before the Supreme Court, a showdown between anthracite coal miners and mine operators swung popular opinion against big business and behind Roosevelt. About 150,000 miners had been on strike in Pennsylvania since January. By the following September, eastern city dwellers who needed coal for the upcoming winter were frantic. The strikers' leader repeatedly offered to negotiate, but the mine operators steadfastly refused, hoping to starve the miners into capitulating.

The government had no power to intervene in the affair, but Roosevelt concluded that the public interest demanded action. Perhaps more important, he also concluded that in the upcoming midterm election voters would blame Republicans for their lack of heat, just as western farmers had blamed Republicans in 1890 for their lack of rain. This latter point gave him ammunition to get recalcitrant mine owners, who were overwhelmingly Republicans, to a bargaining table. In October, Roosevelt brought together the owners and labor leaders. At first, the owners refused to negotiate and demanded the Sherman Antitrust Act be enforced against the workers, but Roosevelt threatened to send the army to take over the mines unless owners accepted the decision of a commission convened to find a solution to the crisis. While the commission deliberated, the men went back to work. Coal fires again warmed chilly homes across the Northeast.

When the commission reported the following March, miners got a 10 percent wage increase and owners got an open shop. But the biggest winner was Roosevelt, who had demonstrated that an active government could steer warring factions toward solutions that benefited everyone. The *London Times* congratulated him for his bold experiment and advised: "Let the Americans stick to their President and strengthen his hands. If there is any living man who can show them the way out of the dangers threatening them, that man is Mr. Roosevelt."[47]

His popularity soaring, Roosevelt began to return government to the people, as he said, rather than to a plutocracy or to the mob. Patterning himself on Lincoln, he sought to use an active government to regulate business and make it possible for individuals to rise. His overarching goal was to create a nation of strong, moral, and economically secure individuals. The Republicans kept their congressional majority in both houses in the midterm elections; although the Democrats won more seats, the reapportionment based on the 1900 census enabled Republicans to stay in power. It looked like a new era had begun.

But the Old Guard wanted no part of a new era. The Senate was increasingly the province of wealthy men who represented the interests of big business. During the McKinley and Roosevelt presidencies, four elderly senators—Nelson W. Aldrich of Rhode Island, John C. Spooner of Wisconsin, Orville H. Platt of Connecticut, and William B. Allison of Iowa—had worked closely with Republican Party chairman Mark Hanna, now a senator, to boost the interests of Wall Street. Aldrich led the group, clinging to high protectionism as the centerpiece of American prosperity. A nondescript man, despite his bright black eyes and walrus moustache, Aldrich passed on the street unnoticed, but he was one of the most powerful men in the country. His manipulation of street railways and politics had made him a multimillionaire, and he carefully represented the interests of moneyed men. In 1901, his only daughter married J. D. Rockefeller's only son—an elite marriage of politics and business. Aldrich was a cheerful fellow, all affability and attention, so long as people did what he wanted. "Aldrich does not convince, nor does he persuade," wrote a journalist, "he dominates."

He also controlled vast amounts of campaign money donated by corporations, forcing congressmen to kowtow to him.[48]

In 1902, the Republican majority in the House elected another member of the Old Guard, Illinois's Joseph G. Cannon, as Speaker. "Uncle Joe," as he was known, had served in Congress almost continuously since 1873. Dictatorial and condescending, he ruled the House with an iron fist, controlling the organization of committees and the management of bills on the House floor to keep old-fashioned Republicans on top.

Led by these powerful men, this Old Guard hamstrung Roosevelt. The president had to fight to get Congress to demand even the simple transparency he had called for in his first message, although it did eventually create a Department of Commerce and Labor that could investigate corporate operations. As Roosevelt's first term ground down, the Old Guard gathered in the Adirondacks to grumble about the hothead in the White House. They talked of nominating Senator Hanna to replace the president in 1904. While they fulminated, Roosevelt quietly used patronage appointments to undercut the old Republican machine in crucial states. When Hanna obligingly died of typhoid in February 1904, Roosevelt's way to renomination was clear. When the Democrats nominated a virtually unknown and lackluster New York judge, Alton B. Parker, so was his way to a landslide. Roosevelt won more than 56 percent of the popular vote and recaptured the western states that had supported Bryan in the past. The Republicans won a greater majority in Congress than they had had since the Civil War. The nation, it seemed, liked Roosevelt and the progressive principles he inherited from Lincoln.[49]

With the people behind him, Roosevelt in his 1904 message to Congress called for reworking industrial America according to the principles Lincoln had embraced a generation before. He proposed dramatic new legislation to nurture good citizens and restore fairness to American society. He called for federal oversight of labor and business, railroad safety laws, slum clearance, schools for urban children, and city parks and playgrounds. He encouraged immigration, but only of "the right sort": people who would become good citizens. Turning to the West, he called for establishing forest preserves to protect water and timber supplies, and for game preserves to protect the conditions that gave such "distinctive character to the American wilderness." This hearty Americanism was also his goal for the Philippines, where Americans still fought to stave off the idea that the Filipinos could rule themselves.[50]

Congress ignored him.

But Roosevelt had given progressive reform momentum. In December 1905, he complained about the profits made by railroad men in secret deals, and several muckraking articles corroborated his complaints. By 1906, people were fed up with Old Guard congressmen, especially Aldrich's gang. Wisconsin sent Governor La Follette, that champion of the people, to the Senate. "Fighting Bob" took his seat on January 2, 1906, and the next month, *Cosmopolitan* magazine made the contest over progressive reform national. It began a series of muckraking articles titled "The Treason of the Senate," focusing on Aldrich's corruption and dictatorial power. On March 15, 1906, Roosevelt wrote, "The dull, purblind folly of the very rich men; their greed and arrogance...and the corruption in business and politics, have tended to produce a very unhealthy condition of excitement and irritation in the popular mind." Railroad men and their senators recognized that they were going to have to bow to popular pressure, Roosevelt's secretary of war William Howard Taft mused, since Roosevelt had so "roused the people that it was impossible for them to stand against the popular demand."[51]

In 1906, the publication of Upton Sinclair's *The Jungle*, a novel that told of bankers and employers who abused a family of naive Lithuanian immigrants until those hopeful hard workers fell into homelessness, prostitution, and death, turned into the catalyst Progressives needed. Sinclair's descriptions of diseased beef canned and sold, of meat dyed with chemicals to hide the rot, of workers who fell into rendering vats packaged and sold as "Durham's Pure Leaf Lard," made outraged constituents pressure Congress to take on the corporations.

In rapid succession in June 1906, Congress passed three major pieces of progressive legislation over the Old Guard's vehement protest. The Hepburn Act gave the federal government power to set maximum rates for the railroads. The Pure Food and Drug Act made it illegal to make, sell, or transport adulterated or fraudulently labeled foods or drugs. The Meat Inspection Act gave the federal government power to regulate and inspect factories that packed meat for shipment across state lines. This trio of laws marked an epochal change in the power of the federal government to protect individuals against the abuses of industrial capitalism. The *Chicago Tribune* noted that these laws were "a radical departure from previous governmental methods."[52]

But they were not enough for the president. By 1907, Roosevelt had had it with the refusal of businessmen to give ground, worrying that their recalcitrance could destroy the nation by sparking workers into revolution. He railed against "malefactors of great wealth" and called for government to rein them in for the good of the people. He wanted stronger regulation of big business, an inheritance tax, and an income tax. When Congress ignored him, he resubmitted, in January 1908, all of the previous year's recommendations plus a call for the federal regulation of the stock market. He slammed the pro-business Supreme Court, which continued to strike down measures intended to protect workers. Finally, he called out oil and railroad executives by name, complaining, "Every measure for honesty in business that has been passed during the last six years, has been opposed by these men...with every resource that bitter and unscrupulous craft could suggest and the command of almost unlimited money secure." Roosevelt was increasingly adamant that the country simply must be steered toward reform.[53]

But someone else would have to take the reins. After the 1904 election, Roosevelt had announced quite dramatically that he would not run again, throwing the 1908 presidential field wide open. The majority of Americans were united behind progressive ideals, with both parties endorsing Roosevelt's policies (although Roosevelt admitted that laborers had good reason to be mad at the Republicans). The election would be one of personalities. After their disastrous experiment in 1904 with Alton B. Parker, the Democrats lined up again behind perennial candidate William Jennings Bryan. The Republicans nominated Roosevelt's secretary of war and the former governor of the Philippines, the phlegmatic, plodding William

Howard Taft. Taft might not inspire the popular loyalty that Bryan did, but he inspired the loyalty that mattered in 1908: Roosevelt's. He was generally considered the president's hand-picked successor.

Who would best carry out Roosevelt's vision? Bryan wanted more regulation and lower tariffs. Taft said he would simply enforce the laws already on the books and allowed that a tariff "revision" was in order. Businessmen sided with the Republicans, threatening to close plants and cancel orders if Bryan were elected. According to Taft, Bryan's election "will mean a paralysis of business and we should have a recurrence of the disastrous business conditions of the last Democratic administration."[54]

In a rather lackluster election, Taft won with about 7.5 million votes to Bryan's 6.5. The real winner in 1908 was progressivism. With the main candidates endorsing Roosevelt and a slew of minor candidates arguing that his reforms did not go far enough, the 1908 election showed that the nation backed reform. In his final message to Congress shortly after the election, Roosevelt attacked the Old Guard and warned congressmen that workers deserved a larger share of the wealth they produced. By 1908, there were a significant number of Progressive congressmen who agreed with him.

There was also a new constituency. The focus on cleaning up American society gave women political influence. Women had been agitating for the vote since they had been excluded from the Fourteenth Amendment, but while they had won some success in western territories, the movement had not gained traction at the national level. By the early twentieth century, though, female reformers had reworked the argument for women's suffrage. No longer did they demand the vote because of their inherent right to it, as older suffragists Elizabeth Cady Stanton and Susan B. Anthony had advocated. Now reformers argued that women should vote because they could clean up the country from the excesses of industrialization. With their morality and their motherly instincts, the argument went, women would counterbalance the corruption of grasping male voters who wanted only to redistribute wealth. In the years to come, women would add their voices to the call for progressive reforms.

With his heavy build and his legalistic mind, Taft was an odd successor to the energetic and imaginative Roosevelt. Roosevelt had managed to steer between the Old Guard and the Progressives because he was loyal both to the party and to progressive principles and, frankly, because he didn't give a damn what anyone else thought. Taft, in contrast, had neither the personality nor the inclination to bridge the widening party split. Taft's true goal was to sit on the Supreme Court, and he considered the presidency a poor second to that position. His fascination for the intellectual puzzle of legal problems gave him a legalistic approach to governance that kept him from making the leaps of imagination that Roosevelt had.[55]

Taft did just what he had said he would do: he applied laws already on the books to curb trusts, initiating ninety lawsuits against monopolies to Roosevelt's forty-four antitrust suits. But Taft did not like conflict, or crowds, or politics. He preferred to spend time with a few cronies playing bridge or golf, or sleeping, or eating. He placed his faith not in an active government, which he feared was too easily corrupted by democracy, but in the courts, where educated men sat in peace and quiet and debated precedent. It illustrated his approach to the presidency that, as soon as he was safely elected, he went to Augusta, Georgia, for six weeks to play golf and to rest.[56]

Taft's conservatism came to the fore over a new tariff measure. Roosevelt had avoided a fight over the tariff, but almost as soon as Taft took office, he called Congress into special session to revise the tariff downward. House members had been working on a new bill for weeks before the session convened, and congressmen had discovered that the problem with promising a lower tariff was that voters liked the idea of lower tariffs on everything except the items they produced. This meant there were few industries willing to take a rate cut and few congressmen ready to accept cuts that would affect their districts. Progressives demanded significant revisions, but Old Guard Republicans passed their own bill after only days of debate.[57]

In the Senate, Aldrich and the Old Guard faced off against the Progressives, led by La Follette and a group of western insurgents. In the process of reviewing the House's tariff rates, the Senate Finance Committee "revised" more than eight hundred rates upward. Outraged Progressives voted repeatedly against the revisions, but because high-tariff Democrats sided with Aldrich and the Old Guard on the different pieces of the measure that affected their own constituents, the Old Guard could ignore the Progressives. With La Follette and the western Progressives howling, the Payne-Aldrich Tariff sailed through Congress in less than a month.[58]

The new tariff was not, in fact, a downward revision at all; to the contrary, it hurt westerners and favored eastern businessmen. But President Taft threw his considerable weight behind it. Complaining that western Progressive Republicans were shrill, forward, stupid, demagogic, and helping the Democrats, Taft sided with Cannon and Aldrich. He called the tariff "the best bill that the Republican party has ever passed." Touring the West, Taft refused to mention the local Progressive Republicans who had voted against the tariff or to pay them the traditional courtesy of permitting them to visit with him on the presidential train. In Washington, the irreverent Gridiron Club—whose members roasted political figures and whose attention Taft hated—offered guests a receipt for Roosevelt's policies, which would be kept in cold storage for the next eight years.[59]

The fight over the tariff split the Republican Party. Progressives had hammered home the idea that the Old Guard was deep in the pockets of big business. In the wake of the new tariff, Cannon and Aldrich became for westerners the symbols of trusts, financiers, and railroads. They represented the "malefactors of great wealth" who were destroying the nation, against whom Roosevelt had warned. Finally, when Taft's secretary of the interior was accused of allowing development on lands the Roosevelt administration had protected, Progressives went into open revolt.[60]

Roosevelt had wanted to stay out of Taft's way in the first years of his administration and had gone to Africa to hunt big game (prompting J. P. Morgan to quip, "Let every lion do his duty"). In his absence, on Lincoln's birthday in February 1910, Cannon gave a widely reprinted speech that attacked Roosevelt and his call for government to rein in big business and protect workers. Uncle Joe insisted that the principles of the

Republican Party had made the nation prosperous, that the heart of those principles had come from Lincoln, and that Lincoln's political philosophy was based in strict adherence to the Constitution. Anyone suggesting that the government could operate in new ways, he announced in a chummy, good-old-boy sort of way, was a wild-eyed radical.[61]

In June 1910, Roosevelt returned to the United States, furious at the conservative turn Taft had taken and stewing over Cannon's insult. Lincoln was "a great radical" who moved the country forward by hewing to a middle course that enabled all men to rise, Roosevelt countered. "To-day many well-meaning men who have permitted themselves to fossilize, to become mere ultra-conservative reactionaries, to reject and oppose all progress, but who still pay a conventional and perfunctory homage to Lincoln's memory, will do well to remember exactly what it was for which this great conservative leader of radicalism actually stood," he admonished the older men of his party.[62]

Invited to speak at a John Brown celebration in Osawatomie, Kansas, in August, Roosevelt opened both barrels at his party's Old Guard. He threw in Cannon's teeth the idea that Lincoln would have stood with big business. Before an audience of Civil War veterans in Osawatomie, Roosevelt claimed Lincoln's mantle as his own. Lincoln, Roosevelt pointed out, had stood against the special interests that had perverted government to their own ends and robbed hard workers of what they had earned. In Lincoln's day, the threat to government had come from the Slave Power; in 1910 it came from business interests. America was currently governed by "a small class of enormously wealthy and economically powerful men, whose chief object is to hold and increase their power." This must stop, or the country was doomed. Roosevelt was not advocating a redistribution of wealth to the lazy, he insisted, but trying to guarantee that men actually earned their money rather than accumulating it through stock manipulation and financial shenanigans permitted by a compliant government. He, like Lincoln, believed that every man deserved a chance to work hard and rise. To permit a special interest to dominate the economy and reduce everyone else to virtual slavery would destroy the country.

At Osawatomie, Roosevelt demanded an active government to restore an even economic playing field. For the good of the country, the government should regulate both big business and the terms of labor. Roosevelt called for transparency in corporate operations, regulation of businesses, and abolition of corporate funding of political campaigns. To prevent the accumulation of huge fortunes, he called for both graduated income taxes and inheritance taxes. He insisted that the government must protect natural resources for future generations rather than permit industrialists to grab them all. To guarantee that all men could rise, he called for minimum wage and maximum hours measures, as well as for better factory conditions. And to make sure that future citizens grew up healthy and sound, he called for the regulation of child labor and women's work.[63]

This fundamental defense of a just government and a healthy citizenry required a strong national government. States and cities had been passing child labor laws, cleaning up factories, and limiting women's work hours for a decade, but Roosevelt wanted to replace the patchwork of local and state regulations with a national code. Roosevelt labeled his plan the "New Nationalism." Everyone in America had the same interests in a strong, healthy nation, he declared, and it was time to create a national government that acted in those interests, as Lincoln's had, rather than in the service of the rich. Of course, such a progressive vision required a strong leader, and Roosevelt was pretty sure he knew who was the best man for the job.[64]

By fall 1910, Progressivism was in full swing, and the Republican Old Guard appeared to be on the ropes. In the November midterm elections, Democrats took control of Congress. Two months later, La Follette and the congressional Progressives organized the National Progressive Republican League. The reform impulse continued to spread, and by December 1911, Roosevelt had decided to oppose Taft for the Republican nomination. When party regulars excluded Roosevelt's delegates from the convention in June 1912 and renominated Taft, Roosevelt coolly shucked the party apparatus and joined the Progressive Party, which nominated him for president in August. In a blistering speech that excoriated Taft for selling out to business, Roosevelt told his audience, "We stand at Armageddon, and we battle for the Lord." Democrats nominated their own reformer, New Jersey governor Woodrow Wilson, history professor and former president of Princeton University. The American Socialist Party also fielded a presidential ticket in 1912, led by labor leader Eugene V. Debs. All three major party platforms called for progressive reforms, and the Socialists went further, calling ultimately for an end to capitalism and for workers to seize control of the government.

There was not much daylight between any of the major party candidates in the 1912 election. Of the three, Taft, with his golfing vacations and his support for the new tariff, was popularly perceived to be the representative of big business, despite his ongoing and successful campaign against trusts. The unpopularity of business-as-usual showed when he garnered the fewest votes of any of the three major candidates, winning only about 3.5 million votes. Still, Taft managed to pull votes from Roosevelt, who came in next, with slightly more than 4 million votes. Together, these two received more votes than the winner, Governor Wilson. Although his 6.2 million votes represented only a plurality, Wilson won the largest electoral majority up to that time, with 435 votes to Roosevelt's 88 and Taft's 8. Debs garnered more than 900,000 votes, 6 percent of the popular vote.

Voters gave control of Congress and the White House to Democrats for the first time since 1893, in the hope they would divorce the government from big business. As crowds thronged the Washington streets in early March 1913 to greet the newly inaugurated President Wilson, Democrats took a last dig at Taft. On their hatbands they wore ribbons that read, "Nobody loves a fat man!"[65]

7

The Business of America Is Business

As soon as voters elected Wilson and progressive Democrats in 1913, an observer declared to the *Washington Post* that progressivism had won the day, and the old Republican Party was "dead—dead as Caesar, dead as a door nail, dead beyond all hope of resurrection." He was dead wrong. Wilson's presidency would so horrify Republicans that they would retreat back to the ideas of the Old Guard. Instead of embracing Wilson's progressive legislation, which embodied the reforms Roosevelt had called for, they stood against it. As soon as they could reclaim the government, they put the Old Guard's policies, untrammeled, into practice. In the Twenties, for the first time, big business Republicans would govern without interference from Democrats or from Republican reformers. The results made America just as prosperous as they had always dreamed.[1]

Or so it appeared.

The Wilson presidency was a great trial for Republicans, who abandoned their commitment to progressivism almost as soon as Wilson was in office. Unable to conceive of working with a Democrat, especially one who right away started threatening the tariff, they fell back on the idea that any government action intended to level the economic playing field was socialism. Their opposition would reach a crescendo in 1918, when they howled that Wilson's proposed League of Nations was a socialist plot to destroy the Declaration of Independence and the Constitution and impose "internationalism" on America.

To all but the most progressive Republicans—men like La Follette, who had not been welcome in the Taft White House—Wilson's election was anathema. For the first time since 1897, a Democrat was in the White House. And Wilson was no northern Democrat as Cleveland had been. Wilson was from Virginia, the son of a slaveholder who had served as a chaplain in the Confederate army, and from 1872 to 1874 he had lived in Columbia, just down the block from the South Carolina State House.

Worse, Democrats had captured Congress, making 1913 only the second time since the Civil War that Democrats had controlled the national government without a Republican check. For Republicans who remembered the Civil War, or the Democratic threats in 1876 to inaugurate Tilden by force, or the rhetoric their own party papers had used during the Cleveland administration, it seemed that the very existence of the nation was at risk. "The South is in the saddle," the *Washington Post* exclaimed. "One who desires to get along here will do well to say 'you all.'" The long-standing fears of men like Henry Cabot Lodge that Confederates would take over the government seemed to have been realized. Indeed, Wilson promptly segregated the federal offices that had been desegregated since Reconstruction.[2]

Wilson inherited Roosevelt's progressive momentum, but what Republicans had seen as admirable in one of their own now seemed dangerous in the hands of a Democrat. Americans wanted to move the government away from big business, and Wilson's men set out to do it. But many Republicans who had lined up behind La Follette and Roosevelt simply could not support Wilson. When the new president named William Jennings Bryan as secretary of state, they shuddered that the dangerous socialist they had barely managed to keep out of power since the 1890s had ended up in power after all.

Wilson called for the restoration of a world of small business and free enterprise, and his apparent desire to move backward raised the incredulity of Republican Progressives. From their perspective, it was ludicrous to imagine the country could resurrect an economy based on small businesses. Even if, by some miracle, that could happen, it would only re-create the conditions that had led to the rise of trusts in the first place. In practice, Wilson's New Freedom looked very much like Roosevelt's New Nationalism, relying on a strong federal government to break up the trusts, but by the time that similarity became clear, Republicans had even bigger complaints about the Democratic president.[3]

Above all, Republicans objected to Wilson's economics. Wilson called Congress into special session in April 1913 to revise the tariff. In the month before Congress was to meet, he strong-armed congressmen to support a lower tariff by the softball method of conferring with them, and by the hardball method of withholding appointments until they voted for his measure. So strongly did he feel about a tariff revision that he took the shocking step of appearing before Congress to make his appeal, becoming the first president to address Congress in person since John Adams in 1801. Republican congressmen, used to ignoring presidential messages and constructing legislation in backroom negotiations, had to endure a lecture from college professor Wilson, informing them that their party's signature issue—the tariff—needed to be scrapped.[4]

During spring and summer 1913, Democratic congressmen overturned the Republican theory of economic development through protective tariffs. In its stead, they adhered to the conviction held by Democrats before the Civil War—that tariffs should be used solely to raise revenue. The new Democratic tariff cut rates almost in half, from close to 50 percent to 25. Predictably, Republicans loathed the revisions. As soon as a preliminary bill was published, Henry Cabot Lodge declared it "very radical" and warned that it would destroy all Massachusetts industries. "The tariff just goes smash at them," he told the *Boston Globe*. "The more you study this bill the worse it gets." This is what the country got, he concluded, from flirting with the Progressive movement.[5]

The revenue bill had another piece that raised Republican hackles: an income tax. Reducing the tariff meant less revenue, and to make up the difference Democrats put a progressive tax on incomes over three thousand dollars. When Democrats had tried to impose an income tax in 1894, the Supreme Court had declared it unconstitutional. But the Democratic plan had gotten a boost from Taft, who had backed a constitutional amendment to permit an income tax because he thought federal taxing power—which, after all, the government had used from 1861 through 1895—was important. The ratification of the Sixteenth Amendment the month before Wilson took office made it constitutional to impose an income tax. The Democrats' revenue bill shifted the cost of government from poorer to richer Americans, and Old Guard Republicans hated it. They complained that it was socialistic and discriminated against capitalists, especially New York City's Wall Street community.[6]

The very wealthy soon had even more reason to despise Wilson Democrats. The financial panics that had roiled the economy since the 1890s convinced everyone that something had to be done to stabilize currency markets. In 1908, when Roosevelt was still in office, Congress created a commission to reform the nation's banking and currency laws. Republicans dominated the commission, and its January 1912 report reflected the recommendations of the financiers who had advised them. It called for a national association of bankers who would support each other with emergency loans, print currency, and act as the financial arm of the government.

Democrats instantly cried foul at a plan that seemed to hand the finances of the country to a few wealthy bankers and organized a committee, chaired by Louisiana Democrat Arsene Pujo, to investigate the power of financiers. It promptly exposed the workings of the "Money Trust," a small group of powerful bankers led by J. P. Morgan, who managed the nation's banking, business, and industry, and controlled over twenty-two billion dollars. Drawing from the Pujo Committee report, young lawyer Louis Brandeis wrote *Other People's Money and How the Bankers Use It*, describing how an oligarchy of financiers influenced the nation. By combining the bank deposits of individuals into huge sums they were able to buy up corporations, which in turn used their power to support tariffs and trusts. Ultimately, the Money Trust used the people's money against them. The book was popular enough to stay in print for a hundred years.[7]

When Congress revised the banking and currency system in 1913, the Democrats' plan reflected a growing national distrust of wealthy financiers. While the new plan preserved the private Federal Reserve banks that Republicans wanted, it provided for an oversight board drawn not from the banking industry but from presidential appointments confirmed by the Senate. National banks would be required to join the Federal Reserve System, and the government, rather than banks, would issue a new national currency, the Federal Reserve note. Wilson signed the Federal Reserve Act into law in December 1913.[8]

The new system promised to stabilize the economy, just as Republicans had advocated in 1908, but party members turned against it. The new banking act did not nationalize the banking system but rather took the far more moderate step of trying to stop the booms and busts of financial speculation by providing government oversight of private banking concerns and allowing for financial expansion and contraction across regions. Nonetheless, Republicans declared that it was Bryan's easy money system resurrected. It would create inflation by permitting the government to issue unlimited currency, which would destroy economic confidence and drain money from the country as skittish European financiers took their money home. The banking measure, Republicans claimed, would destroy America.[9]

Progressive legislation continued to come from Democrats and continued to annoy Republicans. In May 1913, Secretary of State Bryan acknowledged the states' ratification of the Seventeenth Amendment to the Constitution, providing for the direct election of senators. This measure had been a favorite reform of Populists, and it promised to end the power of big business to buy the election of senators like Nelson Aldrich. In 1914, the Clayton Antitrust Act outlawed price fixing and interlocking corporate directorates and made corporate officials personally responsible for illegal actions of the entities they oversaw; it also protected labor unions from antitrust legislation. ("This is not a time for toying with the delicately poised machinery of American business," the *Washington Post* fretted.) In 1916, the Federal Farm Act extended credit to farmers at lower rates than those previously charged by commercial banks. The Farm Act would, at long last, put farmers on the same footing as other businessmen, its supporters cheered. Wilson also endorsed women's suffrage, and in 1919 Congress would approve the Nineteenth Amendment, guaranteeing that women could vote. The amendment was ratified and went into effect in 1920. No longer would politicians be able to ignore the needs of women and children, a neglect that had sparked progressivism in the first place.[10]

While Wilson complained that the Republicans were "a party of masterly inactivity and cunning resourcefulness in resisting change," Republicans coalesced around the idea that Wilson was a Confederate and a socialist whose presidency threatened the nation. In the election of 1916, the Democrats retained control of the government, but only by a whisker. Wilson won the popular election comfortably with half a million more votes than his Republican opponent, former Supreme Court justice Charles Hughes, but the outcome in the Electoral College was in doubt until California went Democratic by fewer than four thousand votes.[11]

The outbreak of World War I in 1914 gave Republicans grounds to argue persuasively that Wilson was determined to destroy America. It was hard for Republicans to win by attacking the president on domestic legislation that was widely popular and had been endorsed at some point by members of both parties. But the realm of foreign affairs was different: there, the Republicans had the popular position of imperialism whereas the Democrats, to the extent they had any position, were defined by the unpopular anti-imperialism of Cleveland and Bryan.

Wilson initially advocated American neutrality in the war, a neutrality that the imperialist wing of the Republican Party insisted was treason. Wilson and the Democrats had left Americans unprepared to fight a war that would determine the nation's future, Theodore Roosevelt roared. Flexing his militaristic muscles, he demanded that American boys fight for right and insisted that Wilson was ultimately worse than the Germans because he had undermined American morality, lulling Americans into thinking that there was no difference between the two warring sides. In that, Roosevelt claimed, Wilson was just like the socialists, who had also played Germany's game by striking at American industry and thus weakening the country so that when it came time to fight, Americans would not be ready. Comparing the president to Pontius Pilate, Roosevelt claimed that Wilson was downright un-American.[12]

But Wilson would not be able to avoid war for long. After Germany made the desperate decision in early 1917 to engage in unlimited submarine warfare, German torpedoes sank five American ships. Then intelligence leaked that the German government was urging Mexico to fight the United States. In April 1917, Wilson asked Congress to declare war against Germany. A year later, American troops began to pour into Europe to bolster the war-weary Allied forces.

Paradoxically, the war fought under the progressive Wilson strengthened the hands of the Old Guard Republicans. The 1917 Bolshevik Revolution in Russia seemed to Old Guard Republicans to prove that Wilson Democrats were part of a conspiracy to undermine America's unique values. Democrats, like the Bolsheviks, had backed reforms to help labor and to ameliorate the corporate excesses of unregulated late nineteenth-century industrialism. But when the Bolshevik Revolution turned a major European nation into a communist state, progressive reforms no longer seemed an effort to save capitalism but rather an attempt to destroy it. To Old Guard Republicans, the Bolsheviks proved once and for all that anyone calling for industrial reforms intended to overthrow capitalism, the system that had made America so prosperous.

And then, thanks to Republicans' hatred of Wilson, a quirk of timing changed the course of Wilson's presidency, American history, and the world. The November 1918 midterm elections coincided with the end of the war. Going into the election, Wilson warned voters that electing Republicans would hurt the war effort. Republicans instantly expressed outrage, although Roosevelt and Lodge had used virtually identical language to call for a Republican Congress in 1898. Claiming that the Democrats were trying to "Make the U.S. Safe for Democrats," Republicans raged that Republicans were

"Loyal Enough to Die; Not to Help Run U.S." and charged that Wilson was an autocrat who wanted unlimited powers.[13]

The Republican fury over Wilson's call for a Democratic Congress, which by chance coincided with the end of World War I, was used to kill Wilson's signature issue: the League of Nations. Proposed by Wilson during the treaty negotiations at Versailles, within weeks of the election, the League of Nations was designed to be a community of nations that would agree to protect each other's borders, resolve international disputes, reduce arms, and set up a court of international justice. It was a progressive solution to international conflict: open discussion of simmering issues with the goal of arriving at a just and informed solution before men resorted to guns. But, in the election season of 1918, before any details of the League had been hammered out, Republicans led by Lodge and Roosevelt spun rumors of the plan into an accusation that Wilson intended to impose an unfavorable peace treaty on America. He could do that, they said, only if Republicans were cut out of the negotiations, which was precisely what Wilson was trying to do by getting voters to return Democrats in 1918. In their hands, the prospective League of Nations became a weapon to drum up Republican votes.

Their spin worked. Voter outrage turned the election against the war president. Republicans won a majority of forty-eight seats in the House and gained control of the Senate. Their margin in the Senate was slim—two seats—but it was enough. Ratification of a peace treaty would require Republican cooperation, and Republicans had no intention of cooperating. The League of Nations was a form of communism, they said, and would destroy America. "Conjure in your mind, if you can, a world without the Declaration of Independence, without our Constitution and free institutions, without our proclamations of emancipation of races and of nations, without this nation itself," one charged, and you would have the world with a League of Nations. Republicans across the board claimed that the League of Nations replaced nationalism with "internationalism." Internationalism was, Lodge pointed out, the goal of communism. One senator saw a more direct communist link: Wilson was a professor, and a government of professors would ultimately lead to Bolshevism. Republicans saw it as their job to stop the man in his tracks.[14]

Republican opposition not only killed the League of Nations—especially when a debilitating stroke left Wilson unable to defend it—but it also convinced many Americans that any form of international cooperation would destroy the America they knew, putting it under socialist control. That formulation would resurface at crucial moments for the rest of the century and beyond. It made diplomacy vulnerable to critics who insisted that negotiation was a cover for socialism and that Americans must assert international authority through independent military action alone or risk losing control over America.

Back in control of Congress, Republicans reignited fears of communism at home. Right away, they took aim at the power the Wilson administration had assumed during the war. As soon as the guns fell silent on the eleventh hour of the eleventh day of the eleventh month of 1918, the Republican Congress slashed the military budget. The sudden reduction threw the country into an economic slump that created 20 percent unemployment. Prices had more than doubled since 1914, and squeezed between underemployment and high prices, workers across the nation struck.

In the strikes Republicans saw not an economic crisis sparked by the sudden cutbacks in federal spending, but rather communism, socialism, or anarchism. Their reaction was not as far-fetched as it might seem in retrospect. No one really understood how a modern economy worked in 1918. And, after all, anarchists had killed McKinley in 1901 and had set off World War I by killing Austrian Archduke Franz Ferdinand in 1914. They had not necessarily been neutralized by the war. When anarchists sent bombs to prominent Americans, including congressmen and J. D. Rockefeller, in April and June 1919, Republicans believed the anarchist virus remained virulent in the United States.

A September strike by more than two-thirds of Boston's fifteen hundred police officers, who wanted the right to unionize, confirmed Republicans' fears. With most of the city's officers away from their posts, thugs caroused through the streets, overturning fruit carts, taking spare tires from parked cars, smashing store windows and stealing jewelry, hats, shirts, neckties, and, above all, shoes. Men played craps in the streets, shooting dice in front of police stations. A group of toughs pulled a trolley car off its wires. The looters overall caused an estimated thirty-four thousand dollars in damage—about the cost of a small fire—but newspapers across the country described the events in Boston as a "Bolshevist nightmare," with lawless mobs roaming through a civilized city, shooting, raping, and pillaging. Newspaper articles from California to Pennsylvania screamed "terror reigns in the city" and

"Bolshevism in the United States is no longer a specter." The *Wall Street Journal* warned, "Lenin and Trotsky are on their way." The *New York Times* repeated a senator's warning that something had to be done, or "the nation will see a Soviet Government set up within two years."[15]

On September 11, over the protest of Boston's Democratic mayor, who sympathized with the strikers, the Republican governor of Massachusetts took control of the city, declaring, "There is no right to strike against the public safety by anybody, anywhere, any time." With this dramatic statement, Calvin Coolidge, the unremarkable, dour politician, stepped into the limelight as the bulwark of civilization against anarchy. Newspapers across the country reprinted his picture and his message. Seventy thousand of his fellow citizens were so moved by this acidic Yankee that they sent letters and telegrams to his office, lauding his brave stance. Labor had gone too far, commentators explained, and threatened the very existence of American government. Governor Coolidge had taken a stand against "Bolsheviks" in the nation and had stopped "the beginnings of Soviet government."[16]

Although President Wilson joined the chorus condemning the strikers, Republican Party leaders blamed Wilson and his party for the strike. Democrats had encouraged the "insolence of organized labor," the Republican Publicity Association insisted. It warned, "Unless the drive against the Republic is crushed the country will be Russianized." Just as they had in the previous century, newspapers and business leaders charged that any group advocating government activism was plotting to destroy America. Labor unions bore the brunt of their assault, but dislike of unions also swept in church agencies whose members defended labor organization. It included African Americans, whose demand for improved conditions led the *New York Times* to sigh that there was "no use in shutting our eyes to facts.... Bolshevist agitation has been extended among the Negroes." Educators, too, were accused of preaching communism: just look at the socialist professor in the White House. "A majority of the college professors in the United States are teaching socialism and Bolshevism," insisted oil baron Edward L. Doheny in 1919; he went on to list executives who were sliding into the swamp: men who led J. P. Morgan's enterprises, Republican bankers, and even a man who would later become a fervent admirer of Adolf Hitler. Republicans insisted that Democrats had been "over-lenient... toward anarchists and murderous communists."[17]

Attacks on the tentacles of communism were not just rhetorical. During 1919 and 1920, the two years of what became known as the Red Scare, mobs surged against labor organizers and African Americans. Fights broke out in New York at Madison Square Garden and at the Waldorf-Astoria Hotel; in West Virginia, a mob forced 118 striking steelworkers to kiss an American flag; in Centralia, Washington, angry citizens led by local businessmen lynched a member of the new radical union Industrial Workers of the World—called Wobblies—after a fight between the mob and the union men left four people dead.[18]

It seemed there was a full-scale class war going on. In May 1920, police arrested two Italian immigrants believed to be associated with anarchists responsible for planting bombs. Police charged Nicola Sacco and Bartolomeo Vanzetti with armed robbery and the murder of two men in Braintree,

Massachusetts. Then, in September, a drayman parked a wagon packed with dynamite and metal slugs across from J. P. Morgan's bank at the busiest corner of Wall Street. The explosion killed thirty-three people and destroyed two million dollars in property. Although historians now think there was something in the charges against Sacco and Vanzetti, people on the street saw their arrest as the incarceration of two poor men by the country's wealthy power brokers. The Wall Street bombing further encouraged the sense that regular people were under attack. The destruction was on Wall Street, but the 33 dead and 200 wounded were clerks and stenographers. Not one was a financier.[19]

The lesson Republicans took from their anxiety about communism was that government should work harder to protect business interests. During the war, the Wilson administration had overseen and coordinated food and fuel production as well as all industries tied to the war effort. Rather than rebelling against this control, when the war ended businessmen celebrated the efficiency of the past months and called for yet more cooperation—but now without oversight. They demanded that the government repeal the antitrust measures that had made large-scale cooperation within industries difficult since the 1890s.[20]

Their task was made easier because the Wilson years had decimated the Progressive Republicans. Roosevelt had moved out of the party, and La Follette had so fervently opposed American intervention in the war that he became one of the most hated men in the country. Albert Beveridge, whose "The March of the Flag" speech had helped Progressives rise to power, had generally backed Wilson's policies until the League of Nations, which he loathed. He had been turned out of the Senate in 1911; in the 1920s he gave up politics altogether and turned to writing history. By 1920, Progressive Republicanism had lost all coherence and significance as a movement.

At the 1920 Republican Convention, held in Chicago in early June, Republicans resurrected their late nineteenth-century worldview. Roosevelt had died the year before, and though the delegates said all the right things about their departed leader, it was clear he had taken his ideas with him. Instead the attendees celebrated the few surviving members of the Old Guard—Uncle Joe Cannon and Henry Cabot Lodge, who were eighty-four and seventy. When a Wisconsin Progressive called for legislation that would relieve farmers, workers, and people generally from the intolerable economic pressures of the time, delegates laughed at him, heckled him, threatened to throw him out, and called him a socialist. The only person who drew greater disdain from the delegates was Wilson himself, who, in their view, led a party that was un-American and should be thought of as "the enemy." Republicans called for a return to a high tariff and cheap government.[21]

The Republicans were determined to nominate a businessman because, as one delegate said, "Our National government should be run as a business is run." No more flirting with highly educated professors or using the Wisconsin experiment to direct policy to achieve optimal social outcomes; it was time to go straight to a businessman. Other than that requirement, the delegates were searching for someone "restful," as one said, after the turmoil of the Progressive Era. What they wanted was a return to a vanished America, the world before Roosevelt, when government had nurtured the economy solely by supporting big business, in the belief that booming businesses would create jobs and improve life for everyone. Republican delegates believed that the government's only job was to promote business prosperity. None of this mucking around with social welfare legislation, which only muddied the waters.[22]

Delegates nominated one man after another. The three front-runners were all lackluster, and the next tier of nominees was even less impressive. With the tide running against Wilson, the Republicans were looking for someone who could fog a mirror and who, once elected, would feel obliged to do little else.

Finally, the former governor of Ohio nominated favorite son Warren G. Harding, a sitting senator. In his exceedingly short speech full of smooth platitudes, he called Harding "Ohio's second McKinley": quiet, unassuming, and electable. He could carry the key state of Ohio, whose loss in 1916 had cost Republicans the presidency. As the former governor finished, pictures of Harding fluttered from the ceiling. The speech seconding Harding's nomination was even briefer than the nomination speech, making it clear how little the candidate mattered. "Back to Normal" and "America first" should be the slogans of the campaign, one man said; the country needed someone "safe and sane." Still, it took ten ballots and a late-night conference in a "smoke-filled room" to secure the nomination for Harding, even though delegates were anxious to check out of their expensive Chicago hotels and escape the unseasonably hot weather. As soon as the nomination was announced, delegates rushed out of the meeting hall, red in the face and sweating, in shirtsleeves, bawling for taxis to start the trip home.[23]

Harding was a perfect figurehead for 1920s America: an old-fashioned small-town man with a veneer of sophistication. He was a handsome, back-slapping, card-playing neighborly fellow from Marion, Ohio, about as far from the austere Wilson as it was possible to be. When asked how he felt about his nomination, Harding said he felt like a man who held a pair of eights and had drawn a full house. Wilson was a smart, condescending, internationally connected college professor ("a kind of frozen flame of righteous intelligence," a journalist called him); Harding was the nice guy who would keep an eye on your house while you were away. He was "a wheelhorse of the old Old Guard" who hated Roosevelt's apostasy. He was undistinguished and indistinguishable, the *New York Times* spat: it called him a very respectable second-class politician. Indeed, the only people really ecstatic about Harding's nomination were the townspeople of Marion, whose enthusiasm was so marked it made most of the national papers.[24]

The real headliner on the ticket was the vice presidential nominee: Massachusetts governor Calvin Coolidge. Thanks to his handling of the Boston police strike, Coolidge was the man of the hour, the man who would preserve America from Bolshevism.

The election was so lopsided that, as one California Republican commented, if it were a prize fight, "the police would interfere on the grounds of brutality." Harding's chief responsibility in the election was to keep his mouth shut and to look presidential. He was the antithesis of Wilson, and he acknowledged—even celebrated—his anti-intellectualism. He knew nothing about Europe—and admitted it. As for a budding fight over wartime taxes, he told one of his secretaries he couldn't make heads or tails of the problem. He was such a terrible speaker, Wilson's son-in-law remarked, that his speeches "leave the impression of an army of pompous phrases moving over the landscape in search of an idea; sometimes those meandering words would actually capture a straggling thought and bear it triumphantly, a prisoner in their midst, until it died of servitude and overwork." Wilson wanted Democratic candidate James M. Cox to rally voters around the complicated issue of the League of Nations; Harding simply promised a return to "normalcy."[25]

When the votes were tallied, it turned out that most Americans were eager for normalcy. Harding and Coolidge had won more than 60 percent of the popular vote and had captured every state in the North and West. They had even broken into the solid South, taking Tennessee for the Republicans for the first time since Reconstruction. As one observer commented, "It wasn't a landslide, it was an earthquake."[26]

Harding brought his small-town bonhomie to the White House, where he surrounded himself with Ohio cronies who were badly out of their depth. They were known as the "Ohio Gang"; Herbert Hoover, who became Harding's commerce secretary, scornfully called them Harding's "playmates" and complained that they dealt poker all night in the White House. Their vision of government was primarily to see what they could get out of it for themselves and their friends, and before a year had gone by, they were playing fast and loose with the country's laws and resources. In exchange for a suitcase full of cash—to the tune of one hundred thousand dollars—and another twenty-five-thousand-dollar "loan," Harding's secretary of the interior had leased government oil lands in Teapot Dome, Wyoming, and Elk Hills, California, to oil barons. (One of the men happened to be Edward L. Doheny, who was the man obsessed with the threat of socialism encroaching everywhere from colleges to J. P. Morgan's offices.) Other members of the Ohio Gang, led, unfortunately, by the attorney general, were taking kickbacks from liquor dealers and ignoring graft in the Veterans Bureau.[27]

Rumors spread of the drinking and poker playing upstairs at the White House, where the air was heavy with tobacco smoke, tables were covered with trays of whiskey bottles, and cards and poker chips were at hand, and where, one observer noted, the general atmosphere was one of "waistcoat unbuttoned, feet on the desk, and the spittoon alongside." But by summer 1923, even darker rumors swirled: rumors of corruption and lawbreaking. Journalist William Allen White caught Harding one day in despair: "My God, this is a hell of a job!" the president cried. "I have no trouble with my enemies.... But my damn friends, my God-damn friends, White, they're the ones that keep me walking the floor nights!"[28]

In July 1923, the president and Mrs. Harding embarked on a trip to Alaska and the West Coast. The scandals had begun to break, and shortly before the travelers set off, two members of the Ohio Gang committed suicide. Harding broke from his usual boon companions and asked the upstanding Herbert Hoover to accompany the party. Surprised, the commerce secretary agreed, but he soon regretted his decision. Harding was nervous, his gaiety forced as he wrung as much excitement as he could out of the parades and celebrations on his route. When he wasn't enjoying the crowds, he kept his companions tethered to the bridge table through long nights; Hoover came to so hate bridge on this journey that he never played the game again.[29]

On July 27, during a speech, Harding faltered and dropped the pages of his manuscript. He seemed to recover but then quickly deteriorated. The presidential train shot down to San Francisco, where the president died in his bed, most likely from a heart attack. "Harding was not a bad man," Roosevelt's daughter Alice later summed him up. "He was just a slob."[30]

The schemes of the hapless Ohio gangsters would soon attract national attention, but their pillaging of the Treasury was petty compared to the reordering that was going on in the real hallways of power. With such a weak president, power might well have slid back to Congress, but twenty years of obstructing the course of first Roosevelt, then Taft, then Wilson had split Congress into factions and made its members far more adept at working against measures than for them. Into the vacuum stepped administration officers, notably Commerce Secretary Herbert Hoover and Secretary of the Treasury Andrew Mellon. On their watch, the government implemented policies of which pro-business Republicans previously could only dream.

While Harding played cards and congressmen squabbled, administration men turned the government over to businessmen. For commerce secretary, Harding had tapped Hoover, who had successfully managed world food supplies during and after World War I. Facing the postwar economic slump, Hoover was dead set against government support for unemployed workers, believing it would cause "paternalism" and destroy America. The best solution for unemployment, he thought, was for the government to spur private economic investment through foreign trade agreements that would increase exports. Hoover immediately began to organize and expand his department. During his tenure it grew to fifteen thousand employees with a budget of more than thirty-seven million dollars and became an important liaison between business and the government.[31]

While Hoover was busy conferring with businessmen and strengthening the Department of Commerce, Andrew Mellon undertook to fix the war debt. Mellon was not a politician but a Pittsburgh banker whose enormous wealth seemed to indicate he knew how to handle money. A cadaverous-looking man who was close to seventy when he took the Treasury post, Mellon had started his career in the 1870s in lumber and coal, backed by his wealthy father. By 1880, he had joined his father's banking firm and shortly afterward took it over. At first, he invested in land, coal, and iron. Then he turned to steel, oil, shipbuilding, water companies, and aluminum. In the mid-1920s, he was one of the richest men in America.[32]

Mellon's first concern was the extraordinary taxation Congress had levied to fight the war. In September 1916, as Europe's conflagration threatened to engulf America, Congress had passed an emergency revenue act to raise $200 million for defense. A year later, it passed steeply progressive taxes to raise a huge sum: more than $2.5 billion. Those in the top bracket paid a tax rate of 63 percent. Early estimates were that the progressive taxes would raise about $850 million from incomes—$500 million of that from Wall Street—and about $1 billion from excess profits. The 1916 tax measure had borne grumbling that it weighed too heavily on the rich, but in 1917, with war fever boiling, the second bill passed both the House and the Senate without a negative vote. This extraordinary tax measure—at the time the largest revenue measure in the history of the American government—was generally popular as Americans took pride in their willingness to put their shoulders to the wheel to defend the nation.[33]

But as soon as the war ended, Republicans insisted that the heavy taxes would destroy the economy, a position with which many Democrats agreed. When they took control of Congress in 1919, Republicans cut the tax rates for the top income brackets, and when Mellon took over the Treasury in 1921, he cut them still further. Touting "the Government's New Thrift Campaign," he wrote extensively in popular magazines, explaining to readers that the only way to increase productivity after the war was to increase investment in industry. And the only way to do that was to free up capital. The government must slash its budget and taxes must go down to enable wealthy men to invest in the economy. "The Government is just a business, and can and should be run on business principles," Mellon announced.[34]

Harding's death increased, rather than decreased, the influence of businessmen in government. Once Calvin Coolidge became president, businessmen associated with Mellon entirely eclipsed Republican nineteenth-century statesmen like Henry Cabot Lodge. With Coolidge in the White House, Mellon stepped up his efforts to kill the taxes that he maintained were slowing investment in the economy. In a 1924 book, he tried to rally support for his cause, quoting industrialist Henry Ford's assertion that "high taxes on the rich do not take burdens off the poor. They put burdens on the poor." Taxing the wealthy destroyed individual initiative and thus destroyed the country, he explained. If America did not get rid of the taxes on the rich, it would become a nation of followers, not leaders.[35]

Privately, Mellon asked the head of the Internal Revenue Service for tips on how to avoid the income tax, used the man's advice for his own finances, then turned around and warned Americans that the only way to keep the wealthy from dodging taxes was to get rid of progressive taxes altogether, taking away their incentive to cheat. The Republican Congress agreed with Mellon. In 1926 it slashed income and estate taxes for the wealthiest Americans. In 1928, Congress left income rates the same but gave Mellon the legal authority to make any decisions he thought appropriate "relating to the internal revenue laws." Mellon used this authority freely, as he had always used his ability to give refunds, credits, and abatements. From 1921 to 1929, he returned $3.5 billion to wealthy men. Much of this largesse went to Republicans. There were seventeen men who gave ten thousand dollars to the 1930 Republican campaign; they all received Mellon's help.[36]

The Coolidge administration worked to promote business not just by freeing capital but also by direct action. As the head of the Department of Commerce, Hoover worked with trade associations to develop codes of business practice. The idea was to enable businesses to avoid unfair practices; in reality the codes allowed industry to avoid antitrust lawsuits. The Federal Trade Commission (FTC), established under Wilson to attack monopolies and trusts, became a full-throated advocate of business collaboration. The old FTC had been a "publicity bureau to spread socialistic propaganda," the new head complained. Under his direction it would no longer hurt businessmen, he said; it would help them. Under the new FTC, business mergers took off. Eight thousand businesses disappeared between 1919 and 1930. Local utilities, stores, and movie theaters merged into national concerns, proud that they were replacing bumbling local management with sophisticated national organizations. Chain stores—Montgomery Ward, Woolworth, and American Stores—popped up across the nation.[37]

Meanwhile, the administration aggressively developed foreign markets while protecting American business. Under Harding, Congress had restored tariff rates to their former Republican levels from the lows of the Wilson years. It also gave the president power to raise or lower tariffs at will. Harding and Coolidge changed tariff rates thirty-seven times; thirty-two times they moved rates upward (they dropped the rates on paintbrush handles and bobwhite quails). At the same time, Hoover urged European countries to buy American. Under these measures, business boomed. More than twenty-two thousand new manufacturing companies were formed between 1925 and 1926, and industrial production took off. Business profits rose, and if wages didn't rise much, they didn't fall, either. Businessmen applauded the Republican program.[38]

Coolidge has gone down in history as a do-nothing president who worshipped business almost as a religion. This is largely true, and if Republicans were right, nothing was precisely what a good president should do. After 1880, Republicans had stood against government activism for social welfare while throwing the weight of the government behind industry. They had recoiled from Cleveland's rhetoric about rebalancing the power of the rich in government and had managed to neutralize his administration even before it took office. They had politely ignored the demands of their fellow Republican Roosevelt for government to level the playing field between different groups in society. But they had panicked over Wilson. Riding on the momentum Roosevelt had launched, Wilson had passed strong progressive legislation. The Republican leadership had not liked the new laws and liked even less the idea of an active executive creating a government that meddled in the economy. With his silence and inactivity, his eagerness to let business and government work together without interference, Coolidge was acting exactly as Republicans thought a president should.

At last, it seemed, government and business had managed to combine the efficiencies of an industrial economy with the protection of property. The experience of World War I had enabled the government and business to leave behind the old world of robber barons roiling the economy while they duked it out for supremacy, and to figure out how to run a national economy. The way to a prosperous future seemed clear.

And what a future it would be! The war had decimated Europe, but it had strengthened America. It unleashed new technologies and gave businessmen and government officials the bright confidence to develop those innovations and new tools to sell them. Fittingly, radio burst into public consciousness on November 2, 1920, when the East Pittsburgh radio station KDKA broadcast the election returns announcing that voters had chosen Harding and Coolidge. Electricity revolutionized the nation in the 1920s; by 1929, electric lights lit more than two-thirds of American homes, extending the hours of light everywhere but in the benighted rural countryside. Electricity brought refrigerators, washing machines, vacuum cleaners, sewing machines, and toasters, which spread as rapidly as consumers could afford them. Americans rushed to buy the new products, which modern advertising presented as objects that would bestow on their owners glamour, sophistication, romance, and power. Social reform and religion fell into disfavor because it appeared that prosperity was wiping out the economic differences at the heart of social strife. Men aspired not to change the world but to belong to a well-run organization. A best-selling book in the mid-1920s suggested that Jesus was not a meek spiritual leader but rather "the Founder of Modern Business" who had "picked up twelve men from the bottom ranks of business and forged them into an organization that conquered the world."[39]

When Coolidge wrote that "the man who builds a factory builds a temple, that the man who works there worships there," he was not abandoning America's greatest principles for the service of big business. Like other Americans of his day, Coolidge believed that the nation had finally figured out how to marry extraordinary industrial production to human elevation. Business was booming, standards of living were rising, and Americans were finding the time to read, learn, invent, and improve.[40]

It seemed that Lincoln's vision had finally come true, and Republicans claimed the credit. They had, they said, solved all of the nation's major financial problems. In their 1928 platform, they promised faithfully to continue the policies of the Coolidge administration and nominated Herbert Hoover to do it. In his acceptance speech, he articulated the era's Republican vision. Thanks to Republican policies, he said: "We in America are nearer to the final triumph over poverty than ever before in the history of any land. The poorhouse is vanishing from among us.... Given a chance to go forward with the policies of the last eight years, we shall soon, with the help of God, be in sight of the day when poverty will be banished from this nation."[41]

Republicans warned that turning the country over to Democrats would create a depression, but such a warning wasn't really necessary in the business boom of the 1920s. The American people did not have to be convinced that Republicans had discovered the secret to a winning economy. In 1928 they elected Hoover over the Democratic candidate, New York governor Al Smith, by a whopping 58.2 percent of the vote. The Republicans lost only Massachusetts, Rhode Island, and the Deep South.[42]

In a "victory boom" on the stock market the day after the election, stocks at the top of the market rose 5 to 15 points, and almost 5 million shares changed hands, only a few less than in the market's highest-volume day the previous June. On November 16, the market shattered old records with the exchange of more than 6.5 million shares and the industrial average rising 4.5 points.[43]

Hoover's deep confidence shone in his inaugural address. Speaking in a downpour, he told Americans that the question was not how to prevent falling backward but rather how to progress to even higher standards. "Ours is a land rich in resources, stimulating in its glorious beauty, filled with millions of happy homes, blessed with comfort and opportunity," he said. "In no nation are the institutions of progress more advanced. In no nation are the fruits of accomplishment more secure. In no nation is the government more worthy of respect. No country is more loved by its people. I have an abiding faith in their capacity, integrity, and high purpose. I have no fears for the future of our country," he concluded. "It is bright with hope."[44]

The 1920s represented the ultimate success of that era's Republican vision: government and business working together to accomplish Lincoln's dream of ever-increasing prosperity. By the end of the decade it appeared that the Republicans had brought America to the pinnacle of human achievement.

8

Republicans and the New Deal

What the Republicans could not see in the heady days of the late 1920s was that the prosperity they celebrated was based on two terrible fallacies. First, the rising living standards getting so much attention in the media were not widespread; they affected primarily white, middle-class, urban Americans. And second, 1920s prosperity rested on a speculative bubble, not on solid economic growth. When the bubble burst, there was an explosion the likes of which the world had never seen, proving that the very fundamentals to which the Republican Party had held since the mid-1880s were breathtakingly wrong.

Stunned Republicans attempted to explain the Great Crash of 1929 with their traditional bugbears: a bloated federal government sucking up taxes and greedy workers who demanded more money than employers could afford to pay. Republicans called for the government to cut wages and workers to tighten their belts. But such a weak prescription could not begin to combat the worldwide crisis. It would take a popular Democratic administration to develop the dramatic government action imperative to keep Americans from starving during the Depression. As the Democrats took center stage, Republicans found themselves adrift, unable to conceive of a new ideology to replace the old one, which had turned out to be so disastrous. As members of the party sought to regain relevance, they split into two factions. The growing animosity between the two groups turned into a fight for control of the party that would become increasingly desperate as it reached into the twenty-first century. For the next eighty years, Republicans struggled to come to terms with the ideological crisis caused by the New Deal.

In the 1920s, college educations, refrigerators, and leisure time did not reach far beyond the men who congratulated themselves on their prosperous country. People in rural areas, whose front doors overlooked endless fields and ramshackle outhouses, could only dream of such riches. After World War I and the deadly influenza pandemic of 1918, which killed twenty to forty million people worldwide, farm prices crashed. Prices began to recover by 1925, but world competition and overproduction meant that by 1929 they remained less than half of what they had been in 1919.[1]

Worried western congressmen twice tried to prop up agricultural prices in the 1920s, but Coolidge vetoed both measures, warning that they would put farmers at the mercy of an army of bureaucrats and redistribute tax money to a special interest. If the government went down that dangerous road, he said, it was only a question of time until every special interest experiencing hard times demanded government assistance.

Farmers' best hope, Coolidge told them, was to join the modern economy by finding better ways to market their crops.[2]

Republicans were even less helpful to African Americans. After the Harrison administration's drive for federal protection of Black voters in 1889, lynching in the South had begun to rise as white Americans accused their Black neighbors of corrupting American society. Then World War I and the Twenties exacerbated racial tensions in the North by bringing almost two million southern African Americans to northern factories. White men resented the migrants who settled in Black enclaves in Chicago, Detroit, New York, and other urban areas. They saw the newcomers as awkward yokels willing to work for less money than the men they replaced.[3]

The Great Migration, as it became known, permanently changed race relations in America. Issues of race were no longer a "Southern Problem"; they now were national, and northerners had no more a solution to them than southerners had had. In summer 1919, race riots broke out in cities across the country, leaving dozens dead and thousands homeless. In Chicago at the end of July, white youths stoned to death a Black boy who had drifted toward a whites-only beach; the resulting ten days of violence left thirty-eight dead and more than five hundred wounded. In 1921, rioters in Tulsa burned the country's wealthiest Black community and killed an untold number of African Americans (some estimates are in the hundreds). The Ku Klux Klan re-formed to defend "traditional America," claiming forty thousand members, largely in the North. At the same time, when Black soldiers returned from the trenches of Europe, where they had been fighting for American values, they were unwilling to go back to second-class citizenship.

Republican leaders had no answer for the country's racial tensions. In their 1920, 1924, and 1928 party platforms they offered weak reassurance of safety to African Americans by stating that they wanted a federal anti-lynching law. But by the time Hoover took office, Republicans appeared to worry more about offending white sensibilities than maintaining their traditional ties to the Black community. Hoover committed one racial slur after another. He nominated to the Supreme Court a southerner who had suggested that African Americans should not have been given the vote so soon after the Civil War (the Senate denied the candidate's confirmation). Then Hoover segregated the ships taking Gold Star Mothers, women who had lost sons in World War I, to visit their sons' European graves. He disbanded to menial jobs the celebrated Black Tenth Cavalry. Worst, when a hundred Black leaders visited Hoover during the 1932 campaign, the president would not let them into the White House; he met them outside.[4]

Republicans also turned against immigrants. Their early theory that immigrants were the foundation of a nation's wealth had faltered during the labor protests of the 1870s. In the 1890s, as his vision of reform was developing, Roosevelt made discriminating against immigrants central to his Americanism. In 1909, Roosevelt's friend Lodge had proposed a bill restricting immigration from southern and eastern Europe. In 1917, under Wilson, an immigration act had expanded the ability of the government to reject immigrants it believed undesirable.

The arrival of a Republican Congress in 1919 revolutionized immigration restrictions. In 1921, Congress set a limit on the number of immigrants allowed per year, and it established a quota system for immigrants based on country of origin. The number of immigrants coming to America plummeted in the first year of the act's operation, from more than 800,000 to about 300,000. The 1924 Immigration Act lowered immigration numbers further. It established that, beginning in 1927, total annual immigration to America be lowered to 150,000. Congress designed quotas to keep Jews, southern and eastern Europeans, and Asians from coming to America.

Part of the impulse for excluding the foreign-born was the lingering belief that they brought with them political and economic radicalism. These two strands came together in August 1927 with the execution of Sacco and Vanzetti in Boston. Although it is likely the men were, in fact, involved in some way with the robbery and murder with which they were charged, their show trial turned stomachs across the world. Protests roiled every continent except Antarctica on the day of their execution. When the electric chair had done its work, novelist John Dos Passos recorded the despair of those on the outside of the magical circle of the 1920s: "they have clubbed us off the streets they are stronger they are rich they hire and fire the politicians the newspaper editors the old judges the small men with reputations the college presidents the wardheelers (Listen businessmen college presidents judges America will not forget her betrayers) they hire the men with guns the uniforms the policecars the patrolwagons.... we stand defeated America."[5]

Those celebrating the prosperity of the 1920s dismissed people like Dos Passos as carpers and cavilers, but their critique of the American society in the era exposed a truth that would soon undermine the entire Republican project. The new economy of the 1920s benefited too few Americans to be sustainable. When an ill wind blew, the entire edifice collapsed.

The election of Hoover, the great engineer, seemed to assure a permanent Republican ascendancy and its attendant prosperity. Everyone wanted in on the inevitable growth. It made sense to invest in the industries producing the steel, coal, utilities, transportation, and consumer goods that distinguished the era as a new moment in human history. As investors rushed in, stock prices rose.

And rose, and rose.

By 1929, the rush to buy stocks had become a rush to speculate in the stock market. Prices that had seemed too high to be real in spring 1928 were laughably low by fall. Radio had been at 94½ in March 1928; by September 1929 it was 101 but had split so often that the holdings from 1928 were actually worth 505. Similarly, a share of Montgomery Ward at 132¾ in March 1928 translated to 466½ a year and a half later. American Can had been at 77 in March 1928; eighteen months later it hit 181 (and 7/8). And so it went, down the stock lists. Everyone wanted in.[6]

Relatively easy money fed the speculation. Mellon had remained Treasury secretary under Hoover, and his tax cuts pumped cash into the market. So, too, did his $3.5 billion in rebates. Those with less money to burn could get into the market by buying on margin, putting down 10 or 20 percent of the cost of a stock and borrowing the rest from a broker. The loans could be paid off by the anticipated increase in the value of the stock. By the end of 1928, brokers' loans had pumped almost $6 billion into the economy. For even smaller players, investment trusts rose in the late Twenties. Run by market specialists, these entities bundled together portfolios of common stocks. Small investors could buy shares in trusts, making it possible for anyone to invest in the stock market. By early 1929, a new investment trust was being organized every day in America. That year, trusts handled more than $8 billion.[7]

Few grumbled about the bubble on the stock market, and those who did were attacked as ignorant, anti-American naysayers. When senators nervously suggested better stock market regulation, Princeton scholar Joseph Stagg Lawrence famously dismissed them as biased fanatics whose "provincial ignorance" was attacking "an innocent community" (he meant Wall Street). "Be a bull on America!" boosters urged. "Never sell the United States short!" Cracks appeared in the bull market in September 1929, but they did not worry true believers. On October 17, Irving Fisher, a renowned professor of economics, cheered that stock prices had reached "what looks like a permanently high plateau." Within a few months, he expected to see the stock market "a good deal higher than it is today."[8]

October 24, a Thursday, was the beginning of the end. Heavy trading in the morning made the ticker tape that recorded prices run behind. Fearful of getting caught with overvalued stock as prices dropped, brokers sold more and more heavily. The tape fell further behind, and brokers stampeded to sell. As the market fell, stop-loss orders—price triggers at which brokers automatically sold—poured more and more stocks into the cascade, driving the market still lower. Many investors were sold out of the market entirely. When the ticker tape finally caught up, at eight and a half minutes past seven that night, it showed that an astonishing 12,894,650 shares had changed hands.[9]

In fact, leading bankers had worked to stabilize the market by afternoon on the twenty-fourth, and the total stock drops that day were actually quite minor as the afternoon market regained the ground the morning had lost. But those dreadful early hours had wiped out hundreds of thousands of small investors. Not only had their imagined fortunes disappeared, but their rosy futures had gone, too. The market seemed to recover on Friday and Saturday, but over Sunday, people reconsidered where to place their faith. On Monday, October 28, prices slid far in heavy trading. The Times industrial average fell forty-nine points. Financial men were no longer boasting of their confidence. They held their breath.[10]

And then it hit. October 29 has gone down in history as Black Tuesday. When the gong in the great hall of the Stock Exchange struck at ten o'clock, the market opened with heavy trading, all of it downward. Huge blocks of stock came on the market, and brokers asked only for someone to bid anything at all. No one did (except, according to rumor, one bright messenger boy who bid a dollar a share on a block of stocks and got it). When the ticker finally revealed its last transactions two and a half hours late, it showed that 16,410,030 shares had changed hands, and the industrial average had dropped another forty-three points. If October 24 had been a slaughter of the innocents—as some called it—October 29 was the slaughter of everyone else.[11]

The market continued to drop. Three days in mid-November cut fifty more points off the industrial average, until it stood at less than half of what it had been two months before. Frantic for money, brokers demanded that clients deposit funds to cover the stock they had bought on margin;

these margin calls wiped out anyone who had survived the early catastrophes. Worse, sanguine investors who had missed the first collapse rushed in to pick up cheap deals and were ruined along with everyone else as the market continued to fall. The number of Americans speculating in the stock market was probably less than a million and a half out of a population of about 120 million. But even those who did not play the stock market watched the drop and suddenly went bearish on the economic future.[12]

Republican leaders might have been able to explain the crash as a normal correction to an inflated market, but the depression that followed it convinced most Americans that the modern Republican economic vision was wrong. Since the 1880s, Republicans had been saying that enacting their program of hard money, high tariffs, low taxes, and no regulation would create endless American growth and prosperity. In the 1920s, they put that vision into place. When the result was a depression of unimaginable depths and duration, it undermined Americans' faith in the Republican Party.

The ruin on Wall Street revealed the central weakness in Republicans' economic vision. The business boom of the 1920s had increased worker productivity by about 43 percent, but wages did not rise, and the increasing profits from that productivity went to business owners. Combined with the Mellon tax policies and the dividend payoffs from the stock market, this meant that wealth moved upward dramatically. In 1929, 5 percent of the population received one-third of the nation's income. The stock market crash wiped out the purchasing power of this group, and the rest of the population did not have the income to fuel the economy.[13]

Also devastating was the corporate structure that tied all the major industries together. Just as the collapse of Reading Railroad took down everyone in 1893, so the collapse of a major firm during the Depression started a chain reaction that wiped out entire segments of the economy. The cooperation that Hoover championed strengthened industry when times were good, but it brought everyone down together when times were bad.

The banking structure that Mellon had overseen had even worse structural problems. The failure of independent banks created a run on other banks to cover the losses of the first, and they all collapsed together. Worse, unlike manufacturers who had to produce something, banks had provided for their customers, as one observer said, everything but a roulette wheel. Old-fashioned banking, whose hallmark had been caution, had been replaced in the Twenties by entrepreneurial banking that focused on spectacular growth. In the last week of Hoover's administration, nine million savings accounts vanished. At the same time, credit abruptly contracted: the end of brokers' loans alone dried up nearly three billion dollars.[14]

In 1932, manufacturing output was less than it had been in 1913; the output of pig iron was lower than it had been since 1896. Foreign trade plummeted, dropping from $10 billion to $3 billion in the three years after 1929. Agricultural prices fell correspondingly: from 1929 to 1932, wheat dropped from $1.05 to 39 cents a bushel; corn from 81 to 33 cents; cotton from 17 to 6 cents a pound. By 1932, a million people in New

York City were out of work; 60 percent of the workforce in Akron couldn't find jobs; only 277 out of almost 14,000 workers in Donora, Pennsylvania, had regular paychecks. By 1933, 1 person in every 4 in the labor force was out of work: 13 million people. Unable to pay rent or mortgages, people lost their homes and lived in shelters made of packing boxes.[15]

So much for the Republican miracle.

Treasury Secretary Mellon, whose theories had done much to create the crisis, believed he knew exactly what the government must do: nothing. "Liquidate labor, liquidate stocks, liquidate the farmers, liquidate real estate," he told Hoover. "It will purge the rottenness out of the system. High costs of living and high living will come down. People will work harder, live a more moral life. Values will be adjusted, and enterprising people will pick up the wrecks from less competent people." Handled this way, the pain would be severe but brief. Mellon tried to impress on Hoover that government inaction had worked in the 1870s.[16]

With his history of feeding hungry Europeans, Hoover had reservations about deliberately starving Americans. He also recognized that the world had changed in the past fifty years. Being able to go home to family farms had cushioned people in the 1870s, an option no longer available in the urban 1920s. But the Hoover administration's initial answer to the crisis was straight out of Mellon's financial theories: it cut taxes and raised tariffs. Unfortunately, taxes were already too low for tax cuts to free up much capital—most people would see only a few extra dollars a year—and higher tariffs only choked off trade.[17]

As Americans lost their jobs, their homes, their faith, and their hope, the Hoover administration preached thrift, morality, and individualism. The problem was not Republican ideas, party leaders insisted; it was the big government that served greedy constituencies. Government was wasteful; it had overstaffed public offices. Republicans declared that to restore economic growth the government must restore confidence among businessmen, who were worried their profits might disappear through the taxation necessary to support a host of lazy government employees. To that end, the nation must slash government spending. The very first thing that must happen was to lay off public workers and to insist that those who remained accept lower wages.[18]

Most Americans agreed that they were responsible for their own economic troubles, but they no longer trusted Republican policies. From being economic and political oracles, Republicans suddenly became outcasts. It did not help that they tried desperately to ignore the trouble. After the October 24 panic, Hoover had announced, "The fundamental business of the country, that is, production and distribution of commodities, is on a sound and prosperous basis." Although this wasn't strictly true, actual production numbers were no worse than they had been in the recessions of 1892 and 1907 or, for that matter, in 1920. When things didn't recover, the president continued to declare that things were getting better. They weren't.[19]

In 1930, the chairman of the Republican Party, Ohio senator Simeon D. Fess, noted that a Republican leader only had to say something to make voters believe the opposite. Unable to understand why voters had turned against Republicans, Fess darkly hinted at a conspiracy against his party. He complained that "persons high in Republican circles are beginning to believe that there is some concerted effort on foot to utilize the stock market as a method of discrediting the Administration.... Every time an Administration official gives out an optimistic statement about business conditions, the market immediately drops." Ridiculing Fess, the *New York Times* suggested that if Republican leaders believed in such a conspiracy, the only proper course for them was to shut up.[20]

Suddenly, Republicans' close relationship to business seemed diabolical. In 1928, bankers had been pillars of society; after the crash, they became parasites. When, after October 1929, men began to look for their money, they often discovered that bankers and brokers had stolen it. Worse than the thousands pilfered by little players were the deals and valuable severance packages awarded to big ones. In 1932, as breadlines stretched around city blocks, the executive committee of the Chase National Bank voted its retiring chairman a lifetime yearly salary of one hundred thousand dollars. Richard Whitney, a Republican and former president of the Stock Exchange, preached to senators that the way to fix the crisis was to balance the budget by cutting government salaries and veterans benefits. (His own salary couldn't be cut because he made "very little"—only sixty thousand dollars—six times a senator's pay.) Six years later, people learned that he had stolen assets and poured them into failing companies. When Whitney finally went under, it became clear the great emperors of Wall Street were not, after all, clothed.[21]

Since the Civil War, Republicans had usually managed to convince voters that a Democratic government meant a devastated economy, but in 1932 things were different. The Republican program had been enacted fully, and the result was unparalleled economic disaster. Hoover did channel some money into public works programs to aid the unemployed, but fundamentally he believed that local and state charity was the solution to tiding victims over until things improved. The Democratic presidential candidate that year, New York governor Franklin Delano Roosevelt, promised a "New Deal" to the American people, using the government to combat the Depression. But Hoover denounced such government activism as dangerous radicalism that would destroy America. The election was not about men or even parties, Hoover insisted: it was "a crucial battle between two conflicting theories of American government."[22]

Roosevelt's proposed New Deal work programs would "enslave" taxpayers, Hoover insisted in an echo of Andrew Johnson, and create an army of bureaucrats. It was a "soak the rich program" that would introduce class distinctions into America, whereas Republicans stood for the tradition that all were created equal. Roosevelt's plans would "crack the timbers of the Constitution." Bankers and businessmen nodded sagely at Hoover's warning that Democrats would destroy the country and called for the president's reelection, but other voters listened when Roosevelt scoffed at Republicans' fear mongering. Their "chorus of fear" was nothing short of a threat, Roosevelt said; it was un-American, and it endangered political freedom.[23]

Franklin Roosevelt swept the 1932 election with nearly 58 percent of the popular vote. Hoover had a pretty shrewd idea he was going to lose, and lose badly, but he felt obliged to fight it out. He truly believed, as Republicans had insisted since the

1870s, that Democrats would destroy America. Their government activism was socialism, he believed, while Republican insistence on small government and private enterprise was the true American way. So horrified was he by FDR's victory that Hoover refused to issue the president-elect the customary invitation to dinner at the White House the night before the inauguration. He substituted an awkward afternoon tea only when the White House usher put his foot down and insisted that Roosevelt must be allowed to pay his respects.[24]

The policies of the Roosevelt administration prompted Republicans to split into two groups over the next decade. On one hand were party members who clung with a stranglehold to the idea that government activism was socialism and that FDR's attempts to address the calamities of the Depression with work and relief programs would destroy the country. President Taft's son, Senator Robert Taft, a member of Hoover's staff and a staunch admirer of the engineer president, led this die-hard faction, which took its inspiration from the small-town Midwest. On the other hand were Republicans who gradually came to accept that the modern economy required government intervention, although they always maintained that Republicans could manage that process better than the Democrats who had instigated it. This faction centered in eastern cities and took its direction by 1940 from Thomas E. Dewey, the Manhattan district attorney famous for taking on organized crime.

In the early days of FDR's administration, Republicans stood together against the Democrats' plans for public programs. As Democrats began to pass laws endorsing workers' rights and providing government jobs and relief for impoverished Americans, Republicans in Hoover's mold, especially the businessmen who had prospered under the Republican policies of the 1920s, insisted that Democrats were redistributing wealth, pure and simple. Labor laws were bad enough, but worse was the Democrats' deficit spending. Roosevelt's "Brain Trust" of advisers championed the economic theories of John Maynard Keynes, who argued both that government investment in infrastructure would promote employment and that deficit spending during economic downturns would stimulate growth without crowding out private enterprise. Those deficits would eventually have to be paid, and Republicans eyed Democratic taxes, which fell primarily on corporate profits and the wealthy, with loathing. "Our revenue laws have operated in many ways to the unfair advantage of the few, and they have done little to prevent an unjust concentration of wealth and economic power," FDR told Congress in 1935. The new revenue act of that year provided for taxes of up to 75 percent on incomes of over five million dollars.[25]

In the early years of the New Deal, Republicans greeted FDR's initiative with the cry that the president was a socialist. He was destroying free enterprise, and it was only a question of time until individual freedom died, too. Democrats, whom Republicans had always believed were in the pockets of organized labor, were using the government to redistribute wealth from the haves to the have-nots, just as Republicans had predicted since the 1880s. Almost as soon as he took office, FDR reestablished diplomatic ties to Russia, which had been severed by the 1917 revolution, a move Republicans insisted showed his sinister motives.[26]

They also saw a red flag as African Americans abandoned the Republicans to back FDR. Leaders like Robert L. Vann, editor of the widely influential Black newspaper the *Pittsburgh Courier* and former Republican Party official, encouraged those African Americans who could still vote to support FDR. In a September 1932 speech, Vann famously prophesied: "I see millions of Negroes turning the picture of Lincoln to the wall." New Deal programs disproportionately helped people in the bottom third of the economic scale, and African Americans were disproportionately stuck in that bottom third. Up to a million African American families—one-seventh of the Black population—survived on government salaries during the 1930s, and three hundred scholars interviewed former slaves about their lives, an invaluable resource for today's historians—but also a symbolic act that validated the importance of those marginalized people.[27]

Roosevelt and his wife, Eleanor, made it a point to treat African Americans as equal citizens. Whereas Hoover had refused to welcome Black supporters in the White House, FDR invited African American visitors and dignitaries inside. He appointed a number of Black advisers and visited Black organizations on his travels. On one occasion, a poor Black farmer named Sylvester Harris, facing foreclosure, called the White House. Overhearing the call, FDR picked up the receiver, promised help, and then followed through—a dramatic gesture to a group that had been ignored at the highest levels of government since the 1890s.[28]

In 1936, to embarrass FDR and the African American community, southern whites circulated a photograph of Mrs. Roosevelt standing with Black Reserve Officer Training Corps

(ROTC) cadets. When asked about it, Mrs. Roosevelt replied that she had no problem with the photograph—quite a contrast to Hoover's reception of the Black delegation on the White House lawn. "[We]…need to…work for equality… of opportunity regardless of race, color or creed," she later commented.[29]

Mrs. Roosevelt was echoing the language of Lincoln and the early Republican Party, but anti–New Deal Republicans fretted that the Black community was getting benefits from government. This belief harked back to the concerns about communism in the early Reconstruction years and tied into James Henry Hammond's insistence that, given political power, a Black underclass would force the redistribution of wealth. In reality, the New Deal retained a number of racially discriminatory policies and never addressed race and ethnicity evenly, but its imperfect record was enough to send traditional Republicans into a frenzy.

The shrill fury of the Republicans worried observers. In Italy, Benito Mussolini had developed fascism, a form of government based on staunch nationalism and the creation of a police state ruled by a political and economic elite. Inspired by Mussolini's example, Adolf Hitler was building a similar system in Germany. Few Americans were paying attention to Japan, but some diplomats familiar with Asia were beginning to worry that the political assassinations in that country looked a lot like the fascism in Europe. When Japan invaded Manchuria in 1937, then demanded total loyalty from its people during the war, it was clear that in Japan, as well as in Italy and Germany, the government was stamping out socialism, as well as any sort of democratic impulse, harshly.

Could that form of government come to America? Many worried that the answer was yes. In 1933, Walter Huston, founder of the Huston acting dynasty, starred in *Gabriel over the White House*, a film in which the angel Gabriel possesses the Hoover-like president and makes him a dictator, who dissolves Congress, destroys civil liberties, and summarily executes criminals. Shockingly, the film was not a cautionary tale; it was a prescription. In 1936, FDR faced a strong challenge for control of the Democratic Party from Louisiana senator Huey Long, who had come to wield dictatorial power in his state and boasted more than 7.5 million followers. Father Charles Coughlin, the "radio priest," was another potential dictator. He had begun as a staunch supporter of FDR, but by the mid-1930s his diatribes had slid away from social justice into virulent anti-Semitism, nationalism, and fascism. Father Coughlin's radio audience was huge; by the mid-1930s he was receiving more than ten thousand letters a day.[30]

By 1935, Americans flirting with fascism were numerous enough that Sinclair Lewis penned his famous novel *It Can't Happen Here*, the picture of a horrific world in which an elected president becomes a dictator, rounds up opponents and throws them into prison camps, and creates an American version of the German SS, called the MM—the Minute Men—a "patriotic" army. Lewis is often credited with saying that when fascism came to America it would come wrapped in the flag and carrying a cross, but in fact that language came from a Methodist minister, Halford E. Luccock, who taught at Yale. In 1938, in a speech the *New York Times* reprinted, Luccock warned that when fascism came to America it would be called "Americanism." "The high-sounding phrase 'the

American way' will be used by interested groups, intent on profit, to cover a multitude of sins against the American and Christian tradition, such sins as lawless violence, tear gas and shotguns, denial of civil liberties," he intoned. Never, he said, "has there been a time when there was a more vigorous effort to surround social and international questions with such a fog of distortion and prejudice and hysterical appeal to fear... to whip up fear and prejudice against many causes of human welfare, such as a concern for peace and the rights of labor to bargain collectively."[31]

In 1936, the anti–New Dealers controlled the Republican Party. In that year's presidential election, Republicans went before the country arguing that the Democratic administration's policies threatened freedom and individual enterprise and made people dependent on government. Democrats had started a class war against the rich and were breeding such "fear and hesitation in commerce and industry" that they were prolonging the Depression. The real reason for the New Deal was not to relieve those destroyed by the economic crash, Republicans insisted, but rather to build up a bureaucracy to keep Democrats in power. The Republican Party's platform invited "all Americans, irrespective of party, to join us in defense of American institutions."[32]

For president, Republicans nominated Kansas governor and wealthy oil executive Alf Landon, who worried that the New Deal was wasteful and stifled business and who retained the Republican hatred for labor organization. Even Landon, though, was willing to accept the idea that 1920s Republicanism could not reign unchanged, and he grudgingly endorsed some mild adjustments to Mellon's values. He still went down to defeat in a landslide, with only 36.5 percent of the vote to FDR's 60.8 percent (he carried only Maine and Vermont).

After the party's disastrous experiment with Alf Landon, its members turned to a new leader who would do what Landon could not: he would resurrect 1920s Republicanism for the future. Ohio Senator Robert A. Taft, President Taft's son, was a ready-made standard-bearer, well-off and with a well-known name, with consistent and well-established ideas. As a young man, Taft had served with Hoover in Europe after World War I, and he had never abandoned Hoover's vision of an old-fashioned world in which individuals worked their way up on their own. A shy, upper-crust midwesterner, Taft had little patience for the new ideas coming from the East, especially eastern cities, about how the government should approach the volatile new economy. He also deeply resented reformers—like Theodore Roosevelt—who had denied his father reelection in 1912.[33]

Taft represented the Republicanism of the late nineteenth century, with its emphasis on small government, fiscal solidity, and isolation from the world. It was lost on men of Taft's stamp that the Republican Party's original expansion of government powers to help business was a deliberate rejection of southerners' strict interpretation of the Constitution. Taft thought that the pro-business slant the party had developed after the Civil War was dictated by the Constitution itself. He believed himself to be a staunch defender of that founding document and that anyone wanting to expand government power for anything other than business growth was striking at the very heart of the nation.[34]

Taft and his supporters believed they were the only true Republicans; others who called themselves Republicans but

were willing to flirt with New Deal reforms were dratted reformers like Theodore Roosevelt, whose unorthodoxy had
split the party in 1912 and handed government to that dangerous Democrat Wilson.[35]

Taft and his ilk found common cause with conservative
southern Democrats, who could not stand the New Deal's
support for African Americans. Anyone agitating against
segregation was "un-American," claimed the president of the
Federation of Citizens Associations. According to him, Black
people weren't poor because they were underprivileged; they
were poor because they were thriftless. This tentative alliance
between Taft Republicans and southern Democrats, launched
in the 1930s, would create a seismic shift in American politics
in the second half of the twentieth century.[36]

As the country became more and more comfortable with
Democratic reforms, the Taft men gripped more and more
tightly to 1920s Republicanism, believing that the New Deal
was socialism, pure and simple. For the rest of the century,
these men and their intellectual heirs would fight any sort of
government activism as an attack on America itself.

Not all Republicans backed the Taft faction. During the first
few years of the New Deal, most Republicans, in fact, gradually came to recognize that the problems of the 1920s had
come from exactly what Lincoln and Theodore Roosevelt had
warned against: the control of government and the economy
by the wealthy. Although that system had brought extraordinary profits for some—just as slavery had—it was not sustainable for a society based on the idea of equality. Some would
be able to manipulate the system so that they would have too

much; the rest would have too little. For the survival of America, these Republicans came to think, the government must keep the legal and economic playing field level.

Leading the moderate Republicans was Thomas E. Dewey, the young Manhattan district attorney who rocketed to fame in 1936 after he successfully prosecuted former Stock Exchange president Richard Whitney—the same man who had told the Senate his sixty-thousand-dollar salary was inadequate—for embezzlement. Members of the Dewey faction accepted government activism to trim the excesses of business. They recognized the value of New Deal policies that employed more than 8.5 million people—whose paychecks saved their families from starvation—built more than 650,000 miles of highways, built or repaired more than 120,000 bridges, and put up more than 125,000 public buildings. They saw that a social safety net, including unemployment and old-age insurance and regulation of food and drug safety, was important in a world where individuals did not control their own food security, housing, or environmental conditions.

This faction of the party accepted the importance of government regulation of banking and the stock market. In 1933, the Democratic Congress tried to prevent another stock market bubble by passing the Federal Securities Act, which required that new issues of stock be registered with the Securities and Exchange Commission (SEC) and that companies issuing stock provide full disclosure to potential investors. It empowered the SEC to curb speculation by regulating margin requirements. In the same year, Congress tried to protect people's money by passing the Glass-Steagall Act, which separated investment banks from deposit banks; expanded the Federal

Reserve System to include savings banks; and created the Federal Deposit Insurance Corporation (FDIC) to insulate individual bank accounts from bankers' mismanagement.

These Republicans were even willing to regulate business in order to expand the middle class. They accepted the Democrats' National Labor Relations Act, popularly known as the Wagner Act, which upheld the right of workers to organize and to bargain collectively, defined unfair labor practices on the part of employers, and established a new National Labor Relations Board that could issue cease and desist orders if workers testified that employers were engaging in unfair labor practices. They also bowed to Democratic establishment of a minimum wage—seventy-five cents an hour—and a maximum work week of forty hours and to the abolition of child labor for youngsters under sixteen.

Where Dewey and his people parted company with Democrats was over, as Dewey said, "faith." He argued that Democrats were defeatists who believed the nation's great days were over and the economy limited, whereas Republicans had "faith in ourselves, in our system, and in our own traditions." The genius of America was private enterprise, Dewey said, but Democratic hostility and repressive taxation had prevented businessmen from restarting the nation's great economic engine. He accepted the government reforms under FDR but called on voters to "restore America's greatness" by rejecting "the decay of the New Deal" and returning to "the vitality of a live and forward-looking America."[37]

Dewey and his supporters took a stand in favor of foreign intervention on the side of Britain and France in the years before

America's entry into World War II, whereas Taft and his men were staunch isolationists. As the war marched closer, the Dewey faction gained the upper hand in the party. By 1940, the Dewey men commanded the presidential nomination, and in 1945, Republicans shaped one of the greatest pieces of social welfare legislation in American history—the G.I. Bill, a law that mirrored the ideology of Abraham Lincoln and that helped to make the 1950s the most prosperous era ever. But as Americans embraced an activist government, the increasing isolation of the Taft men from the modern trend of society, including the opinions of their fellow Republicans, would feed their growing fury.

Their isolation began as the split over America's entry into World War II strengthened the hand of the Dewey men. Taft Republicans echoed Henry Cabot Lodge and deplored the idea of foreign entanglements, but Dewey saw the need for armaments as a great opportunity to rebuild the American economy. He condemned what he saw as FDR's isolationism and called for the nation to pour money and business expertise into defense spending.

When the Japanese bombing of Pearl Harbor in December 1941 ended the American debate over intervening in the war, the Dewey wing's focus on preparation seemed prescient and its power in the party increased. Caught flat-footed, Taft Republicans hinted darkly that FDR had deliberately engineered the attack to involve America in the war in Europe, an accusation that, over time, would become a popular American myth. Taft continued to insist that Americans must leave the Europeans to their own devices and focus on Asia, where American industrialists had done business since the 1870s, and where, if the United States must get involved, he thought it could win with ease. The Dewey faction, with its emphasis on building the military, willingly went along with the administration's focus on Europe and the Allied forces. When that focus turned out to be successful, the Dewey faction gained ground over the Taft faction.[38]

The split over foreign intervention that strengthened the Dewey men also made it difficult for them to develop a coherent Republican vision during World War II. Stand in favor of the war and they would alienate Taft isolationists, who continued to dislike a fight they thought the nation had been tricked into; stand against the war and they would alienate voters. Republicans did pick up proportional strength as workers who supported FDR migrated to the West Coast for jobs in war industries and neglected to register to vote. But the tendency of workers to drop out of the wartime electorate prevented Republicans from developing a strong position; they couldn't attack the New Deal because any assault they made on workers' programs might induce migrants to register to vote, which would cut into the gains the party had made because of their absence.[39]

Even without a strong platform, the Dewey faction beat out the Taft men in 1940 to nominate Wall Street attorney Wendell Willkie for president. This was a wildly dangerous nomination: everyone knew that the looming war would require a brilliant and delicate hand, and Willkie had never held public office. Still, he was a good tactician. Unlike those in the Taft faction, Willkie recognized that the Republican Party had come to an ideological crossroads. He saw that the tariff was no longer a winning political issue and that Republicans must find new causes and supporters. He accepted the New Deal, although he vowed to clean up its inefficiencies and corruption. He also accepted the idea of American involvement in world affairs and blasted FDR for neglecting to prepare the military adequately for war. To bolster the party, he proposed to court the Black vote that Coolidge and Hoover had alienated.

But Willkie's prescription for the party did not convince voters to abandon FDR. The president won reelection with 55 percent of the popular vote to Willkie's 45 percent. Willkie's formula did not get more popular as time went on: when the Republicans nominated Dewey himself in 1944, his share of the vote was almost exactly what Willkie had garnered four years before.

In 1945, Republicans bowed to popular pressure for government activism and sponsored a piece of legislation that transformed the nation: the Servicemen's Readjustment Act, popularly known as the G.I. Bill. Congress had developed the precursor to the Republicans' version of the bill in 1943, when Democrats worried that the 15 million soldiers returning from the war would flood the labor market and bring back the Depression. Democrats wanted unemployment benefits for soldiers, as well as education benefits to keep some in school and out of the job market. They also wanted to guarantee home or business loans of up to two thousand dollars to help returning service men and women transition back to civilian life. Republicans objected to what they saw as a socialist welfare program, but after a great deal of pressure from veterans' groups, they recognized that opposing a measure to help veterans would be political suicide. Almost all Republicans came around to support the bill on the grounds that they were not endorsing a general social welfare program but rather helping veterans, as the government had always done. The Democrats' version of the G.I. Bill passed in 1943, but only two years later it was revised to reflect Republican beliefs.

The end of the war in 1945 revealed that fears of a returning Depression were unwarranted. Most veterans found work: on average, they spent fewer than three months looking for a job; only 14 percent were unemployed for a year. This meant that the unemployment benefits of the bill were far less important than the educational provisions. In late 1945, Congress revised the bill to reflect Republicans' focus on economic growth rather than Democrats' fears of returning unemployment. The new bill increased both the reimbursement amounts the government provided schools and the stipends it offered veterans. The G.I. Bill was no longer a defense against recession; it had become an agent for economic growth.

The G.I. Bill helped four million veterans buy homes. House construction pumped up building trades. Once built, the homes continued to boost the economy. Soon they would fill with children who wore diapers and clothes, ate, played with toys, rode bikes, went to school, wore out the furniture, and before long would watch television. The baby boom that followed the war created such demand for domestic products that one commercially produced 1962 card to congratulate parents on a new baby read: "Wonderful News!!...for the diaper service...greeting card publishers...Toy Shops...orthodontist...infants wear department...carriage makers...milk man...super market...pediatricians...furniture manufacturers...shoe salesmen...department stores...p.s. also good for Income Tax Deductions...congratulations!"[40]

The G.I. Bill enabled veterans to get vocational training or a college degree. Fifty-one percent of veterans—7.8 million—went back to school. Women and African Americans were eligible for the provisions of the bill, but its benefits went largely to white men. Colleges and universities built apartment complexes and new academic buildings to accommodate the mature students who were, in some cases, more than doubling the student body. Returning soldiers tended to be serious students, determined to succeed. The G.I. Bill added to the American workforce not only skilled managers but also 450,000 engineers, 180,000 medical professionals, 360,000 teachers, 150,000 scientists, 243,000 accountants, 107,000 lawyers, and 36,000 clergymen.[41]

By providing homes and higher education to almost 8 million Americans, the G.I. Bill transformed America. Millions of families vaulted into the middle class and enjoyed a standard of living unimaginable before the war. Initially forced into supporting the G.I. Bill by veterans' groups, Republicans helped to resurrect the vision of the original Republicans, who in 1862 passed the Homestead Act and the Land-Grant College Act to provide poorer Americans with the means to fund homes and get an education. In doing so, they laid the foundation for an economic boom of astounding proportions.

The sudden death of FDR from a massive cerebral hemorrhage on April 12, 1945, just after the start of his fourth term, relieved Republicans' political paralysis. Because FDR was so personally popular, the Democratic Party had not built up much of a grassroots organization, and the elevation of Vice President Harry S. Truman to the presidency without a strong machine behind him opened the way for a Republican resurgence, especially when Truman had to deal with the inevitable turmoil of a society demobilizing from a world war. Republicans gained ground, which, in turn, strengthened the Taft wing of the party. As their power grew, Taft Republicans joined with conservative southern Democrats to begin dismantling the New Deal.

The end of the war shocked the American economy. The story went that you could not make a phone call in Washington the day after Japan surrendered in August 1945 because the telephone lines were jammed by officials calling to cancel contracts. At the same time, unions, which during the war had enrolled more than thirteen million members out of a total employed population of about fifty-four million—about 22 percent of the labor force—struck for higher wages and for pensions. Also in the mix was inflation, for by 1946, the government was ending wartime price controls and rationing, and pent-up demand drove prices up. The combination of ending government contracts, labor agitation, and rising prices spelled trouble for the president.[42]

With Truman's popularity at an all-time low, Republicans swept the 1946 midterm election. For the first time since 1928, they commanded both houses of Congress. Finally, after more than a decade in the wilderness, they were emerging back into the light. No one was happier about the change in the party's fortunes than Senator Taft, who as chairman of the Republican Policy Committee was the party's de facto leader. Although people had voted for Republicans in the usual rejection of the party occupying the White House during the midterms, and the G.I. Bill to which Republicans had signed on was enormously popular, Taft interpreted the election as a mandate to dismantle the New Deal entirely and to stop government from meddling—as he put it—with business.[43]

In 1947, confirming a new alliance that would recast American politics for the next two generations, Taft men began to work with wealthy southern Democrats who hated the New Deal's civil rights legislation and taxes. Together, they blocked initiatives to expand government programs, convinced that Truman and his New Deal–type policies were leading America to the communism that was spreading across eastern Europe. Echoing the arguments of 1871 that had broken the original Republican vision, they claimed that the president wanted to tax Americans for the support of a huge government, to destroy individual enterprise, to ruin "home rule"—this was a veiled reference to southern racial laws—in short, to become a dictator. Furious when Congress stopped him at every turn, Truman dubbed the Eightieth Congress the "Do Nothing Congress."[44]

Taft Republicans stymied Truman, and their alliance with southern Democrats enabled them to push through their own measures to restore Republican policies of the 1920s. Over Truman's veto, Taft and his Democratic allies cut income and estate taxes—a $4.8 billion tax slash, according to the *New York Times*—although they continued to rail at the nation's huge debt. Old-line conservatives complained that cutting taxes would create inflation and ruin the nation's ability to pay off its debt, but Taft Republicans responded with Mellon's argument: cutting taxes would boost business, and a strong business sector would take care of everything else.[45]

Also over Truman's veto, they passed the Reed-Bulwinkle Act, which permitted railroads to collude on rates without fear of antitrust suits, as long as the Interstate Commerce Commission (ICC) approved. This would, the *New York Times* calculated, save railroads one hundred million dollars annually and knock the bottom out of ongoing antitrust suits against big carriers. The news instantly boosted railroad stocks, and the railroads immediately applied to the ICC to raise rates.[46]

In 1947, Republicans joined with southern Democrats to attack the heart of New Deal principles. Over Truman's veto, they passed the Taft-Hartley Act, undermining the Wagner Act, which had been a central piece of FDR's reworking of the American economy; it gave workers a unified voice in American politics and leveled the playing field between them and employers. Taft men hated the Wagner Act because it established that if a majority of a company's workers voted to join a union, that union would represent all the workers in the company. This provision was intended to increase the power of organized workers, but, paradoxically, it created a problem for unions: if workers were going to get the benefits of union representation without joining, why should they pony up dues? Labor leaders responded by writing "union shop" provisions into contracts, requiring that everyone employed in a company must join the union. Taft men hated this system because it put large sums of money into the hands of labor officials, who used them to influence politics.[47]

Taft claimed that the Taft-Hartley Act would simply equalize power between workers and employers, a relationship that had been skewed when the "completely one-sided"

Wagner Act gave all the power to labor leaders. Taft-Hartley weakened labor organizations' ability to strike and outlawed the closed shop that hired only union men. It enabled the government to stop strikes that affected public safety. Taft-Hartley also prevented unions from donating to national political campaigns, and it required labor leaders to swear they were not communists.[48]

Republicans directly attacked the communism they believed had infiltrated the highest levels of American government. They prodded Truman's Justice Department to make a list of subversive organizations, membership in which—either current or past—would indicate disloyalty and be grounds for firing from federal jobs. When the list emerged in October 1947, it included a number of civil rights and labor organizations, including one endorsed by Eleanor Roosevelt. Clearly, Republicans expected to find communists in government. Abraham L. Pomerantz, senior counsel at the Nuremberg war crimes trials, pointed out that even accused Nazis received more constitutional protections than federal employees.[49]

Even more visibly, under the glare of television floodlights, Congress went after communists in Hollywood who were, congressmen alleged, spreading propaganda to undermine American capitalism. With the Republican victory in 1948, the House Committee on Un-American Activities became the congressional arm of the Taft Republicans' anticommunism campaign, the place where a new representative from California, Richard M. Nixon, would gain visibility.

On October 20, 1947, the committee began hearings to show that communists had wormed their way into Hollywood and that FDR's men had promoted communist propaganda.

The committee commanded a number of people engaged in film production to testify. The hearings split the country. On one hand, Walt Disney insisted that communists had inspired his workers to strike and were trying to ruin him, and Gary Cooper explained that he had been shocked by the "pinko scripts" he saw. On the other hand, Henry Fonda and Katharine Hepburn declared their utter opposition to what they saw as a smear campaign. Republican congressmen in turn attacked as disloyal anyone suggesting that the hearings offended free speech and the right to defend oneself in court. Ten of those commanded to appear refused to testify, citing their right to free speech and free assembly. They were cited for contempt of Congress. The Hollywood Ten, as they were known, were blacklisted and shut out of the film industry.[50]

Once under way, the hunt for communists in California led the Screen Actors Guild to require its officers to swear they were not communists. The union's president, a handsome thirty-six-year-old actor named Ronald Reagan, loved both his union and his country. He testified before Congress that there were indeed communists in Hollywood but that they couldn't gain much ground. He gave similar information to the FBI—although he was in no position to know anything that wasn't already public—but at the same time had a reputation in Hollywood as being kind, fair, and caring of the actors in his union.[51]

It seemed the Republicans were gaining momentum to win back the White House in 1948. Indeed, Taft was ready to bank on the idea that he was going to be the next president. The Taft-Hartley debates had made him the most prominent Republican in the country, and he fully expected the nomination. He was heartbroken when Republicans at the sweltering Philadelphia convention in June recognized that his victories had been carefully staged in a Washington bubble and that his old-fashioned stances would never fly in New Deal America. They again nominated Thomas Dewey for president, with California governor Earl Warren as his running mate. In the first televised national convention, the party wrote a platform that included calls for expanding Social Security and education, federal civil rights legislation, equal pay for women, farm price supports, and international involvement, as well as Taft's lower taxes and anticommunism.[52]

Republicans went into the election with a great structural advantage. The Democrats had split—not just in two, but into three. Truman led the regular party. Progressive Democrats opposed him with their own candidate, Henry A. Wallace, who had been FDR's vice president before Truman. Finally fed up with their party's support for Black rights—which the convention included in the 1948 platform in an attempt to attract new Black urban voters—southern white Democrats ran their own "Dixiecrat" candidate: South Carolina's forty-five-year-old governor Strom Thurmond, who stood against civil rights and backed segregation (although unbeknownst to the public for decades to come, he had fathered a biracial daughter in his early twenties).

Pollsters trumpeted that Dewey would win. So sure was the editorial board of the staunchly Republican *Chicago Tribune* of Dewey's victory that it allowed a few hundred copies of the November 3, 1948, edition onto newsstands announcing DEWEY DEFEATS TRUMAN. But the laugh was on them. It was a jubilant and reelected Truman who stood holding the issue above his head for a cameraman in St. Louis.

Taft and his followers had been wrong. Americans liked the New Deal reforms—especially those that defended laborers—and did not want them expunged. The vote was not even particularly close. Truman captured 49.5 percent of the popular vote to Dewey's 45.1 percent. Thurmond's segregationists won 2.4 percent of the vote, capturing more than a million votes in the Deep South; Wallace's Progressives peeled off another 2.3 percent. The Democrats regained control of both houses of Congress. It seemed the old-fashioned vision of the Taft Republicans was not the way to compete with the New Deal.

9

A New Republican Vision

A new Republican vision to compete with FDR's Democratic worldview came from an unexpected quarter: the victorious Allied general of World War II. Dwight Eisenhower had given a great deal of thought to the true nature of American government as he planned and executed the war in Europe. His conclusions reshaped Lincoln's vision for the modern world. In Eisenhower's hands, an active American government would promote a strong middle class, just as Lincoln had planned, but its reach would not be bounded by the nation's borders; under Eisenhower, America would promote prosperity across the globe.

Born in rural Texas in October 1890 and transplanted to Abilene, Kansas, as a toddler, Eisenhower grew up in a hardscrabble family of six boys whose parents barely managed to keep them fed. When Eisenhower and his brothers were tussling with neighbor boys and sneaking out of school, Abilene was still a typical nineteenth-century town. Its streets were unpaved, it had a single police officer, and its few storeowners made no effort to advertise: they knew that people would come to them when they needed something. A nickel would buy a dozen eggs; three cents, a loaf of bread.[1]

In the traditionally Republican state of Kansas, Eisenhower was a Republican both by geography and by heritage— his uncle was named Abraham Lincoln Eisenhower—and his life echoed Lincoln's vision for America. The family kept chickens, cows, and horses as well as a garden, and Eisenhower's father worked as an engineer at a creamery to earn the cash necessary to keep his household running. He encouraged his sons to work, too. Dwight raised corn and cucumbers to sell; as he grew older, he picked apples, harvested wheat, riveted grain bins, and packed ice. In such a small town, even the few men with office jobs also worked with their hands. There was little social stratification, and the richest man in town—according to local legend, at any rate—made only $125 a month.[2]

Eisenhower went to West Point for college, and the army educated him outside the classroom as well as inside it. His superior officers recognized that he was brilliant at organization, and during World War I they placed him in charge of a camp to prepare men for deployment overseas. He came to disdain the interference of politicians whose eagerness to keep their supporters happy came up against his own determination to apply regulations impartially. Eisenhower did not take kindly to political arm-twisting. Encounters with politicians convinced him that they often put the good of their constituents and their own careers over the good of the country.[3]

In 1919, Eisenhower volunteered to take part in a truck convoy—from Washington, D.C., to San Francisco—designed to dramatize America's need for better highways. Unsafe wooden bridges, terrible grades, mud, and breaking equipment meant that the convoy proved its point: in the two months it took to cross the country, it never averaged above ten miles an hour. As the trucks leaped and balked down the main streets of small towns and cities across the middle of the country, Eisenhower had plenty of time to look around. He saw people recovering from the war and the devastating influenza epidemic that followed but who were optimistic about their future and looked forward to it. Welcoming committees greeted the officers, and Eisenhower drew the men out about local interests and industries. What he saw would later enable him to reconceive the nation's role in the world.[4]

The army's greatest contribution to Eisenhower's education was the three years he spent in Panama as an aide to General Fox Connor. Connor recognized the young man's intelligence and encouraged him to explore military history, tactics, and philosophy. They discussed the Battle of Gettysburg, terrain, and Shakespeare. Eisenhower later called his years with Connor "a sort of graduate school in military affairs and the humanities." The older man quietly trained the younger one in logistics by making him write daily field orders. A keen student of foreign affairs, Connor impressed on his young aide that America's refusal to join the League of Nations meant another world war was on the horizon. He warned Eisenhower to be ready.[5]

Connor arranged for his protégé to attend the Command and General Staff School at Fort Leavenworth in August 1925. Eisenhower graduated first in his class, then spent time under General John J. Pershing writing a guide to American World War I battlefields in Europe. From there, he was assigned to

the Army War College, where he studied strategy and continued to prepare to be a military leader. To his dismay, his
talents—including the writing skills he had developed under
Pershing—made him a good candidate to become the chief
aide to the army chief of staff, General Douglas MacArthur.
When his superiors conspired to get rid of the difficult MacArthur by sending him off to advise the Philippine government
on the organization of their military, Eisenhower went with
him. From 1935 to 1939, he steamed in Manila.

In 1939, Eisenhower was posted back to the United States.
After the Japanese bombing of Pearl Harbor, his climb through
the upper ranks of the army was swift. While rivals sniped at
his lack of experience in active command, superiors recognized his genius for long-range planning. In November 1942,
the Combined American and British Chiefs of Staff made him
the supreme commander of the Allied forces in North Africa.
A year later, they made him the supreme Allied commander
in Europe. Two years later the war was over, on Eisenhower's
terms.

A new era in world history had begun.

Eisenhower understood that new era more profoundly than
most of his contemporaries. He had grown up in small-town
America, in a world that looked much like that of the nineteenth century. America in his childhood was still bounded by
tariff walls and looking inward, isolated from other countries.
He had grown up as Theodore Roosevelt pulled the nation
into the war against Spain and onto the international stage,
and he had fidgeted when he wasn't deployed to fight in Europe in World War I.

The end of World War I did not usher in the era of peace and prosperity for which Americans had hoped. Just over a decade after the guns stopped firing, the Western world was mired in the worst depression it had ever seen. For Eisenhower and most other Americans, the Great Depression profoundly changed the way they thought about the government and the economy. After the Civil War, the government had repressed those perceived to be "socialists" or "communists": the railroad strikers in 1877, the "armies" marching on Washington with Coxey and Kelly during the recession of the 1890s, the Wobblies in 1919. In the post–World War II years, the perspectives of men like Eisenhower were dramatically different. They did not see disaffected workers as a threat to the American way; rather, protesters identified important inequalities the government must address. Protecting equality had come to rank above all else in Eisenhower's worldview.

Eisenhower's experiences in World War II convinced him that nothing—literally nothing—was more important in the modern world than political and economic equality. For him, the war was not simply a military conflict; it was an illustration of what could happen when societies were destabilized by inequality.

In April 1945, US soldiers liberated Ohrdruf, the Nazi concentration camp that funneled prisoners to Buchenwald. They were unprepared for what confronted them: stacks of bodies still smoldering from a last-minute attempt to destroy evidence of mass murders, living men so starved they could not move. Eisenhower visited the site a week later, and he was shocked to the core. "I never dreamed that such cruelty, bestiality, and savagery could really exist in this world!" he wrote.

Determined to do all he could to guarantee that such atrocities never happened again, he urged reporters and congressmen to visit the camp to ensure there were witnesses, pictures, and films to gainsay anyone who might, in the future, try to deny the horrors had taken place. He ordered every soldier in the area not on the front lines to visit both Ohrdruf and Buchenwald, and he ordered every citizen of Gotha, the town nearest Ohrdruf, to go see what had happened on their watch (the mayor and his wife went home from their visit and hanged themselves).[6]

Eisenhower had faith in America, and, like other Republicans before him, he staunchly believed that economic freedom underpinned everything else. The American ideal was economic opportunity for all, and he was convinced it must be exported to the world to prevent the extremes of wealth and poverty that permitted the rise of political extremism within nations. He opposed communism, but he equally feared the fascism that had produced Ohrdruf and a world war of dizzying proportions.[7]

Eisenhower recognized that economically dispossessed people were natural targets for political and religious extremists. They could easily be manipulated by a strong leader to back a cause—any cause—that promised to resurrect a world in which they had enjoyed prosperity and cultural significance. Such extremism had been dangerous enough in the hands of the Nazis, but 1945 gave quite specific shape to Eisenhower's fears. The atomic bomb, unleashed by the United States over Hiroshima and Nagasaki in summer 1945, changed the meaning of human conflict. If a charismatic political or religious extremist roused a dispossessed population behind another war, and if that leader got his hands on a nuclear weapon, he could destroy the world.[8]

Democracy, Eisenhower believed, was at a crisis. Future global wars would be ideological, he thought: a struggle between individualism and "statism." The USSR was exporting its state-centered ideology to other countries as quickly as it could, putting individualism "under deadly, persistent, and constant attack." To counter the spread of Soviet ideology, Americans must promote democracy, and the way to do this was by showing its great ability to increase economic productivity and standards of living. Guaranteeing prosperity to the world was no longer just about peace or justice. It was the only way to save humankind.[9]

Eisenhower's worldview would not become public right away. Truman's reelection in 1948 had convinced Taft men that the problem with the Republican Party was that it continued to be a "me too" party. Republicans had done everything right in the 1920s, they insisted, and should not cave in to pressure for government programs. True Republicans believed in small government and pro-business policies; anyone who advocated government action to bolster the position of anyone but businessmen was not a Republican. In their view, any government activism aside from the promotion of business took America down the road to communism. Republicans must not tag along behind Democrats into an immoral morass; they must stand firm on the principles of Coolidge and Hoover.[10]

Taft had been hurt when Republican kingmakers bypassed him to nominate Dewey in 1948, and he was horrified when Dewey refused to repudiate the New Deal and seemed, in

Taft's view, to run a "me too" candidacy. Dewey's ignomini-
ous defeat convinced Taft that he was right: Republicans must
take a hard line back to the past, drawing a clear distinction
between themselves and New Deal Democrats. When eastern
Republicans talked of bowing to popular pressure for a social
safety net, he saw them and anyone else who disagreed with
him as an enemy, both of him and of America—someone
who wanted to use the government to redistribute wealth. A
communist.

Taft's characterization of anyone but a 1920s Republican
as having communist tendencies drew from Republican history all the way back to Reconstruction, but it had new power
during the 1950s. Republicans had worried about communism
since the 1870s, when news of the Paris Commune had made
them fear that politically active Black workers in the South
and white workers in northern cities would try to redistribute
wealth in America as the Communards had tried in France.
Since then, Republicans had interpreted virtually every attempt to use government to level the playing field between
workers and employers as the creeping tentacles of communism. The Russian Revolution of 1917 had sparked the Red
Scare in America just after World War I, a time when men
like Taft had come of political age. Then, in China in 1949,
the communist forces of Mao Zedong pushed the nationalist
government of Chiang Kai-shek to the island of Formosa (now
Taiwan) and established a communist government on the
mainland.

The Communist takeover of China fed the anticommunism of Taft Republicans. In the tense years before the outbreak of World War II, Taft men and their allies who had

business interests in China had insisted that America must involve itself in Asia rather than Europe, but they had been overruled by the Democratic president and lawmakers. Taft men saw the Communist takeover in China as evidence that, at best, the Democrats had been misguided in their foreign policy. At worst, government officials had deliberately colluded to allow communism to spread. Few, if any, Americans were happy about the revolution in China, but for Republicans already afraid that New Deal reforms were domestic communism, the addition of the huge country of China to the ranks of international communism was horrifying.[11]

An undistinguished Republican junior senator from Wisconsin helped Taft men spread their political fears across the nation. On February 9, 1950, Joseph McCarthy stood before a group gathered to celebrate Lincoln's birthday in Wheeling, West Virginia. He announced that there were 205 members of the Communist Party working in the State Department to shape national policy, and that the Democratic secretary of state, Dean Acheson, knew it. McCarthy said he didn't have time to mention the names of all those individuals, but he assured his audience that the Truman administration was refusing to investigate "traitors in the government."[12]

The staunchly Republican *Chicago Tribune* trumpeted the story, and the next day McCarthy pledged to share the names of "57 card carrying Communists" in the State Department with Acheson, so long as the secretary would let Congress investigate the loyalty records of the people in his department. Acheson had been instrumental in developing the Marshall Plan to rebuild Europe after World War II, and the previous year he had worked hard to bring twelve Western countries together as the North

Atlantic Treaty Organization (NATO) to counter the military might of the USSR. Taft Republicans, who wanted no part in foreign involvement, especially in Europe, hated both plans. McCarthy's clear message was that Secretary of State Acheson was deliberately protecting communists within his own ranks. The next day, McCarthy telegraphed Truman, charging him with protecting communists in government; the *Chicago Tribune* showcased the accusations on the front page, and McCarthy had his office send out copies of the missive. "Failure on your part will label the Democratic party as being the bed-fellow of international Communism," McCarthy wrote.[13]

State Department officials demanded that McCarthy substantiate his claims; the *Washington Post* condemned McCarthy's "Sewer Politics" and charged him with trying to undercut the State Department's accurate assessment of Asian politics; and the *New York Times* bemoaned his "hit-and-run" attacks on the State Department. But their outrage gained far less attention than the senator's claims themselves. McCarthy had perfected the art of staying one step ahead of the reporters checking his stories. By the time the reporters called him on his fabrications, the lies were already old news, and the fact checking got buried deep in the papers. On the first page would be McCarthy's newest accusation.[14]

Taft Republicans jumped on board. Taft himself—the one man who might have toned down McCarthy's extremism— praised the senator. The *Chicago Tribune* attacked President Truman and insisted that McCarthy's charges "cannot be laughed down or pooh-poohed away."[15]

Dewey Republicans pushed back against the senator from Wisconsin but had little success. On June 1, 1950, Maine senator Margaret Chase Smith stood up two rows in front of Senator McCarthy to deliver what she called a "Declaration of Conscience." "I speak as a Republican, I speak as a woman. I speak as a United States Senator. I speak as an American," she began. Smith wanted Republicans to win the upcoming elections as much as anyone, she explained, but she did not want to see "the Republican Party ride to political victory on the Four Horsemen of Calumny—Fear, Ignorance, Bigotry and Smear." She concluded, "As an American, I condemn a Republican 'Fascist' just as much as I condemn a Democrat 'Communist.' They are equally dangerous to you and me and to our country." The Dewey wing of the party quietly applauded Smith, but only six Republican senators concurred in her declaration. For his part, McCarthy sneered at "Snow White and the Six Dwarves."[16]

McCarthy was not worried about Dewey Republicans. He had gained enormous power in the country at large, and the outbreak of the Korean War in June 1950, when communist North Korea, backed by the Soviet Union, invaded South Korea, stoked anticommunism even further. Before the 1950 midterm elections, he spoke widely, and every candidate he endorsed won. His message of staunch anticommunism harmonized with what Taft Republicans had been saying for years: only Republicans would fight communism both abroad and at home.

Taft was reelected to the Senate on just such a platform in 1950, and his reelection convinced him that the American people wanted a revival of old-fashioned Republican policies. The waffling "Me Too" Republicans had their chance in 1948, and the result was embarrassing. As the undisputed leader of the old-fashioned Republican faction, the faction that had produced McCarthy's winning formula, he fully expected the Republican nomination for president in 1952.[17]

Taft was in for a nasty surprise. His rock-ribbed conviction that 1920s Republicanism was the only true course for the nation horrified Eisenhower, who saw clearly that the safety of the world depended on American leadership abroad. Coming out of World War II, the general had no interest in politics. He had seen how politicians were hamstrung by the need to please interest groups, and he believed the problems of the day were too big for political machinations. Repeatedly, he insisted he would not run for president, a refusal many dismissed as posturing but to which he held even in his most private writing. It took a strong push to make him launch a political career. Ironically, that push came from Taft, the man most interested in keeping Eisenhower out of politics.

Eisenhower's sole foray into the political world had been carrying a torch in a McKinley parade when he was six. Convinced that the military should stay above the political fray, the general had never voted, and he kept his political cards close to his vest. No one knew which party claimed his loyalties. Both Democrats and Republicans asked him to become their presidential candidate in 1948. He refused.[18]

Instead, Eisenhower accepted the presidency of Columbia University, a seemingly odd choice for a victorious general but a fitting one for a man whose approach to war had been shaped by understanding history, foreign affairs, and philosophy. Like Progressive Republicans who had put their faith in expert advice, Eisenhower believed academic study could inform intelligent approaches to the grave problems of economic fairness in a post–World War II world. He accepted the Columbia presidency with the understanding that he would devote much of his time to developing a think tank to bring together the nation's greatest minds to solve the problems of the postwar nation. In 1950, he founded the American Assembly, an organization he considered one of his greatest accomplishments.

Eisenhower soon left Columbia and turned his hand to politics. He worried about the increasing power of the federal government and the growing budgets under the Democrats but was even more concerned about the isolationism of Taft Republicans. Eisenhower finally decided he had to oppose the Taft wing of the party publicly over Korea. As soon as North Korea had launched the invasion, the United States had committed troops to stop the advance, launching America into a new foreign war only five years after the end of World War II.

American officials worried that the communist advance into South Korea was a feint to enable the USSR to invade a woefully underprepared Western Europe. When the North Koreans advanced, NATO, which had organized the previous year, wasn't much more than a piece of paper. Truman asked Eisenhower to travel to Europe to oversee the region's rearmament.[19]

After a tour of Europe, Eisenhower returned to America to report. He tried to enlist Taft's support for NATO, but Taft wanted to cut all foreign aid, not increase it. Taft was a shoo-in for the 1952 Republican presidential nomination. If he won the presidency, he would kill American efforts to undercut political and religious extremism by raising living conditions around the world. Eisenhower saw Taft's isolationism as catastrophic. He promised Taft that if the senator would back NATO, Eisenhower would not challenge him for the presidency. Taft refused. Eisenhower seemed to have no choice but to yield to those insisting that he run for president. In 1952, as one reporter wrote, the general "put aside his five stars and tried for forty-eight."[20]

The Republican Convention met in the broiling heat of a Chicago July. Taft had the machinery of the Republican Party behind him and 530 of the 630 delegate votes he needed to win the nomination. Eisenhower had the enormous popularity of the man who had won D-Day. He also had the support of the Dewey Republicans, who controlled the key state of New York. Dewey and Henry Cabot Lodge Jr. (the grandson of Henry Cabot Lodge) worked to swing the nomination to Eisenhower. After a bitter contest between the two factions, including fistfights and accusations by Taft men that the Eisenhower boom would, once again, lead the party down the road to defeat, Eisenhower emerged as the party's 1952 candidate for president.[21]

For vice president, the convention nominated a fierce anticommunist who had gained the approbation of the Taft camp, Senator Richard Nixon of California. The addition of Nixon to the ticket did not quell the fury of the Taft men. They condemned what they called the "Eastern Establishment": the Dewey New Yorkers who called themselves Republican, but were polluting the party and the true meaning of what it meant to be an American.

In the sweep of American history, Eisenhower's nomination seems almost inevitable, but because of the tension between the Taft and Dewey-Eisenhower wings of the party it sparked a profound crisis. Taft had expected the nomination, and Eisenhower's contention for it infuriated Taft loyalists. The bitter rift between Eisenhower men and Taft support-ers would reverberate in American politics for the next two generations, as the very success of Eisenhower and his poli-cies would convince Taft men and their heirs that they were the embattled victims of an international conspiracy to spread communism. Over the next decades, Republicans in the Taft mold would come to believe that they, and they alone, were good Americans. Everyone else must be purged first from the government, then from the Republican Party, and eventually from America's political system.

Eisenhower, the last president born in the nineteenth century, spoke in the classic nineteenth-century Republican style, but he had at his disposal technologies that would drag politics into a new era. Despite the profundity of his worldview, Ei-senhower's campaign message was simple and easily com-municated. As Theodore Roosevelt had done before him, Eisenhower promised to stop government corruption. He pledged to appoint to office honest men and women. He also told voters he would go to Korea himself to end the simmering war. The Republican campaign committee ran on what they called the K1C2 message: Korea, Communism, and Corrup-tion. Republicans had an attractive message and Eisenhower's enormous personal popularity to back it. "I Like Ike" was the campaign's catchphrase.[22]

But what Republicans really had going for them was new technology to shape and communicate their message across the nation. Eisenhower, with his love of travel and people, met cheering crowds with enthusiasm. As candidates had done for decades, he stumped the country by train, meeting with local politicians to boost local tickets and shake as many hands as possible. In 1952, though, for the first time ever, both Eisenhower and the Democratic nominee, Illinois governor Adlai Stevenson, also used airplanes. Eisenhower traveled 30,505 air miles on the campaign and 20,871 by train.[23]

The candidates also began to use the new medium of television. The 1948 political conventions had inaugurated the use of television, but the cameras had simply recorded the regular business of a convention, its sweating delegates, dull speeches, and cheesy hoopla. In 1952, Eisenhower's people staged events for television audiences. They arranged for their candidate to appear with Hollywood entertainers, and they distributed ticker tape and confetti to workers along parade routes to give an air of triumphant procession. (One excited man in Los Angeles nearly brained Eisenhower when he threw his block of confetti still in its unopened package.)[24]

Television allowed the Eisenhower campaign to craft simple messages that would prompt emotional, rather than intellectual, responses. When opponents accused Nixon of accepting gifts from political donors, the Republican National Committee paid for him to address the "Fund Crisis" in a half-hour televised speech. Nixon explained to the television audience that the eighteen-thousand-dollar slush fund used to promote his Senate bid was a reflection of good character, not bad. Most politicians used inherited wealth to pay the costs of their campaigns, he said, but he was a man of modest means. In an unprecedented discussion of a candidate's finances, he explained that he had worked in the family grocery store as a child, had worked to put himself through college, and that he and his wife, Pat, had both worked until he went into the army. They lived cheaply and saved to buy a house. They still paid a mortgage and owed another eighty-five hundred dollars. They drove an old car. "That's about it," Nixon said. "It isn't very much. But...every dime that we've got is honestly ours." Pat doesn't have a mink coat, he went on, "but she does have a respectable Republican cloth coat, and I always tell her she'd look good in anything." The one gift he'd received, he said, was "a little cocker spaniel dog." Nixon's six-year-old daughter had named it Checkers, and "We're gonna keep it."[25]

The Checkers speech reached an astonishing sixty million people, many of whom identified with Nixon's story of hard work and a difficult rise to respectability. Commenters noted that the speech did not really answer the question of the propriety of the fund, but it hardly mattered. Nixon's story had defined him as an honest, hardworking man. When the scandal broke, Eisenhower had considered dropping Nixon, but after the Checkers speech, Nixon's place on the 1952 Republican ticket—and in history—was secure. From then on, no politician would ignore the immense power of a carefully crafted television message.

Eisenhower and Nixon won with almost 55 percent of the vote to Adlai Stevenson's 44.5 percent. Republicans were back in the White House. They also controlled Congress. Eisenhower had the mandate he needed to create a just, prosperous, and safe world. What he did not have was the support of Taft men in his own party, who utterly rejected the popular new concept of American government and who would launch a new kind of political warfare during his administration, in an attempt to kill government regulation and social welfare programs once and for all.

Still, Eisenhower had every reason to expect that he had been given the chance to remake the modern world as he envisioned it. His first message to Congress reclaimed both the ideology of Abraham Lincoln and Theodore Roosevelt and their determination to represent all Americans, not just members of their party. He refused to separate the interests of labor and capital, believing that smart economic policies would benefit everyone. On one hand, he called for a reduction of the national debt, a balanced budget, low inflation, and then, when those things were safely on track, a reduction in taxes. On the other, he insisted on the right of laborers to bargain collectively and recognized that they must have salaries high enough to buy what they needed. Together, both halves of this equation would promote the universal prosperity on which the world depended. "We all—workers and farmers, foremen and financiers, technicians and builders—all must produce, produce more, and produce yet more," he said. Only such productivity could guarantee the economic balance in the world that would produce religious and political stability.

Eisenhower adapted his predecessors' ideology to the modern era. He explained that the new economy had created two great needs. First, he said, individuals must have safeguards against disasters created by forces outside their control. Second, the government must perform certain indispensable social services. It must cover people suffering from unemployment, old age, illness, and accident. It must protect them from unsafe food and drugs. It must address the needs for health care and housing. And, just as Lincoln and Roosevelt had insisted, it must promote education.

Eisenhower gave a new name to this vision of the world. He called it "a middle way between untrammeled freedom of the individual and the demands of the welfare of the whole Nation.... In this spirit must we live and labor," he concluded, "confident of our strength, compassionate in our heart, clear in our mind." The philosophy that underlay modern Republicanism, one of Eisenhower's supporters wrote, was "If a job has to be done to meet the needs of the people, and no one else can do it, then it is the proper function of the federal government."[26]

The president pushed his vision first in international affairs. In early March 1953, soon after Eisenhower took office, Soviet leader Josef Stalin died, giving the president a chance to reset the growing hostility between the United States and the USSR. In mid-April, in a speech to newspaper editors that he insisted on delivering although he was suffering acutely from inflammatory bowel disease, Eisenhower articulated his vision for the world's future.

All people hungered for "peace and fellowship and justice," he said, and he deplored the growing arms race with the USSR. Even if the two superpowers managed to avoid an atomic war, pouring wealth and energy into armaments would limit their ability to raise up the rest of the world. "Every gun that is made, every warship launched, every rocket fired signifies, in the final sense, a theft from those who hunger and are not fed, those who are cold and are not clothed." The sweat of workers, the genius of scientists, and the hopes of children would be better spent on schools, hospitals, roads, and homes than on armaments. World peace could be achieved, Eisenhower said, "not by weapons of war but by wheat and by cotton, by milk and by wool, by meat and by timber and by rice."[27]

Taft Republicans sneered at Eisenhower's "stomach theory" of diplomacy and harped on isolation from Europe and a heavy hand in Asia, but the president insisted on promoting freedom and repulsing totalitarianism around the world with all the tools he had at hand. The post–World War II world was a complicated place, with boundaries shifting and conflicts flaring as smaller countries threw off the colonial powers that had occupied them for generations. Like most other Americans, Eisenhower tended to misinterpret these nationalist movements as communist expansion, and he tried to keep developing countries from embracing totalitarianism.[28]

In his first year in office, Eisenhower had to negotiate perilous events in Europe, Indochina (Vietnam, Laos, and Cambodia), Korea, and Iran. He believed his strongest weapon was humanitarian aid, but he used other means, too. He pledged money to France to continue what he believed was a fight against communism in Indochina, although he refused to commit American troops to a terrain he thought unconquerable. Eager to end the stalemate in Korea, where 21,000 Americans had died and another 104,000 were wounded or missing, without escalating the conflict to the point of forcing China and the USSR to commit fully, Eisenhower quietly threatened to use nuclear weapons in tactical situations. In July 1953 the two sides ended the war by agreeing to an armistice restoring the preexisting boundary between North Korea and South Korea. Eisenhower's least successful ploy was his use of the Central Intelligence Agency to destabilize a democratically elected Iranian leader who planned to nationalize Iran's oil fields, and to replace him with the Shah, Mohammad Reza Shah Pahlavi. The coup worked in the short term, but the Shah's unpopularity would come back to haunt the United States in 1979.[29]

Eisenhower's methods ran the gamut, but they were all designed to ensure international stability by promoting economic prosperity and undercutting totalitarianism.

Eisenhower began his term with great hopes that the Republican Congress would pass his domestic proposals, for even if the Taft Republicans didn't like him, surely they would work with the first president of their own party in twenty years. Eisenhower's first step was to rein in the federal deficit so that tax money would not be swallowed by interest payments on the debt. Eager to balance the budget, he got Congress to extend taxes that had been scheduled to expire and to chop the defense budget. In 1954, the Republicans passed an overhaul of the tax laws: Congress provided for a progressive income tax ranging from 20 percent on incomes under two thousand dollars up to 91 percent on incomes over two hundred thousand dollars. In 1956, Eisenhower presided over a balanced budget, the last Republican president in the twentieth century to do so.[30]

But Eisenhower was not just a fiscal hawk. As had Lincoln and Roosevelt before him, he wanted to create what he called a "progressive" America by using the federal government to promote growth. To free up business development, he got Congress to cut regulations and price controls and to return to the states control over offshore oil drilling. Although critics complained that he was too chummy with businessmen, his private notes suggest that he was increasingly frustrated with men who could not look beyond their bottom lines to see the importance of widespread prosperity. In 1956, he vetoed a bill that he believed had been bought by oil men. He agreed with the objectives of the bill, he noted, but vetoed it because "private persons...have been seeking to further their own interests by highly questionable activities. These...I deem so arrogant and so much in defiance of acceptable standards of propriety as to risk creating doubt [about] the integrity of governmental processes."[31]

Eisenhower used the government to create individual opportunity and a public safety net. He asked Congress to create a Department of Health, Education, and Welfare, which it promptly did. The only Republican Congress of his presidency passed little other welfare legislation. But in 1954 voters turned both houses of Congress over to the Democrats, and with their help, Eisenhower expanded Social Security to about ten million people who had not previously been covered. He named Nelson Rockefeller—grandson of Nelson Aldrich and J. D. Rockefeller—as undersecretary of the Department of Health, Education, and Welfare; Rockefeller promptly tried to create a national health-care system. Eisenhower also called for federal aid to depressed industrial areas, federally funded schools, and a sweeping system of federally funded highways.[32]

The proposals for aid to depressed areas and schools failed because southern Democrats wanted facilities to remain segregated, but the highway bill passed. In 1956, the Federal-Aid Highway Act provided twenty-five billion dollars to construct forty-one thousand miles of highway across the country over a ten-year period—the largest public works program in American history. The act jumpstarted the economy not just by providing jobs and tying together the states, but also by creating a market for new motels, diners, and gas stations along the new roads. As Route 66, the old road across the country, withered, the Interstate Highway System remade America.[33]

Eisenhower's Middle Way worked. Between 1945 and 1960, the gross national product (GNP) grew from two hundred billion dollars to five hundred billion dollars—a jump of 250 percent. The new prosperity was widely shared as newly educated former soldiers joined a rapidly expanding middle class. Their elevation not only helped them to prosper; it also helped less educated workers by creating a healthy market for unskilled labor. Across the economic spectrum, incomes doubled from 1945 to 1970. Although Americans living in rural areas and inner cities did not share equally in the general prosperity, overall the Fifties was a decade of affluence: candy-colored cars and single-family homes, toys and television, steady jobs and advanced schooling. For the rest of the century, politicians would work to bring back the economic prosperity of the Eisenhower era.[34]

10

The Rise of Movement Conservatism

Eisenhower's policies spoke for a vast consensus in the country, but Republicans who had followed Taft stood angrily on the outside even after the senator died in 1953. It had been bad enough when Democrats created an activist government that provided a basic safety net, developed infrastructure, and oversaw business. When a popular Republican president followed the same course, Taft Republicans became convinced that both political parties had been hopelessly corrupted by communism. As Eisenhower tried to advance equality and prosperity at home and across the globe, Taft Republicans scorned the legislation, which they said redistributed wealth, and Eisenhower's willingness to work with foreign governments, which they called appeasement. They took an increasingly hard-line approach to Republicanism.

Supporting the Taft Republicans were the staunch libertarians at the National Association of Manufacturers and the Foundation for Economic Education. They hated government regulation and taxation, and they fought back against Eisenhower Republicanism. They inundated newspapers, magazines, and radio with the message that the government must stay out of the economy; they labeled any kind of economic intervention as communism. Grassroots clubs and organizations coalesced to fight the consensus that was allegedly taking tax dollars away from the people in order to enslave them.[1]

At first, the carping of this older minority seemed to be the meaningless squawks of a dying breed, attracting the notice of only a few unsophisticated followers. But Taft Republicans began to gain ground when a young political writer named William F. Buckley Jr. adopted McCarthy's techniques on behalf of the Taft faction and launched a movement against everyone who did not endorse its principles. He insisted that elites who believed in laissez-faire government must retake control of society and kill government activism. He called this radical reworking of modern America "Conservatism."

Buckley's rants would have been dismissed as fringe lunacy had it not been for one critical factor: race. When Eisenhower used federal troops to enforce court-ordered desegregation at Little Rock's Central High School in 1957, Buckley's new political magazine, *National Review*, resurrected the traditional Republican link between federal aid to African Americans and communism. White Americans who loved what Eisenhower's Middle Way had done for them were not at all sure they wanted the federal government to help their Black neighbors, especially when, as Buckley's *National Review* made clear, tax dollars were paying for the federal troops escorting Black children into white schools.

In response to an equation straight out of the 1870s—that an active government would use tax dollars to help Black people—Americans fell back on their ancestors' solution. In a revision of Republican ideology more thorough than even that of the 1890s, Movement Conservatives by 1960 rejected the worldview of Abraham Lincoln in favor of an explicit echo of James Henry Hammond's. They insisted on a strict interpretation of the Constitution that prevented government from responding to the will of the people: the Founding Fathers, they said, had deliberately created a government that would protect rich men from "the tyranny of the masses," from those who demanded wealth redistribution. America's founding principle was not equality, Movement Conservatives asserted, but the protection of property. The only way to achieve this goal was to dismantle the federal government and return to a system of states' rights.

Like the Americans who had attacked federal activism in the late nineteenth century, Movement Conservatives turned to the idealized image of western individuals, who wanted nothing from the government and embodied hard work and self-made success. That the image was no more valid in the 1950s than it had been in the 1870s made no difference. Over the next generation, Movement Conservatives increasingly turned to images of the American West to sell their brand of politics, helped in no small part by the peculiar demographics of post–World War II America.

Taft Republicans had little hope of attacking Eisenhower's popular economic policies, so they began their effort to slow down his agenda by accusing him of leading America into a fatal communist "internationalism," a loaded word for anyone who remembered the fight over the League of Nations. After World War II, their accusations focused on the United Nations, which had been organized under the aegis of the United States in October 1945 to replace the ineffectual League of Nations and diffuse international conflict. The Taft Republicans hated the new organization. They argued that the opposition of the United Nations to segregation would override southern state laws and that America's participation was the wedge through which foreign communists would take over the country, making the nation part of a new world order, imposing "socialism by treaty." To nail shut the doorway through which a cabal could tie America to communism, in 1953 Ohio senator John Bricker proposed a constitutional amendment that would shift treaty-making power to Congress and guarantee that no treaty could impose policy on America.[2]

Eisenhower recognized that this dramatic change in constitutional power would hamstring the conduct of foreign affairs. Even if Congress could manage to negotiate treaties that could make it through the Senate, each one could be challenged by any state on the grounds that it was imposing policy. States, in effect, would direct foreign affairs, the very situation that had been so disastrous under the Articles of Confederation and which had inspired the Founding Fathers to centralize foreign policy in the executive branch of the federal government. If the Bricker amendment passed, it would become almost impossible for the government to make any foreign agreements. America would be forced into isolationism. Of course, this was precisely what the Taft men wanted. They barnstormed the country, filling meetings, radio programs, and newsletters with warnings of a vast conspiracy to surrender America to communists. Only the Bricker amendment, they said, could protect the nation from falling under foreign control.[3]

Eisenhower was shocked at the gulf between experts who understood what the amendment would mean and voters so gripped by fear that they bombarded him with letters and visits to demand his support for the amendment. Americans across the country came to believe that the entire Constitution could be overridden by a foreign treaty and that a diabolical cabal in government was angling to drag America into a new world order.[4]

The president remained firmly against such a profound revision of the executive's ability to manage foreign affairs, but his opposition simply hardened the Taft Republicans' conviction that communism was taking over the country. When Eisenhower removed one of Brinker's chief allies, Clarence "Pat" Manion, from a minor government position, a Taft newspaper claimed that the president had "finally yielded to the insistent clamor of a vicious internationalist cabal, spearheaded by the *New York Times* and the Henry Luce *Time-Life* smear brigade, *Washington Post* and New Deal columnists."[5]

Manion himself took it further. "Left-wing Communists... have had an unfortunate effectiveness in this administration," he told a TV interviewer. Manion went back to Indiana to write form letters and deliver radio broadcasts designed to drum up opposition to Eisenhower. Remember, he warned his sparse audience, the "Leftwing... is strong, well-organized and well-financed. Many gigantic fortunes, built by virtue of private enterprise under the Constitution, have fallen under the direction of Internationalists, One-Worlders, Socialists and Communists. Much of this vast horde of money is being used to 'socialize' the United States."[6]

The Senate defeated the Bricker amendment in late February 1954, but just barely. Despite their failure to enforce American isolationism, Taft men had convinced at least some Americans that any attempt to engage in foreign cooperation meant a communist takeover was imminent.[7]

A dramatic resurgence of Senator McCarthy's anticommunist crusade began to show Taft Republicans a new way to advance their budding cause. McCarthy's popularity had begun to slip after the 1950 hearings, and he tried to resurrect his fortunes by stepping up his investigations of communists in government. Now, though, instead of going after a Democratic administration, he went after Eisenhower's. McCarthy worked closely with business-funded Taft newspapers and reveled in the media attention he grabbed with outrageous statements and outright lies. His style would eventually destroy him, but not before it gave Taft men the first piece of a new approach to their war on Eisenhower's Middle Way.

In January 1953, McCarthy began to investigate the State Department's International Information Agency. The senator's bullying of witnesses, conviction by innuendo, and destruction of careers is so well known that "McCarthyism"—a term coined in a 1950 *Washington Post* cartoon by Herbert Block (known as Herblock)—is still a widely used synonym for reckless, unsubstantiated, demagogic attacks on individuals, generally weaker ones. McCarthy tended to go after mid-level civil servants who had some connection to leftist politics in their past (one man had belonged to a Great Books program that had read Karl Marx) but who were not members of the Communist Party. The hearings were disorganized and produced little evidence of communists in government. Few of them were ever concluded: they simply petered out when they ceased to produce shocking headlines. Once they had lost publicity value, the senator lost interest in them.[8]

But McCarthy provided news for the Taft Republican press. Reporters who had covered communism found witnesses for him and often coached the witnesses before they testified. The Hearst and McCormick newspaper chains backed him enthusiastically; together they had a circulation of more than seven million. McCarthy also won the support of Alfred Kohlberg, a wealthy importer of Chinese textiles, who fervently supported the nationalist government of Chiang Kai-shek in Taiwan and believed that a cabal in the State Department had deliberately handed China to the communists. Kohlberg funded the three leading right-wing magazines in the country, and he put their research and editorial staffs at McCarthy's service. Willard Edwards of the *Chicago Tribune* recalled that McCarthy "just fitted into what we had been saying long before." So, he went on, "we gave him complete support. We never criticized him in any way."[9]

McCarthy's investigations enlisted social issues on the side of patriotism. True Americans must be heterosexual, for one thing. Before the 1950s, same-sex relationships had been either ignored or accepted in America, from the childless "Boston marriages" of women to the gay culture of working-class men in urban areas. But McCarthy's investigation of "homosexuals and other sex perverts" in government, to "consider reasons why their employment by the Government is undesirable," made heterosexuality central to patriotism. Although his right-hand man, Roy Cohn, was gay, McCarthy insisted that emotional instability and moral weakness, as well as the susceptibility of homosexuals to blackmail, made them security risks. He railed against "those Communists and queers who have sold 400 million Asiatic people into atheistic slavery and have American people in a hypnotic trance, heading blindly toward the same precipice." He denounced "powder puff diplomacy" that appeased communists and contrasted it with his own "bare-knuckle" approach.[10]

McCarthy also added to American patriotism an identification with Christianity. Communists were godless atheists, he and his followers emphasized, and anyone standing against communism must also stand for religion. McCarthy was Catholic, and Catholics—including the Democratic Kennedy family of Massachusetts—tended to support him.

Plenty of newspapers—including the nation's ten top dailies and all major news magazines—criticized McCarthy's antics, but they were in a bind. Beginning in the Progressive Era, newspapers had distanced themselves from partisanship and had striven for "objectivity": they reported events without interpretation. This straight-up reporting meant that reporters spread McCarthy's accusations even when they knew them to be false. A senator accusing members of the government was newsworthy by any standard. "It is difficult, if not impossible, to ignore charges by Senator McCarthy just because they are usually proved exaggerated or false," the *New York Times* explained.[11]

No one could figure out how to grapple with McCarthy's new style of smear. Eisenhower despised the senator and tried to weaken his influence by ignoring him. Privately, the president steamed; publicly, he maintained that McCarthyism would run its course. In the end, McCarthy destroyed himself. In fall 1953, he went after "subversion" in Eisenhower's beloved US Army. In a wild miscalculation, McCarthy bullied and browbeat a decorated World War II battlefield veteran, outraging army veterans and—of much more import to the senator—causing an irreparable breach with the president. Early the next year, the army turned the tables and went after McCarthy, charging that he had pressured army officers to give a friend favorable treatment. Unlike his investigations, which were behind closed doors and reported on McCarthy's terms, the Army-McCarthy hearings were televised. Up to twenty million people watched McCarthy bully, evade, attack, and lie. When the senator tried to shore up his weakening position by accusing a young lawyer of communist sympathies, the opposing counsel, Joseph Nye Welch, responded wearily in carefully crafted words that resonated among disgusted viewers: "Have you no sense of decency, sir, at long last? Have you left no sense of decency?"[12]

McCarthy was finished. His popularity plummeted, and the reporters who had once dogged his steps now ignored him. The Senate "condemned" the senator in December 1954, and he died two and a half years later, only forty-eight years old. Democrat William Proxmire won the special election held to fill McCarthy's seat, telling voters that McCarthy was "a disgrace to Wisconsin, to the Senate and to America."

But McCarthy and his investigations had shown activists within the Taft wing of the Republican Party that they could advance an agenda by use of fiction, as long as that fiction spoke to Americans' fears and could be kept from open scrutiny. McCarthy's demagoguery gave Taft's die-hard followers a new style. He yelled; he made crazy accusations; he leaked fragments of truth that misrepresented reality; he hectored and badgered. He got in the faces of people who mattered. His antics got attention. Although a senator—about as inside a job as one can get—he posed as an outsider taking on what he insisted was a corrupt system. Claiming his opponents were bent on destroying America, he promised to defend it. When his crusade faltered, he gave it up, but he left behind a following of true believers.

McCarthy drank himself to death, but his supporters insisted that he had been worn down by a gang led by "the stinking hypocrite in the White House." One went further: "Joe McCarthy was slowly tortured to death by the pimps of the Kremlin."[13]

After McCarthy, for Taft Republicans, protecting America would increasingly mean wild accusations designed to defend free-market capitalism, heterosexuality, and Christianity in the face of what they insisted was a corrupt leftist and godless government.

No McCarthy supporter was more important than William F. Buckley Jr., who transformed McCarthy's themes into a new political movement. The son of a wealthy Catholic oilman, Buckley found himself out of step with the modern consensus about the role of government. With techniques like McCarthy's, he determined to take on the Eastern Establishment that had stolen the 1952 nomination from Taft. In doing so, he transformed McCarthy's crude egocentrism into an ideology with the stunning premise that the central idea of the European Enlightenment—that societies advanced by reasoned argument—was dead wrong. The fact that Americans had chosen Eisenhower's Middle Way proved that people could not be trusted to choose what was right, he declared. Elites must retake control of America from the misguided masses and push the country toward religion and free-market capitalism.

Buckley launched his career as a radical during his undergraduate years at Yale with a crusade against what he saw as the university's godlessness. After graduating, he took his crusade national with the 1951 publication of *God and Man at Yale: The Superstitions of "Academic Freedom."* Modern universities embraced the Enlightenment tradition of a free search for knowledge in the belief that informed discussion fed by a wide range of ideas was the best way to reach toward truth. As ideas were tested in public debate, people would be able to choose the best of them. Buckley denied this "superstition." Truth would not win out in a free contest of ideas, he said; students would simply be led astray. For proof, he offered the fact that most Americans had chosen the New Deal over Taft Republicanism.

Refusing to acknowledge that the political economy he espoused had dumped the world into the Great Depression, Buckley echoed the Republicans of the late nineteenth century and declared that any government intervention in the economy other than in support of business was socialism. Instead of allowing people a choice through the free contest of ideas, he argued, universities should exclude "bad" ideas like Keynesian economics and instead inculcate individualism and Christianity.[14]

The book was a sophomoric diatribe against a long intellectual tradition of honest examination of facts and arguments. It cherry-picked quotations from professors Buckley despised, taking their comments out of context and showing them in the worst possible light. It imputed sinister motives to administrators who, for example, refused to give him access to other students' exam answers in one of Yale's popular courses. It demonstrated precisely the sort of inculcation Buckley advocated: it defended Christianity and individualism not through a well-reasoned argument but by misrepresenting the opposition, posing as a persecuted minority, and smearing opponents as tools of socialists and atheists.

Buckley followed his first book with *McCarthy and His Enemies*, published in 1954, just after the Army-McCarthy hearings. He wrote this book with his brother-in-law and fellow Catholic Yalie, L. Brent Bozell. Purporting to be an examination of McCarthy's tactics, it concluded that the senator had, perhaps, destroyed some reputations but his ends justified his means. The book recast McCarthyism as a justified crusade not against actual communists, but against anyone who, in the eyes of the book's authors, was not sufficiently opposed to communism: those they called "Liberals." Although the capitalized name that Buckley and Bozell ascribed to this group suggested it was an organized party, in fact there was no such organization. The authors saw almost everyone in America as a member of what they insisted was a dangerous cabal, for Buckley and Bozell conflated Soviet-style communism with the New Deal consensus. McCarthy should be lauded, they insisted, for challenging the "orthodoxy" of Middle Way thinkers.

Buckley and Bozell recognized that they were radicals. Their intention was to create a new "orthodoxy" of strict Christianity and individualism, and if it took the crudeness of a McCarthy to do that, so be it. They foresaw a time when America would purge the country of Liberals as it was currently purging the country of communists. Indeed, "McCarthyism...is a movement around which men of good will and stern morality can close ranks," the authors concluded. Even a journalist who had just written a sympathetic biography of the recently deceased Taft found the arguments in *McCarthy and His Enemies* staggering.[15]

But Buckley was only getting started. In 1955, he launched the *National Review,* a periodical that set out to explode what Buckley saw as the national consensus of creeping communism promoted by Liberals. He maintained that the magazine was funded by a groundswell of support for his ideas, but in fact it was bankrolled primarily by a rich South Carolina mill owner who loathed labor unions and desegregation, by a Los Angeles oil magnate, and by Buckley's wealthy father.[16]

Buckley laid out the precepts of what he called Conservatism, an ideology that could stand against that of his imagined Liberal cabal. Buckley's Conservatism embraced a worldview that closely echoed that of James Henry Hammond and his ilk a century before. Government must limit itself to protecting lives, liberty, and property, Buckley announced. Any further activities would diminish freedom and slow progress. The growth of government—a reflection of the reforms of the twentieth century—"must be fought relentlessly." Buckley castigated his opponents as "Social Engineers" looking to establish a "utopia." Although the ideology he espoused had failed badly only twenty years before, he insisted that he, rather than his opponents, stood on the side of true human experience. He abhorred the conformity of the intellectuals who advised FDR and Eisenhower, claiming they wanted to "impose upon the nation their modish fads and fallacies" and had nearly succeeded.[17]

Those "fads and fallacies" were destroying America, he said. Buckley claimed that a cabal controlled both political parties under "such fatuous and unreasoned slogans as 'national unity,' 'middle-of-the-road,' 'progressivism,' and 'bipartisanship.'" Although American economic indicators were the best they had ever been, he insisted that current government policies were destroying both liberty and material progress by strengthening labor organizations, which had "doctrinaire socialist objectives." The *National Review* proposed to tell the "violated businessman's side of the story." Finally, Buckley took a shot at Eisenhower directly, disparaging the idea of international cooperation to reduce arms and spread prosperity. Freedom depended not on stronger government, he said, but on political decentralization.[18]

Observers pointed out that this version of conservatism seemed quite radical. To them, the Middle Way was truly conservative: it was based in experience; had been tried and succeeded; provided enormous social, economic, and political stability; and was widely popular. Since their origins in the aftermath of the French Revolution, conservative ideals had been governance based on experience and slow change, rather than radical reworking of society according to an ideology.

Buckley might have called his ideas conservative, but they were actually the very radicalism true conservatives opposed.

Buckley's vision was explicitly elitist, and there was little hope of it attracting widespread popular support on its economic merits. But there was one point in Eisenhower's Middle Way policy on which Americans had a long-standing history of disagreement. That point was race. Americans had been primed for generations to conflate the government defense of Black rights with socialism. Thanks to Buckley and his friends, Americans now tied together the struggle for civil rights with postwar communism.

Eisenhower believed that Americans must oppose racial inequality not only because doing so was right but also because until equality became a reality, Communist governments could use racial discrimination to underscore the disparity between American words and deeds. Segregation was not just morally wrong; it was a political liability. As soon as he took office, Eisenhower desegregated schools and hospitals on naval and army bases and pressured private businesses in Washington to desegregate or lose government contracts.[19]

Eisenhower's initial drive for desegregation was limited to areas in which the executive had exclusive control, but his Supreme Court made that drive national. The president inherited a Supreme Court whose justices all identified as Democrats. He believed that the court should be bipartisan and set out to appoint as justices Republicans whose reputations as statesmen would restore public confidence in the court's rulings. In October 1953, Eisenhower appointed the former governor of California, Earl Warren, as chief justice of the Supreme Court. A popular three-term Republican governor, Warren was a politician as much as a lawyer, and he brought to the court great skills at building coalitions. He had also been a district attorney in California during the landmark Lemon Grove court case, in which the California Superior Court determined that schools separating Mexican-American children from white children was illegal.

The principle Warren had seen established in Lemon Grove—that separate schools were inherently unequal—would, in his hands, become the law of the land. In 1954, the Warren Court handed down the *Brown v. Board of Education* decision outlawing the "separate but equal" doctrine that had segregated education in America since the Civil War. Thanks to Warren's coalition building, the vote was unanimous.

Eisenhower put the muscle of the federal government behind desegregation. After a number of schools had peacefully begun the process of integration, Arkansas governor Orville Faubus sent the state National Guard to prevent nine African American students from enrolling at Central High School in Little Rock in September 1957. When the governor, who was under pressure from segregationists, refused to back down, Eisenhower nationalized the Arkansas National Guard and deployed the 101st Airborne Division to protect the Little Rock Nine.

For the first time since Reconstruction, a president had sent troops to the South to protect Black rights. White southern Democrats opposed integration, but it was Buckley's crowd that resurrected the anti-Reconstruction rhetoric of the previous century. Using white racism to garner support for their economic program, they called up old arguments that federal support for Black rights went hand-in-hand with communism. Federal activism cost money, which was taken from taxpayers and redistributed to officeholders and to African Americans.

On racial grounds, the Taft Republicans could tear apart the popular support for New Deal programs. Poor whites had been fans of FDR's Democratic Party, but they were not fans of their Black neighbors. In 1955, as members of the Black community organized to demand their rightful place in American society, protested the torture and murder of fourteen-year-old Emmett Till in Mississippi, and refused to move to the colored section at the back of a Montgomery bus, white southerners fought back. In early 1956, ninety-nine congressmen, led by South Carolina Democrat Strom Thurmond, wrote the "Declaration of Constitutional Principles"—quickly dubbed the "Southern Manifesto"—denouncing desegregation as unconstitutional.

Until this point, the *National Review* had barely stayed afloat, but the foundering publication got a new lease on life when it stepped into the nation's racial fight with an intellectual defense of segregation, giving Virginia newspaper editor James Kilpatrick a platform to assure readers that desegregation challenged traditional American values. African Americans had no right to the equality declared unanimously by the Supreme Court, he said. Rather, the white community had an established right "to peace and tranquillity; the right to freedom from tumult and lawlessness." Desegregation would lead to bloody violence, he promised, implying that Black Americans would rage and riot (although, in fact, it was the white community that was attacking African Americans).[20]

White southerners were willing to heed this warning. They liked the active government that provided an economic safety net after the 1920s had proved that unregulated capitalism was a disaster. They liked the government contracts that brought jobs to their impoverished region. But Eisenhower's willingness to use the government to enforce freedom for all, regardless of race, was a different thing altogether. They believed it had been suggested before the Civil War, then established during Reconstruction, that Black people wanted the government to redistribute wealth. If Eisenhower was going to defend Black rights with federal troops, then perhaps Taft Republicans were right to argue that government activism was communism.

It took a secret movement to spread that argument from the elite *National Review* to regular voters. The year after Eisenhower sent troops to Little Rock, the chairman of the Education Committee of the National Association of Manufacturers, a salesman named Robert Welch, started the John Birch Society. Chock-full of conspiracy theories, Welch had written a potboiler that claimed to expose the government's complicity in the spread of communism. In *The Life of John Birch: In the Story of One American Boy, the Ordeal of His Age,* Welch explained that the State Department had assassinated young missionary John Birch when, at the end of World War II, he uncovered the communist plot to take over China. State Department operatives were secretly aiding the communists, and they rubbed him out before he could let the world know that China was about to fall. With the John Birch Society, Welch linked racial fears and anticommunism together and turned them into a grassroots movement to oppose Eisenhower Republicanism.[21]

Welch started his organization in December 1958 to combat what he believed was the creeping communism of the administration. Using his training in sales, he organized the society like a corporation, with himself at its head. Paid field coordinators recruited local section heads, who then recruited members. Meetings were held in members' homes, which made it easier to encourage friends and family to join. Local chapters split in two whenever their numbers got higher than twenty. The purpose of the organization was to convince Americans that communism was a deadly threat to their everyday lives and to create a grassroots movement to challenge the moderates who controlled the Republican Party. Ironically, Welch drew his inspiration from the Communist Party when he organized the John Birch Society: he tolerated no dissent—he believed that debate weakened power—and insisted on secrecy.[22]

Powerful industrialists who had made their fortunes during and after World War II joined the John Birch bandwagon: William Grede of Milwaukee's Grede Foundries, Fred Koch of Wichita's Koch Engineering and Koch Oil Corporation, and A. G. Heinsohn of Tennessee's Cherokee Mills Manufacturing Corporation. Their abhorrence of government regulation dovetailed nicely with Welch's warning that communism was already snaking through the nation. But the laws protecting workers' safety and wages were generally popular; dislike of government regulation was not going to attract a wide range of support.

So Welch played on the idea that government programs would redistribute wealth to African Americans. According to him, the burgeoning civil rights movement revealed the creeping tendrils of communism. "The trouble in our southern states has been fomented almost entirely by the Communists for this purpose," he explained, "to stir up such bitterness between whites and Blacks in the South that small flames of civil disorder would inevitably result. They could then fan and coalesce these little flames into one great conflagration of civil war. . . . The whole slogan of 'civil rights,' as used to make trouble in the South today, is an exact parallel to the slogan of 'agrarian reform' which they used in China."[23]

Pushed by businessmen, the fervently anticommunist John Birch Society spread quickly through the South and West. The number of members was hard to know because of the group's secrecy, but it ran to at least ten thousand and probably much more—higher than the American Communist Party had ever boasted. Far more important than foot soldiers, though, was the money and attention the Birchers attracted. By 1962, the organization was pulling in more than a million dollars a year. By labeling opponents—including Eisenhower—as communists, the Birchers were able to force politicians to tolerate their extremism out of fear that they would be the next to find themselves under attack. The Birchers might be over-the-top, Republican politicians rationalized, but they were patriots.[24]

In response to the apparent communist threat, Americans began to turn to the image of the individualist cowboy, as they had done almost a century earlier, and that imagery produced for Movement Conservatives a respectable spokesman. Westerns had grown out of the Wild West shows of the late nineteenth century and had always been popular, and in the

340

mid-1950s, with the new medium of television gaining maturity, they took off. Viewers tuned in to *Gunsmoke*, *Rawhide*, *Bonanza*, and *Wagon Train* to see simple stories in which strong white men worked hard and made it on their own. In 1959, there were twenty-six westerns on TV. During one week in March 1959, eight of the top ten shows were westerns.[25]

No politician benefited more from the popularity of the western image in the 1950s than Barry Goldwater, the Republican senator of Arizona. To hear him tell it, he was a product of the Wild West. His grandfather, Michael Goldwasser, had come to America to cash in on the California gold rush, reached San Francisco in 1852, then took a stagecoach "to the newest bonanza town," Goldwater recalled, where he and his brother opened a saloon, surrounded by "gambling, whiskey, and wild, wild women."

By 1880, the Goldwassers had settled in Prescott, Arizona, where they established a successful department store that sold pretty much everything settlers in the new Territory could want. The Goldwassers expanded into Phoenix and created a hugely profitable business, which eventually employed the next two generations (who called themselves Goldwater)—but that was incidental in Goldwater's recasting of the story. Goldwasser "was not seeking riches or power or the easy life," his grandson claimed. "What he sought was freedom and independence."

Barry Goldwater was fond of noting that when he arrived in the world in 1909, the oldest son of Baron Goldwater and his loving wife, Arizona was still a western Territory: "The automobile was a newfangled invention. Steam locomotives and horses pulled our conveyances. For personal transportation we

had the horse and the street railway." But Goldwater's reminiscences reflected more than a quaint past; they represented
a political ideology: "There was no federal welfare system, no
federally mandated employment insurance, no federal agency
to monitor the purity of the air, the food we ate, or the water we drank." Goldwater worried that the expansion of the
federal government meant that Americans had surrendered
their independence. "We didn't know the federal government," Goldwater said. "Everything that was done, we did it
ourselves."[26]

Goldwater's depiction of his history tied into American
images, but it was, in fact, an invention. Goldwater—and his
supporters—were correct to see him as the embodiment of the
Old West. And like people in the real Old West, the Goldwaters had risen through the generosity of the federal government. Army contracts provided the money to build the first
Goldwater store; federal subsidies for the Roosevelt Dam, begun in 1905, funded the population growth in Phoenix that
made the Goldwaters' enterprise boom. World War I and more
reclamation projects in the 1920s poured more money into the
Goldwater business. During the 1920s, the federal government
funded 15 percent of the Arizona economy. Then the New
Deal, with its emphasis on developing the South and West,
arrived. Between the Hoover Dam and the fifty different federal agencies operating in Arizona, the federal government
pumped $342 million into the state during the New Deal,
while it took less than $16 million in taxes out.[27]

Goldwater grew up the wealthy son of a wealthy son, with
a nurse, chauffeur, and live-in maid. He never carried cash in
Phoenix because he could charge anything he wanted to his

father, who had long since handed the day-to-day operations of the business to a professional manager. Goldwater chose to quit college after only a year because he didn't like it. When he married, he married an heiress.[28]

But Goldwater maintained that his fortune came from hard work, and he resented New Deal labor regulations. He hated the Wagner Act, with its stipulation that if a majority of a company's workers voted to join a union, that union would bargain for all the workers in the company. Men like Goldwater accused FDR of ruining workingmen by turning power over to unions. The contracts workers negotiated with powerful labor leaders usually included automatic raises, regardless of economic conditions, which employers thought would create rampant inflation. The same contracts, employers argued, destroyed American individualism by treating all workers as interchangeable. No longer would a man rise or fall according to his own merits; his future would depend solely upon seniority. The rise of organized workers would mean unemployment, riots, bloodshed, and class warfare. Goldwater supported McCarthy, sharing his conviction that the nation was full of communists. At a time when government policies were putting money into the hands of Goldwater's customers, Goldwater complained bitterly about having to pay the taxes that funded those policies.[29]

Taft Republicans like Goldwater fell back on the language of the nineteenth century to oppose unions. Every man should have the freedom to set whatever terms he wished for his labor. They wanted, they said, to protect a man's "right to work." Goldwater made it his mission to destroy the political power of unions because, he said, their leaders were stealing American

343

freedom. They were, he said, "more dangerous than Soviet Russia."[30]

By 1958, Goldwater was ready to turn not only on the Democrats but also on Eisenhower and Middle Way Republicans. When the president released his 1958 budget, which called for expenditures of $71.8 billion, Goldwater denounced him on the floor of the Senate. Eisenhower was no spendthrift, but a recession was looming, and the president and his advisers knew well that eliminating government jobs and slashing government contracts at such a time was a mistake. Unemployment and lack of purchasing power would ripple down through the economy, making a bad situation worse. But Goldwater and Taft Republicans wanted no part of such Keynesian ideas. On the floor of the Senate, Goldwater accused his party's president of embracing "the siren song of socialism."[31]

The fulminations of Goldwater and other Taft Republicans did not catch on. In the midterm elections of 1958, Republicans ran on right-to-work platforms that would break unions in seven states. In six of the states, that platform, and the candidates who backed it, were trounced. Across the nation, the right-to-work initiatives pushed voters away from the Republican Party. They gave Democrats heavy majorities in both the Senate and the House of Representatives. But Arizona was already a right-to-work state, and it continued to lead the way in embracing the ideas of the Taft Republicans. Voters swept Barry Goldwater back into office with 56 percent of the vote, and *Time* magazine heralded "the tall, bronzed, lean-jawed, silver-haired man of 49," whose grandfather "packed in behind a mule to found the mercantile business which now does $6,000,000 a year in five department stores, [and] spawned a robustious breed."[32]

It seemed the Eisenhower wing of the Republican Party had buried the Taft extremists, but the wealthy men who hated the American consensus now had a standard-bearer to carry on the fight. Goldwater was personable, handsome, and well connected. He had publicly denounced the *Brown v. Board of Education* decision as "not based on law" and had criticized Eisenhower's use of troops to desegregate Little Rock Central High. Clarence Manion, that key Taft-faction wire-puller, decided to push Goldwater for the 1960 presidential nomination. Although that effort foundered, Goldwater's contention for the nomination would give ideological coherence to Movement Conservatism.

To launch Goldwater's candidacy, Manion funded the production of a declaration of Taft Republican principles. "We hope to publish a 100 page booklet on Americanism by Senator Goldwater," he wrote to a friend, "which can be purchased by corporations and distributed by the hundreds of thousands." To write the manifesto, he turned to Buckley's brother-in-law, L. Brent Bozell. The final product, published over Goldwater's name and titled *The Conscience of a Conservative*, hit bookstores in spring 1960.[33]

This astonishing book revived the ideas of James Henry Hammond and insisted, as Hammond had, that they were the only true American principles. The laws of God and nature, Bozell wrote, were fixed and unchanging. Conservatives, as he called those who shared his beliefs, must apply those timeless laws to the modern world. His central principle was simple, as it had been for Hammond a century before: the Constitution strictly limited the functions of government. Like Hammond, Bozell argued that the government should only keep order, fight against foreign foes, and administer justice. To those duties, Bozell added another: promote economic growth. Anything beyond these functions took the government down a short road to tyranny.[34]

Like Hammond, Bozell didn't care that a majority of Americans wanted an active government. The Founding Fathers had not set up a democracy, he insisted, because they understood "the tyranny of the masses." Given a chance, he wrote, people would vote for politicians who promised them a better economic deal—Hammond's redistribution of wealth. The Founding Fathers abhorred this idea, according to Bozell, and wanted to make sure that intelligent elites, rather than a mob, ran things. To that end, they had written a document carefully guaranteeing that, no matter what the people wanted, the government could never alter the natural tendency of wealth to accumulate in the hands of society's leaders.[35]

Lincoln had founded the Republican Party to guarantee that a few wealthy elites would not control government at the expense of hard workers, but Bozell insisted that laborers with a political voice meant socialism. He demanded a return to the world before 1860, arguing, as slave owners had, that American liberty depended on property rights. Civil War Republicans had believed the federal government had an unlimited claim on individuals' wealth to fund national policy, but Bozell claimed that taxation to fund government action attacked freedom by undermining property rights. True

Americans must destroy federal government activism and re-turn the nation to its true foundation: states' rights. According to Bozell, only small government, not legislative protection, would restore freedom to African Americans, farmers, and workers. The Supreme Court's unanimous stand against seg-regated schools was unconstitutional, he wrote, and set up a system of rule by men rather than by law. Federal regulation of agriculture was unconstitutional and rewarded farmers for laziness. Federal labor laws had enabled workers to amass too much political power, power they used to encourage ineffi-ciency, decrease production, and raise prices. Taken together, these efforts destroyed liberty and, he claimed, decreased the American standard of living.[36]

Unless voters took the country back to the founding prin-ciples of protection of property by a wealthy elite, America would continue to become a totalitarian state. Lower taxes, though, would "return to the individual the means with which he can assert his freedom and dignity, but also guarantee to the nation the economic strength that will always be its ulti-mate defense against foreign foes."[37]

And therein lay the strange paradox of Bozell's manifesto. For all his talk of lower spending and lower taxes, he was ad-amant that the nation was not prepared for an all-out strug-gle with the Soviet Union. Americans were losing the Cold War, Bozell warned, and "our national existence is once again threatened as it was in the early days of the Republic." Eisen-hower's "stomach theory" for foreign aid propped up commu-nist regimes, and his attempts at an accord with the USSR played into communist hands. As for the UN, it actively un-dercut the nation's security. America must become dominant in all spheres—military, political, and economic—and act preemptively to topple authoritarian governments. Only then would other nations respect the United States, and only respect would keep them from trying to spread communism into the very heart of America itself. Building the strongest military in the world would be expensive, yes, but it would be money well spent.[38]

Bozell did not address the fact that it would not be possible both to cut taxes and to increase American military might without creating crushing debt. His rhetoric hid this paradox under sweeping celebrations of American strength, but the contradiction it embraced would cut more and more deeply into American life in the following decades.[39]

In *The Conscience of a Conservative*, Taft Republicanism turned into Movement Conservatism, laid out in 127 pages. It was the mind-set of wealthy employers, of men who disdained "the mass mind [of] average intelligence" in favor of "the brilliance and dedication of wise individuals." It disregarded that the American economy was producing at an extraordinary rate and that wealth was widespread. It saw the popularity of Eisenhower's Middle Way as a statement not for it, but against it, for its popularity proved that the people could not be trusted to choose the right course for the nation. Given the chance, they had turned away from America's traditional government in favor of socialism. Had this declaration not provided an intellectual argument for segregation, it would never have amounted to more than the fevered rants of a young, well-connected Yale man. But with the defense of segregation added in, it gained enough adherents to become the signature book of a rising political star.

Goldwater did not get the Republican nomination, and the outcome of the 1960 election horrified Movement Conservatives. Eisenhower had been enormously popular, and delegates to the Republican Convention in 1960 chose his vice president, Richard Nixon, as their presidential candidate. Nixon was more moderate than the Movement Conservatives wanted, but they accepted him because of his strong anticommunist background and because they believed he could be elected. When he lost to Senator John F. Kennedy, a Massachusetts Democrat whom Movement Conservatives saw as a brainless stuffed shirt, they were shocked. Initially, they argued that Kennedy was not a legitimate president, though he had won the popular vote by 125,000 votes and the Electoral College 303 to 219, because, Movement Conservatives said, the election had been bought. (This was ironic, coming from members of a party that had seated President Hayes in 1877 with a quarter of a million fewer votes than his opponent, and President Harrison in 1889 with 100,000 fewer votes than his opponent, but so they argued.) When their complaints got no traction, they could only conclude that America had truly fallen to communism.[40]

Insisting that the Republican Party had lost the White House because Eisenhower's Middle Way was simply a warmed-over version of the New Deal, Movement Conservatives vowed that Republicans must take a stronger stand against New Deal apostasy. They must "reverse the whole trend of American intellectual history from the days of Lincoln to those of Franklin Roosevelt and Dwight Eisenhower," as one wrote in the *National Review*. They promised to turn the clock back to the days before the Civil War.[41]

Although in 1960 Movement Conservatives were still a small minority in the country as a whole, the peculiarities of post–World War II demographics helped spread their ideas in the South and the West. The western imagery of Movement Conservatism appealed to Americans in these regions, which were the same ones where cowboy imagery had spread almost a century before. During World War II, people and federal money had flowed south and west as the government spread out military installations and industry to ensure that enemy strikes in the heavily populated East could not immobilize the war effort. Land was cheap in the South and West, and real estate developers and businessmen worked to entice the military to their regions by offering to lease land to the government for nominal rates. Government money continued to pour in after the war, but in a twist much like that of the late nineteenth century, southerners and westerners ignored their dependence on the federal government and instead championed Movement Conservatism.[42]

In the South, Movement Conservatism grew along with new defense industries and the influx of mechanization. Many southern whites whose farms had failed during the Depression climbed out of poverty into steady jobs, and the new industries lured many middle-class northerners south to work as managers. This demographic change revived Republican fortunes in the solidly Democratic South. Men who had been on the receiving end of federal programs in the 1930s now found themselves wage earners who had to pay taxes. To them, especially after the birth of the John Birch Society, it appeared that those taxes went to their African American neighbors, and they resented it. They were a fertile ground for Movement

Conservative rhetoric. At the same time, many transplanted northerners were already Republicans. Reluctant to join the southern Democratic Party, these former northerners offered another inroad for Movement Conservatism south of the Mason-Dixon Line.[43]

White southerners were especially susceptible to Movement Conservatives' defense of segregation. The connection between African American civil rights activism and communism had been present in the South since at least 1957, but it took tangible form in 1962 when Black military veteran James Meredith tried to enter the University of Mississippi and was stopped by a hastily written state law backed by Mississippi governor Ross Barnett. President Kennedy supported Meredith's right to attend Ol' Miss, bucking southern white control of the state by overruling a state governor and ordering federal intervention to make Meredith's registration take place. Kennedy had to call in federally controlled marshals and troops to put down riots during the crisis.

The federal government was advancing the interests of an African American in a Deep South state, just as it had done during Reconstruction. White southerners reacted to that government activism with the same accusation of communism they had made in the 1870s, an accusation that echoed the Movement Conservatives. Who was paying for the troops integrating Ol' Miss? Taxpayers. Bumper stickers cried, "The Castro Bros"—a reference that conflated President Kennedy and his brother, Attorney General Robert Kennedy, with the communist government of Fidel Castro in Cuba—are "in the White House." A Ku Klux Klan billboard in North Carolina was more direct: "Help Fight Communism & Integration."[44]

Demographic changes in the West in the middle of the twenti-eth century were even more dramatic than those in the South. They, too, fed Movement Conservatism, but in the West it grew because of the economic attraction of anticommunism rather than its opposition to integration.

During the war, Congress appropriated more than $70 bil-lion for the West, almost half of it designated for California. More than $1.8 billion went to construct 344 new plants in the West: steel mills, aircraft plants, magnesium factories. By 1943, California's new aircraft industry employed almost a quarter of a million people, while the California shipyards employed 280,000. By 1944, Los Angeles was second only to Detroit as a manufacturing center.[45]

After previous wars, the US economy had abruptly switched away from military production, but after World War II, military spending continued to climb with the rise of the Cold War. Between 1950 and 1959, the budget for defense con-tracts increased 246 percent, up to $228 billion every year. At the same time, American nonmilitary businesses expanded only about 76 percent. By 1962, defense took up 62 percent of the federal budget. Defense spending dominated the Ameri-can economy.[46]

In the 1950s, California received twice as much annual de-fense spending as any other state. Defense contracts, together with the military and civilian payrolls of the Department of Defense, poured more than $50 billion into California in that decade. Los Angeles and its surrounding counties boomed as defense contractors built up the region. People flocked in to build airplanes and electronics. Los Angeles had only 1.5

million residents in 1940; by 1960 the metropolitan region boasted more than 6 million people.[47]

All those people needed food, clothing, housing, appliances, entertainment, and luxuries. The building industry boomed, and property development took off. Retail sales skyrocketed. Doctors and dentists and lawyers and accountants and scores and scores of small businessmen joined the boom. Walt Disney jumped on the bandwagon with Disneyland, an ambitious venture whose success meant that tourists also began to flock to Southern California.[48]

As in the post–Civil War years, the West's extraordinary growth was built on federal spending and, just as before, western entrepreneurs in the twentieth century hated the federal government. Defense contractors knew their livelihood depended on federal contracts, paid for by federal taxation, but the businessmen who came to the region to absorb the paychecks of defense industry employees did not see this connection so directly. In their eyes, they were individual entrepreneurs, and the federal government was stealing their just profits by redistributing wealth through unnecessary labor regulations and taxation. Employees of the defense industry and businesses that sprang up around it, paying mortgages and school bills and consumer debt, were no more anxious for taxes to cut into their paychecks than were their employers.[49]

This peculiar western economy fed Movement Conservatism. In defense-heavy communities, especially in Southern California, anticommunism was good politics. Congressmen could stand firm against communism both by condemning government spending for public works programs and by favoring the strong military that funneled federal money to their constituents.

Eisenhower understood that this new military-industrial system was simply a public works program under a different name, but unlike funding that created schools or roads, building the military indefinitely brought no long-term benefits to society. When he left office in 1961, he focused his farewell address on the peril of the growing ties between armaments industries and the government. For the first time ever, he pointed out, America had a permanent and vast armaments industry. Annually, the nation spent more on military security than the net income of all the corporations in the United States. Fully three and a half million men and women were directly engaged in the defense industry; many others made their livelihoods in communities surrounding those companies. The defense industry exercised economic, political, even spiritual influence everywhere—"in every city, every State house, every office of the Federal government." It affected the very structure of American society. This "military-industrial complex," as he called it, threatened to endanger American liberties and the democratic process.

Eisenhower dismissed the Movement Conservatives who were feeding off this new equation. They were simply wrong. America had not lost its preeminent place in the world, as they kept harping, but leadership and privilege depended on using power for world peace and human betterment. If used in arrogance or lack of comprehension, he warned, power would cause grievous harm. In Eisenhower's view, the last thing America should do was to build up weaponry. Instead it must work for disarmament. There was no miraculous solution to the problems of the modern era, no spectacular and costly action that could forestall the crises that would inevitably arise as time passed. According to Eisenhower, the only way to meet such crises was to use good judgment and to seek balance and compromise, a prescription very different from the absolutist approach of Movement Conservatives. The president who had fought a world war begged partisans within his own party to see that national policies were not a game. Another war could destroy human civilization.[50]

Western Republicans ignored Eisenhower and eastern Republicans who objected to the growing power of the defense industry. They saw those easterners as pro-communist, part of what Taft had scorned as an Eastern Establishment that had been corrupted by the wealthy, well-educated easterners Buckley had denigrated as a "liberal elite." Eisenhower and Kennedy had courted the expertise of Ivy League intellectuals, leaving western businessmen resentful that their views were not adequately represented in Washington and reinforcing their conviction that they were ruled, without their consent, by an effete and arbitrary Eastern Establishment. Western defense communities were prime fodder for the Movement Conservatism articulated by Buckley and his cohort at the *National Review*.[51]

Movement Conservative disgust with the Eastern Establishment grew when eastern businessmen supported Kennedy. The pro-business Democratic president's expansion of trade, the 1963 tax cut, and restraint of antitrust action made him popular with the leaders of multinational corporations in the East, and they drifted toward the Democratic Party. The comfort of eastern businessmen with the Democratic president strengthened Movement Conservatives within the Republican Party. As easterners donated money to the Democrats, westerners gained more say in the national Republican Party.[52]

While Movement Conservatism spread throughout the South and West generally, the demographics of Southern California made people there a prime audience for *God and Man at Yale*, the *National Review*, *The Life of John Birch*, and the growing body of literature, bankrolled by wealthy industrialists, warning that America was falling to communism. From that hotbed of anticommunism would emerge Movement Conservatism's most promising leader.[53]

Southern Californians were overwhelmingly white and affluent, and many of their jobs depended on the defense industry. They had grown up during the depths of the Depression, moved to California to find work, and were now living the American Dream. Ignoring the central role of government spending in their success, they believed that they had risen on their own and developed a corresponding faith in individual achievement. "It was God's country," one woman recalled of her postwar years in Southern California. "It made you so thrilled to be an American that you wanted to do everything you possibly [could] to keep it this way."[54]

People in the booming California suburbs were recent arrivals without community connections, living in sprawling new developments that had been built without town centers. Organizations like the John Birch Society, with its local, homey chapters, helped to foster a sense of community while pushing an ideology that served the economic interests of the suburbanites. So did the coffee klatches, barbeques, and bridge clubs where people shared ideas about individualism and their fears of communism. And so did churches, for central to combatting the godless communists was a strong faith in religion.[55]

One of the Californians who embodied this mind-set was a charismatic transplant from Illinois: Ronald Reagan. The ruggedly handsome charmer was born in 1911, put his mellifluous voice to work in radio, and relocated to Hollywood in 1937 as a B-list actor. He was relatively popular immediately after the war, but his fortunes declined partly because his crisp, clean, good-boy image was falling out of fashion by the 1950s—and also because he spent so much of his time engaged in politics. In 1947, he became the president of the Screen Actors Guild, where he protected his actors and fought against craft unionists he suspected were communists.

Initially a Democrat, Reagan moved to the right in the politically charged atmosphere around him. Three years after his 1949 divorce from his first wife, he married Republican actress Nancy Davis, and his politics began to shift. In 1954, he took a job hosting General Electric's weekly television show. He also made motivational speeches for the company across the country, emphasizing that America's free enterprise system meant that all interests in the community—workers, employers, consumers—operated harmoniously for the good of all unless the government or unions poisoned the well.

In 1955, Reagan became a charter subscriber to the *National Review*, and in 1960 he reacted to Kennedy's acceptance speech with a letter that sounded like Buckley himself. "Shouldn't someone tag Mr. Kennedy's *bold new imaginative program* with its proper age?" he wrote to Richard Nixon. "Under the tousled boyish hair cut it is still old Karl Marx."[56]

Soon Ronald Reagan was giving political speeches to Republican clubs across California, using his calm charm to spread Orange County's anticommunist gospel.

By 1964, Movement Conservatives had moved from the fringe of American politics to become dominant players. The November 1963 assassination of President Kennedy amid hysterical accusations that he was a communist made a wide range of pundits, including Republican Supreme Court Chief Justice Earl Warren, beg Movement Conservatives to stop their hateful rhetoric. But Buckley deftly claimed that his language was pure; it was the rhetoric of Liberals, like Chief Justice Warren, condemning "extremists" on the right, that was stirring up partisanship and destroying the country. According to Buckley, Liberals, not Conservatives, were "hate-mongers" engaged in an "orgy of lynch incitement against the American Right." Movement Conservatives had come to believe they were all that stood between America and the apocalypse, and they set their sights on the White House.[57]

In 1964, Movement Conservatives decided to run Goldwater for president. It seemed at first to be a very long shot. The nomination appeared sewn up by New York's popular four-time governor Nelson Rockefeller, a quintessential Eisenhower Republican who had served extensively in federal office under both Democratic and Republican administrations. He had expanded New York's educational system to become one of the best in the nation, developed the state's transportation systems, backed union wage increases, funded public works programs, and established low-income housing and successful welfare programs in New York. Like Eisenhower, Rocky saw himself primarily as a problem-solver, not a partisan.

In contrast to Rockefeller and his nonpartisan competence, Goldwater was an outspoken advocate of Movement Conservatism, which was widely perceived as radically out of step with the imperatives of modern America. A more difficult obstacle for supporters was Goldwater's categorical refusal to run for the nomination. Undeterred, twenty men organized as a secret team to create a grassroots movement to draft him. They drummed up plenty of support, but had little success convincing the reluctant candidate to run until events pushed him toward the nomination.[58]

Rockefeller's personal peccadillos fed the hopes of the Goldwater boosters beyond their wildest dreams. Rocky had always been a womanizer, but he hardly had a monopoly on that sort of scandal—mistresses, even if they were barely hidden, would not stop his nomination. But in 1962 he divorced his wife of thirty-two years and a year later remarried a newly divorced mother of four children, who left the kids behind to join Rocky. Such behavior suggested Rockefeller was a threat to the stability of the American family, the very foundation of American society. His support for the nomination crumbled. Although there were a number of candidates jockeying for the nomination, the way was open for Goldwater.

In 1964, Republicans held their convention in San Francisco's Cow Palace, indicating the rising power of the West in the party. There, Goldwater delegates held the field. They booed Governor Rockefeller when he spoke, then constructed a platform that closely followed the prescriptions in *The Conscience of a Conservative*. It talked of America's "moral decline and drift" and called for individualism, small government, states' rights, low taxes, and the strongest military in the world. Behind his own bid for the presidency at last, Goldwater urged the Movement Conservatives on. In his acceptance speech he announced, "Extremism in the defense of liberty is no vice... and... moderation in the pursuit of justice is no virtue." Eisenhower was aghast at Goldwater's nomination, but Herbert Hoover rejoiced.[59]

Supporting a candidate they believed to be pure, Movement Conservatives rallied voters to their cause. Two of them brought important new additions to the movement. One wedded the elitism of Movement Conservatives to populist anger; the other gave the movement a genteel sheen.

Phyllis Schlafly, the president of the Illinois Federation of Republican Women, brought anti-elite conspiracy theory to Movement Conservatism. Her short book supporting Goldwater—almost a pamphlet, really—was titled *A Choice Not an Echo*. She accused a cabal of rich easterners of sabotaging the true Republican Party—the Taft Republicans—in order to guarantee an interventionist foreign policy to profit its members. These "secret kingmakers" were the financiers and banking interests who fed off New Deal foreign policies. Schlafly insisted the world was really divided in two: black and white, communism and freedom. But the cabal refused to acknowledge that stark division because it made more money nursing the dangerous idea of world cooperation. And it was significant money: Annual spending on foreign affairs had climbed from thirteen billion dollars in 1941 to one hundred billion dollars in 1964, she pointed out. These men had deliberately undermined Taft Republicans and nominated weaker, Middle Way candidates to maintain the system that made them rich. Even Nixon, who had begun as a firm anti-communist, had been coopted by the internationalist cabal.[60]

The moderate consensus was enormously popular, but Schlafly rejected this fact. She maintained that polls by the new pollster George Gallup showing that voters did not like Goldwater's extremism were part of a "propaganda machine" to maintain internationalist lackeys in office. After the false polls had done their part, she said, the cabal used newspapers and radio to destroy anyone but their chosen candidates.[61]

Goldwater would stand up to the eastern plotters and face down communism. He would offer "a choice, not an echo." Schlafly celebrated the anti-intellectualism of Movement Conservatism that Eisenhower had deplored. Eggheads complained that Goldwater "had one-sentence solutions" for complicated problems, she wrote. But simple solutions were the answer! What should America do about communism? Stop it! The very fact that establishment Republicans opposed Goldwater's nomination proved that he was the right man for the job. He was the grassroots candidate, the candidate for the little guy who supported real Republicans for their principles, not because they wanted a payoff. Like Buckley, Schlafly wanted no part of bipartisanship or cooperation. Political campaigns should be "competitive and adversarial," she wrote, and she set out to do her part to make that happen.[62]

Whereas Schlafly brought populist conspiracy theory and anti-intellectualism to Movement Conservatism, Ronald Reagan brought gentility. In late October, just before the election, he endorsed Goldwater in a televised speech titled "A Time for

Choosing." A popularized version of *The Conscience of a Conservative*, the speech attacked the moderate consensus of the past thirty years and called for both small government and an all-out war on communism. Government regulation of business meant totalitarianism. Reagan extolled individuals and denigrated "a little intellectual elite in a far-distant capitol" that thought it could "plan our lives for us better than we can plan them ourselves."

As Buckley had done when attacking his Yale professors, Reagan cherry-picked anecdotes about individuals hurt by government action and made a blanket dismissal of those the government helped. He ignored the government funding of the burgeoning defense industry that kept his state flush. In his folksy speech, there were only beleaguered individuals and a dangerously intrusive government, run by out-of-touch elites. While Eisenhower had championed education and sought the advice of academics, Reagan's speech was as anti-intellectual as Schlafly's book, taking a potshot at a Harvard education as useless. The problem, he said, was Liberals—anyone, Democrat or Republican, who was not a Movement Conservative. In contrast to those totalitarian-minded elites, Reagan claimed, Goldwater had "faith that you and I have the ability and the dignity and the right to make our own decisions and determine our own destiny."

There was no left or right, Reagan explained. There was only up or down: up to "the ultimate in individual freedom consistent with law and order, or down to the ant heap of totalitarianism." Everyone but Movement Conservatives had started on the downward course. To Lincoln's words of inspiration, Reagan added an apocalyptic warning: "We'll preserve for our children this, the last best hope of man on earth, or we'll sentence them to take the last step into a thousand years of darkness."[63]

To Movement Conservatism, Reagan brought a trump card: his phenomenal ability to make a speech, honed as an actor and as a GE spokesman. He was warm, funny, convincing. The same principles that many dismissed as the rants of the rich when they came from Bozell's hand seemed laudatory and almost self-evident in Reagan's. Movement Conservatism had found the perfect spokesman.

11

Movement Conservatives Capture the GOP

From 1964 to 1980, Movement Conservatives took over the Republican Party. It was not an obvious or inevitable outcome. Observers in November 1964 thought Movement Conservatives were extremists, soon to be relegated to a footnote in history books. Or perhaps they would not warrant that much attention: a history of the Republican Party published in 1967 did not mention William F. Buckley Jr. But anyone who thought Movement Conservatives were done for was wrong. In 1980, they would elect one of their own to the White House.[1]

Movement Conservatism won elections by marshaling a new electoral strategy based on the link between race and government activism. But what Movement Conservatism had going for it, above all else, was that it offered a clear, simple, positive solution to the terrible tangles of the 1960s and 1970s. In those decades, America floundered through the Vietnam War, soaring inflation, social unrest, Watergate, and the Iran hostage crisis. These were complicated issues all, made more complicated by international troubles, but Movement Conservatives explained them in black-and-white terms that made it easy to tell which side a good American should take. In an era of such confusion, Movement Conservatives' anti-intellectualism became a strength. That their rhetoric did not address reality mattered less than that it seemed to offer a comforting route to bring back the prosperity and security voters associated with an idyllic American past.

Helping their cause was that they were so convinced they were right they refused to budge on anything. As they held fast, they forced the rest of America to leave the middle of the political spectrum and move toward them.

Although Goldwater was trounced in 1964, his candidacy laid the groundwork for a Movement Conservative victory sixteen years later. In 1964, most Americans were horrified by the idea of a Goldwater presidency. Goldwater called himself a conservative, but he promised to turn the clock back to the 1920s in a radical rejection of the Keynesian economics that had kept the nation's economy relatively stable since the Depression. He had the support of extremists like the Birchers and Phyllis Schlafly, and he took extreme stances, including his apparent proposal to approve the use of tactical nuclear weapons by commanders in the field. Republican leaders backed him reluctantly, and many jumped ship to support the Democratic candidate.[2]

In 1964, voters returned to the White House in his own right Kennedy's former vice president, Lyndon B. Johnson, the Texas wheeler-dealer who had finished Kennedy's first term. Johnson brought home 61.1 percent of the popular vote to

Goldwater's 38.5 percent. Clearly, Movement Conservatives were not the majority voice they claimed to be.

But the Goldwater candidacy did three important things. First, it gave Movement Conservatives a blueprint for taking power. To promote the Arizona senator's candidacy, his supporters had used direct mail lists and sympathetic media. Circumventing big political donors, who tended to be moderates, the Goldwater team sought small donations from individual voters. The small donations added up—not only in cash but also in the commitment of their donors to show up and vote. Goldwater organizers managed to produce more than twenty-seven million votes for the Arizona senator and to leave his campaign in the black. Their grassroots strategy was a wild success. After the election, Goldwater supporters took their grassroots organization national, forming the American Conservative Union (ACU) to bring together the many different conservative groups and expand their influence. Young Americans for Freedom and the World Youth Crusade for Freedom organized to provide alternatives to the era's burgeoning youth culture.[3]

Second, Goldwater's candidacy cut the Deep South away from the Democrats. Goldwater carried six states: South Carolina, Georgia, Alabama, Mississippi, Louisiana, and his home state of Arizona. White southerners liked Goldwater's defense of states' rights, dismissal of *Brown v. Board of Education* as unconstitutional, and disapproval of the government's use of federal troops to enforce desegregation. They abandoned the Democrats, who had shown a distressing tendency to enforce civil rights, and found a new home with the Republicans. Party leaders did not miss the possibilities of this new constituency.

Finally, the Goldwater implosion gave the Democrats a landslide year. When the Eighty-Eighth Congress met in January 1965, Democrats held supermajorities in both houses. Backed by a decisive mandate, Johnson pushed through Congress a spate of legislation rivaling the New Deal: federal aid to education, housing legislation, antipoverty legislation, rural development aid, Medicare/Medicaid, and the Voting Rights Act, which defended Black voting. He committed ground troops to an ongoing struggle against communist forces in Vietnam.

Johnson's Great Society programs energized Movement Conservatives. Even as Congress was passing laws to combat poverty and increase the access of underprivileged communities to political power, racial violence increased across America. Voting rights had seemed a panacea for ameliorating conditions in the rural South, but they did little for African Americans in the North. There, manufacturing had declined as it had risen in the West, leaving inner-city African Americans jobless. At the same time, middle-class white Americans had moved out of the cities to the new postwar suburbs, eroding the urban tax base and leaving the cities strapped. Stranded in crumbling neighborhoods, Black Americans took to the streets. In August 1965, the Watts neighborhood of Los Angeles disintegrated into a six-day riot that left thirty-four dead, more than a thousand injured, and more than forty million dollars in property destroyed. The confluence of new antipoverty and civil rights legislation with Black rioting convinced white taxpayers that they were handing their hard-earned money to destructive ingrates.

Movement Conservatives' stance against taxes and welfare and civil rights legislation gained adherents. In the 1966 midterm elections, Republicans gained forty-seven seats in the House and three in the Senate. It did not give them a congressional majority, but it did enable them to slow down the passage of Great Society legislation. *U.S. News and World Report* noted that "the big bash" was over. Americans had shied away from Goldwater, but they were increasingly leery of an unchecked New Deal. It seemed they preferred Eisenhower's Middle Way.[4]

But Movement Conservatives believed the election results proved the opposite—that in fact the nation's false infatuation with the Middle Way was ending. The ACU noted that all but 20 of the 153 House candidates it endorsed had won. Republicans had also taken 8 governorships, including that of California, where Ronald Reagan was elected. He won with Movement Conservative language, promising "to send the welfare bums back to work" and "to clean up the mess at Berkeley," where antiwar college protesters were agitating to stop the war in Vietnam. As their voice in the Republican Party continued to grow, Movement Conservatives looked forward to the 1968 presidential election.[5]

The logical choice for the 1968 Republican nomination was Eisenhower's vice president, Richard M. Nixon, but Movement Conservatives did not trust "Tricky Dick." Their opposition forced Nixon, who was a moderate at heart, to embrace what came to be known as the "southern strategy" of race baiting and to let himself be packaged for television by new media strategists, including one named Roger Ailes, who understood how to convey the simple themes of Movement Conservatism in apparently spontaneous town hall TV specials.

Nixon's problems started before he won the nomination. Movement Conservative Ronald Reagan set out to gain the nomination for himself, forcing Nixon to go after Goldwater's southern states to gain the upper hand. He courted southern delegates, especially Strom Thurmond, the former Dixiecrat candidate who had switched to the Republican Party in 1964 to back Goldwater. After winning the nomination, Nixon shifted gears and named Spiro Agnew, the moderate governor of Maryland, as his running mate. Nixon hoped that Agnew's place on the ticket would hold the states bordering the Deep South for the Republicans.[6]

Nixon knew that in the general election he would lose votes in the Deep South to segregationist third-party candidate George Wallace, a former Democratic governor of Alabama, and so he turned for his winning coalition to urban Democrats in the North. Voters there were frightened by rising racial violence and were open to a leader who promised stability and fairness. Nixon promised to restore law and order to America and to bring the warring factions in the nation together.

Nixon's campaign took its theme from Movement Conservatives and championed the average American. This fellow was the new incarnation of William Graham Sumner's 1883 Forgotten Man. He was a hardworking, middle-class taxpayer who got no attention from the government while special interests were snarling for benefits. A logical outgrowth of Nixon's successful Checkers speech, in which he portrayed himself as the champion of the average American, this theme also spoke

to the turbulence of the 1960s. The promise to restore traditional America resonated with people profoundly disturbed
by the growing counterculture movement and the nation's
mounting violence.[7]

Movement Conservatives liked this theme, but it was not
an obvious winner in the late 1960s. To make it one, Nixon
turned to new media. He distrusted television after a televised 1960 debate with Kennedy had injured his candidacy,
but in 1968 he hired a young advertising executive to package him for voters. Harry Treleaven believed that television
had transformed politicians into celebrities, actors with a
narrative that far outweighed any of their potential policy positions. Nixon's staff thought like Treleaven. "Voters are basically lazy," one Nixon media adviser wrote. "Reason requires a
high degree of discipline, of concentration; impression is easier. Reason pushes the viewer back, it assaults him, it demands
that he agree or disagree; impression can envelop him, invite
him in, without making an intellectual demand....When
we argue with him, we...seek to engage his intellect....The
emotions are more easily roused, closer to the surface, more
malleable."[8]

Treleaven gave Nixon's Movement Conservative rhetoric a
visual language that overrode substance. He created a candidate who was calm and presidential, able to solve the nation's
pressing problems. To keep the awkward Nixon from having to
perform for a camera, he hired a brilliant young photographer
to construct TV commercials from stock photographs, shown
in sequence to create a mood. One advertisement flashed stark
images of communist leaders, missiles, and military helicopters across the screen to scary music. Then an image of the

Statue of Liberty took over as an announcer intoned the name "Nixon." Another showed young Americans working together to create "peace and progress for all the people in the world." Still another showed horrific carnage and promised "an honorable end to the war in Vietnam." At the end of every ad ran the words: "Vote like your whole world depended on it."[9]

The campaign hired a young television producer, the blunt-spoken Roger Ailes, to show Nixon in staged town hall events geared to different markets. Ailes handpicked people to question the candidate in carefully managed shows from which the press was pointedly excluded. ("On this one we definitely need a Negro"—Ailes barked, and—"No more farmers. They all ask the same goddam dull questions.") Ailes arranged applause, the set, Nixon's answers, the camera angles, the crowd cheering the candidate, the careful shading of Nixon's makeup. "Let's face it," he said, "a lot of people think Nixon is dull. Think he's a bore, a pain in the ass." But television, carefully managed, could "make them forget all that."[10]

It did, although Nixon's campaign also benefited immeasurably from the chaos surrounding the Democrats, who were worn down by the ongoing war in Vietnam, Johnson's refusal to seek reelection, Robert Kennedy's assassination in June, and protests at their national convention in Chicago. Nixon won the 1968 election, but not by much. He got only about half a million more votes than the Democratic candidate, Vice President Hubert Humphrey, and lost almost ten million votes in the South to segregationist candidate George Wallace. This meant that a majority of the American people had voted for someone other than Nixon. Voters also returned strong Democratic majorities to both the House and the Senate. But

Nixon was in office, and, thanks to his campaign, the message of Movement Conservatism had permeated the nation.

With such a weak mandate, it seemed that Nixon would have no choice but to stand in the middle of the road while he kept Movement Conservatives happy. It was not an easy act to deliver. By the time he took office, post–World War II prosperity was faltering. Strong consumer spending and big defense budgets had mixed together to create rampant inflation. Nixon tried to curb inflation by cutting the budget and raising taxes on the wealthy while dropping nine million poor from the tax rolls. But when spending cuts bumped unemployment up to a politically unpalatable 6.2 percent, Nixon reversed course. He froze prices and wages, cut taxes, and temporarily stopped foreign exchanges of dollars for gold. Reassured, the American public began spending again, and a year-long economic boom began in 1971.[11]

Nixon played to both camps on domestic legislation. He offered social programs to mainstream America, while either undercutting those offers or devolving the power to implement the programs to the states. So, for example, he called for the government to establish a guaranteed income for poor Americans but set the limit so low that advocates for the poor denounced the plan and Congress killed it. He called for the protection of the environment, signing the tough Clean Air Act of 1970, and then made sure that business interests trumped environmental regulations. He poured money into the arts, expanding the budget of the National Endowment for the Arts from $7.7 million to $61 million, but took away the power of eastern cultural organizations to direct the use of that money.[12]

Nixon's use of Movement Conservatives to get himself elected while aiming to keep moderate support put him in a precarious position. It was one he would not be able to maintain.

The events of 1970 pushed the Nixon administration into the arms of Movement Conservatives. In spring 1970, frustrated by his inability to "Vietnamize" the war by replacing American troops with trained South Vietnamese soldiers, Nixon made the decision to bomb North Vietnamese supply bases across the border in Cambodia. Americans had relied on Nixon's promise to find an honorable end to the war and believed it was winding down. Disillusioned and worried when they discovered it was in fact escalating, they began to turn against the president. Americans already opposed to the war, especially the antiwar protesters on college campuses, marched in the streets. On May 4, in a melee at Ohio's Kent State University, National Guard troops shot and killed four students. The Kent State shooting drove the president to abandon all hope of keeping moderates behind him. He threw the weight of his administration behind Movement Conservatism.

As the nation reacted in horror to images of a young woman screaming over a murdered friend and a bereaved father asking how such a thing could have happened, Nixon drew a stark line between himself and the protesters. In a widely reprinted comment, he called the Kent State victims "bums," then made a clipped announcement through his press secretary that seemed to blame the students for the crisis: "When dissent turns to violence it invites tragedy." *Newsweek* noted that "Mr. Nixon's short reign of togetherness has finally burst apart."[13]

After Kent State, Nixon worked actively to divide the nation along the lines Buckley had drawn more than a decade before. The president championed the average American who loved his country, supported the president, and didn't want anything from the government except to be left alone. In 1969, in a speech pleading for Americans to support his course in Vietnam, he had called on the "silent majority" to support him against "a vocal minority," which was imposing its views over "reason and the will of the majority" by protesting in the streets. In 1970, the idea of that silent majority against the vocal minority merged with the idea that it was imperative to hold the line against young radicals, African Americans, and feminists, all special interests determined to destroy America.[14]

On January 5, 1970, *Time* honored Nixon's shift: "The Middle Americans" were *Time*'s "Man and Woman of the Year." These men and women prayed, loved America, and hated protesters. They worried they were losing their grip on the country as Liberals, radicals, and defiant youngsters took over with the help of a lying communications industry. They felt fleeced by taxation while they had less and less say about how tax money was spent. They resented the inflation that destroyed their chance to rise economically. They worried about drugs and sex and violence. They resented that "angry minorities" got government's attention while all they got was condescension.

Middle Americans stood apart from Black Americans, intellectuals, and professionals, and they practiced a cultural solidarity based on what they saw as traditional American values. They worried about women working outside the home and wanted the traditional family structure restored. They applauded Goldwater's ideas and championed politicians like Governor Reagan in California, who took a hard line against dissent, at one point commenting, "if it takes a bloodbath" to end the protests, "let's get it over with."[15]

After 1970, Nixon and his men worked to create a new Republican majority by inflaming these middle-class white voters against special interests who wanted the government to help them out. They divided Americans between hardworking, tax-paying individuals and "detractors of America"—lazy people eager for a government handout. On Labor Day 1971, Nixon contrasted the lazy and slothful with the industrious and purposeful. Those with a strong work ethic had built America, he said, but now unspecified "voices" were attacking the work ethic. "We see some members of disadvantaged groups being told to take the welfare road rather than the road of hard work, self-reliance, and self-respect," he claimed.[16]

In one of the paradoxes of a strong ideology, the power of Nixon's stance as the representative of traditional American values opened up room for him to make a dramatic departure from traditional Republican foreign policy. Republican anticommunists remained angry over the 1949 Communist takeover of China, and the pro-Taiwan China Lobby of American businessmen backed Nixon. But the president knew that Communist China was growing and should not remain isolated. When skirmishes broke out along China's border with Russia in 1969, Nixon and his national security adviser, Henry Kissinger, saw an opportunity to open a dialogue with China. Triangulating foreign diplomacy among the United States, the Soviet Union, and China would give America power to pressure the Soviet Union from a different direction.[17]

After three years of quiet preparation, President and Mrs. Nixon visited the People's Republic of China. For a week in February 1972, they toured historic sites, cities, schools, and factories. Their every move was covered by a large press entourage that sent back ceaseless reports and stunning footage from a country closed to the world for more than two decades. President Nixon talked briefly with Mao Zedong and grew to like and respect the Chinese prime minister, Zhou Enlai. It was a daring visit that changed the course of history by launching a modern relationship between America and China. It was, as Nixon said in a toast to his Chinese hosts, "the week that changed the world." And it was politically possible precisely because he had proven himself to American voters to be such a staunch anticommunist.[18]

The 1972 presidential election should have been a cakewalk for Nixon. His China trip had garnered widespread approval, a brief economic recovery buoyed voters, and the Democrats were still badly divided. But Nixon's black-and-white division of the world led him to grief.

In June 1971, the *New York Times* began to publish what became known as the Pentagon Papers, a secret government study that detailed American involvement in Vietnam. It showed that presidents from Truman to Johnson had lied to the American people about the war. The study ended before the Nixon administration, but Nixon thought the leak revealed a conspiracy to undermine his Vietnam policy. If people broke the same sort of information about him—and there was plenty to reveal—it would destroy his presidency.[19]

The drive to stop his enemies consumed the president. Frustrated that the FBI was not being aggressive enough in hunting down the supposed conspirators, Nixon put together within the White House a Special Investigations Unit to stop leaks: the Plumbers. Hoping to discredit the man who had given the Pentagon Papers to the *New York Times*, Daniel Ellsberg, they broke into the office of his psychiatrist looking for damaging information about him.

The burglarizing of a California psychiatrist's office was only the beginning. By January 1972, administration men were operating an illegal shadow government. The Committee to Reelect the President, dubbed CREEP as its misdeeds became known, sabotaged opponents before the 1972 election. Their methods, called "ratfucking" by one of their legal advisers, involved planting fake letters in newspapers, hiring vendors for Democratic rallies and then running out on the unpaid bills, planting spies in opponents' camps, and wiretapping. On June 17, 1972, they tried to wiretap the headquarters of the Democratic National Committee in Washington's fashionable Watergate complex.[20]

A Watergate security guard noticed doors wedged open and called the police, who arrested five men trying to take photographs of documents and bug the Democrats' office. The White House denied all knowledge of what it called a "third-rate burglary attempt." Most of the press took the denial at face value, but two young reporters for the *Washington Post*, Bob Woodward and Carl Bernstein, followed the sloppy money trail behind the burglars and discovered tracks that ran directly to the White House. Taking another leaf from

Buckley and Movement Conservatives, Nixon blamed Woodward's and Bernstein's mutterings on what he insisted was the Liberal bias of the media.

The fallout from Watergate gained no traction before the election, which Nixon and Agnew won with an astonishing 60.7 percent of the vote. They took 520 electoral votes—those of 49 states. Democratic nominees Senator George McGovern and Sargent Shriver managed to capture only 37.5 percent of the popular vote, and the electoral votes of only the District of Columbia and one state: Massachusetts. Within months, though, voters turned against Nixon with the fury of the betrayed. In March 1973, during his sentencing, one of the Watergate burglars revealed that he and his codefendants had perjured themselves to protect their employers. White House counsel John Dean promptly turned state's evidence. In April, three of Nixon's top advisers resigned, and the president was forced to appoint prominent attorney Archibald Cox as a special prosecutor to investigate the affair. The following month, the Senate began nationally televised hearings that reviewed the sordid elements of the growing scandal.

Things unraveled quickly. As Watergate heated up in mid-1973, Vice President Agnew came under investigation for conspiracy, extortion, bribery, and tax fraud stemming from his years as governor of Maryland and as vice president. He pled guilty to tax evasion to avoid a jail term, and in October 1973 he became the second US vice president in history to resign from office. (John C. Calhoun had resigned in 1832 to get away from President Andrew Jackson and reenter the Senate.)[21]

Meanwhile, the Senate hearings had uncovered the existence of audiotapes of conversations held in the Oval Office.

When Cox subpoenaed a number of the tapes, Nixon ordered Attorney General Elliot Richardson to fire him. In the "Saturday Night Massacre," Richardson and his deputy, William Ruckelshaus, refused to execute Nixon's order and resigned in protest; it was only the third man at the Justice Department—Robert Bork—who was willing to carry out the order to fire Cox. Popular outrage forced Nixon to assure the American people that "I am not a crook" and to appoint a new special prosecutor, Leon Jaworski. Jaworski fought Nixon for access to the tapes all the way to the Supreme Court, which sided unanimously with the prosecutor. Their hand forced, Nixon's people released transcripts of the tapes. They were damning, not just in content but also in style. Nixon had cultivated an image of himself as a clean family man, and the tapes revealed a mean-spirited, foul-mouthed thug. Aware that the tapes would damage his image, Nixon had his profanity redacted. "[Expletive deleted]" became the buzzword of 1974.[22]

The House of Representatives began to develop articles of impeachment, charging the president with obstruction of justice, abuse of power, and contempt of Congress. Still, Nixon insisted he was not guilty, maintaining that he had not known his people were involved in the crimes committed on his watch. Then, in early August, a new tape, recorded days after the Watergate break-in, revealed Nixon and an aide plotting to invoke national security to protect the administration. Even Republican senators who had not wanted to convict their president knew the jig was up. Goldwater went to the White House to deliver the news.[23]

On August 9, 1974, Nixon became the first president in American history to resign. Rather than admitting anything, he told the American people he no longer had enough support in Congress to advance the national interest. He blamed the press, whose "leaks and accusations and innuendo" had been designed to destroy him. The paranoia inherent in Movement Conservatism had so crippled the president that he had had to resign, and yet even at the end, both he and Movement adherents clung to their divisive ideology.[24]

Paradoxically, Nixon's disgrace strengthened rather than weakened Movement Conservatism. His fall reinforced for true believers the idea that there was something badly wrong in America. For some, the Watergate saga proved that there was a Liberal conspiracy, spearheaded by the press, to bring down any Conservative president. For those unable to ignore that Nixon had, in fact, committed crimes, the whole debacle simply proved that big government was evil and must be dismantled.

In August 1974, House minority leader Gerald R. Ford, a popular party wheelhorse from Michigan whom Nixon had chosen to replace Agnew, stepped up to replace Nixon. When his two-year presidency became tangled in inherited problems, it, too, reinforced the impulses of Movement Conservatism.

Ford tried first to put the divisions of the Nixon years behind the country. He issued a preemptive blanket pardon for any crimes the former president might have committed against the United States, pleasing Movement Conservatives but infuriating Americans who thought that the number of administration men in jail (forty-eight) was at least one short. Then Ford tried to assuage moderate Republicans by calling for clemency for draft evaders and naming Nelson Rockefeller as his vice president. The Republicans took a bath in the 1974 midterm elections, losing forty-nine seats and giving the Democrats more than a two-thirds majority in the House. Republicans lost four Senate seats, giving the Democrats sixty in that chamber.[25]

Fallout from the Vietnam War also hobbled Ford. Nixon had ended military action in Vietnam in January 1973 with the Paris Peace Accords, promising nervous South Vietnamese allies that the United States would continue to protect them. But when North Vietnamese troops invaded South Vietnam in December 1974, Congress refused aid. In April 1975, American newspapers printed horrific images of frantic refugees clawing their way to a place on overloaded helicopters lumbering out of Saigon as North Vietnamese troops took the capital city.

Ford also had to manage Nixon's economic jujitsu. Nixon had pumped up the economy to win the 1972 election, promoting unchecked inflation. In 1973, Arab members of the Organization of Petroleum Exporting Countries (OPEC), taking umbrage at American support for Israel during the Yom Kippur War, declared an oil embargo, forcing the price of oil up from three to twenty-one dollars a barrel. By the time Ford took office, the nation was locked into "stagflation," the seemingly counterintuitive situation when a country suffers from both high unemployment and inflation. This creates a catch-22: policies to help one problem exacerbate the other. Ford tried first to curb inflation through tax increases on corporations and high earners. When unemployment then rose to more than 7 percent, he switched to tax cuts of $22.8 billion. Like Nixon's, Ford's administration ran budget deficits.[26]

The financial troubles of the Ford administration changed the economy of the American home. Americans tended to be savers, but the rampant inflation of the early 1970s meant that it made sense to borrow: A consumer could buy at today's lower prices and repay the loan with tomorrow's cheaper dollars. The modern credit card came into being in the mid-1960s and took off in the decade after 1973. Credit card use increased fivefold, hitting $66 billion by 1982. As interest rates climbed, regular Americans looked to cash in on that market, too. The rise of money market accounts, which allowed individuals to invest in bundled short-term, high-interest debt instruments, took off. From 1974 to 1982, American investors increased their holdings of money market funds from $1.7 billion to more than $200 billion. It was only a question of time until stock mutual funds blossomed as well.[27]

This focus on new financial instruments reflected not optimism but rather fear. The prosperity and confidence of the Eisenhower years had been replaced by a weakening economy, social turmoil, and a political debacle. No longer did America seem to be Lincoln's greatest nation on earth. It was no accident that the refrain of the most popular ballad of the 1970s ran "Bye, bye, Miss American Pie...." Don McLean's "American Pie" was, the song's producer later commented, "the funeral oration for an era."[28]

As the 1970s fed Movement Conservatism, Americans increasingly embraced the idea of the post–Civil War American West, with its image of rugged individualism and small government. Western clothing and culture went mainstream. No longer were blue jeans worn only by hoodlums like James

Dean; they were everywhere. Seventy-five million pairs of Levis sold in 1975. As sales of Levis took off, cowboy boots and cowboy hats came off the ranch and into popular culture. These new American "cowboys" flew Confederate flags, which had fallen into disgrace during the Depression and now made a dramatic comeback. In 1975, at a giant outdoor concert with Confederate flags flying, the southern rock band Lynyrd Skynyrd told its audience, "Watergate does not bother me / Does your conscience bother you? Tell the truth."[29]

To promote Movement Conservatism, believers focused on churches and other organizations that emphasized the traditional values Buckley had told them Liberals opposed. Evangelical religious groups across the South and West emphasized individualism and free-market capitalism. Denigrating education and disdaining the Eastern Establishment, they focused on an individual's relationship with God, a traditional family structure with a strong male head, and the idea of economic freedom. They held fervently to this last belief, although their movement centered in regions that received a disproportionate share of government monies. Although the evangelical movement did not explicitly endorse racism, at the heart of their worldview was the conviction that government services were designed to help African Americans. Thus economics reinforced a white-centered view of what it meant to be a good American.

Ford had hewed a moderate line on social issues, advocating an Equal Rights Amendment to the Constitution to protect women's rights and supporting access to abortion, but his party was running toward Movement Conservatism. In addition to their pro-business advocacy, the Republican

Party began to focus on overturning modern social values. In the early 1970s, a secretive Christian organization known as "The Family" began to sponsor prayer meetings in businesses, colleges, and, significantly, Congress and other government offices. By the mid-seventies, Republicans had become committed to mobilizing white Protestants as a voting bloc. The party's slide to the right forced Ford to drop Rockefeller as his running mate in 1976 and replace him with the far less moderate Senator Robert Dole of Kansas. But nothing could save a Republican after Watergate. Democratic challenger Jimmy Carter, a former governor of Georgia, and his running mate, Senator Walter Mondale of Minnesota, captured 50 percent of the popular vote to Ford and Dole's 48 percent.[30]

Movement Conservatism continued to gain ground during Carter's administration. Oil remained expensive; fuel shortages mounted. The economy continued to totter, with inflation racing into double digits. Inflation pushed middle-class Americans into higher tax brackets; they stormed about the cut taken out of their income just when they needed it most. Towns and cities tried to make up their declining fortunes with higher property taxes; angry property owners turned against government. That anger was especially powerful in California. There, in 1978, voters passed Proposition 13, an amendment to the state constitution that limited property taxes to 1 percent of the cash value of the property and required a two-thirds majority of the state legislature to increase state taxes.

America seemed to have begun sliding from its place at the top of the international community. The taking of fifty-two American hostages at the embassy in Iran, when followers of the Islamic leader Ayatollah Khomeini ousted the Shah whom Eisenhower had backed, painfully illustrated America's sinking status. In late 1979, as the nation reeled during the hostage crisis, the Soviet Union invaded Afghanistan. This mountainous country had remained off-limits in the East-West power struggle since the nineteenth century's "Great Game" of world domination between Britain and Russia. The breaking of that tradition by the USSR convinced Americans that they were no longer taken seriously as a world power.

Movement Conservatives blamed these crippling indicators on Buckley's banes: overregulation of the economy, godless Liberalism, and an almost criminal neglect of national defense. The solution to the economic troubles, they believed, was for the government to get out of the way of an individual's desire to work and accumulate wealth. Rather than trying to adjust consumer demand, the government should promote production. Greater productivity would stop inflation and create richer Americans, who would pay taxes to eliminate the budget deficit. To free up money for investment in new businesses, Movement Conservatives argued, the government must cut taxes. Wealthy people would invest their accumulating money, inspiring new businesses that would hire more workers. The principles of the 1920s had come back to life, but this time they seemed to carry the authority of economic science. Led by Professor Milton Friedman at the University of Chicago, economists embraced the Laffer Curve, which purported to prove that tax cuts produced increased revenue. This old vision of the American economy also got a new academic-sounding name—supply-side economics—for it promised to fix the economy not from the bottom, the demand side, but from the top, the supply side.[31]

Movement Conservatives also tied into the growing evangelical movement. Direct marketing specialist Richard Viguerie concluded in 1976 that the best way to push Movement Conservative philosophy was to court evangelical Christians, and in 1979, Movement Conservatives persuaded the Reverend Jerry Falwell to form the Moral Majority, the religious wing of Nixon's silent majority, to bring the moral values of Christianity into politics. Falwell's *Old Time Gospel Hour* was one of many television ministries. In 1979, about 10 percent of all TV broadcasting was religious programming, with televangelists like Falwell, Pat Robertson, and Jim and Tammy Faye Bakker attacking communism, feminism, abortion, homosexuality, and the "humanism" coming from godless eastern Liberals. Adherents of "prosperity theology" argued that God's promise to guarantee Christians' well-being meant that faith would translate into economic prosperity. If you believed, you would get rich.[32]

Movement Conservatives had been arguing since the days of Eisenhower that American weakness had permitted the spread of communism, but they saved their fiercest denunciations for the Carter administration, which they claimed had led the nation to its most vulnerable moment in its two hundred years of existence. They argued that Carter had cut defense spending dramatically—although, in fact, his budgets had increased spending to keep up with inflation—and they promised to pour money into defense.[33]

As long as the government cut taxes, people believed in Jesus, and Congress properly funded the military, Movement Conservatives promised, prosperity and calm would return.

The Republican presidential primaries of 1980 were a showdown between Movement Conservatives and Republican moderates. The front-runners for the nomination were Ronald Reagan, who had vaulted to national prominence when he supported Goldwater, and who had only hardened his beliefs since, and George H. W. Bush, the New England–born, Yale-educated former congressman from Texas, who took more moderate social and economic positions than Reagan. Bush insisted that Reagan's promise that he could fix the economy from the top down was "voodoo economics." The impulses of Movement Conservatism carried the day. Reagan cinched the Republican nomination, although he did nod to the centrists by inviting Bush onto the ticket as the vice presidential candidate.

Reagan launched his general election campaign with a speech in Philadelphia, Mississippi, just miles from where civil rights workers had been murdered in 1964. After some barbed jokes about President Carter, he lauded Movement Conservatism. He blamed federal bureaucracy, and the taxes it required, for stifling the American dream. "I believe in states' rights," the candidate told the cheering audience. "I believe in people doing as much as they can for themselves." "And I believe we have distorted the balance of our government today by giving powers that were never intended in the Constitution to that federal establishment." Fittingly for a nominee embracing a philosophy of the past, the sixty-nine-year-old candidate concluded his speech by pointing to a nearby horse-drawn carriage and noting that he could recall riding one of them for real.[34]

With Carter's presidency dragged down by inflation and the Iran hostage crisis, voters swung toward the Republican ticket. Even then, however, Reagan and Bush got only slightly more than 50 percent of the popular vote to Carter's 41 percent. (Third-party candidate John Anderson got about 6.6 percent of the vote.) Twenty years after Bozell had ghostwritten Goldwater's *The Conscience of a Conservative*, the promise of that document had been fulfilled: a full-fledged Movement Conservative had taken the White House.

With Reagan's election, the uncompromising views of Movement Conservatives took over the government. Although Reagan himself would not take the hard lines that some of his followers did, he was a master of portraying events as a struggle between good and evil. Ignoring the aggregate statistics on which Democrats tended to rely for their policies, Reagan personalized Movement Conservatism with folksy anecdotes.

In 1976, he had summed up the argument of Movement Conservatives against government activism with the idea of a "welfare queen," a Cadillac-driving, unemployed moocher from Chicago's South Side—a geographical reference that implied the woman was Black without actually saying so. "She has 80 names, 30 addresses, 12 Social Security cards and is collecting veteran's benefits on four non-existing deceased husbands," Reagan claimed. "And she is collecting Social Security on her cards. She's got Medicaid, getting food stamps, and she is collecting welfare under each of her names." The story was unique—the woman was, in fact, a dangerous criminal rather than a representative welfare recipient—but it illustrated perfectly the idea that government involvement in the economy bled individual enterprise and handed tax dollars to undeserving African Americans.[35]

Whereas his campaign rhetoric reflected America's divisive lows, Reagan's inaugural address cast his ascension to the presidency in heroic terms. The nation was in a crisis that rivaled the Great Depression, he said, brought on not by unregulated capitalism, but by taxes and the public spending they supported. Promising to defend the average American, he warned that "government is not the solution to our problem; government is the problem." He promised to reduce the size of the federal government and to return power to the states.[36]

Just as Goldwater had done, Reagan quite deliberately drew on the post–Civil War image of the Old West. During his campaign, he had portrayed himself as an American cowboy. An accomplished horseman who had been in the cavalry branch of the Army Reserve, he traded the English riding clothes he preferred for jeans and a cowboy hat. In his western clothing, Reagan embodied the values associated with the Old West: individualism and small government. Fittingly, Reagan delivered his inaugural address not from the East Front of the Capitol, where it had always been held in the past, but rather from the West Front. That switch had been made for practical reasons, but it also reflected the rising power of the West and the western image on the nation.[37]

Once in office, Reagan put into action the prescription for individualism that Buckley, Bozell, and Goldwater had written thirty years before. He prohibited federal agencies from hiring new personnel; then he turned to cutting the government regulations businessmen hated, and appointed staunch deregulators to head the Commerce and Interior departments—the ones most closely responsible for economic affairs—and to head the Securities and Exchange Commission and the Federal Communications Commission.[38]

The next item on the agenda was to cut both spending and taxes. As soon as he was elected, Reagan had tapped a young Michigan congressman, David Stockman, to be his budget director. Raised on *The Conscience of a Conservative*, Stockman was a firm believer in the principles of Movement Conservatism. "The whole thing is premised on faith," he told a reporter. "On a belief about how the world works."[39]

Stockman slashed through domestic programs: food stamps, education, unemployment benefits, job training. In February 1981, Reagan proposed to cut $47 billion from the previous year's budget, taking money primarily from antipoverty programs. The administration then turned to tax cuts. Stockman promised that the cuts would so stimulate the economy that growth would wipe out the $55 billion budget deficit projected for 1981 and produce surpluses by 1984. When the computer simulations at Stockman's own Office of Management and Budget showed that, far from balancing the budget, his plan would create budget deficits of up to $116 billion by 1984, Stockman solved the problem by reprogramming the computers to reflect his beliefs. "None of us really understands what's going on with all these numbers," he rationalized. He tried to assure businessmen nervous about growing deficits by inserting what he called a "magic asterisk" in the budget to mark unspecified cuts that would be announced by the president in the future.[40]

Even within the administration, not everyone bought into the supply-side dogma, but a botched attempt on Reagan's life gave the president great political capital. On March 30,

1981, less than three months into Reagan's presidency, John Hinckley Jr., a mentally ill young man obsessed with movie star Jodie Foster, tried to get her attention by shooting the president. As Reagan left the Washington, D.C., Hilton after making a speech, Hinckley unloaded six bullets into the president's entourage. His first five bullets hit the White House press secretary, a police officer, and a Secret Service agent. The sixth ricocheted off the presidential limousine into the president, lodging in his lung an inch from his heart. The nation watched, transfixed, as the genial Reagan joked with his wife—"Honey, I forgot to duck"—and with the doctors who saved his life. In the wake of the assassination attempt, his popularity soared to 73 percent.[41]

The president used that popularity to sell his economic program. His first public appearance after the shooting was a televised address in late April in which he challenged Congress to pass budget and tax cuts to reduce the debt, stop inflation, and put the nation back into economic prosperity. Hammering on the idea that special interests had perverted the government, he announced, "When I took the oath of office, I pledged loyalty to only one special interest group—'We the people.'" To keep that faith, he said, it was imperative to get rid of the New Deal–type government programs that drained tax dollars from hardworking Americans.[42]

His appeal worked. Over the summer, Congress developed a bill that cut thirty-five billion dollars from the next year's budget. It also passed a sweeping tax cut that shaved 23 percent off individual tax rates over three years and slashed capital gains and estate taxes. Stockman admitted that the broad tax cuts were cover for cutting top income tax rates from 70 to 50 percent. The whole idea of supply-side economics was really just new language for the old pre–New Deal Republican idea of cutting taxes for the rich and letting the good effects "trickle down" to everyone else, Stockman explained. But "It's kind of hard to sell 'trickle down,'" he said, "so the supply-side formula was the only way to get a tax policy that was really 'trickle down.' Supply-side is 'trickle down' theory." Stockman had counted on closing corporate tax loopholes to realize about twenty billion dollars of additional revenue to help balance the budget, but the president refused to back that plan, and the final measures left the loopholes untouched. Reagan signed the bills at his sprawling 688-acre western ranch in August 1981.[43]

In that same month, the president took a stand against unionized labor, whose existence had tormented Movement Conservatives since Goldwater. In August, the thirteen thousand members of the Professional Air Traffic Controllers Organization (PATCO) struck for better conditions, pay, and work hours. Although PATCO had endorsed him in 1980, Reagan ordered the strikers back to work, invoking Taft-Hartley's provision enabling the government to stop strikes that affected public safety. When most of the strikers refused, he fired them and barred them from ever again holding a government job. Americans who believed that unionized workers were crippling business cheered.[44]

Reagan also dramatically increased defense spending. The 1980 Republican platform attacked Carter for cutting military funding, and Reagan's first budget proposed spending increases that would, in the first five years of his administration, create a 40 percent real increase in defense spending. For 1982,

Congress approved seventeen billion dollars in new defense appropriations even as it was cutting domestic spending.[45]

Reagan's construction of national policy based in Movement Conservatism almost failed immediately as the country fell deep into a recession. Carter had appointed Paul Volcker as chairman of the Federal Reserve Board in August 1979. In October of that year, Volcker raised interest rates sharply to curb inflation. By 1981, the prime rate—the interest rate on money borrowed from a bank—was more than 21 percent. Higher interest rates made inflation plummet from 13.3 percent in 1979 to 3.2 percent in 1983. As economists had warned, though, higher interest rates spurred unemployment. By 1982, it hit over 10 percent, its highest level since the Great Depression, and Reagan felt obliged to back off on his earlier supply-side policies. He raised taxes, including taxes on gasoline, to try to make up some of the budget deficit. But this gesture didn't help the president's plummeting popularity. In the midterm elections, the Democrats picked up twenty-six seats in the House, making up some of the thirty-six seats they had lost in 1980 and solidifying their majority.[46]

Rather than turning away from the Movement Conservatism that had failed to deliver economic prosperity and balanced budgets, the president embraced its ideology even more closely in foreign affairs. In January 1983, he issued NSDD-75, a directive outlining what would come to be known as the Reagan Doctrine. Changing America's long-standing policy of containing communism, NSDD-75 called for rolling it back by pressuring the Soviet Union through a military buildup, economic destabilization, and supporting local insurrections fighting communist governments in third world countries. This meant backing the mujahideen anti-Soviet forces in Afghanistan, as well as antigovernment forces in Angola and Nicaragua. Anticommunist guerrillas were "freedom fighters," in Reagan's parlance.[47]

Two months later, the president explained the connection between his new foreign policy and Movement Conservatism when he spoke to the National Association of Evangelicals in Orlando, Florida. Conflating religion, traditional morality, and capitalism as Bozell had in *The Conscience of a Conservative*, Reagan's Orlando speech denigrated politicians and told his religious listeners that America could be great only if it remained "good." Modern-day secularism was destroying America, he said, because it had replaced morality with bureaucracy. He went on to decry abortion, the lack of prayer in schools, and what he insisted was creeping infanticide and insisted that the majority of Americans—who, he said, opposed these trends—must return religion to public life.

There was sin and evil in the world, Reagan assured his audience in a turn back to Republican politics, and it was embodied by the Soviet Union. Communism was godlessness, and god-fearing Americans must never come to an accommodation with it. America was engaged in a titanic struggle between "right and wrong and good and evil." The Soviet Union was the "evil empire." It was important to pray for the Soviets, but Americans must never forget that "while they preach the supremacy of the state, declare its omnipotence over individual man, and predict its eventual domination of all peoples on the Earth, they are the focus of evil in the modern world."[48]

In October 1983, the United States invaded the small Caribbean island nation of Grenada—one of the world's great producers of nutmeg—after Reagan officials began to worry that political turmoil in that nation would enable Cuban communism to spread. Operation Urgent Fury was the first major mobilization of American military forces since Vietnam. It quickly overwhelmed the local soldiers. Although it installed a stable government on the island and was largely popular in America, the operation drew the wide condemnation of the international community; the United Nations called it a "flagrant violation of international law."[49]

The conjoining of the war against communism and the struggle for the soul of America continued. In summer 1984, moviegoers were treated to what was at the time the bloodiest movie ever made. *Red Dawn* was the story of regular Americans fighting communists who were overtaking their community with the collaboration of the government. An embattled group of high school football players in Colorado, the Wolverines, fought off a communist invasion of Soviets, Cubans, and Nicaraguans. The politician mayor and his son cooperated with the communists, making the heroic Wolverines the underdogs fighting both world communism and their own government. The apocalyptic film boasted 134 violent acts per hour, and it inspired disaffected young Americans. Significantly, Reagan's first secretary of state, the hawkish Alexander Haig, had helped the director with, as he put it, "some political advice" during the filming. *Red Dawn* took the Movement Conservative emphasis on a coordinated popular message to a new level.[50]

In the presidential election of 1984, Republicans sold Reagan as the embodiment of all of America's best qualities. The administration had made much of its stance in favor of what it called the majority of Americans—the hardworking, presumably white, taxpayers—against special interests—those lazy Americans, presumably people of color and women, who wanted government to provide for them. An economic recovery that took off in 1983 helped to cement the idea that cutting programs that helped special interests while also cutting taxes on hardworking Americans would restore old-fashioned American prosperity.

The recovery had many contributing factors. Dropping oil prices combined with Volcker's dramatic contraction of the economy made inflation plummet after Reagan took office. As soon as it did, the Federal Reserve Board slashed interest rates just as the dramatically increased defense spending pumped money into the economy. Another $160 billion or so poured into the economy from savings and loan banks, on which Congress had lifted lending and deposit restrictions to enable them to compete with the high-interest money market accounts that were beginning to soak up deposits. The result of this backdoor Keynesianism was an economic boom that saw unemployment drop to 7.5 percent in 1984 while annual economic growth moved up almost three percentage points to 7.2 percent.[51]

Although the deficit spending that fueled the boom was racking up a huge national debt, administration supporters insisted that the extraordinary economic growth under Reagan proved that supply-side economics worked. That was exactly what voters wanted to hear. When Democrats tried to raise

taxes to fill budget deficits, workers squeezed by the recession joined the "antitax" movement. In November 1983, voters in Michigan took advantage of a little-used law to recall
two Democratic state senators after they voted for a tax hike.
The lesson politicians had to learn, according to an up-and-
coming Republican spokesman named Grover Norquist, was
that voters didn't want to be taxed to pay down deficits. Movement Conservatives told them they didn't have to be; the government could spend money without having to pay for it.[52]

"Paint Reagan as the personification of all that is right
with or heroized by America," read a 1984 Republican campaign memo. "Leave [the Democrats] in a position where an
attack on Reagan is tantamount to an attack on America's
idealized image of itself." "It's morning again in America," a
popular TV advertisement intoned. "America today is prouder
and stronger and better. Why would we want to return to
where we were less than four short years ago?"[53]

In the 1984 campaign, Democrats railed against the growing deficits and called for higher taxes and defense cuts to
balance the nation's books, as well as for investments in education and the environment—Eisenhower Republican stances,
all. But compared to Reagan's upbeat faith in America, Democrats sounded gloomy, anti-business, anti-American. The
wide-open Democratic presidential field reinforced the idea
that the party was a coalition of special interest groups. The
party finally settled on Carter's vice president, Walter Mondale; when he made history by tapping a woman—New York
representative Geraldine Ferraro—to be his running mate, 60
percent of voters thought he had done so not because she was

the best candidate, but because he was under pressure from women's groups.[54]

The election of 1984 was a Republican romp. Reagan and Bush took almost 59 percent of the popular vote. Mondale and Ferraro won only about 40 percent of the popular vote. They carried only Washington, D.C., and Mondale's home state of Minnesota, and that by only about four thousand votes. It seemed that Movement Conservatism had finally won the popular enthusiasm Buckley had anticipated years ago. "I think the revolution is happening," Grover Norquist mused.[55]

Although Reagan had been forced to raise taxes to address ballooning deficits—he would do so eleven times in his presidency—he continued to believe that tax cuts were the key to economic prosperity. As deficits continued to rise in 1983, the president had endorsed tax reform to forestall calls for a tax hike. A final bill relieved about six million Americans from paying income taxes by increasing deductions; it removed loopholes and cut the capital gains tax. On the other side of the equation, it cut the marginal tax rate for the highest tax bracket from 50 percent to 28 percent and raised it for the bottom bracket from 11 percent to 15 percent. It also cut the corporate tax rate from 48 percent to 34 percent.[56]

To put pressure on Congress to agree to tax reform, Reagan backed the creation of an organization that brought together big business, evangelicals, and social conservatives under the leadership of Grover Norquist, who had been an economist for the Chamber of Commerce. "Traditional Republican business groups can provide the resources," Norquist explained, "but these groups can provide the votes." Americans for Tax Reform stood staunchly against higher taxes...ever, by any amount, for any reason.[57]

The 1986 tax overhaul showed that the populism behind the Reagan Revolution was a screen for the business interests behind Movement Conservatism. When a senator pointed out that the bill gave 16 percent of the tax relief to the richest 0.5 percent of Americans, while most Americans would get relief of only 6.4 percent, the Republican chairman of the Senate Finance Committee stormed that anyone wanting higher tax brackets for the rich was simply trying to run "social welfare schemes." The bill's deductions to poor families led Movement Conservatives like Phyllis Schlafly to protest vehemently that such a benefit was "just an idea of liberal bureaucrats who want to redistribute the wealth." In their view, the deductions were "anti-growth" and therefore "anti-family" by definition.[58]

The tax cuts went through, and the mushrooming debt meant that Movement Conservatives could—and did—attack any social spending proposed by Democrats as more proof that their opponents were spendthrifts. Budget cuts hit African Americans especially hard because the loss of union jobs in industrial areas disproportionately affected them. In the past, cities had been engines for job creation; now they were idle and rusting. "Black people see one thing, whites see another," a Wisconsin state representative said. "We are not included in this new prosperity. The struggle is, how do we fit into the new order?"[59]

And yet, despite the administration's determination to keep from providing for special interests, it promoted policies that distributed government largesse to those it considered good Americans. It did so primarily through what are known as tax expenditures: deductions and "tax breaks" that cost the nation three hundred billion dollars a year by 1990. That figure equaled one-half the cost of welfare programs and three out of every ten dollars the US government collected in individual and corporate income taxes.[60]

These virtually invisible benefits—tax-deferred corporate pensions, Social Security benefits, individual retirement accounts, guaranteed student loans, mortgage interest deductions (which the 1986 tax overhaul significantly increased), charitable contribution deductions, health-care subsidies—disproportionately flowed to the wealthier end of the economic spectrum and could be enjoyed without any of the stigma of accepting welfare. They could be tucked into appropriations bills without new legislation or debate. They appeared to prevent the growth of the "welfare state" and could be characterized as "tax relief." When the Republicans tried to reduce Social Security payments, voters turned against them in the 1986 midterm elections, searing the sanctity of tax expenditures into the thinking of Republican Party leaders.[61]

Movement Conservatism received another boon from the administration's continuing deregulation of the economy. Since the earliest days of radio communication, the cost of receiving a public license was the promise that stations would present information honestly and fairly, balancing different points of view. Movement Conservatives attacked this tradition, arguing that the Fairness Doctrine in fact pushed a Liberal media bias, just as Buckley and his ilk had charged. In 1987, the Federal Communications Commission abandoned the rule.[62]

The end of the Fairness Doctrine opened the door for the kind of public education Buckley had advocated almost forty years before. Rather than presenting informed debate and encouraging listeners to make their own decisions, public media could now exclude "bad" ideas—like government activism—and inculcate individualism and Christianity. Within a year, talk radio had gone national, with hosts like Rush Limbaugh electrifying listeners with his attacks on femi-nazis, hatred of affirmative action, scorn for Liberals, and warnings that socialism was creeping through America.

The president also brought what Movement Conservatives believed was traditional morality firmly into politics. Although he himself had been divorced and was rather more tolerant than not of homosexuality, Reagan urged social and religious conservatives to back Movement Conservatism. Norquist had begun to recruit white evangelical Christians into Americans for Tax Reform, but the sought-after coalition of big business and southern and western Christians was uneasy.

In 1989, Norquist's friend Ralph Reed addressed that disjunction by turning evangelical Christians into a permanent political pressure group. With Reed as executive director, the Christian Coalition, as the group was called, rallied evangelicals behind the Republican Party with great success. By 1992, it would have a quarter of a million members and spend ten million dollars on that year's political campaigns. It recruited evangelicals to run for local and state offices, and it effectively spread the religious and economic tenets of Movement Conservatism. The "pro-family movement," Reed explained, could win political control only by addressing "the concerns of average voters in the areas of taxes, crime, government waste, health care, and financial security" and by tackling abortion and homosexuality. Seemingly counterintuitively, evangelicals' solutions to these problems often seemed to exacerbate them—they vehemently opposed government health-care reform, for example, which would actually help families—but they always followed the Movement Conservative line.[63]

Perhaps most important, Reagan managed to enshrine the principles of Movement Conservatism in such a way that they would last far beyond his administration: he appointed lots of judges. In his eight years in office, Reagan appointed more judges than any other president in history: 3 Supreme Court justices and 1 chief justice, as well as 368 district and appeals court justices. Accepting the idea that the economic and civil rights decisions of the Warren Court were "judicial activism" rather than a fair interpretation of the law, Reagan promised to return the court to those who believed in a strict interpretation of the Constitution and in "family values."[64]

To the outrage of older members of the Justice Department, who believed that the enforcement of the law should not be politicized, the Reagan appointees at Justice systematically quizzed candidates for judgeships about their views on abortion and affirmative action. The aim, the president's attorney general, Ed Meese, said, was to "institutionalize the Reagan revolution so it can't be set aside no matter what happens in future presidential elections." Those justices carried water for the movement: in 1988, in *Communications Workers of America v. Beck*, Reagan's Supreme Court limited the ability of unions to spend money in political campaigns.[65]

Movement Conservatism elevated American individualism in much the same way Americans had in the 1890s and the 1920s. And in the 1980s, as in the earlier eras, Americans tended to put on a pedestal those with money and power. The 1987 film *Wall Street* featured the corporate raider Gordon Gekko, whose famous line "greed . . . is good" encapsulated the popular vision of the era.

The intellectual justification for the pursuit of money was both economic and religious. According to the economic argument, people "growing" the economy were creating wealth to invest in new businesses, which would in turn hire more people, who would themselves be able to climb the economic ladder. Wealthy Americans as job creators was an idea that came from the original free labor economy, but it did not take into consideration the role government played in underwriting that success through favorable legislation. The religious justification came from the idea that those with money were favored by God. These ideas translated into a conviction that America, with its vaunted wealth and power, was blessed by God and had a mission to spread American values.[66]

Such views made it a religious as well as an economic and political duty to oppose communism, and Reagan and his advisers, including Vice President Bush, took that charge seriously. A Marxist revolution in Nicaragua in 1979 made them fear that communists might gain control of Central America. Once in office, Reagan's men began to fund opposition groups in Nicaragua—the Contras—to overthrow the Sandinista government. The Democratic Congress was less enthusiastic than the White House about funding the Contras, partly because congressmen objected to the CIA meddling in a Latin American country, partly because the Contras themselves were no prizes: their scorched-earth tactics included kidnapping, arson, rape, and murder. In 1985, Congress firmly prohibited further aid to the Contras.[67]

Half a world away from Nicaragua, terrorists in Lebanon, backed by Iran, had been kidnapping Americans and Europeans. By 1985, they held seven Americans. This hostage crisis seemed to have no solution: the prisoners were too closely guarded to be rescued. Israeli officials suggested selling arms to Iran, a plan that might soften moderate Iranians toward the United States and encourage Iranian leaders to pressure the terrorists to release hostages. The Reagan administration agreed, and Israeli agents made the sales. Soon, though, Colonel Oliver North, an evangelical military aide to National Security Council head John Poindexter, proposed cutting Israel out of the middle and selling directly to Iran, although it was illegal under US law to sell arms to countries on the State Department's terrorism list. Cutting out Israel meant the United States could charge a high mark-up. The proceeds could then be used—off the books—to aid the Contras.

This was just the sort of plan that appealed to Reagan-era individualists: a handsome army colonel finding a too-clever-by-half way to do what was morally "right," rather than allowing America to be bound by the weak-kneed elite Democrats in Congress. It was the stuff from which Red Dawn had been shaped. The administration executed the plan. (The sales of about four thousand missiles to Iran did not, in the end, result in any great change in the hostage crisis, which ceased with the conclusion of the Iran-Iraq War, when Iran released the hostages to attract Western aid for rebuilding.)

When the story of the Iran-Contra affair broke in November 1986, it revealed the dark underside of a government driven by ideology rather than by respect for law. The investigation of the affair was shocking less for the revelation of administration officials breaking laws than for the continued willingness of government employees to engage in illegal behavior. North and Poindexter concealed, altered, and shredded so many documents—"one and a half feet" of them, according to North's secretary—that the full story could never be pieced together. Still, fourteen administration officials were indicted and eleven convicted (the latter would be pardoned by George H. W. Bush, himself implicated in the scandal, when he was president). And yet, to many, Oliver North—and the administration that backed him—seemed the face of all that was right in America: a strong, moral man, taking military action to spread American capitalist values over the objections of communist-sympathizing congressional Democrats.[68]

The image of Reaganism also overawed its reality in the domestic economy. The Republican Party talked about helping the average American, but, in fact, under Reagan it pulled together a religious, social, and cultural movement that fueled policies to benefit the very wealthy. Money flowed to defense industries in the South and West while wages of workers in the East and the middle of the country stagnated. From 1975 to 1980, private wealth had grown 31 percent; from 1983 to 1988, it grew by only 8 percent. Those not thriving in the new economy participated in the boom times either by becoming the very two-income households social conservatives opposed or by borrowing: from 1983 to 1988, household debt as a percentage of GNP grew by more than 20 percent.[69]

The Republican rhetoric about protecting the average American by cutting taxes, endorsing strict constitutionalism, and blocking the power of special interests bolstered economic policies that redistributed wealth upward. The lowering of marginal tax rates started wealth flowing not down, as supply-side economics promised, but up, reversing what economists have called the "great compression" of wealth in America from the New Deal to the 1970s and turning it into the "great divergence" in wealth after the 1980s. At the same time that Republicans slashed the tax base, which funded the social welfare legislation and kept the way open for individuals to rise, they endorsed tax expenditures that favored the wealthy. Federal taxes did not, in fact, go down; they remained steady at about 19.4 percent of the national income. But state and local governments had to raise taxes to make up for federal cuts. What changed was not the level of taxation, but who paid it. In 1979, 1 percent of Americans held 20.5 percent of the nation's wealth; by 1989, the top 1 percent held 35.7 percent.[70]

Although federal taxes did not go up, the size of the federal government or its budgets did not go down. They grew. Reagan increased the number of federal workers faster than Carter had. Budgets, too, increased. Reagan's people insisted this was the fault of the Democrats, who refused to make sufficient cuts, but in fact the administration never submitted a balanced budget—its dramatic increase in defense spending, which equaled the highest percentage of GNP ever in peacetime, meant that it could not. The administration made up the difference between taxes and spending through extensive borrowing, turning America from a creditor to a debtor nation. The federal debt tripled from $994 billion to $2.8 trillion during the Reagan years. Taxpayers had to pay interest on this debt, further stripping their tax dollars of potency.[71]

By 1987, cracks were appearing in public support for Reaganism. *Wall Street's* Gordon Gekko sent up the Reagan era's economy:

> The richest one percent of this country owns half our country's wealth, five trillion dollars. One third of that comes from hard work, two thirds comes from inheritance, interest on interest accumulating to widows and idiot sons and what I do, stock and real estate speculation. It's bullshit. You got ninety percent of the American public out there with little or no net worth. I create nothing. I own. We make the rules, pal. The news, war, peace, famine, upheaval, the price per paper clip. We pick that rabbit out of the hat while everybody sits out there wondering how the hell we did it. Now you're not naive enough to think we're living in a democracy, are you buddy? It's the free market. And you're a part of it.[72]

By 1987, it was clear that relaxing the rules governing the savings and loan banks had permitted speculation and downright theft that had allowed wealthy men, including Vice President Bush's son Neil and a number of congressmen of both parties, to emerge wealthy from the wreckage of people's retirement accounts. Government insurance would have to bail out the savings and loans, to the tune of more than a hundred billion dollars. Then, in October 1987, the booming stock market crashed, revealing the underbelly of the Reagan econ-omy. Perhaps, naysayers noted, supply-side economics didn't work after all. Perhaps the whole idea was just what Stockman had admitted in 1981: a justification for the age-old trick of gaming the system to benefit the rich. But Movement Con-servatives saw it differently. The problem with Reagan, they thought, was simply that he had not cut government enough.[73]

12

The West as an Idea

In the years after Reagan, Movement Conservatives lashed
the Republican Party to an ideology that was based on image
rather than reality and created a government constructed on
the same principles James Henry Hammond had espoused a
century and a half before. The people who guided the Republican Party in the 1990s and 2000s claimed to be trying to cut
government down to an acceptable size. But in truth they were
destroying the New Deal government, which they saw as socialism, and replacing it with an even bigger government that
served the ideals of Movement Conservatism: promoting big
business, religion, and the military. Their allegiance to their
ideology overrode party considerations as they turned on their
own president for being insufficiently Republican. Their ideology overrode voters' will: they tried to destroy a Democratic
president whose policies promoting growth and balancing
the federal budget made him enormously popular. Ultimately,

their ideology would override reality, setting both the party and the country up for disaster.

Wedded to their take-no-prisoners approach to politics, Movement Conservatives turned on Republicans they believed were insufficiently dedicated to destroying the social welfare state. In 1988, they forced Republican presidential candidate George H. W. Bush, whom they perceived as too moderate, to adopt their language and then rejected him when he persuaded Congress to pass a tax hike to fix Reagan's dire budget deficits.

In 1988, when Bush ran to succeed Reagan, Movement Conservatives dismissed him as a wishy-washy moderate Republican whose support for expanded government services, abortion, and civil rights they disliked. In the important Iowa caucuses, Bush ran eighteen points behind conservative Kansas senator Bob Dole and six points behind televangelist Pat Robertson. To court Movement Conservatives, Bush adopted a campaign slogan that echoed the clear declarations of principle put forth by Phyllis Schlafly in 1960: "Read my lips: No New Taxes." Further, he tapped a young Movement Conservative, Indiana senator James Danforth ("Dan") Quayle, who had well-established ties to evangelical religious groups, to be his running mate.[1]

Bush's swing to the right did not overcome voters' lack of enthusiasm for this mild-mannered patrician, and he had to adopt Movement Conservative imagery. In mid-summer, the Democratic ticket held a lead of almost twenty points over Bush and Quayle. The Democratic nominee was Massachusetts governor Michael Dukakis, a technocrat who had presided over the dramatic 1980s recovery of the ailing

Massachusetts economy by overseeing its switch from heavy industry to high tech and finance; his running mate was Texas senator Lloyd Bentsen, an older centrist Democrat. The ticket conjured up memories of the JFK-LBJ ticket of 1960 and carried a refreshing air of competence and moderation.

To reverse the devastating poll numbers, Bush's chief of staff, Lee Atwater, decided to run a viciously negative campaign, garnering voters not by illuminating national policies but by focusing on the central image of Movement Conservatism: special interests—especially Black people aided by Liberals like Dukakis—were literally killing Americans. Led by Roger Ailes, the man who had packaged Nixon in 1968, Bush's team produced the devastating "Willie Horton" advertisement.

Presented like a news story, the television ad featured a mug shot of Willie Horton, a convicted Black murderer. A voice-over explained that Governor Dukakis had allowed Horton a weekend furlough from prison, during which he attacked a couple, stabbing the man and raping his girlfriend. Horton was white middle-class America's worst nightmare: a Black killer turned loose on society by a Liberal. In fact, the Massachusetts furlough program had been signed into law by Dukakis's Republican predecessor, and the most progressive furlough program at the time was the federal program under Reagan and Bush, but Atwater and Ailes encapsulated in thirty seconds the argument that Democrats were socialists working for dangerous Black Americans.[2]

The Willie Horton ad swung the campaign. Dukakis's numbers plummeted. On November 8, Bush and Quayle took 53.4 percent of the popular vote to Dukakis and Bentsen's 45.6 percent, although Democrats kept control of the House and

Senate. Dukakis later called the Republicans' winning tactics "despicable."[3]

Although Movement Conservative imagery had put him in the White House, Bush's inaugural address signaled that he would back away from the movement's extremes. He promised to bring the budget into balance. But since popular programs— Medicare, Social Security, veterans' benefits, food stamps— took up 65 percent of the budget and defense spending took up most of the rest, there was very little room for cuts. Bush suggested hopefully that volunteerism could replace expensive social programs. He told Americans the nation had a "high moral principle" to "make kinder the face of the Nation and gentler the face of the world." He deplored the rise of partisanship in Congress and called for bipartisan cooperation.[4]

Bush tried to repair the damage to the nation's finances wrought by Reagan's policies. Between 1980 and 1989, the federal debt had tripled to $2.8 trillion, interest payments cost $200 billion a year, and budgets were still badly out of balance. The debt problem had been bad when Reagan left office, but it got worse almost immediately as the federal government stepped in to clean up the mess of collapsing savings and loan institutions to the tune of $132 billion.[5]

In 1990, Bush faced an estimated $171 billion deficit for the next fiscal year. This amounted to 4 percent of GNP, less than the deficits of the 1980s but a greater problem for Bush than deficits had been for Reagan because a 1985 law that went into effect in 1991 would require automatic cuts of 40 percent across the board if something weren't done. "I'm willing to eat crow," Bush wrote in his diary. "But the others are going to have to eat crow. I'll have to yield on 'Read My Lips,' and they're going to have to yield on some of their rhetoric on taxes and on entitlements."[6]

But Bush had badly underestimated Movement Conservatives. In fall 1990, he and his lieutenants in Congress hammered out a deal with congressional Democrats that made deep spending cuts, demanded that future appropriations be paired with a way to pay for them, and called for $134 billion in new taxes. Movement Conservative congressmen signed on in private, but in public they launched a broadside against the deal as an affront to economic growth, common people, and Reagan.[7]

Leading the Movement Conservatives was Georgia Republican Newt Gingrich. A consummate egotist, Gingrich believed he could put the Republicans in control of Congress for the first time since 1954. To do that, he took a hard Movement Conservative line, accusing anyone who stood against him of elitism, socialism, or corruption—either personal or in the traditional sense of corrupting the body politic by representing "special interests." "You are killing us," Bush told him. "You are just killing us."[8]

That was exactly Gingrich's intention: to knock off the remaining Republican moderates, whom he and his lieutenants were beginning to think of as RINOs—Republicans in Name Only—and marshal Movement Conservatives to take over the party and the country. First to his side was Grover Norquist, who had developed a pledge designed to guarantee that Reagan's 1986 tax reform measure would not be "subverted." Elected officials who signed the pledge vowed to oppose any increase in tax rates or any elimination of tax deductions or tax credits from the 1986 law. The pledge had been such a powerful talisman for voters in 1988 that 101 House Republicans and 2 House Democrats had signed it. Norquist warned that anyone elected based on the pledge who then voted for Bush's budget agreement was elected on a "falsehood" and would be held accountable. He promised that Americans for Tax Reform and other antitax groups would publicize the names of those who broke the pledge.[9]

The tax measure that Gingrich opposed, the Omnibus Budget Reconciliation Act of 1990, as it was formally known, destroyed Bush. With members of his own party carping at him from the right, his popularity fell to 52 percent in October.[10]

Although Movement Conservatives didn't like it, the same pragmatism that made Bush a careful custodian of the country's finances made him a good leader through the crumbling of the Soviet Union and its empire in eastern Europe. Bush had extensive experience in foreign policy. He had led the CIA for a year in the mid-1970s, served for two years as the American ambassador to the UN, and spent fourteen months as an American representative in China. He understood that America must be cautious as the USSR spun apart and its satellites—Poland, East Germany, Czechoslovakia, Bulgaria, Romania, Lithuania, and others—tried to transition out of communism. He refused to gloat over the nation's former foes and tried to institute a "new world order" in which America and former communist countries cooperated to solve international problems.[11]

The splintering of a superpower raised an important question: with national boundaries shifting almost daily, would America permit larger countries to swallow up smaller ones?

That question ceased to be academic in August 1990, when Iraq's Saddam Hussein invaded neighboring Kuwait. Swayed by British prime minister Margaret Thatcher to conclude that if Iraq were permitted to keep Kuwait, no small country would be safe, Bush backed sanctions against Iraq and then its invasion by a coalition of thirty-three countries allied to remove Saddam from Kuwait.

On January 17, 1991, Operation Desert Storm began with air strikes against Baghdad. On February 24, US Marines advanced into occupied Kuwait. Prepared for a bloody struggle against the best troops in the Arab world, coalition forces were astonished when the Iraqi army melted away, in retreat even before the invasion. Only 243 coalition soldiers—147 of them American—died in combat. Four days after the fighting began, it was over; Iraqi forces had abandoned Kuwait, and the Bush team declared a cease-fire. Bush hoped that disaffected Iraqis would remove Saddam from power, but he offered only humanitarian aid to the rebelling Shiites and Kurds who tried to do just that. Saddam's forces killed between fifty and eighty thousand of those rebels, created a mass exodus of Kurds from Iraq, and laid the groundwork for another invasion under another President Bush twelve years later.[12]

In the buildup to the Gulf War, Bush's popularity soared to an astonishing 89 percent. But his goose was cooked with Movement Conservatives, who warned that anyone who had voted for the 1990 tax measure—or signed it—was a RINO who would pay for his or her apostasy at the polls. In the election of 1992, they backed the independent candidate, billionaire businessman Ross Perot, while the Democratic governor of Arkansas, the charismatic William Jefferson Clinton, whipped up cheering audiences with his relentless focus on the economy, which was in a short-term recession sparked primarily by the savings and loan crisis. Bush clung to the vain hope that he could come from behind.[13]

That November, Clinton and his running mate, Tennessee senator Albert Gore III, garnered 43 percent of the vote to win the White House. Republicans had the powerful language of individualism and prosperity against special interests, but Democrats had the even more powerful facts that the Reagan years had left poor and middle-class Americans falling behind the wealthiest of their countrymen. Bush captured only 37 percent of the electorate, and Ross Perot siphoned off more than nineteen million votes, almost 19 percent of the voters, who were fed up with what seemed to many to be the interchangeability of the politicians in Washington. Democrats retained control of the House and Senate. With Republican policies driving more and more voters toward Democrats, the election of 1992 demonstrated that Republicans could not win without the votes of Movement Conservatives. They would have to harden their positions even further.

If they hated RINOs, Movement Conservatives were apoplectic about Democrats, those Liberals who were pushing America toward socialism. They worried that Clinton would find a way to erase the gains of the Reagan years. They had spent forty years fighting "statism" on two fronts: in America and against the Soviet Union. Now that the Soviet Union was gone, they noted, they could concentrate their firepower at home.[14]

And they did. Although polls suggested that the public was not greatly concerned about taxes, Movement Conservatives' rhetoric against taxes continued to mount as they pushed supply-side economics. Promising to slash budgets and cut taxes, regardless of the effect on state and local governments, was almost always a recipe for victory. In 1993, Republican Christine Todd Whitman, a woman with, as even the supportive *Wall Street Journal* noted, "no recognizable economic credentials," came from twenty points behind to win the governorship of New Jersey when she called in Grover Norquist to craft a tax-cut promise. Norquist simply fought the supply-side fight: "We worked from the assumption that our economic policies worked and theirs didn't.... We ran on this message... and we won."[15]

Movement Conservatives continued to insist that social welfare legislation was simply Democratic vote buying. When Clinton proposed a national health-care plan, they worried that health-care benefits would cement more voters to the Democrats, and they attacked it with the same sort of vicious misrepresentation that had worked in the Willie Horton ad.[16]

But it was not just health care they opposed. A law designed to protect women against domestic violence was portrayed as an attempt to create more government jobs; support for education was called a payoff for teachers' unions or a plot to indoctrinate children into Liberal ideas. Movement Conservatives called for "school choice," the privatization of the educational system, or homeschooling to guarantee children's moral safety. Support for affirmative action for minorities was "reverse discrimination"; Movement Conservatives suggested that the real people at risk in America were white men, against whom the government had consistently stacked the rules.[17]

These arguments had a wide reach as Rush Limbaugh's Movement Conservative talk show—only one of many—was aired on 659 radio stations. To extend that reach further, in 1992 Limbaugh began to host a television show—produced by Roger Ailes—which was carried on 225 television stations by 1994.[18]

From the very beginning of Clinton's administration, Movement Conservatives demonized the president as fiscally and morally bankrupt: James Johnson, for example, who had challenged Orville Faubus for the governorship of Arkansas in 1956 on the grounds that he was too soft on racial integration, told the Conservative Political Action Committee that he had proof Clinton was a "queer-mongering, whore-hopping adulterer; a baby-killing, draft-dodging, dope-tolerating, lying, two-faced, treasonable activist." Republicans searched for a scandal that would stick, but had no luck with anything other than a land development project in the Ozarks. The Whitewater story was thin—the Clintons had invested in a land development project in which they had lost forty thousand dollars, and they had no connection to the developer's later shady deals—but that tenuousness did not matter to Republicans.[19]

Clinton appointed a special prosecutor to look into the Whitewater matter, fully confident it would be put to rest. He figured wrong. Hard-line Movement Conservatives brushed aside his own appointee—a Republican with a reputation for fairness—and replaced him with one of their own, Kenneth Starr. Starr had no prosecutorial experience, but he was connected to the Arkansas Project, a group funded by billionaire

Richard Mellon Scaife to get rid of Clinton. The Arkansas Project had urged a former government employee, Paula Jones, to charge that Clinton, during his term as governor, had sexually harassed her. With his broad power to subpoena witnesses as a special prosecutor, it was a sure-fire bet that Starr would dig through the Arkansas stories.[20]

In the 1994 midterm elections, an astonishing 175 House seats were in play. Republican National Committee Chairman Haley Barbour went for broke, pouring fifteen million dollars into House races.[21]

Republicans offered voters a "Contract with America," produced primarily by Newt Gingrich and his adviser Grover Norquist, along with Texas representative Dick Armey. It was a "contract" because, they said, Americans were tired of having politicians break promises; the language of contract promised that the items in it would be binding. The contract called for small government and claimed that if given control of Congress, Republicans would immediately—on their first day— enact eight changes, including an audit of Congress, a cut of one-third of House committees and their staffs, and a rule to require a three-fifths majority to pass a tax increase. In the following ninety-nine days of a new Congress, they promised they would pass a balanced budget amendment, a line-item veto, welfare cuts, an anticrime bill, and a whole host of the tax expenditures—tax breaks—Americans seemed to love.[22]

The Contract with America sounded good, especially as talk show hosts like Limbaugh pushed it hourly on their stations and kept up the attacks on Clinton. That November, voters swung fifty-four seats from Democrats to Republicans, giving Republicans control of the House for the first time since

1954. In the Senate, Republicans picked up eight seats, gaining control there, too. The election results made Republicans, but especially Movement Conservatives, giddy. "Speaker Gingrich," read a T-shirt selling in Washington. "Deal with it."[23]

The Republican sweep of 1994 gave Movement Conservatives a free hand to set the terms of political debate, although reporters noted that they seemed to articulate only what they opposed, not what they favored. What they opposed was very clear: they hated what they claimed was the socialist system that was turning America into a nation of dependents. Destroying it, they thought, was simple: just get rid of the taxes that paid for it.[24]

Rush Limbaugh, whose support had been so instrumental that the Republican revolutionaries of 1994 made him an honorary member of their incoming congressional freshman class, outlined their agenda. They must "begin an emergency dismantling of the welfare system, which is shredding the social fabric," bankrupting the country, and "gutting the work ethic, educational performance, and moral discipline of the poor." Next, Congress should cut capital gains taxes, which would drive economic growth, create hundreds of thousands of jobs, and generate billions in federal revenue. Limbaugh kept staff in Washington to make sure the positions of the Movement Conservatives got through to voters. In exchange, every congressman knew that taking a stand against Limbaugh would earn instant condemnation on radio stations across the country.[25]

The Gingrich revolutionaries hit the ground running. They took over control of key positions in the House— Gingrich became Speaker; Armey, House majority leader;

Texas's Tom DeLay, majority whip. In April 1995, an internal memo laid down the theme of cutting taxes, rather than paying down the national debt, as the main principle of Republicanism. "Mr. Norquist has become one of the main power brokers in the new Republican majority," a writer for the *Wall Street Journal* noted. "His rise helps explain both the power of Newt Gingrich and the ideological makeover of Republicans."[26]

A balanced budget amendment to the Constitution passed by Congress two months later was the next step. It was, Norquist said, "the containment strategy," a mirror of the national security strategy the nation had used to contain communism during the Cold War. "All reductions in federal government spending weaken the left in America," Norquist continued. "Defunding government is defunding the left." His plan was, he said, to "run up 100 yards and blow [up] the train tracks."[27]

In the end, the inability of Gingrich's revolutionaries to compromise meant they went too far. Pieces of the agenda triumphantly passed in the House were watered down in the Senate and fell to the president's veto. Frustrated when Clinton refused to sign the Republican budget slashing funding for Medicare, public health, the environment, and education, Gingrich refused to compromise. The federal government shut down all nonessential activity for twenty-eight days between November 1995 and January 1996: national parks shut down, government contracts were suspended, applications for visas and passports went unanswered. The crisis pushed Clinton's poll numbers higher than they had been since his election as Americans blamed Republicans for the shutdown. The Contract with America, announced with such fanfare, withered. By March 1996, Republicans themselves were ignoring it.[28]

But the apocalyptic rhetoric of Movement Conservatism had taken on a life of its own. Newly empowered by talk radio and by fax machines that gave easy access to their representatives and to like-minded activists, people who had fallen behind in the Reagan economy blamed their troubles not on the policies that were drawing wealth upwards, but on the taxes that the Republicans insisted were the root of America's problems. Disaffected Americans began to see plots everywhere: politicians were selling out America to socialism. It was imperative for regular citizens to take matters into their own hands, just as the boys in *Red Dawn* had done, and return the nation to the traditional values Buckley had asserted in the 1950s: religion, the free market, and a strong military.[29]

Antigovernment extremism forced its way into American consciousness on the morning of April 19, 1995, when a bomb exploded in front of the Alfred P. Murrah Federal Building in downtown Oklahoma City. The blast killed 168, including 19 children younger than six, and injured more than 800. Timothy McVeigh, the chief bomber, had grown up on *Red Dawn*, had been a gunner in the Gulf War, and had become increasingly disaffected when he got home, convinced that America was turning socialist. "Taxes are a joke," he wrote to a newspaper. "Regardless of what a political candidate 'promises,' they will increase. More taxes are always the answer to government mismanagement. They mess up. We suffer. Taxes are reaching cataclysmic levels, with no slowdown in sight....Is a Civil War Imminent? Do we have to shed blood to reform the current system? I hope it doesn't come to that. But it might." When the police captured him shortly after the bombing, McVeigh was wearing a T-shirt that featured a picture of Abraham Lincoln and the words of presidential assassin Booth: *sic semper tyrannis.*[30]

The Republican revolution took on a life outside official channels in Washington, too. Gingrich, Armey, and DeLay, together with Norquist, launched the K Street Project, designed to change the culture of Washington to favor Republicans, rather than the congressional Democrats who had built up long-standing ties to businessmen and lobbyists over their many years in power. DeLay pointed out to lobbyists that Republicans were now in charge, and that if they wanted access to the channels of power, they had better remember Republicans and forget Democrats when they were hiring and making political contributions. K Street, the address of Washington lobbying firms, quickly got the message.

At the same time, the budget cuts the revolutionaries pushed through Congress led to congressional staff cuts, meaning that representatives increasingly turned to lobbyists, rather than staffers, to explain issues and write bills. Government pay stagnated, making the private sector an attractive alternative for former congressional staffers, and the space between congressional offices and K Street became a revolving door. By 1998 there were more than ten thousand registered lobbyists in Washington, spending $1.45 billion to advance their industries' interests. As the business community wrote legislation, congressmen justified it with the language of Movement Conservatism, emphasizing that only businessmen knew what was best for their industries.[31]

In October 1996, the movement gained its own television network, with Roger Ailes as its founding CEO. The Fox News

Channel (FNC) was the brainchild of Australian-born media mogul Rupert Murdoch, who recognized the frustration of Movement Conservatives with what they insisted was a Liberal media biased against their version of the world. Buckley had outlined this argument initially, and followers like Schlafly and later Limbaugh amplified it until followers believed that anything coming from a mainstream reporter was Liberal propaganda. Calling Fox News "fair and balanced," Murdoch played on Movement Conservatives' idea that their views had been dismissed by a cabal of elitist "leftist and anti-American" news outlets. By giving a voice to those ideas, Fox News promised to restore fairness and balance to American politics.[32]

Ailes used his trademark visual skills to set up an information system based on a clear, simple narrative. Stories used colorful graphics with bullet-pointed information. Newsreaders were handsome men or young, beautiful women; their stories created a narrative uncluttered with nuance. To hurry the spread of the new channel, Murdoch offered ten dollars per subscriber to each cable company that carried FNC. The FNC presented a mythologized America based on the ideology of Movement Conservatism. Its Americans were overwhelmingly white and rural and wanted just to be independent individuals. They hated taxes and intrusive government, and they would do fine if they could just get the socialistic Democrats to leave them alone.[33]

This vision had resonated in America since 1872, but it was even less real in the 1990s than it had been a century before. The 1990 census showed that more than three-quarters of the US population lived in cities of more than one hundred thousand people. Whites were the slowest-growing racial group in America (although they still made up about 80 percent of the population). And Americans across the board liked government services; they just didn't like paying for them, something Movement Conservatives since Reagan had said they didn't have to do.[34]

Fox News quickly became a major political player. By election 2000, 17.3 percent of Americans were watching FNC, and 3 to 8 percent of its voting viewers moved into the Republican column. FNC charged all other news stations with bias, forcing them to air the views of Movement Conservatives in self-defense. This technique had driven McCarthyism in the 1950s, and in the 1990s it acquired a new, scientific-sounding name. A vice president for the Movement Conservative think tank, the Mackinac Center for Public Policy, Joseph P. Overton, came up with the idea of the Overton Window, a span of ideas the public would accept. To move that range rightward, Movement Conservatives had to promote their views aggressively, until arguments and policies that had previously been considered outrageous would become acceptable. FNC moved the Overton Window by keeping up a constant stream of media chatter charging Democrats with socialism, elitism, and anti-Americanism.[35]

Clinton won reelection in 1996 because no matter how Republicans tried to spin it, the economy boomed during the Clinton years. Indeed, it put the Reagan economy to shame. The budgets of Reagan and Bush had run $290 billion in the red, and at the end of his term, Bush suddenly announced that that year's budget deficit would be $60 billion higher than projected. To address the deficits while also promoting his goals of social welfare, Clinton pushed through a 1993 budget that raised marginal tax rates on incomes over $250,000—affecting about 1 percent of Americans—to 39.6 percent, increased the highest corporate tax rate by 1 percent, and increased the tax on gasoline by 4.3 cents. He made small cuts to defense and overall spending but increased the earned income tax credit for low-income households with children. Although Clinton groused that his administration was full of "Eisenhower Republicans" trying to push back against Reagan Republicans, not a single Republican voted for the budget measure.[36]

Republicans howled that Clinton was destroying the economy by raising taxes on all Americans to fund special interests, but in fact the economy jumped back from its weak performance in 1991–1992 to perform brilliantly. Per capita GDP climbed and would climb 3 percent each year after 1997; unemployment dropped from 7.3 percent in 1993 to 4 percent in 2000; inflation fell from 3 percent to 1.6 percent in 1998. The raging deficits that had plagued the country since the Eisenhower years began to shrink. By 1998, thanks both to Bush's 1990 Omnibus Budget Reconciliation Act and Clinton's 1993 tax reform, the government was producing a budget surplus. In 1997, the booming economy gave Clinton room to expand health care for poor children, provide tax credits for college tuition, and cut the capital gains tax rate from 25 percent to 20 percent.[37]

The very fact that the economy was doing so well under a Democrat convinced Movement Conservatives that Clinton had to be stopped. If the Democratic program worked, Americans would continue it, just as they had chosen Eisenhower Republicanism in the 1950s. The country would be right back where it had been when William F. Buckley Jr. had despaired that people could not be trusted to choose the right thing: a government that worked hand-in-hand with business and religion.

In 1997, having turned up nothing on Whitewater, Kenneth Starr turned to the Paula Jones case in Arkansas. It, too, produced nothing that he could use, until Jones's lawyers gave him the name of a White House intern, Monica Lewinsky. They had gotten her name after her friend Linda Tripp secretly recorded Lewinsky's heartfelt conversations about her encounters with Clinton, then shared them with a man who had been part of Nixon's dirty-tricks team in 1972, who took them to Jones's lawyers (who played them to Movement Conservative hit woman Ann Coulter). Subpoenaed by Jones's lawyers, Lewinsky signed an affidavit denying any sexual relationship with the president. Jones's lawyers took the tapes to Starr. When he deposed Clinton in the Paula Jones case on January 17, Starr questioned him closely about his relationship with Lewinsky and elicited from him a statement, under oath, "I have never had sexual relations with Monica Lewinsky." With the secretly recorded Tripp tapes in hand, Starr promptly concluded he could get the president on charges of perjury and obstructing justice.[38]

For the next year, Starr called witnesses and leaked damaging gossip in techniques that looked much like McCarthy's. When Starr issued his report on September 9, 1998—just in time for the 1998 midterm election—it was an excruciatingly detailed account of every intimate encounter between Clinton and Ms. Lewinsky. Designed to shock and to confirm every hint that the president's actions would horrify moral

427

Americans, it read like pornography. Clinton, it appeared to jubilant Republicans, was coming down.[39]

But Movement Conservatism had always been based in ideology, not reality. As far as Movement Conservatives were concerned, Clinton was a mistaken president, an abomination, and they had finally been able to prove it. Most Americans, though, were disgusted less by the president's sexual encounters than by the prurience of his tormentors. Clinton's popularity remained high throughout 1998; it was above 65 percent before the elections. In those elections, after Gingrich had pumped ten million dollars into House races to pound on the Lewinsky scandal, the Democrats actually picked up five seats in the House and held even in the Senate—an outcome virtually unheard of in a midterm election in the sixth year of an administration. The last time it had happened was in 1822.[40]

Gingrich had promised his supporters a House pickup of ten to forty seats. Disgraced by the election results, already tainted by a reprimand and fine for ethics violations, and well aware that he was politically vulnerable himself because of his own extramarital affair, he resigned from Congress within a week of the election.[41]

But once again, Movement Conservatives believed that the problem was not their ideology, rather that Gingrich had been insufficiently committed to it. Power in the House went to Texas's Tom DeLay, a former pesticide salesman who had replaced a fondness for alcohol and women with evangelical Christianity. DeLay enforced his will by threatening to back a primary challenger against any Republican who opposed him. He demanded a vote for impeachment, and nervous moderate

Republicans complied. DeLay and House Judiciary Committee Chairman Henry Hyde—sponsor of a congressional measure prohibiting federal funding for abortion and himself soon to admit to an extramarital affair—wanted to force Clinton out of office.[42]

On December 19, 1998, the House of Representatives voted to impeach President Clinton for perjury and obstruction of justice, based on his statement under oath that he had not had sex with Lewinsky when there was evidence that the two had, in fact, engaged in oral sex. The case went to the Senate for trial, where, after all the hoopla that had raged around the case for a year, the Senate called no live witnesses and deliberated in private, acquitting the president—whose popularity was now at 70 percent—on all counts.[43]

Clinton's continuing popularity made Movement Conservatives despair. Why couldn't Americans see how awful he was? They swung toward conspiracy theories and pure Clinton-bashing, aided by talk radio and by new websites, especially the Drudge Report. In 1997, Matt Drudge and his assistant, Andrew Breitbart—who was a fan of Limbaugh—began aggregating anti-Democratic gossip and news. They sensationalized rumor and began to build a community of like-minded right-wing radicals on the increasingly powerful Internet.[44]

The election of 2000 forced another showdown within the Republican Party. Americans' disillusionment with the Gingrich Republicans dictated moving back toward the center. But the whole point of Movement Conservatism was that there was no such thing as a moderate Republican. As Buckley had laid out in the 1950s, anyone who accepted any part of the New

Deal was a socialist. There was no middle ground. Either you believed in the purity of Movement Conservatism or you were a heretic. The term RINO—Republican in Name Only—had been invented in the early 1990s, but the idea took off in the 2000 election: The party must be purged of RINOs.

The conflict came down to a fight over the nomination. While both of the main candidates—Arizona senator John McCain and Texas governor George W. Bush, the son of President Bush—were antiabortion conservative Republicans, they attracted different constituencies. McCain tried to run from Movement Conservative extremists to pick up the centrist Reagan Democrats and build a coalition closer to the political center. He raised the ire of Norquist's Americans for Tax Reform, the American Conservative Union, and the National Rifle Association, among others, when he called for limiting the amount of money corporations could spend in a political campaign.[45]

Those groups turned to Bush, who jumped to attract the Movement Conservative coalition and enlisted Norquist as an adviser. Bush—who had worked on his father's campaign with Lee Atwater—and another Atwater disciple, Karl Rove, destroyed McCain's candidacy by spreading rumors in South Carolina that McCain had fathered an illegitimate Black child (in fact, he and his wife had adopted their daughter from South Asia). Bush won the South Carolina primary; McCain's campaign never recovered.[46]

Bush repackaged the Gingrich-Norquist Movement Conservative plan with "a certain winsome cowboy charm," as one reporter put it. The Connecticut-born, Yale- and Harvard-educated son of a president had bought a ranch in Crawford,

Texas, in 1999, put on cowboy boots, and presented himself to voters as a Texas cowboy, drawing on the hatred of activist government that the western image represented. Even his hard-drinking, dissolute past looked iconic to supporters, for he could point to a good woman—his wife, Laura—and his recent sobriety as a sign that he had led a hard life and been redeemed.[47]

The Republican convention, carefully staged to highlight minorities and women, was awash in cowboy hats as Bush tried to appeal to moderates with promises that he would be "a uniter, not a divider." He promised never to raise taxes, calling instead for a large tax cut and the privatization of Social Security.[48]

Against Bush's folksy cowboy imagery, the Democratic nominee, Al Gore, Clinton's vice president, came across as a smart, experienced technocrat, out of touch with everyday Americans. His choice of Connecticut senator Joseph Lieberman, the first Jewish candidate named to a national ticket, reinforced the idea that the Democrats were up to their usual special interest politics. Gore's wooden style made it hard for supporters to swoon with enthusiasm, and his obvious disdain for Bush made it easy for Bush supporters to accuse him of elitism.

In the end, the election of 2000 was as deeply problematic as the election of 1876. Gore and Lieberman won the popular vote by more than half a million votes, despite the fact that consumer advocate Ralph Nader, who ran to show that all politicians were alike, peeled almost 3 million votes from the Democrats. But Gore was four votes short in the Electoral College. The winner of the 2000 election would be decided in Florida, where Bush's brother Jeb was the governor. In one heavily Democratic Florida county, a confusing ballot meant that about ten thousand votes thought to be intended for Gore were actually cast for the far-right candidate Pat Buchanan. In minority districts, ballot machines malfunctioned. The original vote count in Florida showed Bush ahead by 1,210 votes. A machine recount reduced that to 327. The Gore campaign requested a manual recount.[49]

Republicans howled that Bush had won and that Democrats were trying to steal the election. The issue pitted different levels of the government against each other. When the Florida Supreme Court ordered a recount, the US Supreme Court stepped in, announcing that recounting the votes would create "irreparable harm" to Bush and the country by "casting a cloud upon what he claims to be the legitimacy of his election." Although this seemed to suggest that the court thought Gore would win if there were a recount, in a five-to-four decision the Supreme Court upheld Bush's election. All five justices who voted in favor of Bush were Republican appointees; three had been appointed by Reagan, one by the first President Bush. Florida's electoral votes went to Bush, and he became president. For the first time since the Eisenhower administration, the Republicans had control of the White House and both chambers of Congress, although by squeakily narrow margins.[50]

Rather than seeing his weak support as a sign that he needed to steer a moderate course, Bush appeared to believe—as Benjamin Harrison had under similar circumstances—that God had eked out a surprise victory for him and that he should take a stronger, not a weaker, stance because of it. As soon as he took office, he pushed the agenda of Movement Conservatives aggressively. He prohibited doctors and nurses in family planning programs funded by the government from counseling pregnant women about abortion. He established the White House Office of Faith-Based and Community Initiatives, designed to enable religious charities to receive federal funding. He overturned so many regulations protecting labor that organizers suspected he was retaliating for their endorsement of Gore. Businessmen, land developers, and opponents of gay rights and affirmative action clamored for executive orders overturning Clinton's policies. Norquist commented, "Many conservatives believe we need to steam-clean the White House to get rid of everything Clinton did."[51]

Bush's father might have been a disappointment to Movement Conservatives, but his son's administration was "more Reaganite than the Reagan administration," one cheered. "Part of what we're doing is bringing K Street and the business community in," Norquist explained. "They should be an integral part.... What does the business community want? Deregulation. Free trade. Tax cuts." "Business is in complete control of the machinery of government," a Democrat railed. "The House, the Senate and the White House are all run by business-friendly Republicans who are deeply indebted to American business for their electoral victories.... It's payback time, and every industry and trade association is busily cashing in."[52]

The ties between business and government were illustrated most dramatically by Bush's vice president, Richard Cheney of Wyoming. Cheney, a former congressman, had been secretary of defense for the first President Bush during the Gulf War.

In 1995, he took the Middle East connections he had developed during the conflict to the Halliburton Company, the world's largest oil services corporation, where he became chief officer. Halliburton did 70 percent of its nearly fifteen-billion-dollar annual oil business overseas. The company had begun to branch out into construction work for the US military at its overseas installations, including logistical support for American forces.[53]

Cheney brought to the White House a strong business sensibility and a strong inclination for secrecy. One of the first things he did as vice president was to convene a White House energy task force with the heads of corporations, although he insisted on keeping the list of attendees secret. By April 2001, only three months into the Bush presidency, observers noted that it was "scoring big with business."[54]

The administration sold its policies with the help of Movement Conservative organizations. Every Wednesday, White House officials met with Norquist and one hundred leaders from religious, social, and economic groups that made up the Movement Conservative regulars. "There isn't an us and them with this administration," Norquist boasted. "They is us. We is them." A request for support from the Bush administration could marshal hundreds of thousands of constituents led by the members of the Wednesday meetings.[55]

Even before he prepared a budget, the president prepared a $1.6 trillion tax cut to wipe out the surplus. As long as there was money to spend, Norquist told a *New York Times* reporter, it would go to welfare legislation. The Bush administration wanted that money gone fast so there would not be a spending spree that would expand the government. The administration muscled the bill through the Republican House by a party vote. The first of the Bush tax cuts passed in June, cutting $1.3 trillion over ten years. The Movement Conservatives were getting their way. But those who had believed Bush would be a "uniter, not a divider," were increasingly disillusioned by his extremist course, and his already precarious popularity slid downward.[56]

Nine months after Bush took office, one of the most dramatic events in American history resurrected Bush's standing and enabled him to establish Movement Conservatism in full force into government. In August, Bush took off for a month's vacation at his Crawford ranch. On August 6, he received a CIA briefing titled "Bin Laden Determined to Strike Inside U.S." The president thought it routine. Osama bin Laden had been part of the CIA-funded anti-Soviet mujahideen in Afghanistan in the 1980s but had turned against his American benefactors during the Gulf War, resenting American support for Israel and the presence of American troops in his native Saudi Arabia.

On September 11, 2001, nineteen terrorists from the radical Islamic al-Qaeda network led by bin Laden hijacked four commercial jets and flew three of them into the twin towers of New York City's World Trade Center and the Pentagon. They tried to hit the US Capitol but missed when the passengers in the fourth plane crashed it in a Pennsylvania field. The attacks killed nearly three thousand Americans. Within a month, US and allied forces invaded Afghanistan to overthrow the Taliban regime that had sheltered al-Qaeda.

The 9/11 attacks intensified the Bush administration's sense of mission. The Cold War had ended, but America was still in a death struggle, now against an even more implacable foe. To defeat the nation's enemies, America must defend free enterprise and Christianity at all costs. "In our grief and anger we have found our mission and our moment," Bush announced. His popularity, which had been slipping as his loyalty to Movement Conservatism had become obvious, soared to 90 percent. Quickly, he and his advisers saw that popularity as a mandate to change America, and the world, along ideological lines.[57]

After 9/11, President Bush divided the world into his supporters and those he believed were anti-American, much as Nixon had done. "Either you are with us, or you are with the terrorists," he announced. To protect the "homeland," as it now called America, the Bush administration assumed extraordinary powers. The president created the Office of Homeland Security without congressional input, and it had no congressional oversight until Congress made it a cabinet-level department a year later. Although he sat at the highest levels of government, the new director, former Pennsylvania governor Tom Ridge (who had no experience in intelligence or security but was Bush's jogging buddy), did not have Senate confirmation. In the wake of the attacks, Congress had appropriated forty billion dollars to beef up American security. The Bush administration staffed this new, massive bureaucracy with true loyalists, Movement Conservatives with ties to Cheney and to his good friend Secretary of Defense Donald Rumsfeld, people who were evangelicals and fervent believers in the American military mission, regardless of their skills.[58]

After 9/11, the administration intensified its Movement Conservatism. It immediately strengthened business, first shoring up the airline industry and then inviting petroleum industry leaders to confer about how the government could best help protect energy infrastructures. Their solution was less regulation and more drilling—and subsidies for ethanol, which the president pressed Congress to permit. Next, the Securities Exchange Commission suspended part of the New Deal–era Securities Exchange Act that prohibited "manipulative and deceptive devices," thus enabling companies to manipulate their stock prices. Then Bush insisted on more tax cuts to stimulate the economy, which had been weakened by the economic dislocation resulting from the attacks.[59]

Bush's proposed $2.13 trillion 2003 budget dramatically increased military spending—by $48 billion—and slashed highway funding, environmental initiatives, job training, and other domestic spending. It would also throw the budget $80 billion in the red. In 2003, Congress elevated the Office of Homeland Security to a government department, consolidating within it twenty-two agencies, including those concerned with customs, immigration, transportation, and the Federal Emergency Management Agency (FEMA). The administration tried—unsuccessfully—to take the union rights from 180,000 employees of those agencies on the grounds that union rules would hurt national security.[60]

"By its very nature, homeland defense requires close cooperation between government and industry because much of the nation's vital infrastructure—from telecommunications networks to power plants to water supplies—is in private hands," the *New York Times* noted. Recognizing a new market, corporations opened homeland security offices to tailor their products to national security needs and began to huddle with

Director Ridge, for it was clear that huge government contracts would be forthcoming.[61]

State governors and urban mayors pled in vain for money to help them meet their new security expenses; Democrats pled in vain for money to strengthen existing security programs like police and firefighters, and the security around power plants and ports. Bush and his Republican allies derided such requests as proposed "pork barrel spending" that would weaken the nation. The president threatened to veto any such bills. Instead, security protection would come from the new programs administered at the federal level. In December 2001, Congress had added to the $40 billion it had appropriated immediately after the attacks, allocating another $318 billion for military and homeland security needs, all to be overseen exclusively by the executive branch. The era of big government was back, but this time, the big government would be run by Movement Conservatives.[62]

With the momentum of 9/11 behind him, Bush consolidated executive power far beyond what Nixon had managed. Cheney adhered to the idea that the executive branch could operate without any oversight and that with the domestication of the war on terror, the president was bound neither by Congress nor by law. The Bush administration assumed the power to wiretap citizens without a court warrant and to suspend the writ of habeas corpus indefinitely, as well as the power to torture prisoners.[63]

The administration also almost immediately began to reinterpret congressional action as it saw fit. In the past, presidents had used "signing statements" as a way to note the significance of the legislation at hand or as a way to thank particular individuals for their part in crafting the law. By November 2001, Bush had begun to use signing statements to redefine congressional laws according to his wishes. One of his first significant signing statements was on a bill providing appropriations for the Interior Department. Congress had required congressional approval before the executive carried out the different provisions in the measure. Bush announced that he would "interpret such provisions to require notification only." The Bush administration would not be bound by Congress.[64]

Bush's men equated the administration with America. Only two days after Ridge took office, the Republican National Committee (RNC) sent an email to Republican activists describing the Office of Homeland Security and asking recipients to reply to the RNC with a message supporting Bush and supplying contact information for future communications, an easy way to expand Republican mailing lists as original recipients forwarded the email to friends and family. An RNC spokesman declared that the Republican Party might well benefit from the apparent link between Homeland Security and the Republicans, but he thought that benefit entirely appropriate. Then, in January 2002, Karl Rove announced that the Republican Party would claim the war on terror as a partisan issue in the midterm elections because Americans trusted the Republican Party "to do a better job of protecting and strengthening America's military might and thereby protecting America."[65]

This theme bled into domestic policy; Republicans attacked Democrats' reluctance to rubber-stamp Bush's economic plans as an attack on "the homeland." In a refrain oddly reminiscent of the late nineteenth century, Republicans took the stand that they were the only ones who could be trusted to govern America. Even odder was the degree to which this image conflicted in 2002 with reality: it was, after all, under Bush himself that the nation suffered the 9/11 attacks and under supply-side economics that the economy had suffered profound economic dislocation. But the beauty of Movement Conservatism was that it offered a neatly packaged story about government, unencumbered by facts.[66]

In October 2001, John Dilulio, the director of the Office of Faith-Based and Community Initiatives, noted the power of the Movement Conservative story. He resigned from his post, complaining that the Bush administration made speeches, not policy, that it was obsessed with the press, communication, media, and strategizing with congressmen, rather than with discussing anything of substance. "The lack of even basic policy knowledge" on the part of Bush's senior staff was "somewhat breathtaking—discussions by fairly senior people who meant Medicaid but were talking Medicare; near-instant shifts from discussing any actual policy pros and cons to discussing political communications, media strategy, et cetera," he explained. Even the creation of the Office of Homeland Security, "the most significant reorganization of the Federal government since the creation of the Department of Defense," received nothing more than "talking-points caliber deliberation."

The Bush administration's rigid division of the world into us and them, said Dilulio, "gave rise to what you might call Mayberry Machiavellis—staff, senior and junior, who consistently acted as if the height of political sophistication consisted in reducing every issue to its simplest, black-and-white terms for public consumption, then steering legislative initiatives or policy proposals as far right as possible."[67]

In the short term, the vision of Bush's Movement Conservatives worked. In 2002, the Republicans won the midterms, picking up eight seats in the House of Representatives and two in the Senate. The administration immediately tried to push its agenda further, calling for more tax cuts. When the secretary of the Treasury, Paul O'Neill, worried that the nation was headed for a fiscal crisis as budgets and debts soared out of control, Cheney shot back: "Reagan proved that deficits don't matter." As O'Neill sat shocked, Cheney continued: "We won the midterms. This is our due." The disillusioned secretary—who would resign—later mused that the Bush administration was operating solely on ideology. That made for easy governing, he commented, "because you don't have to know anything or search for anything. You already know the answer to everything. It's not penetrable by facts. It's absolutism."[68]

Nowhere was the Bush administration's Manichean vision of the world clearer than in foreign affairs. Convinced that Bush's father had not gone far enough in the first Gulf War, a group of Movement Conservatives—dubbed "neocons"—urged his son to stabilize the Middle East by getting rid of Iraq's Saddam Hussein.

The neocons, organized in 1997, when political commentator William Kristol brought together Dick Cheney, Donald Rumsfeld, and a number of other Movement Conservatives to protest Clinton's foreign policy, wanted America to take international preeminence in the wake of the Cold War. They demanded significantly increased defense spending and

American-backed "regime change" in countries that did not have "political and economic freedom." They wanted to see a world order "friendly to our security, our prosperity, and our principles." They had demanded that Clinton remove Iraq's Saddam Hussein from power, for they believed he was destabilizing the entire Middle East. At Cheney's urging, Bush had made Rumsfeld his secretary of defense.[69]

As soon as he heard of the 9/11 attacks, Rumsfeld asked his aides to see if there was enough evidence to "hit" Saddam Hussein as well as Osama bin Laden. In fact, Saddam had not been involved in the attack on America: the al-Qaeda terrorists of 9/11 were from Saudi Arabia, Egypt, and the United Arab Emirates. But the Bush administration pushed so hard on the idea that the terrorists were affiliated with Iraq that many Americans—especially those who watched Fox News—came to believe, incorrectly, that the 9/11 terrorists either were Iraqi or were working with Saddam Hussein.[70]

In September 2002, the administration outlined what became known as the Bush Doctrine. Based largely on the philosophy of the neocons, the doctrine argued that the new conditions of terrorism required the government to act pre-emptively to forestall hostile acts rather than wait for an attack. It embraced the idea that there was "right and wrong" in foreign affairs and demanded that America wage "a war of ideas" by spreading pro-American economic and cultural policies. It warned that there were few greater threats to America than a terrorist attack with weapons of mass destruction (WMDs), meaning nuclear, chemical, or biological weapons.[71]

To convince recalcitrant foreign policy realists that it was worth ousting Saddam Hussein from power, Bush administration officials warned that the dictator was amassing WMDs, including nuclear devices. In a television interview, National Security Advisor Condoleezza Rice warned of mushroom clouds rising over American cities and insisted that Saddam was on the brink of world annihilation.[72]

On February 5, 2003, Secretary of State Colin Powell, a former chairman of the Joint Chiefs of Staff added to the president's cabinet to reassure foreign policy realists but generally ignored by neocons Cheney and Rumsfeld, spoke passionately before the United Nations. Powell provided what he insisted was evidence that Saddam had chemical WMDs and had obtained the resources to create nuclear weapons. He hinted that the Iraqi leader had worked with al-Qaeda in 2001 or that he might in the future. Powell was well known and trusted as a moderate; if he said Iraq was deadly dangerous, it must be true. What those listening could not know was that he had not himself vetted the "evidence" he presented, and that it was almost entirely either discredited or made up of rumor. Powell later referred to "getting had."[73]

But his speech did the trick. Enough countries to call it a "coalition of the willing"—although the only major power that participated was the United Kingdom—backed an invasion of Iraq. On March 20, 2003, American troops invaded Iraq with the intention of overthrowing Saddam Hussein's government. The operation would be a "cakewalk," the administration thought; desperate Iraqis who hated their leader would welcome coalition forces with open arms. Like cowboy heroes—and often publicized as cowboys—American soldiers would bring democracy and capitalism to the benighted Iraqis. Indeed, Saddam's forces crumbled in little over a month. By

May the United States had set up a transitional government in Iraq overseen by L. Paul Bremer.[74]

On May 1, 2003, Bush landed in a fixed-wing aircraft on the USS *Abraham Lincoln*, an aircraft carrier. Wearing a flight suit, he posed for photographs with the vessel's crew, which had just returned from the Persian Gulf. Bush then gave a speech announcing the end of major combat operations in Iraq. Festooning the aircraft carrier was a giant banner emblazoned "Mission Accomplished." From then on, the administration farmed out many of the tasks of supplying and protecting the transitional government—as well as rebuilding Iraq—to private contractors. These included Halliburton, which by the end of 2004 had received more than ten billion dollars in no-bid contracts.[75]

The carefully staged Mission Accomplished event symbolized the triumph of image over substance that had begun in the Reagan years. Combat operations in Iraq would continue until August 2010, with the majority of American casualties coming after May 2003. The mingling of image and reality in the Bush administration became clearer when it decided to search for Saddam Hussein himself, who had eluded American troops. On December 13, 2003, it launched Operation Red Dawn to begin the hunt. The soldiers began by looking in two sites also named after the Reagan-era film: Wolverine 1 and Wolverine 2.

Saddam's eventual capture inspired Rush Limbaugh to wax rhapsodic about what it meant to be a true American, using as examples Movement Conservative presidents Bush and Reagan. They were both cowboys, Limbaugh insisted, in an online piece that drew from the TV shows of the 1960s.

Cowboys, he said, were never looking for trouble, but when it came, they faced it with courage. They were always on the side of right, defending good people against bad people. They had high morals, had good manners, and were honest. They spoke the truth, without regard for "political correctness." They were "a beacon of integrity in the wild, wild West." They were respected, they didn't drink, and bad guys kept their distance. In a fistfight or a gunfight, they always won. In victory, they rode off into the sunset. They lived in a time when there was right and wrong, a distinction blurred in the modern world.

Ronald Reagan was a cowboy, Limbaugh continued. "He was brave, positive, and gave us hope. He wore a white hat.... Liberals hated Ronald Reagan." Limbaugh continued:

> They also hate President Bush because he distinguishes between good and evil. He calls a spade a spade, and after 9-11 called evil "evil," without mincing any words, to the shock of the liberal establishment. That's what cowboys do, you know.... In the old West, might did not make right. Right made might. Cowboys in white hats were always on the side of right, and that was their might. I am glad my President is a cowboy. He got his man! Cowboys do, you know.[76]

The Bush presidency represented the triumph of Buckley's vision for the Republican Party. Christianity and free enterprise had merged, and politicians who understood and endorsed Buckley's program were in full control of the government. They set out to oppose Democrats, moderate Republicans, and the social welfare programs that to them represented communism. They did so, effectively, by rallying voters to a mythologized image, much as the southern Democrats, whose ideas they echoed, had forged a constituency in the 1850s.

The merging of Republicanism, Americanism, and religion was clearly expressed in an extraordinary quotation recorded by journalist Ron Suskind in a *New York Times Magazine* article in 2004. A senior adviser to Bush told Suskind that people like him—Suskind—were in "the reality-based community": they believed people could find solutions based on their observations and careful study of discernible reality. But, the aide continued, such a worldview was obsolete. "That's not the way the world really works anymore.... We are an empire now, and when we act, we create our own reality. And while you're studying that reality—judiciously, as you will—we'll act again, creating other new realities, which you can study too, and that's how things will sort out. We're history's actors... and you, all of you, will be left to just study what we do."[77]

This admission marked a historical circle. Despite its wide base of religious, social, and cultural support, the Movement Conservatism that had taken over the Republican Party was an ideology that permitted wealth to concentrate at the top, just as the defense of antebellum slavery had been. The Republican Party in the twenty-first century adhered to the position it had organized in the nineteenth century to fight. And like their southern predecessors in the 1850s, Movement Conservatives in 2004 were boasting that "Republican hegemony" would last "for years, maybe decades." Like their predecessors, they were wrong. A looming crisis soon revealed that their devotion to an ideology divorced from reality meant they no longer knew how to govern.[78]

The Republican Party's roots lay in the struggle to control the destiny of the American West, and in one of the odd coincidences of Republican history, 2004 gave that western theme a closing scene. In June of that year, President Reagan died after a long struggle with Alzheimer's disease. To honor the recently deceased actor-president, the funeral director carefully arranged for the funeral to have a Hollywood ending. On a warm June afternoon, the airplane carrying Reagan's body reached the naval base at Point Mugu, California, and a cortege made the twenty-five-mile trip to the Reagan Presidential Library in Simi Valley. Seven hundred or so dignitaries and family members gathered to pay their last respects. After eulogies, a twenty-one-gun salute, and four naval fighter jets flying over in missing man formation, the service concluded just as the sun dropped below the horizon.[79]

Conclusion

In the 1850s, rising young men created the Republican Party to stand against a system of government that privileged the wealthy. Early Republicans wanted a government that would promote economic opportunity for men like them, rather than one that would allow a rich elite to monopolize the nation's assets. Yet by 2004, as the country mourned the death of the Republican hero Ronald Reagan, a Republican administration was pouring tax money into corporations while weakening regulations and protections for individuals: the party had embraced the very ideology its founders had opposed.

The US economy, after years of Republican control, looked much like that of the American South before the Civil War. The wealthy enjoyed enormous political clout, and there seemed little chance that would change. Business and wealth were entrenched in the nation's political and judicial system. It appeared likely Congress and the courts would move in only one direction: to strengthen the tax policies and defense spending that served business, and to loosen restraints on the ability of corporations to influence elections. In 2004, it was easy to imagine that Lincoln's vision was finally, and irreparably, doomed.

But, just as in the 1850s, this state of affairs could not last. It had broken apart before the Civil War and twice afterward—in the Progressive Era and during the New Deal— when Americans had demanded an end to the use of government in the service of the wealthy and a return to Lincoln's concept of government as a tool to enable all Americans to rise.

At the beginning of the twenty-first century, as in earlier eras when the government had helped a favored few, most Americans found themselves burdened with debt and stagnating incomes. In the short term, easy money pumped into the economy through relaxed regulation of lending kept people voting Republican, but lending was already stretched alarmingly. Cracks in the economy were starting to show.

Easy money had fed a real estate boom in the early years of the century, but the boom was unsustainable. After a Republican Congress allowed commercial and savings banks to consolidate, with its repeal of the New Deal's Glass-Steagall Act in 1999, it seemed money couldn't be invested quickly enough. But when the market for safe mortgages began to dry up, banks began lending money to borrowers who were likely to have a hard time keeping current on their loans. The risk that entailed was hidden as the loans were "bundled" and exchanged widely in financial markets. When the economy softened in 2006 and home values fell precipitously, the resulting mortgage defaults left banks saddled with bad loans and worthless real estate, further weakening a fragile economy.

Republican policy, based solely on Movement Conservative ideology and imagery, had no answers for the worsening economic crisis, and people were souring on the Bush administration anyhow. President Bush's lackluster response to Hurricane Katrina, which hit the Gulf region in 2005 and left more than eighteen hundred Americans dead, made people doubt his administration's competence, and the exposure in Iraq not of WMDs but of corruption and huge payoffs to Halliburton made Americans wonder if their patriotism had been enlisted in the service of crony capitalism. By the end of his term, Bush's approval ratings, at 22 percent, were the lowest of any sitting president.[1]

The Movement Conservative star faded as the 2008 presidential campaign got under way, and Republicans turned to Arizona senator John McCain, who had conservative credentials though he cultivated the image of a maverick. Needing to court Movement Conservative voters, McCain named Alaska's evangelical Christian governor, Sarah Palin, as his vice presidential choice. Palin promised to go to Washington as an outsider, to oust out-of-touch elites from policy making.

But on September 17, 2008, the financial world began to collapse. Over the next four days, banks failed, and the stock market plummeted. McCain had neither the policy nor language to address a crisis that threatened to destroy the world economy. At first he seemed stunned, and then, like Hoover before him, he tried to reassure Americans that all was well. He succeeded only in sounding out of touch. His running mate didn't help, revealing her reliance on image and talking points in her response to a question about congressional efforts to fund the failing banks and stem the tide of the worst financial crisis since the Great Depression. Palin said, "Ultimately, what the bailout does is help those that are concerned about the health-care reform that is needed to help shore up our economy to help, uhhh, it's gotta be all about job creation, too."[2]

In the midst of the crisis, financiers managed to impress upon Bush that it was imperative to bail out the big banks, whose collapse, they claimed, would destroy the world economy. Bush, along with most congressmen, got behind the Troubled Asset Relief Program, but Movement Conservatives in Congress opposed it as yet another big government program. McCain could not save both the economy and the election. The rift in the party between reality and image was too deep.

As unemployment climbed, housing prices fell, and the stock market plummeted, erasing Americans' retirement savings, voters turned to a relative newcomer, a Democratic senator from Illinois, Barack Hussein Obama. Obama and his running mate, Democratic Party veteran Joseph Biden of Delaware, won the election handily, garnering 52.9 percent of the popular vote to McCain and Palin's 45.7 percent. Obama's election marked the end of an era.

Movement Conservatism had taken the Republican Party to the brink of extinction. The election was an explicit—and overwhelming—rejection of an ideology that had engulfed the Republican Party with Reagan's election in 1980, and although on the wane since 1996, had retained power thanks to the Supreme Court's 2000 decision in *Bush v. Gore* and the 9/11 attacks of 2001. Obama and Biden represented everything Movement Conservatives had so vehemently opposed since the Eisenhower administration.

Democrats though they were, Obama and Biden supported a return to the vision of Republicans Lincoln, Theodore Roosevelt, and Eisenhower. They wanted to use government to level the playing field between big business and workers, and they sought to rebuild a vibrant middle class through education, fair labor practices, and business regulation.

Obama's election revealed the hollow core of the twenty-first-century Republican Party. Immediately, opponents shrieked that the president-elect was a socialist or a communist. They denied that he had been fairly elected, and they denied that he was an American, insisting he was born in Kenya and was therefore constitutionally barred from becoming president. They claimed he was stupid, uneducated, inexperienced; he had been elected only because he represented a special interest. They used the Internet to push conspiracy theories revealing how a "Kenyan Muslim socialist" was planning to destroy the American nation he hated. (Obama was, in fact, a Christian, born in Hawaii.) They circulated hideous racist propaganda, for President Obama was America's first African American president.

In President Obama, all the themes Republican leaders had developed since the 1850s came together. A smart, well-educated American—in this case, a biracial American—who had worked hard to get an education and rise to the presidency was the embodiment of the dream Lincoln had articulated, Theodore Roosevelt had adapted to the era of industrialization, and Eisenhower had formulated for the modern world. It was no accident that Obama twice chose to take his presidential oath with his hand on Lincoln's Bible.

But if Obama was a progressive Republican's dream, he was also James Henry Hammond's nightmare come to life: a Black man in charge, with every intention of using the government to help "mudsills." Obama was also the worst fear of late nineteenth- and early twentieth-century Old Guard Republicans. A Democrat who wanted to rein in business, he was Cleveland, Wilson, and FDR combined: anti-American, a danger to prosperity. Obama was an American with a foreign father: a plant to destroy American sovereignty, dragging the country into a UN-sanctioned internationalism in which Americans would be forced to bow and scrape to other nations. President Obama might have represented Lincoln's hopes, but he was also the embodiment of a century and a half of Republican fears.

Republicans' single-minded determination to stop this man, this one man, regardless of the actual nature of his policies and regardless of the very real needs of a nation trying to recover from a devastating economic recession, revealed that, having been captured by Movement Conservatives, the Republican Party could no longer engage with the reality of actual governance. Their world had become all image, no substance, and voters turned to Democrats, who had come to embrace the principles that Lincoln had insisted were the true heart of American equality a hundred and fifty years before.

And so, in the first decade of the new century the Republican Party completed a third cycle, witnessing the abandonment by the party of its founding principles, the precipitation of an economic crash, and a transfer of power to the Democrats. Lincoln's party found itself, once again, far removed from where it had begun.

The seemingly endless circles of the Republican Party reflect the unresolved tension between equality and property in America. The Declaration of Independence established the nation on the principle that all men were created equal, and it seemed to promise equality of opportunity to all based on equal access to resources and equal treatment under law. Then the Constitution established that the nation was also based on the protection of property. These two principles, both central to America's identity, came into conflict almost immediately when the Founding Fathers neglected to guard against the power of wealthy men to swing government policies in their own favor. The Republican Party's founders set out to rectify this oversight, only to be caught by it themselves.

Is it possible for the party to resolve this tension? Can the future be different? Surely the party's argument that economic opportunity for everyone must be advanced by an active government, the idea conceived by Lincoln and adopted by Theodore Roosevelt and Eisenhower, would adapt as easily to the modern global economy as it did to industrialization and to the nuclear world. But can the party shed the opposing argument, developed in the racial and political conflict of the late nineteenth century and recycled ever since, that government activism is socialism?

With today's shift in demographics, bringing an influx of young people, immigrants, and minorities to the voting population, perhaps the cycle will finally be broken. These voters are too young to remember the Cold War and are comfortable across racial and ethnic lines, making it harder to rally them with the specters of communism or racial conflict. With the power of James Henry Hammond's mudsill argument weakened, party leaders may be able to turn to the question left unanswered since the framing of the Constitution: how can America promote individual prosperity without creating a powerful wealthy faction that controls the government? Forced to adapt to a changing nation, in this century, perhaps, the Republican Party will find a way to stay committed to the ideals of its founders.

Afterword

Just over six years after the publication of *To Make Men Free*, insurgents carrying the Confederate flag stormed the US Capitol and tried to overturn the results of a presidential election. They wanted to seize power for the incumbent president, Republican Donald Trump, who had lost his bid for reelection in 2020. How had the Republican Party, which began in the 1850s as a popular movement to stand against the men who would lead the Confederacy in 1861, come to champion the vision they had organized to oppose?

Although Republicans themselves often tried to lay the blame (or credit, depending on their position) for the Trump years at the feet of Trump himself, in fact the rise of a reality television star to the presidency held a mirror to what the Republican Party had become by 2016. Trump was never a career politician. He was a salesman, and a terrific one. A wealthy young man who had inherited money from his father, he had survived multiple bankruptcies only to launch his reality TV show, *The Apprentice*, which branded him as a rich, successful businessman. By offering Republican voters an over-the-top, headline-grabbing version of Ronald Reagan's promise to get rid of active government, he read the 2016 Republican Party perfectly.[1]

Two generations after Movement Conservatives had taken over the leadership of the party under President Reagan, rank-and-file voters had entirely absorbed their worldview. Republicans had effectively married business deregulation and tax cuts to racism and sexism. They had convinced their supporters that the so-called "liberal consensus" with its widely supported business regulations, social safety net, and investment in infrastructure would redistribute wealth from hardworking white men to lazy people of color and feminists. In the 1990s and 2000s, as wealth moved upward, party leaders purged anyone but true believers from their ranks. And their rhetoric against Democrats and "Republicans in Name Only" became more and more extreme.

By June 16, 2015, when Trump descended the escalator at Trump Tower in New York City to announce his presidential bid, the idea that the federal government had been lost to socialism was an article of faith among Republicans, especially after voters elected Democrat Barack Obama in 2008. The ascension of a Black man to the White House, along with his promise to make health insurance affordable for all Americans, was seen as a threat to the very foundations of the country. Republicans—including Trump—suggested that Obama was an illegitimate president. They promoted the fantasy that he had not been born in America but was, in fact, a "Kenyan Muslim socialist" born in Africa.

For many Republican voters, Trump's claim in his announcement that Mexican immigrants to the United States are drug dealers, criminals, and rapists and, later, the leak of a recording in which he boasted of sexual assault were proof that he would stand up to the people of color and women who were destroying the country. Trump told supporters he would give government back to "the forgotten men and women of our country" by "transferring power from Washington, D.C., and giving it back to you, the people."

Appropriating a slogan that Ronald Reagan made famous, he promised to Make America Great Again.

Republicans had become increasingly convinced that saving the nation meant keeping Democrats out of power. Since the 1980s, they had worked tirelessly to skew the electoral system in their own favor, and by the time Trump ran for office, massive structural resistance to Democratic governance was built into the machinery of government.

In 1986, worried that voters would turn against Reagan's tax cuts of that year, Republican operatives began to talk about launching a "ballot integrity" initiative that they defended as a way to prevent voter fraud but that an official privately noted "could keep the black vote down considerably." Bill Clinton's election in 1992 added urgency to the idea of limiting the vote to those who would support the Republican program. Not only did Republicans consider Clinton to be wildly inappropriate for the White House, but he also presided over a Democratic control of Congress. When the so-called Motor Voter Law was enacted in 1993, expanding voter registration at certain state offices, they complained that Democrats were simply trying to enroll illegitimate voters in welfare and unemployment offices. And in the next midterm election, in 1994, Republicans who lost claimed that Democrats had engaged in voter fraud.[2]

Then, as now, fraud was vanishingly rare. Yet in 1996, House and Senate Republicans launched separate year-long investigations into what they insisted were problematic elections, one in Louisiana and one in California. The media attention helped to convince Americans that voter fraud was a serious issue and that Democrats were winning elections thanks to illegal voters. Republicans began to talk of passing voter ID laws to ensure that everyone who voted was a citizen. In 1998 the Florida legislature took the lead, passing a voter ID law that led to a purge of as many as 100,000 voters from the system before the election of 2000, resulting in what the United States Commission on Civil Rights called "an extraordinarily high and inexcusable level of disenfranchisement," particularly of African American voters.[3]

When the outcome of the 2000 election came down to Florida, and the election in Florida came down to recounting the ballots in Miami-Dade County, Republican operatives stormed the Miami-Dade polling station where election officials were attempting to recount the confusing ballots. They insisted that the Democrats were trying to steal the election, and their outrage helped to get the recount called off. One of the leaders of the "Brooks Brothers Riot" was a political operative named Roger Stone, who had cut his teeth on Richard Nixon's 1972 reelection campaign. Stone later formed a consulting company with Lee Atwater, the man behind the viciously racist Willie Horton ad that sank Democratic candidate Michael Dukakis in 1988 (Atwater apologized for his actions as he was dying), and Paul Manafort, whom Stone would back as Trump's campaign chair in June 2016.[4]

Stone claimed he was at the riot "as a volunteer," but in fact he was a key operative, eavesdropping on the Democratic recount team with a walkie-talkie. He and his fellow Republicans were determined to undermine the recount and to get Republican candidate George W. Bush into office regardless of the popular vote or the real outcome in Florida. "What I admire about Nixon was his resilience," he later told a reporter. "It's attack, attack, attack. [Democratic candidate] Al Gore thought the recount was a high-minded policy debate. He didn't understand that it was an extension of a war, of a political campaign."[5]

It worked. In a 5-4 decision, the Supreme Court stepped in to stop the count, giving Bush a victory in the Electoral College of 271 to 266, even though he had lost the popular vote by more than half a million votes.

After 2000, the increasingly rightward slide in the Republican Party made a lot of voters unhappy with its policies. This made it even more important for the party to promote the idea that Democrats could win only by cheating. The election of Barack Obama in 2008 made it easier for Republicans to claim that Democrats were destroying America and must be stopped. They put racism to work to justify throwing a wrench into the mechanics of government.

The remarkable unanimity among Republicans against the president and the Democrats helped to concentrate power in the Senate majority leader. Mitch McConnell (R–Kentucky) had taken the top Senate spot in 2007, and as soon as Obama took office, he began urging Republican voters to treat the midterm elections "as the first step in retaking the government...." He would famously state that "the single most important thing we want to achieve is for President Obama to be a one-term president."[6]

The Supreme Court made McConnell's job easier when it handed down its decision in *Citizens United v. FEC* in 2010. The case originated when the Federal Election Commission (FEC) prohibited the right-wing organization Citizens United from airing a film attacking Democratic presidential candidate Hillary Clinton just before the 2008 Democratic primaries. In a 5-4 decision, the court decided that corporations were covered by the First Amendment to the Constitution, which protects free speech. According to political scientists Nour Abdul-Razzak, Carlo Prato, and Stephane Wolton, in states with strong corporations, Citizens United increased Republican seat share by as much as 11.5 points.[7]

This mattered a lot. After the 2010 census, state legislatures would be in charge of redistricting their state for the next decade of congressional elections. Because Republicans controlled the key states of Florida, Wisconsin, North Carolina, Ohio, and Michigan, as well as other, smaller states, they could gerrymander congressional maps using precise computer models. In the 2012 election, Democrats won the White House decisively, the Senate easily, and a majority of 1.4 million votes for House candidates. Yet Republicans came away with a thirty-three-seat majority in the House of Representatives. In the Senate, Republicans had a mechanism, in the filibuster, to stop Democrats from achieving their goals. They could use it to require sixty votes to pass any legislation other than budget bills or judicial appointments.[8]

In 2013, in the *Shelby v. Holder* decision, the Supreme Court gutted the Voting Rights Act (VRA). The VRA had always had bipartisan support. First passed in 1965, it won support from 80 percent of House Republicans and 75 percent of House Democrats (the vote was 333–85). When it was reauthorized in 2006, the vote was 390–33. Immediately after the court handed down its new decision, declaring unconstitutional the rule that states could not change voting laws without prior clearance from the Department of Justice, Republican state officials began to introduce voter ID laws and bills restricting voter registration.[9]

In 2015 Republicans indicated they were swinging behind the idea that Democratic governance was illegitimate when 47 of 54 Republican senators, some of them quite senior, signed a letter written by extremist Senator Tom Cotton of Arkansas warning Iranian officials that they would overturn any agreement Iran made with the Obama administration as soon as they could, presumably after the 2016 election. Cotton had taken his seat just two months before.

Perhaps nothing more fully illustrated the Republican determination to dominate the government by whatever means necessary than the refusal of Senate majority leader Mitch McConnell to permit a hearing on the nomination of Obama's choice to replace Supreme Court justice Antonin Scalia after his death in February 2016. President Obama's pick for the Supreme Court was a well-liked moderate federal judge, Merrick Garland. Likely recognizing that little would fire up Republican voters more than the opportunity to fill a Supreme Court seat, McConnell declared it was too close to a presidential election to fill the seat. He insisted the appointment would have to wait until after the upcoming 2016 election.

And so, with Republican voters convinced that Democrats were deadly dangerous and Republican lawmakers increasingly using the machinery of government to handicap democracy, the stage was set for the 2016 election.

Early on, pundits expected establishment Republican Jeb Bush, son of President George H. W. Bush and brother of President George W. Bush, to pick up the nomination, in part because the Republican primaries had been front-loaded into states dominated by low-information voters deemed likely to vote based on name recognition. But that would work to Trump's advantage, for his name was well enough known that he won half of the delegates awarded on Super Tuesday, March 1, and by the end of May he appeared to have clinched the nomination. To calm horrified members of the GOP, the Trump campaign brought former Indiana governor Mike Pence on board as his running mate. Pence had deep ties to the business wing of the Republican Party, including the Koch brothers, whose libertarian father had backed Movement Conservatism since the 1950s.[10]

At the July Republican Convention, "never-Trump" delegates fought over his nomination, only to come up against rule changes that gave Trump far more delegates than he had earned.[11] Still, they could take some comfort from the 2016 Republican platform, which offered Movement Conservative Republicans everything they had ever dreamed of.

In June, Trump had replaced his first campaign manager with Stone's former partner Paul Manafort, who had deep ties to Russia. Soon thereafter he requested a change to the party platform that would weaken the party's stance against Russian president Vladimir Putin, declaring a "determination to maintain a friendship beyond the reach of those who wish to divide us." A later investigation by the Republican-dominated Senate Intelligence Committee turned up evidence that Manafort had shared secret polling information with a Russian operative and that Russian intelligence had flooded social media with pro-Trump stories. By the end of July, FBI director James Comey, himself a Republican, opened a counterintelligence investigation into Russian interference in the 2016 election.[12]

As a candidate, Trump held 232 campaign rallies, raucous affairs in which he called out the "lying media," bashed immigrants, urged supporters to "rough up" interlopers, and made fun of a disabled reporter. He promised to build a wall on the country's southern border to keep out immigrants, and to make Mexico pay for it, and he catered to evangelical Christians by promising a "a total and complete shutdown of Muslims entering the United States." He called for the Democratic nominee, Hillary Clinton, to be arrested for allegedly misusing an email server and promised to "drain the swamp" of Washington, surrounding himself "only with the best and most serious people."[13]

All bets said the election was Clinton's, but a last-minute reopening of an FBI investigation into her emails swung voters against her. Trump lost the popular vote by more than 2.8 million votes, but slim victories in three key swing states won him the White House by a vote of 306 to 232 in the Electoral College.[14]

From the beginning, Trump set out to bring the image he had created to life. Immediately after his inauguration, he refuted the reality of photographic evidence and insisted that the crowds were larger than at Obama's swearing in. Lying about crowd size was not just a silly quirk; it engaged a key element of psychological dominance, forcing supporters to agree with something that was obviously untrue. Constant gaslighting—the long-term process of lying to destroy someone's belief in reality—was a hallmark of Trump's presidency. Over time, people became weary of correcting his lies. The right-wing media trumpeted his every move, and his supporters increasingly accepted that the fantasy world he created was true.

Trump's war on the Washington swamp meant that he refused to fill the ranks of departments he disliked—such as the State Department—and replaced career officials with businessmen or with unqualified loyalists. Working around nepotism laws, he put his sons Don Jr. and Eric, his daughter Ivanka, and Ivanka's husband, Jared Kushner, into key White House positions, and because he refused to separate his businesses from the presidency, opponents charged that his decimation of the ranks of civil servants was designed to enable him and his family to profit from the office, much as the foreign autocrats he admired. Quickly, though, his attacks on career bureaucrats turned to attacks on the "Deep State" when it turned out that the FBI had continued its investigation of Russia's interference in the election. When FBI director Comey refused Trump's request to stop it, Trump fired him. The outcry forced the acting attorney general, Rod Rosenstein, to appoint a special counsel to continue the investigation. On May 17, Rosenstein appointed the well-respected former FBI director Robert Mueller.

Trump was furious about the Mueller investigation, and it appeared to drive him to seek support from the base voters he had courted, at the outset of his term, with a ban on travel to the United States from six primarily Muslim countries. In August 2017 a white supremacist rally in Charlottesville, Virginia, ostensibly to protest the removal of a statue of Confederate general Robert E. Lee, demonstrated just how powerful and dangerous Trump's rhetoric was. Rioters took to the streets in khakis, carrying tiki torches, swastikas, anti-Semitic banners, Trump/Pence signs, and Confederate battle flags, killing activist Heather Heyer and wounding nineteen others. Apparently siding with the rioters, Trump blamed what he called the alt-left for what he alleged was their participation in the riot and concluded that there were "very fine people on both sides."[15]

Americans began to turn away from Trump's apparent support for white nationalism, and original members of the administration began to leave their posts. But Republican lawmakers stayed on the Trump train as long as he was fulfilling their wish list. And Trump continued to deliver for the Republican establishment. In December 2017 Congress used budget reconciliation to pass a significant tax cut without a single Democratic vote. Lowering the corporate tax rate from 35 percent to 21 percent, the law was expected to deliver $320 billion to corporations over ten years. And in July 2018 Trump nominated the contentious appeals court judge Brett Kavanaugh to the Supreme Court to replace the retiring justice Anthony Kennedy. Republicans confirmed him by a historically close vote, significantly shifting the court to the right.[16]

In September 2019 the news broke that in a July phone call, Trump had tried to pressure Ukraine's new president, Volodymyr Zelensky, into helping him steal the 2020 election by smearing one of Trump's chief political rivals. Zelensky was desperate for the money Congress had approved to help his country fight off Russian incursions. Trump indicated he would release the money only after Zelensky announced an investigation into the actions of former vice president Joseph R. Biden's son Hunter during his time on the board of a Ukrainian business.

Trump's own efforts to extricate himself from the story only made it worse, and the question was this: Would the party follow the lead of the Trump team, or would party leaders acknowledge the president's profound attack on the sanctity of the American electoral process? In October the House of Representatives, dominated by Democrats, began to hold hearings. Trump and his loyalists made no effort to disprove the overwhelming evidence against the president. Instead, they misrepresented what happened and blamed the Democrats for the crisis.

On December 18, 2019, the House of Representatives voted to impeach the president for abuse of power and obstruction of Congress. All Republicans voted with the president. In the Senate, against overwhelming evidence that Trump had used the power of the presidency to try to steal an election, on February 5, 2020, all but one Republican senator—Mitt Romney of Utah, who voted to convict on one count—voted to acquit.

Shortly after the impeachment trial, the weaknesses of Trump's presidency were put fully on display when the novel coronavirus began to ravage the United States in early 2020. Eager to prop up the strong economy that he believed was the key to his reelection, the president initially downplayed the disease that would kill more than 392,000 Americans and infect at least 23 million before the end of his term. In mid-March, as the pandemic spread, Trump fell back on the idea that the federal government should stand aside as the states managed their own needs. Mistrustful of career officials, he put Jared Kushner in charge of finding the medical supplies that were urgently needed by hospitals and health-care workers; then, when the pandemic still continued, he insisted that those eager to fight it were trying to sabotage his reelection by hurting the economy. In April he and his supporters called for patriots to overturn the shutdown orders that Democratic governors had put in place to stop the spread of the pandemic: "LIBERATE MICHIGAN," "LIBERATE MINNESOTA," and "LIBERATE VIRGINIA, and save your great 2nd Amendment. It is under siege!" he tweeted. Supporters took him at his word and stormed the Michigan capitol.[17]

Meanwhile, protests over the deaths of Black Americans at the hands of law enforcement officers increased in numbers and frequency after Minneapolis police officer Derek Chauvin killed George Floyd by kneeling on his neck for 9 minutes and 29 seconds on May 25 after arresting him for allegedly trying to pass a counterfeit twenty-dollar bill. Trump and his supporters characterized the protests across the nation as being organized by dangerous leftists, although more than 90 percent of the arrests at the protests resulted in no charges. Still, Trump supporters coalesced around the "Thin Blue Line" flag: an American flag with a blue stripe on it that had come to represent white supremacy.[18]

In summer 2020, Trump appeared to be in control of the Republican Party, which had coalesced around him and seemed to care only about retaining power. The Republican

National Committee didn't even bother to write a platform for the 2020 campaign; it simply recycled the one from 2016. After the coronavirus disrupted two different convention plans, Trump held the convention at the White House, decking it out with banners bearing his name and using the backdrop of the people's house to produce imagery redolent of dictators: flags, classic architecture, massive spaces.

Could Trump pull off a 2020 win that would cement his power? His polling numbers had never broken 50 percent, and the coronavirus and subsequent economic crisis tanked them even further, but he and his team were putting their thumbs on the scale, doing their best to stop people from using the mail-in ballots to which states were turning because of the pandemic. Still, in a sign that he had little faith that Trump would be reelected, Senate majority leader Mitch McConnell pushed through the confirmation of another right-wing Supreme Court justice, Amy Coney Barrett, on October 26, even as balloting for the November 3 election was already under way.

On November 7, 2020, the US media called the 2020 election for Democrat Joe Biden and his running mate, Kamala Harris. By the time all the ballots were counted, the election was not close: Biden beat Trump by more than 7 million votes and by 306 to 232 in the Electoral College. Trump immediately told his supporters that the election had been rigged. In part, this appears to have been a fund-raising ploy. The Trump campaign had repeatedly boosted revenues by tricking donors into making recurring donations. To keep the money to cover the subsequent refund requests, the former president had to maintain that the election had been stolen.

Over the next few months, Trump or his surrogates filed and lost at least sixty-three lawsuits over the 2020 election, most of which were dropped for lack of evidence. Yet right-wing media continued to hype the idea that the election was stolen, and election officials and ballot counters began to get death threats. Establishment Republicans went along with this charade, both to keep Trump's support for a special runoff election over Georgia's two Senate seats, and seemingly hoping to pick up Trump's supporters for their own political future.

House Republicans began to focus their call to overthrow the results on what was usually a pro forma counting of the certified ballots before a joint session of Congress on January 6. They vowed to question the counts from certain states. Such challenges required a paired vote with a senator, but Senate majority leader McConnell tried hard to keep members of his caucus from joining the radicals in the House. It didn't work. Senator Josh Hawley of Missouri, who saw himself as a top 2024 presidential contender, announced that he, too, would challenge at least one of the vote counts. Not to be undercut, Ted Cruz of Texas led eleven other senators in a revolt to challenge the ballots.

The challenges would slow down the count, but because the ballots were, in fact, legitimate, they would not stop Biden's election. So Trump turned to pressuring Vice President Mike Pence, who would preside over the counting, to throw out the Biden votes. When Pence publicly stated that he had no constitutional power to do any such thing, Trump then tweeted that Pence "didn't have the courage to do what should have been done."

For weeks, Trump had urged his supporters to descend on Washington, D.C., for a "Stop the Steal" rally on the day the votes were to be counted. On the morning of January 6, they began to congregate on the Ellipse near the White House. Trump and his surrogates told the crowd again and again that "emboldened radical-left Democrats" had stolen the election. "We will never give up; we will never concede," he told them. "You don't concede when there's theft involved."

"We're going to have to fight much harder," Trump said, "because you'll never take back our country with weakness. You have to show strength, and you have to be strong. We have come to demand that Congress do the right thing and only count the electors who have been lawfully slated, lawfully slated.... And we fight. We fight like hell. And if you don't fight like hell, you're not going to have a country anymore." He concluded: "So let's walk down Pennsylvania Avenue."[19]

The crowd took him at his word, and a violent mob stormed the Capitol. As Capitol police rushed Vice President Pence, senators, representatives, and staff to safety, the insurrectionists broke into the Senate chamber and roamed the Capitol looking for Pence and other lawmakers they considered to be their enemies. Not finding them, they ransacked offices. One rioter photographed himself sitting with his feet up on House Speaker Nancy Pelosi's desk.

As the rioters stormed the Capitol, carrying the Confederate flag, it seemed that the Republican Party, formed initially to stand against those who wanted to destroy our democracy and form an oligarchy, had come full circle.

When people ask me if the Republican Party can survive, I have always noted that Lincoln's original principle remains deeply embedded in our DNA: the economy works best when the government supports those at the bottom so that they, in turn, can produce enough to support those above them, and on upward to the very top, where those few then employ others just starting out. If the current-day Republican Party disappears tomorrow, that principle will re-form almost immediately.

But today's Republican Party leaders have not honored Lincoln's vision since the rise of Reagan. Now it appears that the merger of the libertarian business wing of the party and the racists and social conservatives, initiated by Goldwater, constructed by Nixon, and enshrined by Reagan, is twisting apart. The party is split between the business Republicans and the Trump wing, and it is not clear who will win. Trump has refused to repudiate the insurrectionists he incited, and even after the crisis of January 6, eight senators and 139 representatives still voted to challenge at least one of the state ballots.

Although Trump did, in the end, leave office, during his tenure as president he shifted the party from flirting with oligarchy to supporting autocracy. Pro-Trump media began to insist that the January 6 attack was a false-flag operation of "Antifa," despite the selfies and videos posted by known right-wing agitators and the fact that Trump had invited, incited, and praised them. Despite pictures of congresspeople and their staff members cowering behind barricaded doors, prominent lawmakers said that the whole thing had been overblown: they had never felt threatened.

When the House of Representatives voted 232 to 197 to impeach the president for incitement of insurrection, ten Republicans did join the majority, but it was clear that the party had become motivated only by power. McConnell refused to bring the article before the Senate until after Trump had left office, leaving Republicans free to vote against it on the grounds it was not possible to convict a president who was no longer in office. On February 13, although seven Republicans voted to convict, the Senate acquitted Trump for a second time, by a vote of 57 to 43.

By spring 2021, Republican legislators in 47 states had proposed 361 voter restriction bills, justifying them by saying that they needed to address concerns about voter fraud. These new laws were designed to strengthen Republican power, permanently. When corporations began to abandon the states that were curtailing voting rights, Florida senator Rick Scott, the head of the National Republican Senatorial Committee, echoed Trump's tone and accused them of trying to "rake in cash" and of feeding "the rabble leftist mob that is shouting that America is racist." He warned that "a day of reckoning" was coming.[20]

Both the business Republicans and the Trump wing remain part of the Movement Conservative faction that took over the party a generation ago. But the outrages of the Trump administration have forced Americans to pay attention to what, exactly, that ideology has produced. They are finally acknowledging the devastation that upward wealth redistribution has visited on women, people of color, and poor white Americans. Changes that were ushered in under Reagan, and have been fed ever since by party leadership, have hollowed out our society and returned us to a system that looks much like the one that dumped us into the Great Depression. After seemingly not being able to see this developing crisis for the past thirty years, Americans regained their voices in 2020 and told legislators that this is not the nation they want.

The coronavirus crisis and the resulting recession have made plain that most people, including many Republicans, liked the liberal consensus after all. The Biden administration did an end run around Republican lawmakers, passing relief and rebuilding measures that were wildly popular. This has put pressure on Republicans, who voted unanimously against those popular measures, either to slash Democratic voting altogether or to rethink their political stance. If the current-day Republicans do not manage to destroy our democracy, the party might well, at long last, return to its roots.

ACKNOWLEDGMENTS

This book could not have been written without the help of Lisa Adams, my wonderful literary agent, who prodded me to write it and, as usual, guided me through the rough spots. Lara Heimert and Roger Labrie edited a behemoth into a book, and Eliza Childs performed brilliant magic on the final manuscript. Through his own work on the history of Brazil, Joel Wolfe helped me rethink the relationship between American politicians, voters, and language, then offered insights on American political and economic strife. Frederick Ahern generously shared with me information about the planning for President Reagan's funeral. Michael S. Green, Felicia Lipson, Robert Lipson, Jim O'Toole, Rob Rapley, and T. J. Stiles read drafts and made insightful corrections, and Lynn Lyerly provided important information I couldn't find. Steven Cromack, Remy Hassett, Christopher Mitchell, Cara Richardson, and Lisa Yarin cheered and prodded and read. Gene Dahmen, Beth LaBerge, Linda Lee, Pat Maney, Jim Matel, Sarah Matel, Damian Mencini, Carol Nowacki, Gillian Pearson, Buddy Poland, Robert Pontrelli, Marshall Pontrelli, Eva Pontrelli, David Quigley, Jetsy Reid, Joe Reid, Joshua Russell, Tony Saich, Donald Shaffer, Daniel J. Travanti, Larry Uebel, Sean Wilentz, and

Mark R. Wilson found books, answered questions, and were remarkably patient in indulging my fascination with Republican history. Katya Partan and Donald Pharr were key in producing this new edition.

Finally, Nancy Evans has been part of this project since its beginning. It was her insight that provided the book's narrative design; that narrative, in turn, shaped the argument. She has weighed each piece I unearthed (learning far more about Warren G. Harding and William F. Buckley Jr. than any classicist should) and helped me figure my way out of swamps. For her endless patience and support—during the past ten years and the forty-seven before it—I dedicate this book to her, with love.

Any errors in this book are my responsibility and the interpretations in it my own.

NOTES

All election results, political party platforms, and presidential addresses are at John T. Woolley and Gerhard Peters, *The American Presidency Project*, at www.presidency.ucsb.edu/ws/?pid=25817, unless otherwise noted.

Notes from a single source appearing at the end of a number of paragraphs on the same subject (the passage of the Land Grant College Act, for example) pertain to the entire discussion above them.

Abbreviations

Abraham Lincoln (AL)
Dwight D. Eisenhower (DDE)
Google Books (GB)
Internet Archive (IA)
Library of Congress (LC)

Introduction

1. Theodore Roosevelt, "A Speech Delivered at the Dedication of the John Brown Memorial Park in Osawatomie, Kansas," August 31, 1910, at http://teachingamericanhistory.org/library/document/new-national ism-speech/. Theodore Roosevelt, "The Trusts, the People, and the Square Deal," in *An Autobiography* (New York: Charles Scribner's Sons, 1920), pp. 560–573. GB.
2. Dwight D. Eisenhower, "A Chance for Peace," April 16, 1953, at http:// www.eisenhower.archives.gov/all_about_ike/speeches/chance_for _peace.pdf.

3. James Henry Hammond, "Speech on the Admission of Kansas" [The Cotton Is King Speech], March 4, 1858, in *Selections from the Letters and Speeches of James Henry Hammond* (New York: John F. Trow, 1866), pp. 301–357. GB.

4. AL to Henry L. Pierce et al., April 6, 1859, in Roy P. Basler, ed., *Collected Works of Abraham Lincoln*, 3: 374–376, Making of America–UMich.

5. Calvin Coolidge, "Address to the American Society of Newspaper Editors," January 17, 1925.

Chapter 1: The West as a Land of Promise

1. Robert Mazrim, *The Sangamo Frontier: History and Archaeology in the Shadow of Lincoln* (Chicago: University of Chicago Press, 2007), pp. 75–119.

2. John Filson, *The Discovery, Settlement and Present State of Kentucke* (1784), an Online Electronic Text Edition, ed. Paul Royster, Libraries at University of Nebraska–Lincoln, at http://digitalcommons.unl.edu/etas/3/, accessed May 28, 2010.

3. Ida M. Tarbell, *The Life of Abraham Lincoln* (New York: McClure, Phillips, 1900), pp. 3–6.

4. William Henry Herndon, Jesse William Weik, *Abraham Lincoln: The True Story of a Great Life*, vol. 1 (Chicago: Belford, Clarke, 1889), pp. 9–10. AL to Jesse Lincoln, April 1, 1854, in Roy P. Basler, ed., *The Collected Works of Abraham Lincoln*, 2: 217–218, Making of America–UMich.

5. David Herbert Donald, *Lincoln* (New York: Simon and Schuster, 1995), pp. 21–22.

6. Ibid., pp. 22–23. Tarbell, *Lincoln*, pp. 6–17.

7. Donald, *Lincoln*, pp. 23–24. Tarbell, *Lincoln*, p. 18.

8. Donald, *Lincoln*, pp. 23–25. Tarbell, *Lincoln*, pp. 18–21. Herndon, Weik, *Lincoln*, pp. 17–29.

9. Donald, *Lincoln*, pp. 25–33. Tarbell, *Lincoln*, pp. 22–44. Herndon, Weik, *Lincoln*, pp. 32–62.

10. Donald, *Lincoln*, pp. 38–54. Tarbell, *Lincoln*, pp. 49–109. Herndon, Weik, *Lincoln*, pp. 70–127.

11. Donald, *Lincoln*, pp. 55–83.
12. Ibid., pp. 83–118.
13. *New York Times*, March 8, 1854, p. 2. *New York Tribune*, January 6, 1854, p. 4. Oliver Joseph Thatcher, *The Library of Original Sources, 1833–1865* (New York: University Research Extension, 1907), pp. 144–152, GB.
14. Elmer Davis, *History of the New York Times, 1851–1921* (New York: New York Times, 1921), pp. 3–11. *New York Tribune*, January 6, 1854, p. 4.
15. Francis Curtis, *The Republican Party: A History of Its Fifty Years' Existence and a Record of Its Measures and Leaders, 1854–1904* (New York: G. P. Putnam's Sons, 1904), 1: 177–178, GB. Henry Wilson, *The History of the Rise and Fall of the Slave Power in America*, vol. 2 (Boston: Houghton, Mifflin, 1874), pp. 409–410. AL, Speech at Peoria, October 16, 1854, in Basler, ed., *Collected Works*, 2: 247–283.
16. Douglass Zevely, "Old Residences and Family History in the City Hall Neighborhood," *Records of the Columbia Historical Society*, vol. 7 (Washington, DC: 1904), pp. 159–160, GB. Gaillard Hunt, *Israel, Elihu, and Cadwallader Washburn: A Chapter in American Biography* (1925; rpt. New York: Da Capo Press, 1969), pp. 30–36. *New York Times*, February 25, 1854, p. 8.
17. *New York Tribune*, June 16, 1854, p. 4. Curtis, *Republican Party*, pp. 214–215.
18. *New York Times*, July 15, 1854, p. 6. Wilson, *Slave Power*, pp. 413–415. Curtis, *Republican Party*, p. 176. Michael S. Green, *Politics and America in Crisis* (California: Praeger, 2010), pp. 74–78.
19. Donald, *Lincoln*, pp. 168–178. AL, October 4, 1854, in Basler, ed., *Collected Works*, 2: 240–247. The Peoria speech cited above was a refinement of the Springfield speech.
20. *New York Tribune*, May 27, 1854, p. 4. Wilson, *Slave Power*, p. 415. Elihu B. Washburne to AL, November 14, 1854, LC. Elihu B. Washburne to AL, December 5, 1854, LC. AL to Elihu B. Washburne, February 9, 1855, LC. Donald, *Lincoln*, pp. 178–185.
21. Donald, *Lincoln*, pp. 187–188.
22. Richard B. Morris, ed., *Encyclopedia of American History* (New York: Harper & Brothers, 1953), p. 220.

23. *Chicago Tribune*, May 15, 1856, p. 2. *New York Times*, May 15, 1856, p. 2. *New York Times*, May 19, 1856, p. 2. *Chicago Tribune*, May 20, 1856, p. 2.

24. Speech of Charles Sumner in the Senate of the United States, May 19 and 20, 1856 (Boston: John P. Jewett, 1856), GB.

25. David Herbert Donald, *Charles Sumner and the Coming of the Civil War* (1960; rpt. New York: Da Capo Press, 1996), pp. 288–289.

26. Donald, *Sumner and Coming of War*, pp. 290–297.

27. Ibid., pp. 297–302.

28. Donald, *Lincoln*, pp. 191–192.

29. Morris, *Encyclopedia*, p. 221.

30. James Buchanan, Inaugural Address, March 4, 1857.

31. *New York Tribune*, March 7, 1857, p. 4.

32. Morris, *Encyclopedia*, p. 224. Abraham Lincoln, "A House Divided": Speech at Springfield, Illinois, June 16, 1858, in Basler, ed., *Collected Works*, 2: 461–469.

33. Donald, *Lincoln*, pp. 209–210. AL, Speech at Chicago, July 10, 1858, in Basler, *Collected Works*, 2: 484–502. AL, Speech at Springfield, Illinois, July 17, 1858, Basler, *Collected Works*, 2: 505–521.

34. Drew Gilpin Faust, *James Henry Hammond and the Old South: A Design for Mastery* (Baton Rouge: Louisiana State University Press, 1985).

35. James Henry Hammond, Speech to the US Senate, March 4, 1858, in *Selections from the Letters and Speeches of James Henry Hammond* (New York: John F. Trow, 1866), pp. 301–322, GB.

36. Robert Whaples, Randall E. Parker, eds., *The Routledge Handbook of Modern Economic History* (New York: Routledge, 2013), p. 279.

37. "Lincoln's 1859 Address at Milwaukee," *Wisconsin Magazine of History* 10 (March 1927): 243–258.

38. AL, "Address Before the Wisconsin State Agricultural Society," September 30, 1859, in Basler, ed., *Collected Works*, 3:471–482. On Lincoln's free labor theories, see Heather Cox Richardson, *The Greatest Nation of the Earth: Republican Economic Policies During the Civil War* (Cambridge: Harvard University Press, 1997), pp. 15–30.

39. AL, fragment on government, 1 and 2 (dated April 1, 1854, and July 1, 1854, by Nicolay and Hay but seeming to belong here, instead of 1854), in Basler, ed., *Collected Works*, 2: 221–222.

40. On the Whig mind-set and Lincoln, see Daniel Walker Howe, *The Political Culture of the American Whigs* (Chicago: University of Chicago Press, 1979). See also AL to Elihu B. Washburne, December 19, 1854, LC. David S. Heidler and Jeanne T. Heidler, *Henry Clay: The Essential American* (New York: Random House, 2010), pp. 205–209.

41. Richardson, *Greatest Nation*, pp. 105–106.

42. Michael S. Green, *Lincoln and the Election of 1860* (Carbondale: Southern Illinois University Press, 2011), pp. 18–28.

43. Harold Holzer, *Lincoln at Cooper Union: The Speech That Made Abraham Lincoln President* (New York: Simon and Schuster, 2004), pp. 9–17, 60–100.

44. Green, *Election*, pp. 43–112.

45. Republican Party Platform of 1856, June 18, 1856.

Chapter 2: Government of the People, by the People, for the People

1. Heather Cox Richardson, *The Greatest Nation of the Earth: Republican Economic Policies During the Civil War* (Cambridge: Harvard University Press, 1997), pp. 31–32.

2. Ibid., pp. 33–38.

3. Ibid., p. 114. William Pitt Fessenden, *Congressional Globe*, 37th Cong., 1st Sess., p. 255.

4. Richardson, *Greatest Nation*, pp. 66–89.

5. Ibid., pp. 46–47.

6. Ibid., pp. 73–75.

7. Ibid., pp. 78, 83.

8. Ibid., p. 102.

9. Ibid., pp. 39, 116.

10. A good recent overview of the early history of American taxation is Steven R. Weisman, *The Great Tax Wars* (New York: Simon and Schuster, 2002).

11. Justin Smith Morrill, *Congressional Globe*, 37th Cong., 2nd Sess., p. 1194.

12. Ibid.

13. Richardson, *Greatest Nation*, pp. 116–125. Justin Smith Morrill, *Congressional Globe*, 37th Cong., 2nd Sess., p. 1196.

14. *Harper's Weekly*, July 26, 1862, p. 466.

15. Richardson, *Greatest Nation*, pp. 49–50.

16. Ibid., pp. 40–44.

17. Galusha A. Grow, *Congressional Globe*, 37th Cong., 2nd Sess., p. 910.

18. *New York Tribune*, February 1, 1862, p. 4. William Windom, *Congressional Globe*, 37th Cong., 2nd Sess., p. 1034.

19. Justin Smith Morrill, *Congressional Globe*, 37th Cong., 2nd Sess., Appendix, p. 257. Richardson, *Greatest Nation*, pp. 139–149.

20. William Pitt Fessenden, *Congressional Globe*, 37th Cong., 2nd Sess., p. 2016. Richardson, *Greatest Nation*, pp. 149–154.

21. Richardson, *Greatest Nation*, pp. 154–160.

22. Albert S. White, *Congressional Globe*, 37th Cong., 2nd Sess., p. 1726. William M. Dunn, ibid., p. 1701.

23. Richardson, *Greatest Nation*, pp. 170–187. *American Railroad Journal* 35 (June 28, 1862): 498. *New York Tribune*, May 7, 1862, p. 4.

24. David Herbert Donald, *Lincoln* (New York: Simon and Schuster, 1995), pp. 382–383. W. Holmes to AL, January 22, 1863, in AL MSS, LC, series 1.

25. Abraham Lincoln, Annual Message to Congress, December 1, 1862.

26. F. B. Carpenter, *Six Months at the White House with Abraham Lincoln* (New York: Hurd and Houghton, 1867), pp. 269–270.

27. *New York Times*, January 3, 1863, p. 4.

28. James McPherson and James K. Hogue, *Ordeal by Fire: The Civil War and Reconstruction*, 4th ed. (New York: McGraw-Hill, 2009), pp. 374–375, 388. *New York Times*, July 13, 1863, p. 4.

29. *New York Times*, July 14, 1863, p. 1.

30. McPherson, Hogue, *Ordeal by Fire*, p. 389.

31. Ibid., p. 390.

32. Henry Wilson, *Congressional Globe*, 38th Cong., 1st Sess., p. 1324. Richardson, *Greatest Nation*, pp. 241–242.

33. S. S. Cox, *Congressional Globe*, 38th Cong., 1st Sess., p. 1858.

34. Richardson, *Greatest Nation*, pp. 16–27.

35. Ibid., pp. 162–163. Joseph Baldwin to John Sherman, December 7, 1861, in J. Sherman MSS., LC.

36. Richardson, *Greatest Nation*, pp. 160–168.

37. Ibid., pp. 131–134.

38. Glyndon G. Van Deusen, *Thurlow Weed: Wizard of the Lobby* (Boston: Little, Brown, 1947), pp. 282–294.
39. William Livingstone, *Livingstone's History of the Republican Party* (Detroit: Livingstone, 1900), pp. 148–150, GB. John Savage, *The Life and Public Services of Andrew Johnson* (New York: Edward O. Jenkins, 1865), pp. 290–291, GB. Van Deusen, *Thurlow Weed*, pp. 307–308.
40. Livingstone, *Republican Party*, p. 145. *New York Times*, June 8, 1864, p. 1.
41. Adam I. P. Smith, *No Party Now: Politics in the Civil War North* (New York: Oxford University Press, 2006). Livingstone, *Republican Party*, pp. 146–148.
42. Horace Greeley to AL, July 7, 1864, AL MSS, LC. McPherson, Hogue, *Ordeal by Fire*, pp. 472–474.
43. McPherson, Hogue, *Ordeal by Fire*, pp. 492–493. Livingstone, *Republican Party*, pp. 163–164.
44. Abraham Lincoln, Message to Congress, December 6, 1864.
45. Thomas A. Jenckes, *Congressional Globe*, 38th Cong., 2nd Sess., p. 225. Richardson, *Greatest Nation*, pp. 247, 249.
46. James Ashley, *Congressional Globe*, 38th Cong., 2nd Sess., p. 141.
47. Richardson, *Greatest Nation*, p. 249. George W. Julian, *Political Recollections, 1840 to 1872* (Chicago: Jansen, McClurg, 1884), pp. 251–252.
48. Richardson, *Greatest Nation*, pp. 237–240.
49. *New York Times*, March 4, 1865, p. 1. *New York Times*, March 5, 1865, p. 1.
50. *New York Times*, March 3, 1865, p. 1. *New York Times*, March 4, 1865, p. 4. *New York Times*, March 5, 1865, p. 1.
51. Walt Whitman, Specimen Days 79. "The Weather—Does It Sympathize with These Times?" in *Walt Whitman's Prose Works* (Philadelphia: David McKay, 1892), on Bartleby.com.
52. Ulysses S. Grant, *Personal Memoirs of U. S. Grant* (New York: Library of America, 1990), pp. 731, 740. "Impeachment Investigation," 39th Cong., 2nd Sess., and 40th Cong., 1st Sess. (Washington, DC: Government Printing Office, 1867), p. 286.
53. Hugh McCulloch, *Men and Measures of Half a Century* (New York: Charles Scribner's Sons, 1888), p. 222. William M. Stewart, *Reminiscences* (New York: Neale Publishing, 1908), p. 190. Nora Titone, *My Thoughts Be Bloody* (New York: Free Press, 2010), pp. 329–372.

Chapter 3: Republicans or Radicals?

1. Andrew Johnson, Remarks at an Interview with the Committee of the Legislature of Virginia, in Edward McPherson, *A Political Manual for 1868* (Washington, DC: Philp & Solomons, 1868), pp. 56–58, GB. *New York Times*, April 17, 1865.

2. James McPherson and James K. Hogue, *Ordeal by Fire: The Civil War and Reconstruction*, 4th ed. (New York: McGraw-Hill, 2009), p. 506. Andrew Johnson, Order Appointing William W. Holden Provisional Governor of North Carolina, May 29, 1865, and similar orders for Mississippi, Georgia, Texas, Alabama, South Carolina, and Florida, in McPherson, *Political Manual*, pp. 11–12.

3. "Legislation Respecting Freedmen," in McPherson, *Political Manual*, pp. 29–44.

4. Davidson, Gienapp, et al., *Nation of Nations*, vol. 2 (New York: McGraw-Hill, 1990), pp. 627–628. Heather Cox Richardson, *West from Appomattox* (New Haven: Yale University Press, 2007), pp. 55–57. W. A. Carey, "The Federal Union—Now and Hereafter," *De Bow's Review* (June 1866): 588, Making of America–UMich.

5. *New York Times*, November 19, 1865, p. 2.

6. Andrew Johnson, Message to Congress, December 4, 1865.

7. *New York Times*, January 13, 1866. *New York Times*, January 21, 1866. Edward McPherson, *Political History of the United States . . . During . . . Reconstruction* (Washington, DC: Philp & Solomons, 1871), GB, pp. 72–74.

8. McPherson, *Political History*, pp. 78–81.

9. *New York Times*, January 25, 1866.

10. For a look at the technical argument in his message, see Heather Cox Richardson, "Abraham Lincoln and the Politics of Principle," *Marquette Law Review* 93 (Summer 2010): 1383–1398.

11. Andrew Johnson, Veto Message, February 19, 1866, in McPherson, *Political History*, pp. 68–72, GB. Andrew Johnson, Veto Message, March 27, 1866, in McPherson, *Political History*, pp. 74–78.

12. For more on this, see his extraordinary exchange with Frederick Douglass, in "Interview with a Colored Delegation Respecting Suffrage," on February 7, 1866, in McPherson, *Political History*, pp. 53–56.

13. McPherson, *Political History*, pp. 74, 78–81. "Report of the Special Committee of the House…[on the] Riots at Memphis," 39th Cong., 1st Sess., H. Rpt. #101, p. 23.

14. Benjamin B. Kendrick, *The Journal of the Joint Committee of Fifteen on Reconstruction* (New York: 1914), pp. 292–293, 303. GB.

15. Hans L. Trefousse, *Andrew Johnson: A Biography* (New York: W. W. Norton, 1989), pp. 241–248.

16. James G. Hollandsworth, *An Absolute Massacre: The New Orleans Race Riot of July 30, 1866* (Baton Rouge: Louisiana State University Press, 2001). Richardson, *West from Appomattox*, p. 56. George C. Rable, *But There Was No Peace: The Role of Violence in the Politics of Reconstruction* (Athens: University of Georgia Press, 1984), pp. 33–58.

17. McPherson, *Political History*, pp. 58–63.

18. *Harper's Weekly*, January 18, 1868, p. 34.

19. James G. Blaine, *Twenty Years of Congress*, vol. 2 (Norwich, CT: Henry Bill Publishing, 1893), p. 262.

20. Michael W. Fitzgerald, *The Union League Movement in the Deep South: Politics and Agricultural Change During Reconstruction* (Baton Rouge: Louisiana State University Press, 1989). Heather Cox Richardson, *The Death of Reconstruction: Race, Labor, and Politics in the Post–Civil War North, 1865–1901* (Cambridge: Harvard University Press, 2001), pp. 52–57. Heather Cox Richardson, *West from Appomattox*, pp. 59–63.

21. Fitzgerald, *Union League*, pp. 16–23. *Philadelphia Inquirer*, May 23, 1867, p. 4.

22. Richardson, *Death of Reconstruction*, pp. 55–57. *Montgomery Advertiser*, July 28, 1867.

23. *Columbus (Ohio) Crisis*, March 13, 1867, p. 52.

24. Richardson, *Death of Reconstruction*, pp. 57–62, 59.

25. Ibid., p. 59.

26. Ibid., p. 60.

27. Ibid., pp. 68–69.

28. Terence V. Powderly, *Thirty Years of Labor, 1859–1889* (Columbus, OH: Rankin and O'Neal, 1890), p. 57. Grace Palladino, *Another Civil War: Labor, Capital, and the State in the Anthracite Regions of Pennsylvania, 1840–68* (Urbana: University of Illinois Press, 1990).

29. Richardson, *Death of Reconstruction*, p. 44.

30. *New York Times*, July 1, 1867, p. 4.
31. Ibid.
32. Ibid. *New York Times*, July 9, 1867, p. 4.
33. *New York Times*, July 6, 1867, p. 4. Richardson, *Death of Reconstruction*, p. 65.
34. David Herbert Donald, *Charles Sumner and the Rights of Man* (1970; rpt. New York: Da Capo Press, 1996), pp. 297–299.
35. Ibid., pp. 299–302.
36. McPherson, Hogue, *Ordeal by Fire*, pp. 535–536. Richardson, *Death of Reconstruction*, pp. 65–67.
37. Michael Les Benedict, *The Impeachment and Trial of Andrew Johnson* (New York: W. W. Norton, 1973). David O. Stewart, *Impeached* (New York: Simon and Schuster, 2009). Richardson, *West from Appomattox*, pp. 85–86.
38. McPherson, *Political Manual*, p. 365, GB.
39. Henry H. Smith, ed., *All the Republican National Conventions* (Washington, DC: Robert Beall, 1896), pp. 30–32, GB.
40. Ibid., p. 32.
41. McPherson, *Political Manual*, pp. 365–366.
42. Richardson, *Death of Reconstruction*, pp. 75–76. Philadelphia *Daily Evening Bulletin*, January 29, 1869, p. 4.

Chapter 4: Abandoning Equality

1. *New York Times*, March 5, 1869, p. 3.
2. Ulysses S. Grant, Inaugural Address, March 4, 1869. Joan Waugh, *U. S. Grant: American Hero, American Myth* (Chapel Hill: University of North Carolina Press, 2009), pp. 116–119.
3. George Henry Hynes, *Charles Sumner* (Philadelphia: George W. Jacobs, 1909), pp. 329–340, GB. David Herbert Donald, *Charles Sumner and the Rights of Man* (1970; rpt. New York: Da Capo Press, 1996), p. 433.
4. Waugh, *Grant*, pp. 124–126.
5. Carl Schurz, *The Reminiscences of Carl Schurz* (New York: McClure, 1908), 3: 305–307. Alfred Ronald Conkling, *Life and Letters of Roscoe Conkling* (New York: Charles L. Webster, 1889), p. 44, GB.
6. U. S. Grant, December 5, 1870, Message to Congress.

7. Donald, *Sumner and the Rights of Man*, pp. 434–435.

8. Ibid., pp. 436–439, 444–448.

9. Ibid., pp. 450–467.

10. AL to Charles D. Drake and Others, October 5, 1863. Eugene Morrow Violette, *A History of Missouri* (Boston: D. C. Heath, 1918), pp. 404–410, GB.

11. J. J. Samuels, in Rev. W. M. Leftwich, D.D., *Martyrdom in Missouri: A History of Religious Proscription, the Seizure of Churches, and the Persecution of Ministers of the Gospel, in the State of Missouri*, vol. 2 (Saint Louis: Southwestern, 1870), p. 339, GB. Violette, *History of Missouri*, pp. 412–417.

12. Schurz, *Reminiscences*, 1: 109–236.

13. Ibid., 1: 138–141.

14. Ibid., 3: 292–294; 3: 255–257.

15. Ibid., 3: 294–302. Howard Louis Conard, *Encyclopedia of the History of Missouri*, vol. 5 (New York: Southern History, 1901), p. 171.

16. Heather Cox Richardson, *West from Appomattox: The Reconstruction of America After the Civil War* (New Haven: Yale University Press, 2007), pp. 113–116. Richard White, *"It's Your Misfortune and None of My Own": A New History of the American West* (Norman: University of Oklahoma Press, 1993).

17. Richardson, *West from Appomattox*, pp. 145–147.

18. Frank Triplett, *The Life, Times, and Treacherous Death of Jesse James* (1882; rpt. New York: William S. Konecky Association, 2002), pp. 66, 81, 90–91, 223, 254, 264–266. T. J. Stiles, *Jesse James: Last Rebel of the Civil War* (New York: Vintage, 2002), pp. 350, 385–392.

19. Schurz, *Reminiscences*, 3: 316–317.

20. Ibid., 3: 321–323. Conard, *Encyclopedia of . . . Missouri*, p. 173.

21. Carl Schurz, *Congressional Globe*, 41st Cong., 3rd Sess., December 15, 1870, pp. 123–128.

22. Donald, *Sumner and the Rights of Man*, pp. 467–472.

23. Ibid., pp. 472–480.

24. Ibid., pp. 481–498.

25. Royal Cortissoz, *The Life of Whitelaw Reid* (New York: Charles Scribner's Sons, 1921), vol. 1, pp. 191–192, Hathitrust. *New York Tribune*, January 6, 1871, p. 4.

26. *New York Tribune*, January 23, 1871, p. 1. Xi Wang, *The Trial of Democracy: Black Suffrage and Northern Republicans, 1860–1910* (Athens: University of Georgia Press, 1997), pp. 82–83. U. S. Grant, Message to Congress, December 5, 1870.

27. *New York Tribune*, January 2, 1871, p. 4; January 19, 1871, p. 4; January 21, 1871, p. 1; January 23, 1871, p. 1; January 30, 1871, p. 4; January 26, 1871, p. 4.

28. See, for example, *New York Tribune*, January 2, 1871, p. 4; January 14, 1871, p. 4; January 16, 1871, p. 4; January 17, 1871, p. 4; January 18, 1871, p. 4; January 21, 1871, p. 4; February 8, 1871, p. 4.

29. Thomas Holt, *Black over White: Negro Political Leadership in South Carolina During Reconstruction* (Urbana: University of Illinois Press, 1979). Carole K. Rothrock Bleser, *The Promised Land: The History of the South Carolina Land Commission, 1869–1890* (Columbia: University of South Carolina Press, 1969). Heather Cox Richardson, *The Death of Reconstruction: Race, Labor, and Politics in the Post–Civil War North, 1865–1901* (Cambridge: Harvard University Press, 2001), pp. 89–90.

30. Richardson, *Death of Reconstruction*, pp. 92–93.

31. Ibid., pp. 85–86.

32. http://www.marxists.org/glossary/orgs/f/i.htm#first-international, accessed April 29, 2011. Karl Marx, Address of the International Working Men's Association to Abraham Lincoln, President of the United States of America, January 28, 1865, at http://www.marxists.org/history/international/iwma/documents/1864/lincoln-letter.htm. *Boston Evening Transcript*, December 13, 1871, p. 2. *Philadelphia Inquirer*, October 25, 1871, p. 4. Richardson, *Death of Reconstruction*, p. 87. Frank Norton, "Our Labor System and the Chinese," *Scribner's Monthly* 2 (May 1871): 62, emphasis in original.

33. *New York Tribune*, May 1, 1871, p. 1. Richardson, *Death of Reconstruction*, pp. 94–95.

34. *New York Tribune*, May 1, 1871, p. 1. Richardson, *Death of Reconstruction*, pp. 94–96.

35. *New York Tribune*, June 10, 1871, p. 1. Richardson, *Death of Reconstruction*, p. 97.

36. Richardson, *Death of Reconstruction*, p. 97.

37. Ibid., p. 104.
38. Ibid., pp. 100, 105. *Nation*, October 5, 1871, pp. 221–222. Richardson, *Death of Reconstruction*, p. 98. Charles Loring Brace, *The Dangerous Classes of New York* (New York: Wynkoop & Hallenbeck, 1872), p. 29, GB.
39. Richardson, *West from Appomattox*, pp. 121–122.
40. *New York Tribune*, February 9, 1871, p. 4. Cortissoz, *Whitelaw Reid*, pp. 199–213. Mark Wahlgren Summers, *The Press Gang: Newspapers and Politics, 1865–1878* (Chapel Hill: University of North Carolina Press, 1994), pp. 237–255.
41. Richardson, *West from Appomattox*, p. 122. *New-York Tribune,* April 12, 1872.
42. Richardson, *Death of Reconstruction*, p. 102.
43. Heather Cox Richardson, "What on Earth Was a 'Bourbon Democrat'?" March 15, 2011, at the Historical Society, www.histsociety.blog spot.com, accessed December 12, 2012. Cortissoz, *Whitelaw Reid*, p. 207.
44. *Proceedings of the Liberal Republican Convention . . .* (New York: Baker & Godwin, 1872), pp. 18–21, GB.
45. Karl Schriftgiesser, *The Gentleman from Massachusetts: Henry Cabot Lodge* (Boston: Little, Brown, 1944), pp. 34–35, IA. Cortissoz, *Whitelaw Reid*, pp. 209–210. *New York Times*, May 31, 1872.
46. *North American Review* 15 (October 1872): 401–422. *New York Times*, May 31, 1872.
47. Henry Clews, *Twenty-Eight Years in Wall Street* (New York: Irving Publishing, 1888), pp. 313–315.
48. *New York Times*, April 20, 1872, p. 5. Clews, *Twenty-Eight Years*, pp. 316–319.
49. *New York Times*, April 19, 1872, p. 2. *New York Times*, April 20, 1872, p. 5. Clews, *Twenty-Eight Years*, pp. 316–319.
50. *New York Times*, April 18, 1872, p. 6. See also *New York Times*, April 25, 1872, p. 4.
51. Richardson, *Death of Reconstruction*, p. 103. Republican Party Platform, June 5, 1872.
52. *Official Proceedings of the National Democratic Convention* (Boston: Rockwell & Churchill, 1872), GB.

53. Clews, *Twenty-Eight Years*, pp. 297–306, 303.
54. Richardson, *West from Appomattox*, p. 132.
55. Ibid., pp. 132–133.
56. Ibid., p. 134.
57. *New York Sun*, September 4, 1872, p. 3.
58. Ibid., p. 1.
59. Richardson, *West from Appomattox*, p. 137.
60. James M. McPherson, "Grant or Greeley: The Abolitionist Dilemma in the Election of 1872," *American Historical Review* 71 (October 1965): 43–61. Richardson, *Death of Reconstruction*, p. 103.

Chapter 5: Republicans and Big Business

1. Heather Cox Richardson, *The Death of Reconstruction: Race, Labor, and Politics in the Post–Civil War North, 1865–1901* (Cambridge: Harvard University Press, 2001), pp. 104–106.
2. U. S. Grant, Message to Congress, December 2, 1872.
3. Heather Cox Richardson, *West from Appomattox: The Reconstruction of America After the Civil War* (New Haven: Yale University Press, 2007), pp. 162–163.
4. Richardson, *Death of Reconstruction*, pp. 106–109.
5. Richard B. Morris, ed., *Encyclopedia of American History* (New York: Harper & Brothers, 1953), p. 510. Henry Clews, *Twenty-Eight Years in Wall Street* (New York: Irving, 1888), pp. 513, 696–708, GB.
6. Republican Party Platform, June 14, 1876.
7. *New York Times*, July 30, 1894. John A. Garraty, *Henry Cabot Lodge: A Biography* (New York: Alfred A. Knopf, 1953), pp. 40–50. Platform of the Democratic National Convention, June 22, 1876.
8. Robert V. Bruce, *1877: Year of Violence* (Indianapolis: Bobbs-Merrill, 1959), p. 26.
9. On Tilden-Hayes election, see Roy Morris Jr., *Fraud of the Century: Rutherford B. Hayes, Samuel Tilden, and the Stolen Election of 1876* (New York: Simon & Schuster, 2003).
10. C. Vann Woodward, *Reunion and Reaction: The Compromise of 1877 and the End of Reconstruction* (Boston: Little, Brown, 1951), pp. 51–121.
11. Ibid., pp. 110–112.

12. Richardson, *West from Appomattox*, pp. 177–178.
13. J. S. Black, "The Electoral Conspiracy," *North American Review* 125 (July 1877): 1–35. Woodward, *Reunion and Reaction*, pp. 230–237.
14. Richardson, *West from Appomattox*, p. 178.
15. Allan Pinkerton, *Strikers, Communists, Tramps and Detectives* (1878; rpt. New York: Arno Press, 1969), pp. 19–20. Thomas A. Scott, "The Recent Strikes," *North American Review* 125 (September 1877): 351–363.
16. *Washington Post*, September 27, 1878, p. 1. James G. Blaine, in *Appletons' Annual Cyclopaedia . . . of 1878* (New York: D. Appleton, 1882), p. 202, GB; discussion of Posse Comitatus Act on pp. 196–213. Stephen Young, comp., *The Posse Comitatus Act of 1878: A Documentary History* (Buffalo, NY: William S. Hein, 2003). *Chicago Tribune*, June 8, 1878, p. 2. See also *New York Times*, June 11, 1878, p. 4.
17. G. F. Hoar, *Autobiography of Seventy Years* (New York: Charles Scribner's Sons, 1903), 1: 388. Garraty, *Lodge*, p. 66.
18. Democratic Party Platform, June 22, 1880.
19. James D. Doenecke, *The Presidencies of James A. Garfield and Chester A. Arthur* (Lawrence: University Press of Kansas, 1981), pp. 41–45.
20. Richardson, *West from Appomattox*, pp. 194–195.
21. Ibid., p. 195.
22. Morris, *Encyclopedia*, p. 502.
23. John Hay, *The Bread-Winners* (New York: Harper & Brothers, 1883). William Graham Sumner, *What Social Classes Owe to Each Other* (New York: Harper & Brothers, 1883). *Harper's Weekly*, January 12, 1884, p. 19. *New York Times*, September 3, 1883, p. 3.
24. Raymond Polin and Constance Polin, eds., *Foundations of American Political Thought* (New York: Peter Lang, 2006), pp. 446–447.
25. Garraty, *Lodge*, pp. 77–78. Richardson, *West from Appomattox*, p. 212.
26. *Chicago Tribune* quoted in *Harper's Weekly*, February 9, 1884, p. 86. Nevins, *Cleveland*, pp. 342–345. *New York Times*, December 30, 1894.
27. Heather Cox Richardson, *Wounded Knee: Party Politics and the Road to an American Massacre* (New York: Basic Books, 2010), pp. 87–88.
28. Ibid., p. 88. John Sherman, *Recollections of Forty Years in the House, Senate and Cabinet*, vol. 2 (Chicago: Werner, 1895), pp. 1022–1034. Harry J. Sievers, *Benjamin Harrison: Hoosier Statesman* (New York: University Publishers, 1959), pp. 345–347.

29. Richardson, *Wounded Knee*, p. 88.
30. Sievers, *Benjamin Harrison*, pp. 426–427.
31. Grover Cleveland, Fourth Annual Message, December 3, 1888.
32. Andrew Carnegie, "Wealth," *North American Review* 148 (June 1889): 653–665.
33. Richardson, *Wounded Knee*, pp. 100–102, 109–110. *New York Times*, February 13, 1888, p. 1; February 24, 1888, p. 3; February 15, 1889, p. 5; February 17, 1889, p. 4; February 25, 1889, p. 1. *Frank Leslie's Illustrated Newspaper*, January 5, 1889, p. 346; March 2, 1889, p. 39; March 16, 1889, p. 91; June 1, 1889, p. 287; October 19, 1889, p. 191; November 2, 1889, pp. 223, 230; December 14, 1889, p. 331. Hubert Howe Bancroft and Frances Fuller Victor, *History of Washington, Idaho, and Montana, 1845–1899* (San Francisco: History Company, 1890), pp. 781–806, GB.
34. Richardson, *Wounded Knee*, pp. 142–144. Merle Wells, "Idaho's Season of Political Distress: An Unusual Path to Statehood," *Montana: The Magazine of Western History* 37 (Autumn 1987): 58–67.
35. Richardson, *Wounded Knee*, p. 101.
36. *Frank Leslie's Illustrated Newspaper*, March 16, 1889, p. 87; May 18, 1889, p. 254; April 6, 1889, p. 134.
37. Richardson, *Wounded Knee*, pp. 136–142.
38. Ibid., p. 93. *New York Times*, April 27, 1889, p. 4; February 24, 1889, p. 16; March 16, 1889, p. 2. *Frank Leslie's Illustrated Newspaper*, May 11, 1889, p. 223; May 18, 1889, p. 254; November 16, 1889, p. 270.
39. *Frank Leslie's Illustrated Newspaper*, December 14, 1889, p. 330; December 21, 1889, p. 354; January 4, 1889, p. 387. Richardson, *Wounded Knee*, p. 94.
40. *Frank Leslie's Illustrated Newspaper*, April 6, 1889, p. 134 (Harrison's men bought the moderate *Frank Leslie's Illustrated Newspaper* and turned it into an administration paper shortly after this quotation appeared). Richardson, *Wounded Knee*, pp. 136–144. *Harper's Weekly*, July 19, 1890, p. 551. *New York Times*, April 29, 1890, p. 4; June 19, 1890, p. 4.
41. Davidson, Gienapp, et al., *Nation of Nations*, vol. 2 (New York: McGraw-Hill, 1990), pp. 678, 688.
42. Gunther Peck, *Reinventing Free Labor: Padrones and Immigrant Workers in the American West, 1880–1930* (Cambridge: Cambridge University Press, 2000).

43. Richardson, *West from Appomattox*, p. 241.
44. Richardson, *Wounded Knee*, pp. 148–154. *Frank Leslie's Illustrated Newspaper*, June 14, 1890, p. 395; July 5, 1890, pp. 462–463.
45. Mary Elizabeth Lease, quoted in John D. Hicks, *The Populist Revolt* (Lincoln: University of Nebraska Press, 1961), p. 160.
46. Richardson, *Wounded Knee*, pp. 150–153. Sherman, *Recollections*, 2: 1062–1069, 1073.
47. Richardson, *Wounded Knee*, p. 158. *New York Times*, April 1, 1890, p. 1.
48. Richardson, *Wounded Knee*, pp. 158–159. *New York Times*, May 16, 1890, p. 5; May 22, 1890, p. 1.
49. *New York Times*, November 1, 1892, p. 5. *Atlanta Constitution*, November 2, 1892, p. 1. See also *Boston Globe*, November 10, 1892, p. 10.
50. *New York Times*, November 10, 1892, p. 4.
51. *Chicago Tribune*, November 12, 1892, p. 13. R. F. Pettigrew, quoted in *Chicago Tribune*, November 16, 1892, p. 9.
52. *New York Times*, November 10, 1892, p. 8. Statement from the Commercial Travelers' Republican Club, quoted in *Chicago Tribune*, November 1, 1892, p. 2. *Chicago Tribune*, November 14, 1892, p. 2. Senator Teller, quoted in *New York Times*, November 15, 1892, p. 1. *Washington Post*, February 16, 1893, p. 7. *Chicago Tribune*, November 21, 1892, p. 4. *Chicago Tribune*, November 11, 1892, p. 4. *Chicago Tribune*, November 13, 1892, p. 4.
53. *Chicago Tribune*, November 21, 1892, p. 10. See story of iron manufacturer cutting back explicitly out of fear of Democratic administration, in *Chicago Tribune*, November 15, 1892, p. 5. *New York Times*, November 12, 1892, p. 6. *Washington Post*, November 12, 1892, p. 7. *Financial Times*, quoted in *New York Times*, November 14, 1892, p. 4. *Chicago Tribune*, November 13, 1892, p. 4. Douglas Steeples and David O. Whitten, *Democracy in Desperation: The Depression of 1893* (Westport, CT: Greenwood Press, 1998), pp. 21, 23.
54. *New York Times*, November 24, 1892, p. 9. *Boston Globe*, November 18, 1892, p. 8.
55. *Washington Post*, February 15, 1893, p. 7. *New York Times*, February 15, 1893, p. 6. *New York Times*, February 16, 1893, p. 6. *Commercial and Financial Chronicle*, quoted in Steeples and Whitten, *Democracy in Desperation*, p. 32.

56. *Boston Globe*, February 18, 1893, p. 7. *Boston Globe*, February 18, 1893, p. 9. *New York Times*, February 18, 1893, p. 6.

57. *Chicago Tribune*, February 19, 1893, p. 14. *New York Times*, February 19, 1893, p. 14. *New York Times*, February 19, 1893, p. 3. *Chicago Tribune*, February 21, 1893, p. 1. *New York Times*, February 24, 1893, p. 6. *Boston Globe*, February 25, 1893, p. 9.

58. *New York Times*, February 18, 1893, p. 6. *New York Times*, March 3, 1893, p. 9. *New York Times*, March 4, 1893, p. 6. *Chicago Tribune*, March 8, 1893, p. 1.

59. Grover Cleveland, Inaugural Address, March 4, 1893. E. Benjamin Andrews, "A History of the Last Quarter-Century in the United States, XII. The Democracy Supreme," *Scribner's Magazine* 19 (April 1896): 469–490, Making of America–Cornell.

60. Rose Wilder Lane, *American Life Histories: Manuscripts from the Federal Writers' Project, 1936–1940*, Manuscript Division, LC, Online at American Memory. Robert V. Bruce, *1877: Year of Violence* (Indianapolis: Bobbs-Merrill, 1959).

61. General Nelson A. Miles, "The Lesson of the Recent Strikes," *North American Review* 159 (August 1894): 180–188, MOA–Cornell.

62. Andrews, "A History of the Last Quarter-Century in the United States," 469–490. *Brooklyn Union*, quoted in *Chicago Tribune*, September 4, 1894, p. 6.

63. Republican Congressional Committee, *Republican Campaign Text Book* (Washington, DC: 1894), GB. *New York Times*, November 2, 1894, p. 5. Henry Cabot Lodge, in *Boston Globe*, November 1, 1894, p. 2.

64. *Chicago Tribune*, November 7, 1894, p. 9. *New York Times*, November 9, 1894. *New York Times*, November 7, 1894, p. 1.

65. *New York Times*, November 3, 1894, p. 4. *Chicago Tribune*, November 7, 1894, pp. 11–12.

66. *Chicago Tribune*, September 2, 1894, p. 2. *Chicago Tribune*, September 4, 1894, p. 6.

67. Francis R. Jones, "Pollock v. Farmers' Loan and Trust Company," *Harvard Law Review* 9 (October 1895): 198–211.

68. Pollock v. Farmers' Loan & Trust Company, 158 U.S. 601, 15 S Ct. 912. David P. Currie, "The Constitution in the Supreme Court: The

Protection of Economic Interests, 1889–1910," *University of Chicago Law Review* 52 (Spring 1985): 324–388.

69. William Jennings Bryan, "Cross of Gold Speech," July 9, 1896, at *History Matters*, Roy Rosenzweig Center for History and New Media (George Mason University), at http://historymatters.gmu.edu/d/5354/.

70. Republican Party Platform, June 16, 1896.

71. *New York Tribune*, September 30, 1896, p. 6. Howard Lawrence Hurwitz, *Theodore Roosevelt and Labor in New York State, 1880–1900* (New York: Columbia University Press, 1943), pp. 177–187. *New York Tribune* excerpted the Utica Speech on September 30, 1896, p. 3. *New York Tribune*, September 30, 1896, p. 2.

Chapter 6: Republicans Become Liberals

1. National People's Party Platform, July 4, 1892, at http://historymatters .gmu.edu/d/5361/, accessed May 4, 2014.

2. Henry Cabot Lodge, *Early Memories* (New York: Charles Scribner's Sons, 1913), p. 125. Karl Schriftgiesser, *The Gentleman from Massachusetts: Henry Cabot Lodge* (Boston: Little, Brown, 1944), p. 23, IA.

3. Schriftgiesser, *Gentleman from Massachusetts*, p. 46. John A. Garraty, *Henry Cabot Lodge: A Biography* (New York: Alfred A. Knopf, 1953), pp. 75–81.

4. Garraty, *Lodge*, p. 76.

5. Joseph B. Foraker, *Notes of a Busy Life* (Cincinnati, 1916), vol. 1, p. 167, GB.

6. Garraty, *Lodge*, pp. 79–81, 84, 86–87.

7. Schriftgiesser, *Gentleman from Massachusetts*, pp. 101–104, 119.

8. Aida D. Donald, *Lion in the White House: A Life of Theodore Roosevelt* (New York: Basic Books, 2007), pp. 77–78. Schriftgiesser, *Gentleman from Massachusetts*, pp. 110–114.

9. Schriftgiesser, *Gentleman from Massachusetts*, pp. 111–114.

10. Heather Cox Richardson, *West from Appomattox* (New Haven: Yale University Press, 2007), pp. 312–313.

11. H. Wayne Morgan, *McKinley and His America* (Syracuse: Syracuse University Press, 1963), p. 274. Theodore Roosevelt, quoted in Donald, *Lion in the White House*, p. 81.

12. Theodore Roosevelt, *The Rough Riders* (1899; rpt. New York: Modern Library, 1999), pp. 3–5. Richardson, *West from Appomattox*, pp. 313–319. Morgan, *McKinley and His America*, p. 277. Arthur Wallace Dunn, *Gridiron Nights* (New York: Frederick A. Stokes, 1915), p. 72, GB.

13. Donald, *Lion in the White House*, pp. 88–89. Richardson, *West from Appomattox*, pp. 321–322.

14. David Trask, *The War with Spain in 1898* (New York: Macmillan, 1981), p. 156. Richardson, *West from Appomattox*, pp. 319–322. Theodore Roosevelt, quoted in *New York Times*, September 22, 1898, p. 1.

15. Roosevelt, *Rough Riders*, pp. 124–130, 199–202. Richardson, *West from Appomattox*, pp. 322–323, 319–320.

16. John Hay to Theodore Roosevelt, quoted in Frank Friedel, *The Splendid Little War* (Boston: Little, Brown, 1958), p. 3.

17. *Indianapolis Sentinel*, quoted in *New York Times*, July 4, 1898, p. 7. T. St. John Gaffney, in *New York Times*, August 22, 1898, p. 6.

18. Richardson, *West from Appomattox*, pp. 332–333.

19. Andrew Carnegie, "Distant Possessions—The Parting of the Ways," *North American Review* 167 (August 1898): 239–249. Andrew Carnegie, "Americanism Versus Imperialism," *North American Review* 168 (January 1899): 1–14. Andrew Carnegie, "Americanism Versus Imperialism—II," *North American Review* 168 (March 1899): 362–373. All on Making of America–Cornell.

20. Albert J. Beveridge, "Grant, the Practical," in Albert J. Beveridge, *The Meaning of the Times, and Other Speeches* (Indianapolis: Bobbs-Merrill, 1908), pp. 37–46.

21. Albert J. Beveridge, "The March of the Flag," September 16, 1898, in Beveridge, *The Meaning of the Times*, pp. 47–57, GB.

22. Theodore Roosevelt, *An Autobiography* (New York: Macmillan, 1913), pp. 41–44.

23. Theodore Roosevelt, *Foes of Our Own House* (New York: George H. Doran, 1917), pp. 97–107.

24. Claude G. Bowers, *Beveridge and the Progressive Era* (Cambridge, MA: Houghton Mifflin, 1932), p. 63.

25. Roosevelt, *Autobiography*, pp. 132–133. Richard White, *It's Your Misfortune and None of My Own* (Norman: University of Oklahoma Press, 1991), pp. 285–288.

26. Richardson, *West from Appomattox*, pp. 331–332. Quotation from *Charleston News and Courier*, quoted in *New York Times*, October 3, 1898, p. 6.

27. Theodore Roosevelt, quoted in William Roscoe Thayer, *Theodore Roosevelt: An Intimate Biography* (Boston: Houghton Mifflin, 1919), pp. 133–139, GB.

28. Democratic Party Platform, July 4, 1900.

29. Morgan, *McKinley and His America*, pp. 372–381. Thayer, *Roosevelt*, pp. 150–153.

30. William McKinley, Message to Congress, December 3, 1900. *Boston Globe*, November 14, 1901, p. 9. *New York Times*, November 14, 1901, p. 1. *New York Times*, November 15, 1901, p. 1. *Washington Post*, November 15, 1901, p. 1. *Chicago Tribune*, November 14, 1901, p. 1. *Washington Post*, November 21, 1901, p. 5. *Chicago Tribune*, November 28, 1901, p. 7.

31. Roosevelt to Henry Cabot Lodge, September 23, 1901, in *Selections from the Correspondence of Theodore Roosevelt and Henry Cabot Lodge, 1884–1918* (New York: Charles Scribner's Sons, 1925), 1: 506. Eric Rauchway, *Murdering McKinley: The Making of Theodore Roosevelt's America* (New York: MacMillan, 2007), p. 38.

32. *Chicago Tribune*, March 30, 1901, p. 10. Joseph Bucklin Bishop, *Theodore Roosevelt and His Time Shown in His Own Letters*, vol. 1 (New York: Charles Scribner's Sons, 1920), pp. 154, 165–170.

33. Theodore Roosevelt, Message to Congress, December 3, 1901.

34. *Chicago Tribune*, December 4, 1901, p. 12.

35. *Chicago Tribune*, November 17, 1901, p. 1. *Atlanta Constitution*, November 21, 1901, p. 1. Theodore Roosevelt, Message to Congress, December 3, 1901. On transparency as a way to end the need for business combinations, see *New York Times*, November 15, 1901, p. 8.

36. *Chicago Tribune*, December 4, 1901, pp. 1, 12.

37. *Chicago Tribune*, February 21, 1902, p. 12.

38. *New York Times*, January 8, 1902, p. 9. *Washington Post*, February 21, 1902, p. 3. *Boston Globe*, February 20, 1902, p. 9.

39. *Chicago Tribune*, February 21, 1902, p. 5. Bishop, *Roosevelt*, pp. 182–184, GB.

40. *Boston Globe*, February 21, 1902, p. 9. *Washington Post*, February 21, 1902, p. 3. *Chicago Tribune*, February 25, 1902, p. 12. Balthasar Henry

Meyer, "A History of the Northern Securities Case," *Bulletin of the University of Wisconsin*, no. 142 (Madison, WI, 1906), pp. 258–261, GB.

41. *Boston Globe*, August 27, 1902, p. 6.
42. Robert M. La Follette, *La Follette's Autobiography* (Madison: University of Wisconsin Press, 1960), pp. 4, 9–12.
43. Ibid., pp. 3–8, 12, 18–20.
44. Ibid., pp. 12–15. Theodore Roosevelt, "Introduction," in Charles McCarthy, *The Wisconsin Idea* (New York: MacMillan, 1912), pp. vii–xi, GB.
45. Doris Kearns Goodwin, *The Bully Pulpit: Theodore Roosevelt, William Howard Taft, and the Golden Age of Journalism* (New York: Simon & Schuster, 2013), pp. 157–202.
46. Ellen Fitzpatrick, ed., *Muckraking: Three Landmark Articles* (Boston: Bedford Books, 1994).
47. Bishop, *Roosevelt*, pp. 198–220.
48. George E. Mowry, *The Era of Theodore Roosevelt, 1900–1912* (New York: Harper & Brothers, 1958), pp. 115–117. Orlando Oscar Stealey, *Twenty Years in the Press Gallery* (New York: 1906), p. 175, GB. Orlando Oscar Stealey, *130 Pen Pictures of Live Men* (Washington, DC: 1910), p. 26. Claude G. Bowers, *Beveridge and the Progressive Era* (New York: Literary Guild, 1932), pp. 317–324.
49. Louis Arthur Coolidge, *An Old-Fashioned Senator: Orville H. Platt, of Connecticut* (n.p.: 1910), pp. 563–569, GB. Mowry, *Era of Roosevelt*, pp. 133, 171–180.
50. Theodore Roosevelt, December 6, 1904.
51. Mowry, *Era of Roosevelt*, pp. 202–203. Theodore Roosevelt to William Howard Taft, March 15, 1906, Elting E. Morison et al., eds., *The Letters of Theodore Roosevelt*, vol. 5 (Cambridge: Harvard University Press, 1951), p. 183, as quoted in John Braeman, "Albert J. Beveridge and the First National Child Labor Bill," *Indiana Magazine of History* (March 1964): 1–36. *New York Times*, December 18, 1905, quoted in Mowry, *Era of Roosevelt*, p. 203.
52. John Ely Briggs, *William Peters Hepburn* (Iowa City: State Historical Society of Iowa, 1919), pp. 251–287, GB. *Chicago Tribune*, June 24, 1906, quoted in Braeman, "Albert J. Beveridge," p. 1.
53. Mowry, *Era of Roosevelt*, pp. 220–223. Theodore Roosevelt to Bonaparte, January 2, 1908, quoted in Roosevelt, *Autobiography*, p. 292. See

also Roosevelt, Message to Congress, January 31, 1908, in *Addresses and Papers of Theodore Roosevelt*, ed. by Willis Fletcher Johnson (New York: Unit Book, 1909), p. 416.

54. Edgar A. Hornig, "Campaign Issues in the Presidential Election of 1908," *Indiana Magazine of History* 54 (September 1958): 237–264.

55. Goodwin, *Bully Pulpit*.

56. Mowry, *Era of Roosevelt*, pp. 232–235.

57. Claude E. Barfield, " 'Our Share of the Booty': The Democratic Party Cannonism, and the Payne-Aldrich Tariff," *Journal of American History* 57 (September 1970): 308–323.

58. Ibid.

59. Mowry, *Era of Roosevelt*, pp. 243–249. Dunn, *Gridiron Nights*, p. 217.

60. Mowry, *Era of Roosevelt*, pp. 247–249.

61. "The Return of Colonel Roosevelt," *Moody's Magazine: The Investors' Monthly* 9 (January 1910): 431–432, GB. Joseph Gurney Cannon, "Abraham Lincoln ... Speech of Hon. Joseph G. Cannon of Illinois," February 12, 1910 (Washington, DC: 1910).

62. Roosevelt, *Foes*, p. 92.

63. Theodore Roosevelt, New Nationalism Speech, August 31, 1910, at http://teachingamericanhistory.org/library/document/new-nationalism-speech/.

64. Ibid.

65. *New York Times*, March 3, 1913, p. 1.

Chapter 7: The Business of America Is Business

1. *Washington Post*, March 29, 1913, p. 6. See also *Chicago Tribune*, April 6, 1913, p. 2.

2. *Washington Post*, March 9, 1913, p. 4.

3. Theodore Roosevelt, *Foes of Our Own House* (New York: George H. Doran, 1917), pp. 121–142.

4. *Boston Globe*, April 7, 1913, p. 1. *Chicago Tribune*, April 7, 1913, p. 1. *Washington Post*, April 7, 1913, p. 1.

5. *Boston Globe*, April 8, 1913, p. 4.

6. Edwin R. A. Seligman, *The Income Tax: A Study of the History, Theory, and Practice of Income Taxation at Home and Abroad* (New York: Macmillan, 1914), p. 701. *New York Times*, September 3, 1913, p. 11.

7. Louis D. Brandeis, *Other People's Money and How the Bankers Use It* (New York: Frederick A. Stokes, 1913), p. IA.

8. *New York Times*, November 21, 1913, p. 13. *Washington Post*, November 22, 1913, p. 9.

9. Elihu Root, in *Washington Post*, December 14, 1913, p. 1.

10. *Washington Post*, April 9, 1913, p. 1. *Atlanta Constitution*, April 11, 1913, p. 4. *Washington Post*, July 9, 1914, p. 1. *Washington Post*, September 11, 1914, p. 6. *Boston Globe*, July 18, 1916, p. 11. *Atlanta Constitution*, July 18, 1916, p. 8.

11. *Atlanta Constitution*, September 3, 1916, p. 4.

12. Theodore Roosevelt quoted in *Chicago Tribune*, September 1, 1916, p. 1. Roosevelt, *Foes*, pp. 14–85. Theodore Roosevelt quoted in *New York Times*, September 1, 1916, p. 6.

13. *Atlanta Constitution*, October 27, 1918, p. B4. *Boston Globe*, October 28, 1918, pp. 1, 5. *Chicago Tribune*, October 20, 1918, p. 10. *Chicago Tribune*, October 21, 1918, p. 9. *Washington Post*, October 21, 1918, p. 5. Alice Roosevelt Longworth, *Crowded Hours* (New York: Charles Scribner's Sons, 1933), pp. 274–275. *Chicago Tribune*, October 26, 1918, p. 4. *New York Times*, October 29, 1918, p. 1. *New York Times*, October 27, 1918, p. 10. Roosevelt in *Chicago Tribune*, October 29, 1918, p. 1.

14. Longworth, *Crowded Hours*, p. 275. Speech of Henry Cabot Lodge, February 28, 1919, and speech of Philander C. Knox, March 1, 1919, in *League of Nations* (Boston: Old Colony Trust, 1919), GB. Ralph A. Stone, "Two Illinois Senators Among the Irreconcilables," *Mississippi Valley Historical Review* 50 (December 1963): 443–465. Ralph A. Stone, "The Irreconcilables' Alternatives to the League of Nations," *Mid-America* 49 (July 1967): 163–173.

15. *Boston Globe*, September 10, 1919, pp. 1–2. Robert K. Murray, *Red Scare: A Study in National Hysteria, 1919–1920* (Minneapolis: University of Minnesota Press, 1955), pp. 122–134. *Boston Globe*, September 10, 1919, p. 2. Last quotation from *New York Times*, September 12, 1919, p. 1.

16. Murray, *Red Scare*, pp. 122–134.

17. *Boston Globe*, September 22, 1919, p. 11. Arthur M. Schlesinger Jr., *Crisis of the Old Order* (1957; rpt. New York: History Book Club, 2002), pp. 77–89.

18. Murray, *Red Scare*, pp. 181–189.

19. William E. Leuchtenburg, *The Perils of Prosperity, 1914–1932* (1958; rpt. Chicago: University of Chicago Press, 1993), pp. 79–80.
20. Grosvenor B. Clarkson, *Industrial America in the World War* (Boston: Houghton Mifflin, 1923). *Washington Post*, May 23, 1923, p. 6.
21. *Official Report of the Seventeenth Republican National Convention* (New York: Tenny Press, 1920), pp. 14–33, 19–20, 109–114, 169, IA.
22. *Official Report*, p. 119.
23. *Official Report*, pp. 168–172, 224. *Chicago Tribune*, June 13, 1920, p. 2. *New York Times*, June 12, 1920, p. 1. *Chicago Tribune*, June 13, 1920, pp. 1, 6, 10.
24. *Chicago Tribune*, June 13, 1920, p. 1. Thanks to Adam Easley for explaining to me what Harding's slang meant. William Allen White, *The Autobiography of William Allen White* (Simon Publications, 1946), p. 615. *Boston Globe*, June 13, 1920, p. 13. *Chicago Tribune*, June 13, 1920, p. 6. *New York Times*, June 13, 1920, p. 1. *Washington Post*, June 13, 1920, p. 2.
25. Hiram Johnson, quoted in Leuchtenburg, *Perils of Prosperity*, p. 87. White, *Autobiography*, p. 616. Leuchtenburg, *Perils of Prosperity*, p. 89.
26. Leuchtenburg, *Perils of Prosperity*, p. 88.
27. Herbert Hoover, *The Memoirs of Herbert Hoover: The Cabinet and the Presidency, 1920–1933* (New York: Macmillan, 1952), p. 48.
28. White, *Autobiography*, p. 619.
29. Hoover, *Memoirs*, pp. 48–51.
30. Longworth, *Crowded Hours*, pp. 324–325.
31. White, *Autobiography*, p. 616. Schlesinger, *Crisis of the Old Order*. Hoover, *Memoirs*, pp. 36–46.
32. *The Administration of a New Era* (Boston: George H. Ellis, 1922), pp. 24–26.
33. *Atlanta Constitution*, September 8, 1916, p. 1. *Boston Globe*, September 8, 1916, p. 4. *The Statutes at Large of the United States of America from December, 1915 to March, 1917*, vol. 39 (Washington, DC: Government Printing Office, 1917), pp. 756–793. *Boston Globe*, October 4, 1917, pp. 1, 12. *Washington Post*, September 24, 1917, p. 7. *Atlanta Constitution*, October 3, 1917, p. 5. *New York Times*, September 9, 1916, p. 10. *New York Times*, October 3, 1917, p. 1. *Washington Post*, September 29, 1917, p. 6.

34. Andrew W. Mellon, *Taxation: The People's Business* (New York: Macmillan, 1924), pp. 129–130. Andrew W. Mellon, "Thrift and Progress," *World's Work* 44 (May 1922): 36–39, GB.

35. Mellon, *Taxation*, pp. 97–98, 172–173.

36. Schlesinger, *Crisis of Old Order*, pp. 62–63. Mellon, *Taxation*, pp. 74–89.

37. Schlesinger, *Crisis of Old Order*, p. 65. Leuchtenberg, *Perils of Prosperity*, p. 189. John Kenneth Galbraith, *The Great Crash: 1929* (1954; rpt. New York: Time Incorporated, 1961), pp. 48–49.

38. Leuchtenburg, *Perils of Prosperity*, p. 109. Galbraith, *Great Crash*, p. 8.

39. Leuchtenburg, *Perils of Prosperity*, pp. 194–196. Bruce Barton, *The Man Nobody Knows: A Discovery of the Real Jesus* (Indianapolis: Bobbs-Merrill, 1925), introduction, n.pg.

40. Calvin Coolidge, "Speech to the Amherst College Alumni Association, February 4, 1916," in Calvin Coolidge, *Have Faith in Massachusetts* (Boston: Houghton Mifflin, 1919), p. 14.

41. Republican Party Platform of 1928, June 12, 1928. Frederick Lewis Allen, *Only Yesterday* (New York: Harper & Brothers, 1931), p. 303.

42. Galbraith, *Great Crash*, pp. 20–21.

43. Ibid., p. 22.

44. Herbert Hoover, March 4, 1929.

Chapter 8: Republicans and the New Deal

1. William E. Leuchtenburg, *The Perils of Prosperity, 1914–1932* (1958; rpt. Chicago: University of Chicago Press, 1993), pp. 100–103. Richard B. Morris, ed., *Encyclopedia of American History* (New York: Harper & Brothers, 1953), p. 482.

2. Message from the President of the United States, returning without approval the Bill (S. 4808) entitled "An Act to Establish a Federal Farm Board to Aid in the Orderly Marketing and in the Control and Disposition of the Surplus of Agricultural Commodities," February 25, 1927, 69th Cong., 2nd Sess., S. Doc. 214. Message from the President of the United States, returning without approval the Bill (S. 3555) entitled "An Act to Establish a Federal Farm Board to Aid in the Orderly Marketing and in the Control and Disposition of the Surplus of

Agricultural Commodities in Interstate and Foreign Commerce," May 3 (calendar day, May 23), 1928, 70th Cong., 1st Sess., S. Doc. 141.

3. Nicholas Lemann, *The Promised Land: The Great Migration and How It Changed America* (New York: Vintage, 1992).

4. James M. Sears, "Black Americans and the New Deal," *History Teacher* 10 (November 1976): 89–105.

5. John Dos Passos, *USA* (New York: Modern Library, 1937), pp. 460–464.

6. Frederick Lewis Allen, *Only Yesterday* (New York: Harper & Brothers, 1931), pp. 315, 318.

7. John Kenneth Galbraith, *The Great Crash: 1929* (1954; rpt. New York: Time Incorporated, 1961), pp. 25–26, 50–53.

8. Ibid., pp. 43–44, 97–98. Allen, *Only Yesterday*, pp. 311, 323.

9. Galbraith, *Great Crash*, pp. 101–107.

10. Eric Rauchway, *The Great Depression and the New Deal* (New York: Oxford University Press, 2008), pp. 18–20.

11. Allen, *Only Yesterday*, p. 333. Galbraith, *Great Crash*, pp. 214–218.

12. Galbraith, *Great Crash*, pp. 111, 128, 139. Herbert Hoover, *The Memoirs of Herbert Hoover: The Cabinet and the Presidency, 1920–1933* (New York: Macmillan, 1952), p. 30. Galbraith, *Great Crash*, pp. 80–81. Rauchway, *Depression and New Deal*, p. 19.

13. Galbraith, *Great Crash*, pp. 177–179.

14. Leuchtenburg, *Perils of Prosperity*, p. 246. Allen, *Only Yesterday*, p. 338. Galbraith, *Great Crash*, pp. 180–182.

15. Leuchtenburg, *Perils of Prosperity*, pp. 246–249. Galbraith, *Great Crash*, p. 171.

16. Hoover, *Memoirs*, pp. 30–31.

17. Hoover, *Memoirs*, p. 31. Galbraith, *Great Crash*, pp. 139–140.

18. *Chicago Tribune*, July 27, 1932, p. 10.

19. Allen, *Only Yesterday*, pp. 332, 340–341.

20. *New York Times*, October 16, 1930, p. 21. Also quoted in Galbraith, *Great Crash*, p. 145.

21. Galbraith, *Great Crash*, pp. 135–153, 158–160, 161–167.

22. *Chicago Tribune*, November 1, 1932, p. 1.

23. *New York Times*, November 1, 1932, pp. 1, 15. *Chicago Tribune*, November 1, 1932, p. 1.

24. Arthur M. Schlesinger Jr., *Crisis of the Old Order* (1957; rpt. New York: History Book Club, 2002), p. 2.

25. Franklin Delano Roosevelt, Message to Congress, quoted in *New York Times*, June 20, 1935, p. 2.

26. Thomas A. Dewey, "America in a Troubled World," January 20, 1940, in Thomas A. Dewey, *The Case Against the New Deal* (New York: Harper & Brothers, 1940), pp. 115–121.

27. *Chicago Defender*, September 24, 1932, p. 3. Andrew Buni, *Robert L. Vann of the* Pittsburgh Courier: *Politics and Black Journalism* (Pittsburgh: University of Pittsburgh Press, 1974), pp. 193–194. Sears, "Black Americans and the New Deal," 89–105.

28. Sears, "Black Americans and the New Deal," 89–105.

29. Ibid., 89–105.

30. Alan Brinkley, *Voices of Protest: Huey Long, Father Coughlin, and the Great Depression* (New York: Vintage, 1983). Raymond Moley, *After Seven Years* (New York: Harper & Brothers, 1939), p. 305.

31. Sinclair Lewis, *It Can't Happen Here* (New York: P. F. Collier & Son, 1935). Halford E. Luccock, "Disguised Fascism Seen as a Menace," *New York Times*, September 12, 1938, p. 15.

32. Republican Party Platform, June 9, 1936.

33. William S. White, *The Taft Story* (New York: Harper & Brothers, 1954), pp. 4–9, 18–19.

34. Ibid., pp. 41–52.

35. Ibid., pp. 19–20.

36. *Washington Post*, October 15, 1947, p. 1.

37. Dewey, "Social Responsibilities," May 3, 1940, in Dewey, *New Deal*, pp. 97–113. Dewey, "America Is Not Finished," December 6, 1939, in Dewey, *New Deal*, pp. 2–11. Dewey, "Roosevelt Must Go," June 21, 1940, in Dewey, *New Deal*, pp. 152–165.

38. Dewey, "The Defense of America," May 27, 1940, in Dewey, *New Deal*, pp. 121–131. White, *Taft Story*, pp. 150–164.

39. White, *Taft Story*, pp. 158–160.

40. Glenn C. Altschuler and Stuart M. Blumin, *The GI Bill: A New Deal for Veterans* (New York: Oxford University Press, 2009). Richardson Family Trust Archives, by permission of owner.

41. Altschuler, Blumin, *GI Bill*, pp. 52–87.

42. Morris, *Encyclopedia*, p. 526.
43. White, *Taft Story*, p. 51.
44. *New York Times*, June 12, 1948, p. 7. Dwight D. Eisenhower, *The Eisenhower Diaries*, ed. Robert H. Ferrell (New York: W. W. Norton, 1981), p. 195. *Chicago Tribune*, June 15, 1948, p. 5.
45. *New York Times*, April 4, 1948, p. E1. *Washington Post*, June 14, 1948, p. B15. White, *Taft Story*, pp. 60–65. *Wall Street Journal*, April 6, 1948, p. 6.
46. *New York Times*, June 20, 1948, p. F1. *New York Times*, June 19, 1948, p. 21. *Chicago Tribune*, June 18, 1948, p. B7.
47. Rick Perlstein, *Before the Storm: Barry Goldwater and the Unmaking of the American Consensus* (New York: Hill and Wang, 2001), p. 29.
48. White, *Taft Story*, pp. 66–79. *Washington Post*, June 20, 1948, p. B8.
49. *Chicago Tribune*, October 12, 1947, p. 5. *New York Times*, October 27, 1947, p. 22.
50. *Chicago Tribune*, October 24, 1947, p. 1. *New York Times*, October 20, 1947, p. 14. *Washington Post*, October 25, 1947, p. 1.
51. Author interview with Daniel J. Travanti.
52. Republican Party Platform, June 21, 1948.

Chapter 9: A New Republican Vision

1. Dwight D. Eisenhower, *At Ease: Stories I Tell to Friends* (New York: Doubleday, 1967), pp. 68–69.
2. Ibid., pp. 70–71, 74, 79–81, 96–97.
3. Ibid., pp. 104–106, 138–145.
4. Ibid., pp. 157–166.
5. Ibid., pp. 185–187, 195, 201.
6. DDE to Mamie Eisenhower, April 15, 1945, in John S. D. Eisenhower, ed., *Dwight D. Eisenhower, Letters to Mamie* (New York: Doubleday, 1978), p. 248. http://www.eisenhowermemorial.org/stories/death-camps.htm, accessed October 3, 2012.
7. Eisenhower admired Eric Hoffer's *The True Believers: Thoughts on the Nature of Mass Movements* (1951), which explores the role of cultural and economic dislocation in political and religious extremism. See DDE to Robert J. Biggs, February 10, 1959, in L. Galambos and Daun Van Ee, eds., *The Papers of Dwight David Eisenhower*, vol. 19: *The*

Presidency: Keeping the Peace (Baltimore: Johns Hopkins University Press, 2001), pp. 1340–1343.

8. DDE, September 16, 1947, *Diaries*, pp. 143–144.

9. DDE, May 26, 1946, *Diaries*, pp. 136–137.

10. William S. White, *The Taft Story* (New York: Harper & Brothers, 1954), pp. 81–83.

11. Ibid., pp. 156–159. Mary C. Brennan, *Turning Right in the Sixties: The Conservative Capture of the GOP* (Chapel Hill: University of North Carolina Press, 1995), p. 10. *Washington Post*, February 14, 1950, p. 10.

12. *Chicago Tribune*, February 9, 1950, p. 5.

13. *Chicago Tribune*, February 11, 1950, p. 7. *Chicago Tribune*, February 12, 1950, p. 1. *New York Times*, February 12, 1950, p. 5. *Boston Globe*, February 12, 1950, p. C29.

14. *Boston Globe*, February 14, 1950, p. 12. *Washington Post*, February 14, 1950, p. 10. *Washington Post*, February 24, 1950, p. 22. *New York Times*, February 22, 1950, p. 28. *Washington Post*, February 18, 1950, p. B13.

15. White, *Taft Story*, pp. 85–88. *Chicago Tribune*, February 24, 1950, p. 18.

16. Margaret Chase Smith, "A Declaration of Conscience," June 1, 1950, at http://www.americanrhetoric.com/speeches/margaretchasesmithconscience.html. McCarthy comment at: http://www.senate.gov/artandhistory/history/minute/A_Declaration_of_Conscience.htm.

17. White, *Taft Story*, pp. 93–115, 171–174.

18. Eisenhower, *At Ease*, pp. 74–75.

19. DDE, *Diaries*, pp. 184–185.

20. DDE, October 29, 1951, and November 29, 1959, *Diaries*, pp. 203–204, 369–376. *New York Times*, June 17, 1948, p. 4. Merriman Smith, *Meet Mister Eisenhower* (New York: Harper & Brothers, 1954), p. 48.

21. White, *Taft Story*, pp. 171–183.

22. Smith, *Mister Eisenhower*, p. 26.

23. Ibid., pp. 24–28.

24. Ibid., pp. 28, 36–41.

25. "Checkers Speech" audio and text at http://www.americanrhetoric.com/speeches/richardnixoncheckers.html.

26. DDE, February 2, 1953, Message to Congress. Arthur Larson, *A Republican Looks at His Party* (New York: Harper & Brothers, 1956), quotation on p. 159.

27. Dwight D. Eisenhower, *Mandate for Change, 1953–1956* (Garden City: Doubleday, 1963), pp. 143–148. Dwight D. Eisenhower, "The Chance for Peace," April 16, 1953.

28. White, *Taft Story*, pp. 160–168.

29. DDE, "Special Message...Requesting General Legislation Authorizing the Use of Agricultural Commodities...," June 30, 1953. DDE, *Mandate for Change*, pp. 159–191. Larson, *Republican Looks at Party*, viii–ix.

30. DDE "Radio Report...on the Achievements of the Administration and the 83rd Congress," August 6, 1953. DDE, "Special Message... Transmitting Proposed Changes in the Social Security Program," August 1, 1953.

31. Robert Griffith, "Dwight D. Eisenhower and the Corporate Commonwealth," *American Historical Review* 87 (February 1982): 87–122. DDE, "Radio Report...on the Achievements of the Administration and the 83rd Congress," August 6, 1953. DDE, "Special Message...Transmitting Proposed Changes in the Social Security Program," August 1, 1953. DDE, *Mandate for Change*, pp. 555–556.

32. DDE, "Special Message...Transmitting Reorganization Plan of 1953 Creating the Department of Health, Education, and Welfare," March 12, 1953. DDE, "Radio Report...on the Achievements of the Administration and the 83rd Congress," August 6, 1953. DDE, "Special Message...Transmitting Proposed Changes in the Social Security Program," August 1, 1953, American Presidency Project.

33. DDE, *Mandate for Change*, pp. 547–553.

34. Claudia Goldin and Robert A. Margo, "The Great Compression: The Wage Structure in the United States at Mid-Century," *Quarterly Journal of Economics* 107 (February 1992): 1–34. Alan Brinkley and Ellen Fitzpatrick, *America in Modern Times: Since 1890* (New York: McGraw-Hill, 1997), p. 407.

Chapter 10: The Rise of Movement Conservatism

1. Mary C. Brennan, *Turning Right in the Sixties: The Conservative Capture of the GOP* (Chapel Hill: University of North Carolina Press, 1995), pp. 12–13.

2. Dwight D. Eisenhower, *Mandate for Change* (New York: Doubleday, 1963), pp. 278, 594.

3. Ibid., pp. 278–281. Rick Perlstein, *Before the Storm: Barry Goldwater and the Unmaking of the American Consensus* (New York: Hill and Wang, 2001), pp. 8–11.

4. DDE, *Mandate for Change*, pp. 281–283.

5. DDE, February 2, 1953, State of the Union. DDE, *Mandate for Change*, p. 135.

6. Perlstein, *Before the Storm*, pp. 9–11.

7. DDE, *Mandate for Change*, pp. 284–285.

8. Roy Cohn, quoted in *Executive Sessions of the Senate Permanent Subcommittee on Investigations of the Committee on Government Operations*, vol. 1 (1953; Washington, DC: Government Printing Office, 2003), p. xvi, available at: http://www.senate.gov/artandhistory/history/resources/pdf/Volume1.pdf. Donald A. Ritchie, Introduction to *Executive Sessions of the Senate Permanent Subcommittee*, pp. xiii–xxviii.

9. Frank Luther Mott, *American Journalism* (New York: Macmillan, 1962), pp. 816–817. Robert Griffith, *The Politics of Fear: Joseph R. McCarthy and the Senate*, 2nd ed. (Amherst: University of Massachusetts Press, 1987), pp. 60–65. David M. Oshinsky, *A Conspiracy So Immense: The World of Joe McCarthy* (New York: Free Press, 1983), p. 182.

10. Ritchie, Introduction, p. xxv. "Employment of Homosexuals and Other Sex Perverts in Government," December 15, 1950, 81st Cong., 2nd Sess., S. Doc. 241.

11. Mott, *American Journalism*, p. 720. Oshinsky, *Conspiracy So Immense*, pp. 182–185.

12. Dwight E. Eisenhower, *The Eisenhower Diaries*, ed. Robert H. Ferrell (New York: W. W. Norton, 1981), pp. 233–234. DDE to "Swede," July 21, 1953, in Robert Griffith, ed., *Ike's Letters to a Friend, 1941–1958* (Lawrence: University Press of Kansas, 1984), pp. 107–111. Henry Cabot Lodge, *As It Was: An Inside View of Politics and Power in the '50s and '60s* (New York: W. W. Norton, 1976), pp. 131–137. DDE to "Swede," March 18, 1953, in *Ike's Letters to a Friend*, pp. 120–121. "Have You No Sense of Decency," the Army-McCarthy Hearings (transcript excerpt), at http://historymatters.gmu.edu/d/6444/, accessed May 8, 2014.

13. Richard Rovere, *Senator Joe McCarthy* (1959; rpt. Berkeley: University of California Press, 1976), pp. 250–251.

14. William F. Buckley Jr., *God and Man at Yale: The Superstitions of Academic Freedom* (Chicago: Henry Regnery, 1951).

15. William F. Buckley Jr. and L. Brent Bozell, *McCarthy and His Enemies: The Record and Its Meaning* (Chicago: Henry Regnery, 1954), pp. 267–335. William S. White, "What the McCarthy Method Seeks to Establish," *New York Times Book Review*, April 4, 1954.

16. Rick Perlstein, *Before the Storm: Barry Goldwater and the Unmaking of the American Consensus* (New York: Hill and Wang, 2001), p. 73.

17. William F. Buckley Jr., "Our Mission Statement," *National Review*, November 19, 1955.

18. Ibid.

19. DDE, *Mandate for Change*, pp. 234–236.

20. David L. Chappell, "The Divided Mind of Southern Segregationists," *Georgia Historical Quarterly* 82 (Spring 1998): 45–72. James Jackson Kilpatrick, "Right and Power in Arkansas," *National Review*, September 28, 1957, pp. 273–275.

21. Perlstein, *Before the Storm*, p. 113.

22. Ibid., pp. 114–116. Lisa McGirr, *Suburban Warriors: The Origins of the New Right* (Princeton: Princeton University Press, 2001), pp. 76–79.

23. Welch, quoted in Perlstein, *Before the Storm*, p. 115.

24. Perlstein, *Before the Storm*, pp. 116–118.

25. "Westerns," *Time*, March 30, 1959, p. 52.

26. Barry M. Goldwater, *With No Apologies: The Personal and Political Memoirs of United States Senator Barry M. Goldwater* (New York: William Morrow, 1979), pp. 15–25. Goldwater, quoted in Rick Perlstein, *Before the Storm*, p. 19.

27. Perlstein, *Before the Storm*, pp. 19–20.

28. Ibid., pp. 19–21.

29. Ibid., pp. 20, 29–31. Goldwater, *No Apologies*, pp. 59–61.

30. Perlstein, *Before the Storm*, pp. 36–38.

31. Dwight D. Eisenhower, *Waging Peace, 1956–1961* (New York: Doubleday, 1965), pp. 378–381. Perlstein, *Before the Storm*, p. 33.

32. Perlstein, *Before the Storm*, pp. 41–42.

33. Ibid., p. 48.

34. Barry Goldwater [L. Brent Bozell], *The Conscience of a Conservative* (1960; rpt. Princeton: Princeton University Press, 2007), Foreword.

35. Ibid., pp. 15–24.

36. Ibid., pp. 24–59.

37. Ibid., pp. 60–127.

38. Ibid., pp. 88–127.

39. Ibid.

40. *National Review*, December 3, 1960, pp. 334–335. *National Review*, November 19, 1960, pp. 298–300.

41. Frank S. Meyer, "Principles and Heresies: Hope for the '60s," *National Review*, January 14, 1961, p. 19.

42. McGirr, *Suburban Warriors*, p. 25.

43. Brennan, *Turning Right*, pp. 41–42.

44. Photograph of billboard in Walter Hubbard Collection, Winchester, Massachusetts.

45. Gerald D. Nash, *The American West Transformed* (Bloomington: Indiana University Press, 1985), pp. 17–20. Richard White, *It's Your Misfortune and None of My Own* (Norman: University of Oklahoma Press, 1991), pp. 496–499.

46. McGirr, *Suburban Warriors*, pp. 25–26.

47. Ibid., pp. 25–26.

48. Ibid., pp. 27–28.

49. Ibid., pp. 28–29. Perlstein, *Before the Storm*, pp. 124–125.

50. DDE, Farewell Address, January 17, 1961, at http://www.eisenhower .archives.gov/research/online_documents/farewell_address.html.

51. Nash, *West Transformed*, pp. 210–213.

52. Brennan, *Turning Right*, pp. 45–46.

53. McGirr, *Suburban Warriors*, pp. 95–96.

54. Ibid., pp. 81–88.

55. Ibid., pp. 39–43.

56. Perlstein, *Before the Storm*, pp. 122–124.

57. Chief Justice Earl Warren, quoted in *National Review*, December 17, 1963, pp. 513–514. *National Review*, December 10, 1963, p. 6. *National Review*, December 10, 1963, pp. 3–5. Frank S. Meyer, "Principles and Heresies: and Still...Goldwater Can Win," *National Review*, December 24, 1963, p. 528. "RIP," *National Review*, December 17, 1963, p. 511.

William F. Buckley Jr., "Do They Really Hate to Hate?" *National Review*, December 31, 1963, p. 559.

58. Perlstein, *Before the Storm*, pp. 171–200.

59. Republican Party Platform, July 13, 1964. Brennan, *Turning Right*, pp. 74–81.

60. Phyllis Schlafly, *A Choice Not an Echo* (Alton, IL: Pere Marquette Press, 1964).

61. Ibid., p. 45.

62. Ibid., pp. 28–29, 80.

63. Ronald Reagan, "A Time for Choosing," October 27, 1964, available at www.reaganfoundation.org, http://www.reaganfoundation.org/tgc detail.aspx?p=TG0923RRS&h1=0&h2=0&lm=reagan&args_a=cms &args_b=1&argsb=N&tx=1736.

Chapter 11: Movement Conservatives Capture the GOP

1. George H. Mayer, *The Republican Party, 1854–1966* (New York: Oxford University Press, 1967).

2. Mary C. Brennan, *Turning Right in the Sixties: The Conservative Capture of the GOP* (Chapel Hill: University of North Carolina Press, 1995), p. 16.

3. Ibid., pp. 71–72, 114–116. Lisa McGirr, *Suburban Warriors: The Origins of the New American Right* (Princeton: Princeton University Press, 2011), pp. 113–147.

4. *U.S. News and World Report*, quoted in Brennan, *Turning Right*, p. 119.

5. Ibid., p. 119.

6. Ibid., pp. 122–128. Richard Nixon, *The Memoirs of Richard Nixon* (New York: Grosset & Dunlap, 1978), pp. 302–305, 312–313.

7. *Toledo Blade*, September 8, 1968, p. B4.

8. Joe McGinnis, *The Selling of the President, 1968* (London: Andre Deutsch, 1970), pp. 36, 41–45.

9. Ibid., pp. 83–96. These ads are available on YouTube.

10. Ibid., pp. 62–76, 97–111.

11. Richard Nixon, "Special Message to Congress on Fiscal Policy," March 26, 1969. Richard Nixon, "Special Message to the Congress on Reform of the Federal Tax System," April 21, 1969. Richard Nixon,

"Statement on Signing the Tax Reform Act of 1969," December 30, 1969.

12. Bruce J. Schulman, *The Seventies* (New York: Free Press, 2001), pp. 26–37.

13. Matthew Storin, "President Promises to End Verbal Attacks on Students," *Boston Globe*, May 8, 1970, p. 1. *Newsweek*, May 18, 1970, pp. 26–27.

14. Richard Nixon, "Address to the Nation on the War in Vietnam," November 3, 1969.

15. James T. Naughton, "Finch Criticizes Agnew Remarks," *New York Times*, May 10, 1970, p. 1. *Time*, January 5, 1970.

16. Richard Nixon, September 6, 1971, "Address to the Nation on Labor Day."

17. Ronald Reagan, Speech on phone to YAF Convention in Houston, Texas, September 5, 1971, in Kiron K. Skinner, Annelise Anderson, Martin Anderson, *Reagan, in His Own Hand* (New York: Free Press, 2001), pp. 449–453. Henry Kissinger, *The White House Years* (Boston: Little, Brown, 1979), pp. 163–194.

18. Nixon, *Memoirs*, pp. 559–580.

19. Ibid., pp. 508–511.

20. Schulman, *Seventies*, pp. 44–45.

21. Nixon, *Memoirs*, pp. 816, 823, 856, 912–923.

22. Schulman, *Seventies*, p. 46.

23. Barry M. Goldwater, *With No Apologies: The Personal and Political Memoirs of United States Senator Barry M. Goldwater* (New York: William Morrow, 1979), pp. 261–269.

24. Nixon, *Memoirs*, pp. 1044–1045.

25. William F. Buckley Jr., "Let Him Go," *National Review*, August 3, 1974, p. 996.

26. Schulman, *Seventies*, pp. 135–140.

27. Ibid.

28. http://www.don-mclean.com/americanpie.asp, accessed November 6, 2012.

29. Heather Cox Richardson, *West from Appomattox: The Reconstruction of America After the Civil War* (New Haven: Yale University Press, 2007), p. 347.

30. Allan J. Lichtman, *White Protestant Nation: The Rise of the American Conservative Movement* (New York: Grove Press, 2008), p. 342.

31. Ibid., p. 337.

32. Ibid., pp. 342–349.

33. Republican Party Platform, July 15, 1980. Larry M. Bartels, "Constituency Opinion and Congressional Policy Making: The Reagan Defense Buildup," *American Political Science Review* 85 (June 1991): 457–474.

34. "Transcript of Ronald Reagan's 1980 Neshoba County Fair Speech," *Neshoba Democrat*, November 15, 2007, http://web.archive.org/web /20110714165011/http://neshobademocrat.com/main.asp?SectionID=2 &SubSectionID=297&ArticleID=15599&TM=60417.67, accessed November 10, 2012.

35. Bob Herbert, "Impossible, Ridiculous, Repugnant," *New York Times*, October 6, 2005. Josh Levin, "The Welfare Queen," Slate.com, December 19, 2013.

36. Ronald Reagan, Inaugural Address, January 20, 1981.

37. Robert V. Hine and John Mack Faragher, *The American West: A New Interpretive History* (New Haven: Yale University Press, 2000), pp. 530–531. Donald Ritchie, "Who Moved the Inauguration? Dispelling an Urban Legend," OUPblog, January 22, 2009, at http:// blog.oup.com/2009/01/moving_inauguration/, accessed November 25, 2012.

38. Sean Wilentz, *The Age of Reagan: A History, 1974–2008* (New York: HarperCollins, 2008), p. 140.

39. William Greider, "The Education of David Stockman," *Atlantic Monthly*, December 1981.

40. Greider, "Education." Wilentz, *Reagan*, p. 141.

41. Wilentz, *Reagan*, pp. 142–143.

42. Ronald Reagan, "Address Before a Joint Session of the Congress on the Program for Economic Recovery," April 28, 1981.

43. Greider, "Education."

44. Wilentz, *Reagan*, pp. 142–144.

45. Larry M. Bartels, "Constituency Opinion and Congressional Policy Making: The Reagan Defense Buildup," *American Political Science Review* 85 (June 1991): 457–474.

46. Martin Hutchinson, "To Treat the Fed as Volcker Did," *New York Times*, November 4, 2008, at http://www.nytimes.com/2008/11/05 /business/05views.html, accessed November 30, 2012.

47. NSC-NSDD-75, January 17, 1983, Ronald Reagan Library, http://www .fas.org/irp/offdocs/nsdd/23-1956t.gif.

48. Ronald Reagan, March 8, 1983, speech to the National Association of Evangelicals.

49. U.N. General Assembly Resolution 38/7, November 2, 1983, at http:// www.un.org/documents/ga/res/38/a38r007.htm.

50. *New York Times*, September 4, 1984. David Sirota, "How the '80s Programmed Us for War," Salon.com, March 15, 2011. *Washington Post*, August 9, 1984, pp. D1, D14.

51. Timothy Naftali, *George H. W. Bush* (New York: Times Books, 2007), pp. 73–75. Wilentz, *Reagan*, p. 170.

52. John H. Fund and Grover Norquist, "Michigan Taxes Spark a Blue Flame," *Wall Street Journal*, January 25, 1984, p. 32.

53. Wilentz, *Reagan*, pp. 173–174. Frances Fitzgerald, *Way Out There in the Blue: Reagan, Star Wars and the End of the Cold War* (New York: Simon & Schuster, 2000), p. 233.

54. Wilentz, *Reagan*, pp. 171–174. George L. Church, Ed Magnuson, "Geraldine Ferraro: A Break with Tradition," *Time*, July 23, 1984.

55. James Conaway, "Young and Restless on the Right," *Washington Post*, January 25, 1985, p. C1.

56. Wilentz, *Reagan*, pp. 204–205.

57. Jane Mayer, "Ways and Means Panel's Tax-Overhaul Proposal Brings 'Family' Strive to Conservative Coalition," *Wall Street Journal*, November 27, 1985, p. 52. Anne Swardson, "Senate Rejects Proposal for 35% Tax Bracket," *Washington Post*, June 19, 1986, p. A3.

58. Swardson, "Senate Rejects Proposal." Mayer, "Ways and Means."

59. Thomas B. Edsall, "Hill Vote Is Milestone for Forces of Government 'Containment,'" *Washington Post*, June 30, 1995, p. A8. Isabel Wilkerson, "How Milwaukee Has Thrived While Leaving Blacks Behind," *New York Times*, March 19, 1991, p. A1.

60. Christopher Howard, "The Hidden Side of the American Welfare State," *Political Science Quarterly* 108 (Autumn 1993): 413.

61. Howard, "Hidden Side," pp. 403–436. Wilentz, *Reagan*, p. 204.

62. Dan Fletcher, "A Brief History of the Fairness Doctrine," *Time*, February 20, 2009.

63. Lichtman, *White Protestant Nation*, pp. 398–401.

64. Wilentz, *Reagan*, pp. 187–194.
65. Ibid.
66. Ronald Reagan, "Remarks at the Opening Ceremonies of the Statue of Liberty Centennial Celebration in New York," July 2, 1987, at http://www.reagan.utexas.edu/archives/speeches/1986/70386d.htm.
67. Naftali, *Bush*, pp. 43–45.
68. Lawrence E. Walsh, "Final Report of the Independent Counsel for Iran/Contra Matters," vol. 1: Investigations and Prosecutions, August 4, 1993, at Federal Bulletin Board of US Government Printing Office, at https://www.fas.org/irp/offdocs/walsh/.
69. Wilentz, *Reagan*, pp. 206–207, 275.
70. David Altig and Charles T. Carlstrom, "Marginal Tax Rates and Income Inequality in a Life-Cycle Model," *American Economic Review* 89 (December 1999): 1197–1215. Wilentz, *Reagan*, pp. 275–276.
71. Tim W. Ferguson, "So Who Will Cut Spending?" *Wall Street Journal*, August 17, 1988, p. 20. Wilentz, *Reagan*, pp. 206, 274. Jonathan Weisman, "Reagan Policies Gave Green Light to Red Ink," *Washington Post*, June 9, 2004, p. A11.
72. "Quotes for Gordon Gekko," on Internet Movie Database, http://www.imdb.com/character/ch0012282/quotes, accessed February 25, 2014.
73. Naftali, *Bush*, pp. 74–75. Tim W. Ferguson, "So Who Will Cut Spending?" *Wall Street Journal*, August 17, 1988, p. 20.

Chapter 12: The West as an Idea

1. Tim W. Ferguson, "So Who Will Cut Spending?" *Wall Street Journal*, August 17, 1988, p. 20.
2. History Commons, Profile: National Security Political Action Committee (NSPAC), at http://www.historycommons.org/entity.jsp?entity=national_security_political_action_committee_1.
3. Michael Dukakis, interviewed in "Boogie Man: The Lee Atwater Story," at http://www.youtube.com/watch?v=wTdUQ9SYhUw.
4. Timothy Naftali, *George H. W. Bush* (New York: Times Books, 2007), p. 72. George H. W. Bush, Inaugural Address, January 20, 1989.
5. Sean Wilentz, *The Age of Reagan: A History, 1974–2008* (New York: HarperCollins, 2008), p. 306.

6. Naftali, *Bush*, p. 97.

7. Ibid., pp. 115–117. Wilentz, *Reagan*, p. 309.

8. Naftali, *Bush*, p. 117.

9. *Wall Street Journal*, October 2, 1990, p. A26.

10. Naftali, *Bush*, p. 117. Roxanne Roberts, "Still Trickled Pink: 10 Years Later, a Supply-Side Celebration," *Washington Post*, August 14, 1991, p. C1.

11. Naftali, *Bush*, pp. 76–97, 111–113.

12. Ibid., pp. 101–110, 122–129.

13. Ibid., p. 131.

14. "Review and Outlook: Rules of the Game," *Wall Street Journal*, October 16, 1992, p. A14. Grover Norquist, "How Conservatism Stumbled After Reagan: Bookshelf," *Wall Street Journal*, August 3, 1994, p. A8.

15. Matthew Rees, "How Whitman Did It," *Wall Street Journal*, November 9, 1993, p. A18.

16. Robin Toner, "Thinkers on the Right," *New York Times*, November 22, 1994, pp. A1, B7. Rick Wartzman, "Truth Lands in Intensive Care Unit as New Ads Seek to Demonize Clintons' Health-Reform Plan," *Wall Street Journal*, April 29, 1994, p. A16.

17. James Atlas, "Counterculture: They Grew Up Railing Against the Liberal Establishment," *New York Times*, February 12, 1995, p. SM32. "Choice Goes National," *Wall Street Journal*, October 7, 1993, p. A18.

18. Katharine Q. Seelye, "Republicans Get a Pep Talk from Rush Limbaugh," *New York Times*, December 12, 1994.

19. Ibid. Wilentz, *Reagan*, pp. 331, 341–343.

20. Wilentz, *Reagan*, pp. 345–346.

21. Lloyd Grove, "Drawling Power: GOP Chairman Haley Barbour Is Cautiously Counting His Chickens," *Washington Post*, August 11, 1994, p. B1.

22. Peggy Noonan, "Bliss to Be Alive," *Wall Street Journal*, January 9, 1995, p. A14.

23. Ibid.

24. Atlas, "Counterculture," p. SM32. Toner, "Thinkers on the Right," pp. A1, B7.

25. Seelye, "Republicans Get a Pep Talk." "Beyond the Contract: Setting Priorities," *Wall Street Journal*, December 15, 1994, p. A14. Richard L.

Berke, "The Legman for Limbaugh," *New York Times*, March 12, 1995, p. 1. Dale Russakoff, "Fax Networks Link Outposts of Anger," *Washington Post*, August 20, 1995, p. A1.

26. Robin Toner, "Tax Cut Edges Out Deficit as G.O.P.'s Guiding Tenet," *New York Times*, April 3, 1995, p. A1. Paul A. Gigot, "Dole Bows to GOP's New Powers," *Wall Street Journal*, April 14, 1995, p. A8.

27. Thomas B. Edsall, "Hill Vote Is Milestone for Forces of Government 'Containment,'" *Washington Post*, June 30, 1995, p. A8. Thomas B. Edsall, "Right in the Middle of the Revolution," *Washington Post*, September 4, 1995, p. A1.

28. Wilentz, *Reagan*, pp. 363–364. David S. Broder, "When Unity Becomes Division: Party's 'Contract with America' Is Now a Footnote," *Washington Post*, March 1, 1996, p. A1.

29. Russakoff, "Fax Networks."

30. Letter from Timothy McVeigh to *Union-Sun and Journal* (of Lockport, NY), published February 11, 1992, at CNN, http://web.archive.org /web/20080119111020/http://www.cnn.com/US/OKC/faces/Suspects /McVeigh/1st-letter6–15/index.html.

31. Daniel Schuman, "Congress's Diminishing Budget Strengthens Lobbyist Influence," September 14, 2011, Sunlight Foundation, at http:// sunlightfoundation.com/blog/2011/09/14/congresss-diminishing -budget-strengthens-lobbyist-influence/. Lobbying database, at http:// www.opensecrets.org/lobby/index.php, accessed January 3, 2014. Katharine Q. Seelye, "G.O.P. Set to Lead Congress on Path Sharply to Right," *New York Times*, January 3, 1995, p. A16. Mike Mills, "Communications C.E.O.s Invited to Meetings on Hill: Consumer Groups Say G.O.P. Left Them Out," *Washington Post*, January 18, 1995, p. F2.

32. *Financial Times*, Interview Transcript: Rupert Murdoch and Roger Ailes, October 3, 2006, at http://www.ft.com/cms/s/2/5b77af92–548c -11db-901f-0000779e2340.html#axzz2H1qgBIP0.

33. Stefano DellaVigna and Ethan Kaplan, "The Fox News Effect: Media Bias and Voting," *Quarterly Journal of Economics* 122 (August 2007): 1187–1234.

34. 1990 census, racial and urban data, at http://www.census.gov//apsd /cqc/cqc4.pdf.

35. *Financial Times*, Interview Transcript: Rupert Murdoch and Roger Ailes. DellaVigna and Kaplan, "Fox News Effect," 1187–1234.

36. Wilentz, *Reagan*, p. 328.

37. Ibid., p. 371.

38. Ibid., pp. 378–381, 384–388.

39. Starr Report, *Washington Post*, at http://www.washingtonpost.com /wp-srv/politics/special/clinton/icreport/icreport.htm.

40. Wilentz, *Reagan*, p. 396.

41. Katharine Q. Seelye, "Gingrich Draws Fire from the Right," *New York Times*, October 25, 1998, p. 24. Charles R. Babcock and Ruth Marcus, "Offenses Go to Core of Gingrich Probe," *Washington Post*, December 24, 1996, p. A1. Wilentz, *Reagan*, p. 396.

42. Seelye, "Gingrich Draws Fire." David Talbot, "This Hypocrite Broke Up My Family," Salon.com, September 16, 1998.

43. Wilentz, *Reagan*, pp. 393–403.

44. Katharine Q. Seeyle, "Beyond the Clinton-Bashing, Agony Among Conservatives," *New York Times*, January 2, 1999, p. A1.

45. Alison Mitchell, "One Party Quite Divisible: McCain's Attack on Robertson and Falwell," *New York Times*, February 29, 2000, p. A1. Jill Zuckman, "Attack Ad Says McCain's 'Soft Money,'" *Boston Globe*, December 24, 1999, p. A6. Jill Zuckman, "Foes of McCain's Plan Head for New Hampshire," *Boston Globe*, September 20, 1999, p. A3. "Bashing John McCain," *New York Times*, September 23, 1999, p. A28. Dan Van Natta Jr., "Issue Ads, His Target, Are Turned on McCain," *New York Times*, January 14, 2000, p. A22. Anthony Lewis, "Abroad at Home: When Money Is the Measure of All Things," *New York Times*, March 4, 2000, p. A15.

46. Alison Mitchell, "A McCain Mutiny," *New York Times*, September 26, 1999, p. 147.

47. David Nyhan, "After You Catalog the List of His Triumphs," *Boston Globe*, June 28, 2000, p. A15. Tina Cassidy, "Thomas Pink Set for Copley Store," *Boston Globe*, September 19, 2000, p. C1. Jim Yardley, "With Gore Jabbing at Bush, Texas Takes It on the Chin," *New York Times*, July 21, 2000, p. A1. Nicholas D. Kristof, "Learning How to Run: A West Texas Stumble," *New York Times*, July 27, 2000, p. A1. Nicholas D. Kristof, "How Bush Came to Tame His Inner Scamp," *New York Times*, July 29, 2000, p. A1.

48. Yvonne Abraham, "Delegate Floor Stages a Grand, Old Party," *Boston Globe*, August 4, 2000, p. A22. David E. Rosenbaum, "If Elected, Bush Says, He'll Oppose Tax Increase," *New York Times*, June 10, 1999, p. A24. Alison Mitchell, "Kindler, Gentler: A Newt-Less Revolution with a Familiar Agenda," *New York Times*, June 4, 2001, p. WK3.

49. Wilentz, *Reagan*, pp. 419–420.

50. Ibid., pp. 424–426.

51. Steven Greenhouse, "Unions See Bush Moves as Payback for Backing Gore," *New York Times*, March 25, 2001, p. 33. David E. Rosenbaum, "Bush Rules! It's Good to Be the President," *New York Times*, January 28, 2001, p. WK16.

52. Robin Toner, "Conservatives Savor Their Role as Insiders at the White House," *New York Times*, March 19, 2001, p. A1. Robin Toner, "Capitalist Tools: Cutting a Rightward Path Cut to the Right," *New York Times*, March 4, 2001, p. WK1. Robert Reich, "Corporate Power in Overdrive," *New York Times*, March 18, 2001, p. WK13.

53. James Risen, Leslie Wayne, and Richard A. Oppel Jr., "Gulf War Led Cheney to the Oil Boardroom," *New York Times*, July 27, 2000, p. A1.

54. Bob Herbert, "In America: The Mask Comes Off," *New York Times*, March 26, 2001. Anthony Shadid and Sue Kirchhoff, "Bush Policies Scoring Big with Business," *Boston Globe*, April 1, 2001, p. A1.

55. Toner, "Conservatives Savor Their Role."

56. Richard W. Stevenson, "The High-Stakes Politics of Spending the Surplus," *New York Times*, January 7, 2000, p. WK3. Alison Mitchell, "After the Nicknames: Bush's Tactics on Tax Cut Proposal Show Hardball Beating Conciliation," *New York Times*, March 9, 2001, p. A14. Anne E. Kornblut, "Ad Blitz on Tax Cuts Targets 3 New England Republicans," *Boston Globe*, March 2, 2001, p. A10.

57. George W. Bush, "Address Before a Joint Session of the Congress on the United States Response to the Terrorist Attacks of September 11," September 20, 2001.

58. Bush, "Address," September 20, 2001. Eric Pianin, "Ridge Backed by Bush Friendship in New Role," *Washington Post*, October 7, 2001, p. A10. Elizabeth Becker and Tim Weiner, "New Office to Become a White House Agency," *New York Times*, September 28, 2001, p. B5. "Tax Cuts and Homeland Safety," *New York Times*, November 18,

2001, p. WK12. Eric Pianin, "Homeland Security Team's Key Members Announced: Top Appointees Have Close Ties to Senior Bush Officials," *Washington Post*, November 21, 2001, p. A21.

59. Manimoli Dinesh, "US Policy Makers Focus on Energy, Pipeline Security," *Oil Daily*, September 24, 2001. "Corn Growers Praise President Bush for Pro-Ethanol National Energy Plan," *PR Newswire*, November 29, 2001. "Energy Alliance Strongly Applauds President's Call for Senate Action on Energy Bill," *PR Newswire*, October 12, 2001. Gerard Baker, "Bigger Government: The Terrorist Attacks Have Provoked a Startling About-Turn…," *Financial Times*, September 26, 2001, p. 22. "Tax Cuts and Homeland Safety," *New York Times*, November 18, 2001, p. WK12.

60. Eric Pianin, "Bush Budget About to Show Its Darker Side," *Washington Post*, February 3, 2002, p. A1. "The War Budget," *Washington Post*, February 4, 2002, p. A16. "How the Departments Fare Under the Bush Budget," *Washington Post*, February 5, 2002, p. A13. Stephen Barr, "DHS Withdraws Bid to Curb Union Rights," *Washington Post*, February 20, 2008.

61. Alison Mitchell, "Security Quest Also Offers Opportunities," *New York Times*, November 25, 2001, p. B1. "Titan Creates Homeland Security Office Focused on Chemical and Biological Terrorism," *PR Newswire*, October 17, 2001. "SureBeam Selected to Provide Electron Beam Systems for Eliminating Anthrax Threat in US Mail," *PR Newswire*, October 29, 2001. "e-Smart Technologies Forms Alliance with Akal Security to Market the Super Smart Card System," *PR Newswire*, October 30, 2001, p. 7248. "Multiple Technologies Prosper as Homeland Security Concerns Escalate," *PR Newswire*, October 30, 2001, p. 7774.

62. "The Homeland Security Fight," *Washington Post*, December 10, 2001, p. A22. Michael Janofsky, "Additional Budget Cuts as States and Cities Address Safety Issues," *New York Times*, November 15, 2001, p. B9. Dan Morgan, "House Committee Rejects Increase in Emergency Funding," *Washington Post*, November 15, 2001, p. A14. Helen Dewar, "Bush, GOP Prevail on Anti-Terror Spending," *Washington Post*, December 8, 2001, p. A1. Robin Toner, "Now, Government Is the Solution, Not the Problem," *New York Times*, September 30, 2001, p. WK14.

63. Laura Turner, "ABA President Speaks Out Against Limiting Freedoms of Terrorism Suspects," *Nation's Cities Weekly*, December 17, 2001, p. 6.

64. George W. Bush, November 5, 2001, "Statement on Signing the Department of the Interior and Related Agencies Appropriations Act, 2002," in *Weekly Compilation of Presidential Documents*, 37.45 (November 12, 2001), p. 1601.

65. Ben White, "Democrats Criticize RNC E-Mail Petition," *Washington Post*, October 10, 2001, p. A8. Thomas B. Edsall, "GOP Touts War as Campaign Issue; Bush Adviser Infuriates Democrats with Strategy Outlined at RNC Meeting," *Washington Post*, January 19, 2002, p. A2.

66. Edsall, "GOP Touts War as Campaign Issue."

67. Ibid. John Dilulio, to Ron Suskind, October 24, 2002, *Esquire*, May 23, 2007.

68. Ron Suskind, *The Price of Loyalty* (New York: Simon & Schuster, 2004), pp. 291–292.

69. "Statement of Principles," June 3, 1997, Project for a New American Century, at http://www.newamericancentury.org/statementofprinciples.htm. Elliott Abrams et al. to William J. Clinton, January 26, 1998, at http://www.newamericancentury.org/iraqclintonletter.htm.

70. Steven Kull, Clay Ramsay, and Evan Lewis, "Misperceptions, the Media, and the Iraq War," *Political Science Quarterly* 118 (Winter 2003/2004): 569–598.

71. National Security Strategy, September 17, 2002, at http://nssarchive.us/?page_id=32.

72. Wolf Blitzer, "Search for the 'Smoking Gun,'" January 10, 2003, CNN.com, at http://www.cnn.com/2003/US/01/10/wbr.smoking.gun/.

73. Steven R. Weisman, "Powell, in U.N. Speech, Presents Case...," *New York Times*, February 6, 2003. Howard Kurtz, "Winning Hearts and Minds; Powell Speech Plays Well with Newspaper Gatekeepers," *Washington Post*, February 7, 2003. Karen DeYoung, "Falling on His Sword," *Washington Post*, October 1, 2006.

74. Stan Shatenstein, "USA: The Smokin' Marlboro Man of Fallujah," *Tobacco Control* 14 (February 2005): 5–6.

75. Henry A. Waxman, Committee on Government Reform, US House of Representatives, December 9, 2004, "Halliburton's Iraq Contracts Now Worth over $10 Billion," at http://democrats.oversight.house.gov

/images/stories/documents/20050916123931–74182.pdf, accessed January 14, 2013.

76. Rush Limbaugh, "This Cowboy," RushOnline.com, at www.rushonline .com/halloffame/thiscowboy.htm, accessed January 18, 2005.

77. Ron Suskind, "Faith, Certainty and the Presidency of George W. Bush," *New York Times Magazine*, October 17, 2004, at http://www.ny times.com/2004/10/17/magazine/17BUSH.html.

78. Fred Barnes, "Realignment, Now More Than Ever," *Weekly Standard*, November 22, 2004.

79. Author interview with Frederick L. Ahearn, funeral director for the Reagan funeral.

Conclusion

1. "Bush's Final Approval Rating: 22%," CBS *News*, February 11, 2009, at http://www.cbsnews.com/2100–500160_162–4728399.html, accessed July 26, 2013.

2. Monica Langley, "As Economic Crisis Peaked, Tide Turned Against McCain," *Wall Street Journal*, November 5, 2008, http://online.wsj .com/article/SB125586043326400685.html, accessed July 26, 2013.

Afterword

1. Adam Epstein, "'The Apprentice' May Have (Temporarily) Saved Trump from Financial Ruin," *Quartz*, September 28, 2020, https:// qz.com/1909776/how-the-apprentice-saved-trump-from-financial -ruin.

2. Martin Tolchin, "G.O.P. Memo Tells of Black Vote Cut," *New York Times*, October 25, 1986, p. 7. B. Drummond Ayres, Jr., "Feinstein Opponent Hopes to Uncover Ballot Fraud," *New York Times*, November 30, 1994, p. B11. Michael Janofsky, "Loser for Maryland Governor Files Suit to Overturn Election," *New York Times*, December 29, 1994, p. A16. Lizette Alvarez, "Doubts Rising on Election in California, Gingrich Says," *New York Times*, September 26, 1997, p. A23.

3. "Debunking the Voter Fraud Myth," Brennan Center for Justice, January 31, 2017, www.brennancenter.org/analysis/debunking-voter

-fraud-myth. Lizette Alvarez, "G.O.P. Bill Proposes Check on Whether Voter Is a Citizen," *New York Times*, February 27, 1998, p. A22. Mireya Navarro, "Fraud Ruling Invalidates Miami Mayoral Election," *New York Times*, March 5, 1998. Greg Palast, "Florida's 'Disappeared Voters' Disfranchised by the GOP," *Nation*, January 18, 2001. US Commission on Civil Rights, "Voting Irregularities in Florida During the 2000 Presidential Election," June 2001, www.usccr.gov/pubs/vote2000 /report/main.htm, quotation from Executive Summary.

4. Michael Miller, "'It's Insanity!': How the 'Brooks Brothers Riot' Killed the 2000 Recount in Miami," *Washington Post*, November 15, 2018.

5. Beth Reinhard, "Bush Strategist Shares Insight on '00 Recount," *Miami Herald*, May 17, 2008.

6. Glenn Kessler, "When Did Mitch McConnell Say He Wanted to Make Obama a One-Term President?" *Washington Post*, January 11, 2017, www.washingtonpost.com/news/fact-checker/wp/2017/01/11/when -did-mitch-mcconnell-say-he-wanted-to-make-obama-a-one-term -president.

7. Nour Abdul-Razzak, Carlo Prato, and Stephane Wolton, "After *Citizens United*: How Outside Spending Shapes American Democracy," *Journal of Electoral Studies* 67 (2020), https://doi.org/10.1016/j.elect stud.2020.102190.[0].

8. Hedrick Smith, "Gerrymandering May Prove a Pyrrhic Victory for the GOP," *Los Angeles Times*, October 7, 2015. David Daley, *RAT-F**CKED: The True Story Behind the Secret Plan to Steal America's Democracy* (New York: Liveright, 2016), pp. xxi–xxii.

9. "Voting Laws Roundup 2017," Brennan Center for Justice, May 10, 2017, www.brennancenter.org/analysis/voting-laws-roundup-2017.

10. Amita Kelly, "Donald Trump Clinches GOP Nomination," NPR, May 26, 2016, www.npr.org/2016/05/26/479588197/donald-trump-clinches -gop-nomination. Jane Mayer, "The Danger of President Pence," *New Yorker*, October 16, 2017, www.newyorker.com/magazine/2017/10/23 /the-danger-of-president-pence.

11. Leigh Ann Caldwell, "Anti-Trump Delegates Cause Chaos on Opening Day of GOP Convention," *NBC News*, July 18, 2016, https://www .nbcnews.com/storyline/2016-conventions/anti-trump-delegates -cause-chaos-opening-day-gop-convention-n611996.

12. Brian Naylor, "How the Trump Campaign Weakened the Republican Platform on Aid to Ukraine," NPR, August 6, 2016, www.npr .org/2016/08/06/488876597/how-the-trump-campaign-weakened-the -republican-platform-on-aid-to-ukraine. "2016 Republican Party Platform," American Presidency Project, July 18, 2016, www.presidency .ucsb.edu/documents/2016-republican-party-platform.

13. Ishaan Tharoor, "Some Trump Supporters Want a Holy War," *Washington Post*, June 12, 2017, www.washingtonpost.com/news/world views/wp/2017/06/11/some-trump-supporters-want-a-holy-war. Ishaan Tharoor, "Trump's Travel Bans Caused Heartache and Suffering. For What?" *Washington Post*, January 25, 2021, www.washingtonpost .com/world/2021/01/25/trump-muslim-ban-legacy-biden. Philip Bump, "Donald Trump Only Hires the Best People (at Generating Unhelpful Headlines)," *Washington Post*, August 30, 2016, www.wash ingtonpost.com/news/the-fix/wp/2016/08/30/donald-trump-only -hires-the-best-people-at-generating-unhelpful-headlines. Thomas E. Patterson, "News Coverage of the 2016 General Election: How the Press Failed the Voters," Shorenstein Center on Media, Politics and Public Policy, December 7, 2016, https://shorensteincenter.org /news-coverage-2016-general-election.

14. Nate Silver, "The Comey Letter Probably Cost Clinton the Election," *FiveThirtyEight*, May 3, 2017, https://fivethirtyeight.com/features /the-comey-letter-probably-cost-clinton-the-election.

15. Glenn Thrush and Maggie Haberman, "Trump Gives White Supremacists an Unequivocal Boost," *New York Times*, August 15, 2017, www .nytimes.com/2017/08/15/us/politics/trump-charlottesville-white -nationalists.html.

16. Sheryl Gay Stolberg, "Trump Administration Asks Supreme Court to Strike Down Affordable Care Act," *New York Times*, June 26, 2020, www.nytimes.com/2020/06/26/us/politics/obamacare-trump-adminis tration-supreme-court.html.

17. Logan Lutton, "Coronavirus Case Numbers in the United States: January 20, 2021 Update," Medical Economics, January 20, 2021, www.medicaleconomics.com/view/coronavirus-case-numbers-in-the -united-states-january-20-2021-update. Craig Mauger and Beth LeBlanc, "Trump Tweets 'Liberate' Michigan, Two Other States with Dem

Governors," *Detroit News*, April 17, 2020, www.detroitnews.com
/story/news/politics/2020/04/17/trump-tweets-liberate-michigan-other
-states-democratic-governors/5152037002. Ivan Pereira, "Protestors,
Some Armed, Spill into Michigan Capitol Building Demanding End
to Stay-at-Home Order," *ABC News*, April 30, 2020, https://abcnews
.go.com/US/michigan-rally-shelter-place-order-spills-capitol-building
/story?id=70432928.

18. Erica Chenoweth and Jeremy Pressman, "This Summer's Black Lives
Matter Protesters Were Overwhelmingly Peaceful, Our Research
Finds," *Washington Post*, October 16, 2020, www.washingtonpost
.com/politics/2020/10/16/this-summers-black-lives-matter-protesters
-were-overwhelming-peaceful-our-research-finds. Tom Perkins, "Most
Charges Against George Floyd Protesters Dropped, Analysis Shows,"
Guardian, April 17, 2021, www.theguardian.com/us-news/2021/apr/17
/george-floyd-protesters-charges-citations-analysis.

19. Brian Naylor, "Read Trump's Jan. 6 Speech, a Key Part of Impeachment
Trial," NPR, February 10, 2021, www.npr.org/2021/02/10/966396848
/read-trumps-jan-6-speech-a-key-part-of-impeachment-trial.

20. Rick Scott, "Dear Woke Corporate America, Beware of the Backlash
That's Coming," foxbusiness.com, April 19, 2021, www.foxbusiness
.com/politics/sen-rick-scott-work-corporate-america-backlash.

INDEX

Index

Index

Heather Cox Richardson is an American historian and professor of history at Boston College. Her daily newsletter, *Letters from an American*, has over a half million subscribers. The author of *How the South Won the Civil War*, *West from Appomattox*, *The Greatest Nation of the Earth*, and *The Death of Reconstruction*, she splits her time between Boston and Maine.